MANUAL DRIVETRAINS AND AXLES

SEVENTH EDITION

James D. Halderman
Tom Birch

PEARSON

Boston Columbus Indianapolis New York San Francisco Upper Saddle River
Amsterdam Cape Town Dubai London Madrid Milan Munich Paris Montréal Toronto
Delhi Mexico City São Paulo Sydney Hong Kong Seoul Singapore Taipei Tokyo

Editorial Director: Vernon Anthony
Senior Product Manager: Lindsey Prudhomme Gill
Editorial Assistant: Nancy Kesterson
Director of Marketing: David Gesell
Senior Marketing Coordinator: Alicia Wozniak
Team Lead of Program Management: Laura Weaver

Project Manager: Holly Shufeldt
Senior Art Director: Jayne Conte
Cover Designer:
Lead Media Project Manager: April Cleland
Full-Service Project Management and Composition: Integra Software Services, Ltd.
Printer/Binder: Courier
Cover Printer: Moore Langen

Credits and acknowledgments borrowed from other sources and reproduced, with permission, in this textbook appear on the appropriate page within the text.

Library of Congress Cataloging-in-Publication Data

Birch, Thomas W.
    Manual drivetrains and axles/Tom Birch, James Halderman.—Seventh Edition.
       pages cm
    ISBN-13: 978-0-13-351504-6 (alk. paper)
    ISBN-10: 0-13-351504-4 (alk. paper)
    1. Automobiles—Power trains. 2. Automobiles—Axles. I. Halderman, James D.
    II. Title.
    TL260.B57 2015
    629.2'4—dc23

                                                2013048480

10 9 8 7 6 5 4 3 2 1

ISBN 10:   0-13-351504-4
ISBN 13: 978-0-13-351504-6

PREFACE

PROFESSIONAL TECHNICIAN SERIES Part of the *Pearson Automotive Professional Technician Series*, the seventh edition of *Manual Drivetrains and Axles* represents the future of automotive textbooks. The series is a full-color, media-integrated solution for today's students and instructors. The series includes textbooks that cover all eight areas of ASE certification, plus additional titles covering common courses. The series is peer-reviewed for technical accuracy.

UPDATES TO THE SEVENTH EDITION

- All contents are correlated to the latest NATEF and ASE tasks for Manual Drive Train and Axles (A3).
- New color photos and line drawings have been added in this edition.
- A dramatic, new full-color design enhances the subject material.
- New review and chapter quiz questions are included in this edition.
- New step-by-step photo sequences show in detail the steps involved in performing a specific task or service procedure.
- A new chapter Vibration and Noise Diagnosis and Correction (Chapter 17) has been included in this edition.
- Contents have been streamlined for easier reading and comprehension.
- Two new appendixes have been added: Sample ASE-type Certification Test with answers (Appendix 1) and 2013 NATEF Correlation Chart (Appendix 2).
- Unlike other textbooks, this book is written so that the theory, construction, diagnosis, and service of a particular component or system are presented in one location. There is no need to search the entire book for other references to the same topic.

ASE AND NATEF CORRELATED NATEF certified programs need to demonstrate that they use course material that covers NATEF and ASE tasks. All Professional Technician textbooks have been correlated to the appropriate ASE and NATEF task lists. These correlations can be found in an appendix to the book.

A COMPLETE INSTRUCTOR AND STUDENT SUPPLEMENTS PACKAGE All Professional Technician textbooks are accompanied by a full set of instructor and student supplements. Please see page vi for a detailed list of supplements.

A FOCUS ON DIAGNOSIS AND PROBLEM SOLVING

The *Professional Technician Series* has been developed to satisfy the need for a greater emphasis on problem diagnosis. Automotive instructors and service managers agree that students and beginning technicians need more training in diagnostic procedures and skill development. To meet this need and demonstrate how real-world problems are solved, "Real World Fix" features are included throughout and highlight how real-life problems are diagnosed and repaired.

The following pages highlight the unique core features that set the *Professional Technician Series* book apart from other automotive textbooks.

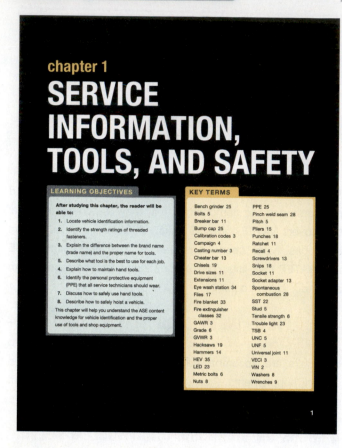

chapter 1

SERVICE INFORMATION, TOOLS, AND SAFETY

LEARNING OBJECTIVES

After studying this chapter, the reader will be able to:

1. Locate vehicle identification information.
2. Identify the strength ratings of threaded fasteners.
3. Explain the difference between the brand name (trade name) and the proper name for tools.
5. Describe what tool is the best to use for each job.
4. Explain how to maintain hand tools.
6. Identify the personal protective equipment (PPE) that all service technicians should wear.
7. Discuss how to safely use hand tools.
8. Describe how to safely hoist a vehicle.

This chapter will help you understand the ASE content knowledge for vehicle identification and the proper use of tools and shop equipment.

KEY TERMS

Bench grinder 25	PPE 25
Bolts 5	Pinch weld seam 28
Breaker bar 11	Pitch 5
Bump cap 25	Pliers 15
Calibration codes 3	Punches 18
Campaign 4	Ratchet 11
Casting number 3	Recall 4
Cheater bar 13	Screwdrivers 13
Chisels 19	Snips 18
Drive sizes 11	Socket 11
Extensions 11	Socket adapter 13
Eye wash station 34	Spontaneous
Files 17	combustion 28
Fire blanket 33	SST 22
Fire extinguisher	Stud 5
classes 32	Tensile strength 6
GAWR 3	Trouble light 23
Grade 6	TSB 4
GVWR 3	UNC 5
Hacksaws 19	UNF 5
Hammers 14	Universal joint 11
HEV 35	VECI 3
LED 23	VIN 2
Metric bolts 6	Washers 8
Nuts 8	Wrenches 9

1

LEARNING OBJECTIVES AND KEY TERMS appear at the beginning of each chapter to help students and instructors focus on the most important material in each chapter. The chapter objectives are based on specific ASE and NATEF tasks.

TECH TIP

It Just Takes a Second

Whenever removing any automotive component, it is wise to screw the bolts back into the holes a couple of threads by hand. This ensures that the right bolt will be used in its original location when the component or part is put back on the vehicle.

TECH TIPS feature real-world advice and "tricks of the trade" from ASE-certified master technicians.

SAFETY TIP

Shop Cloth Disposal

Always dispose of oily shop cloths in an enclosed container to prevent a fire. ● **SEE FIGURE 1–69**. Whenever oily cloths are thrown together on the floor or workbench, a chemical reaction can occur, which can ignite the cloth even without an open flame. This process of ignition without an open flame is called spontaneous combustion.

SAFETY TIPS alert students to possible hazards on the job and how to avoid them.

REAL WORLD FIX

The Case of the Stretched Shift Cable

The clutch on a Dodge Ram pickup (260,000 km) did not release completely. Adjusting the cable helped, but the end of the adjustment was reached. The transmission and clutch were removed. The clutch was carefully inspected, and it showed little wear and no damage.

After reading some similar cases on www.iatn.net a new cable was purchased, and it was determined that the old cable had stretched. Installation of the new cable repaired this problem.

REAL WORLD FIXES present students with actual automotive scenarios and show how these common (and sometimes uncommon) problems were diagnosed and repaired.

FREQUENTLY ASKED QUESTION

How Many Types of Screw Heads Are Used in Automotive Applications?

There are many, including Torx, hex (also called Allen), plus many others used in custom vans and motor homes. ● **SEE FIGURE 1–9**.

FREQUENTLY ASKED QUESTIONS are based on the author's own experience and provide answers to many of the most common questions asked by students and beginning service technicians.

NOTE: Most of these "locking nuts" are grouped together and are commonly referred to as *prevailing torque nuts*. This means that the nut will hold its tightness or torque and not loosen with movement or vibration.

NOTES provide students with additional technical information to give them a greater understanding of a specific task or procedure.

CAUTION: *Never* use hardware store (nongraded) bolts, studs, or nuts on any vehicle steering, suspension, or brake component. Always use the exact size and grade of hardware that is specified and used by the vehicle manufacturer.

CAUTIONS alert students about potential damage to the vehicle that can occur during a specific task or service procedure.

☠ **WARNING**

Do not use incandescent trouble lights around gasoline or other flammable liquids. The liquids can cause the bulb to break and the hot filament can ignite the flammable liquid which can cause personal injury or even death.

WARNINGS alert students to potential dangers to themselves during a specific task or service procedure.

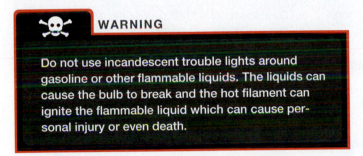

SUMMARY

1. Bolts, studs, and nuts are commonly used as fasteners in the chassis. The sizes for fractional and metric threads are different and are not interchangeable. The grade is the rating of the strength of a fastener.
2. Whenever a vehicle is raised above the ground, it must be supported at a substantial section of the body or frame.
3. Wrenches are available in open end, box end, and combination open and box ends.
4. An adjustable wrench should only be used where the proper size is not available.
5. Line wrenches are also called flare-nut wrenches, fitting wrenches, or tube-nut wrenches and are used to remove fuel or refrigerant lines.
6. Sockets are rotated by a ratchet or breaker bar, also called a flex handle.
7. Torque wrenches measure the amount of torque applied to a fastener.
8. Screwdriver types include straight blade (flat tip) and Phillips.
9. Hammers and mallets come in a variety of sizes and weights.
10. Pliers are a useful tool and are available in many different types, including slip-joint, multigroove, linesman's, diagonal, needle-nose, and locking pliers.
11. Other common hand tools include snap-ring pliers, files, cutters, punches, chisels, and hacksaws.
12. Hybrid electric vehicles should be de-powered if any of the high-voltage components are going to be serviced.

REVIEW QUESTIONS

1. List three precautions that must be taken whenever hoisting (lifting) a vehicle.
2. Describe how to determine the grade of a fastener, including how the markings differ between fractional and metric bolts.
3. List four items that are personal protective equipment (PPE).
4. List the types of fire extinguishers and their usage.
5. Why are wrenches offset 15 degrees?
6. What are the other names for a line wrench?
7. What are the standard automotive drive sizes for sockets?
8. Which type of screwdriver requires the use of a hammer or mallet?
9. What is inside a dead-blow hammer?
10. What type of cutter is available in left and right cutters?

CHAPTER QUIZ

1. The correct location for the pads when hoisting or jacking the vehicle can often be found in the _____.
   a. Service manual   c. Owner's manual
   b. Shop manual   d. All of the above
2. For the best working position, the work should be _____.
   a. At neck or head level
   b. At knee or ankle level
   c. Overhead by about 1 foot
   d. At chest or elbow level
3. A high-strength bolt is identified by _____.
   a. A UNC symbol   c. Strength letter codes
   b. Lines on the head d. The coarse threads
4. A fastener that uses threads on both ends is called a _____.
   a. Cap screw   c. Machine screw
   b. Stud   d. Crest fastener
5. When working with hand tools, always _____.
   a. Push the wrench—don't pull toward you
   b. Pull a wrench—don't push a wrench away from you
6. The proper term for Channel Locks is _____.
   a. Vise Grips   c. Locking pliers
   b. Crescent wrench   d. Multigroove adjustable pliers
7. The proper term for Vise Grips is _____.
   a. Locking pliers   c. Side cuts
   b. Slip-joint pliers d. Multigroove adjustable pliers
8. Two technicians are discussing torque wrenches. Technician A says that a torque wrench is capable of tightening a fastener with more torque than a conventional breaker bar or ratchet. Technician B says that a torque wrench should be calibrated regularly for the most accurate results. Which technician is correct?
   a. Technician A only   c. Both Technicians A and B
   b. Technician B only   d. Neither Technician A nor B
9. What type of screwdriver should be used if there is very limited space above the head of the fastener?
   a. Offset screwdriver   c. Impact screwdriver
   b. Standard screwdriver d. Robertson screwdriver
10. What type of hammer is plastic coated, has a metal casing inside, and is filled with small lead balls?
    a. Dead-blow hammer   c. Sledgehammer
    b. Soft-blow hammer   d. Plastic hammer

SERVICE INFORMATION, TOOLS, AND SAFETY   39

THE SUMMARY, REVIEW QUESTIONS, AND CHAPTER QUIZ at the end of each chapter help students review the material presented in the chapter and test themselves to see how much they've learned.

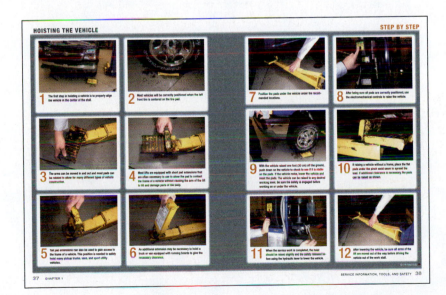

STEP-BY-STEP photo sequences show in detail the steps involved in performing a specific task or service procedure.

RESOURCES IN PRINT AND ONLINE
Manual Drivetrains and Axles

NAME OF SUPPLEMENT	PRINT	ONLINE	AUDIENCE	DESCRIPTION
Instructor Resource Manual 0133516199		✔	Instructors	NEW! The Ultimate teaching aid: Chapter summaries, key terms, chapter learning objectives, lecture resources, discuss/demonstrate classroom activities, MyAutomotiveLab correlation, and answers to the in-text review and quiz questions.
TestGen 0133516180		✔	Instructors	Test generation software and test bank for the text.
PowerPoint Presentation 0133516008		✔	Instructors	Slides include chapter learning objectives, lecture outline of the test, and graphics from the book.
Image Bank 0133515672		✔	Instructors	All of the images and graphs from the textbook to create customized lecture slides.
NATEF Correlated Task Sheets – for instructors 0133515664		✔	Instructors	Downloadable NATEF task sheets for easy customization and development of unique task sheets.
NATEF Task Sheets – For Students 0133516202	✔		Students	Study activity manual that correlates NATEF Automobile Standards to chapters and page numbers in the text. Available to students at a discounted price when packaged with the text.
CourseSmart eText 0133515680		✔	Students	As an alternative to purchasing the print textbook, students can subscribe to the same content online and save up to 50% off the suggested list price of the print text. Visit **www.coursesmart.com**

All online resources can be downloaded from the Instructor's Resource Center: **www.pearsonighered.com/irc**

ACKNOWLEDGMENTS

A large number of people and organizations have cooperated in providing the reference material and technical information used in this text. The authors wish to express sincere thanks to the following organizations for their special contributions:

Acra Electric Corporation
Advance Adapters
Alston Race Car Engineering
American Honda
ARB Air Locker
Band-It
Harold Beck, Yuba City
Borroughs
Tom Broxholm, Skyline College
John Brunner
Borgwarner Inc.
BWD Automotive Corporation
Centerforce Clutches
Chassis Ear, Steelman
Cosmos International, Inc.
CR Services
Chrysler Corporation
Dana Corporation
Darrell Gwynn Racing Team
Dorman Products
Drive Line Service of Sacramento, Jim Scoggin
Durston/Vim Tools
Everco Industries
Exedy/Daikin
Fluke Corporation
Ford Motor Company
Joel Gelfand
Gear Vendors, Inc.
General Motors Corporation
GKN Driveline
HeliCoil
Hyundai Motor America
Jerico Performance Products
John Deere
K-D Tools
Kent-Moore
L & T Slider Clutches, Lanny and Tony Miglizzi
LUK Clutches
Manual Transmission Warehouse, Richard Tinucci
Mark Williams Enterprises
McLeod Industries, Inc., George Koehler
Mighty Mover
Moog Automotive
Neapco
OTC Tools
Perfect Circle
Phoenix Systems
Plews

Quarter Master Industries
Racepak
RAM Automotive
Richmond Gear
Rockland Standard Gear
Snap-on Tools Company
Sta-Lube
Bill Steen, Yuba College
Stock Car Products
Summer Brothers
Thexton Manufacturing Co.
Tilton Engineering, McLane Tilton
Toyota Motor Sales USA
Tractech, Inc.
Transmission Technologies Corporation, TTC
Warn Industries
Warner Electric
Van Norman Equipment Company
Zexel Torsen, Inc.

TECHNICAL AND CONTENT REVIEWERS

The following people reviewed the manuscript before production and checked it for technical accuracy and clarity of presentation. Their suggestions and recommendations were included in the final draft of the manuscript. Their input helped make this textbook clear and technically accurate while maintaining the easy-to-read style that has made other books from the same authors so popular.

Tom Broxholm
Skyline College

Ron Chappell
Santa Fe Community College

Curtis Cline
Wharton County Junior College

Matt Dixon
Southern Illinois University

Kenneth P. Dytrt
Pennsylvania College of Technology

Dr. David Gilbert
Southern Illinois University

Richard Krieger
Michigan Institute of Technology

Russell A. Leonard
Ferris State University

William Milam
Eastfield College

Justin Morgan
Sinclair Community College

Joe Palazzolo
GKN Driveline

Greg Pfahl
Miami-Jacobs Career College

Jeff Rehkopf
Florida State College

Scott Russell
Blue Ridge Community College

Chuck Rockwood
Ventura College

Eugene Talley
Southern Illinois University

Chuck Taylor
Sinclair Community College

Omar Trinidad
Southern Illinois University

Ken Welch
Saddleback College
Special thanks to instructional designer **Alexis I. Skriloff James.**

PHOTO SEQUENCES The authors wish to thank Chuck Taylor of Sinclair Community College in Dayton, Ohio, plus Greg Pfahl and James (Mike) Watson who helped with many of the photos. A special thanks to Dick Krieger and Jeff Rehkopf for their detailed and thorough review of the manuscript before publication and to Richard Reaves for all of his help. Most of all, we wish to thank Michelle Halderman for her assistance in all phases of manuscript preparation.

Jim Halderman

Tom Birch

JIM HALDERMAN Jim Halderman brings a world of experience, knowledge, and talent to his work. His automotive service experience includes working as a flat-rate technician, a business owner, and a professor of automotive technology at a leading U.S. community college for more than 20 years.

He has a Bachelor of Science Degree from Ohio Northern University and a Master's Degree in Education from Miami University in Oxford, Ohio. Jim also holds a U.S. Patent for an electronic transmission control device. He is an ASE certified Master Automotive Technician and Advanced Engine Performance (L1) ASE certified.

Jim is the author of many automotive textbooks, all published by Pearson.

Jim has presented numerous technical seminars to national audiences, including the California Automotive Teachers (CAT) and the Illinois College Automotive Instructor Association (ICAIA). He is also a member and presenter at the North American Council of Automotive Teachers (NACAT). Jim was also named Regional Teacher of the Year by General Motors Corporation and an outstanding alumnus of Ohio Northern University. Jim and his wife, Michelle, live in Dayton, Ohio. They have two children. You can reach Jim at

jim@jameshalderman.com

TOM BIRCH Tom Birch started his automotive service career working as a technician at a Ford dealership. Then, while in the army, he was a Wheel Vehicle Mechanic and worked as a technician on army vehicles when stationed in Europe. He then earned both a Bachelor's and Master's degree from Chico State College, now California State University, Chico and taught in the California school system before going to Yuba College in Northern California. Tom is past president and board member of the California Automotive Teachers (CAT), plus a member and winner of the MVP award of the North American Council of Automotive Teachers (NACAT). He is also a member of the Mobile Air Conditioning Society (MACS) and Automotive Service Council- California (ASC-CA) plus the Society of Automotive Engineers (SAE). Tom is the author of many automotive textbooks, all published by Pearson.

BRIEF CONTENTS

CONTENTS

chapter 1

SERVICE INFORMATION, TOOLS, AND SAFETY

LEARNING OBJECTIVES

After studying this chapter, the reader will be able to:

1. Locate and interpret vehicle and major component identification numbers.
2. Identify the strength ratings of threaded fasteners.
3. Explain the difference between the brand name (trade name) and the proper name for tools.
4. Describe what tool is the best to use for each job.
5. Explain how to maintain hand tools.
6. Identify the personal protective equipment (PPE) that all service technicians should wear.
7. Discuss how to safely use hand tools.
8. Describe how to safely hoist a vehicle.

This chapter will help you understand the ASE content knowledge for vehicle identification and the proper use of tools and shop equipment.

KEY TERMS

Bench grinder 23
Bolts 4
Breaker bar 10
Bump cap 24
Calibration codes 3
Campaign 4
Casting number 3
Cheater bar 13
Chisels 18
Drive sizes 10
Extensions 10
Eye wash station 32
Files 17
Fire blanket 31
Fire extinguisher classes 30
GAWR 2
Grade 6
GVWR 2
Hacksaws 18
Hammers 13
HEV 33
LED 22
Metric bolts 6
Nuts 7

PPE 24
Pinch weld seam 27
Pitch 5
Pliers 14
Punches 17
Ratchet 10
Recall 4
Screwdrivers 11
Snips 17
Socket 10
Socket adapter 13
Spontaneous combustion 26
SST 21
Stud 4
Tensile strength 6
Trouble light 21
TSB 4
UNC 5
UNF 5
Universal joint 10
VECI 2
VIN 2
Washers 7
Wrenches 8

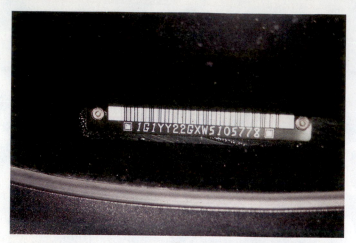

FIGURE 1–1 Typical vehicle identification number (VIN) as viewed through the windshield.

1 = United States	J = Japan	W = Germany
2 = Canada	K = Korea	X = Russia
3 = Mexico	L = China	Y = Sweden
4 = United States	R = Taiwan	Z = Italy
5 = United States	S = England	
6 = Australia	T = Czechoslovakia	
8 = Argentina	U = Romania	
9 = Brazil	V = France	

CHART 1–1

The first number or letter in the VIN identifies the country where the vehicle was made.

A = 1980/2010	L = 1990/2020	Y = 2000/2030
B = 1981/2011	M = 1991/2021	1 = 2001/2031
C = 1982/2012	N = 1992/2022	2 = 2002/2032
D = 1983/2013	P = 1993/2023	3 = 2003/2033
E = 1984/2014	R = 1994/2024	4 = 2004/2034
F = 1985/2015	S = 1995/2025	5 = 2005/2035
G = 1986/2016	T = 1996/2026	6 = 2006/2036
H = 1987/2017	V = 1997/2027	7 = 2007/2037
J = 1988/2018	W = 1998/2028	8 = 2008/2038
K = 1989/2019	X = 1999/2029	9 = 2009/2039

CHART 1–2

The pattern repeats every 30 years for the year of manufacture.

VEHICLE IDENTIFICATION

MAKE, MODEL, AND YEAR All service work requires that the vehicle and its components be properly identified. The most common identification is the make, model, and year of the vehicle.

Make: e.g., Chevrolet

Model: e.g., Impala

Year: e.g., 2008

VEHICLE IDENTIFICATION NUMBER The year of the vehicle is often difficult to determine exactly. A model may be introduced as the next year's model as soon as January of the previous year. Typically, a new model year starts in September or October of the year prior to the actual new year, but not always. This is why the **vehicle identification number**, usually abbreviated **VIN**, is so important. ● SEE FIGURE 1–1.

Since 1981, all vehicle manufacturers have used a VIN that is 17 characters long. Although every vehicle manufacturer assigns various letters or numbers within these 17 characters, there are some constants, including:

- The first number or letter designates the country of origin. ●SEE CHART 1–1.

- The fourth or fifth character is the car line/series.

- The sixth character is the body style.

- The seventh character is the restraint system.

- The eighth character is often the engine code. (Some engines cannot be determined by the VIN number.)

- The tenth character represents the year on all vehicles. ●SEE CHART 1–2.

VEHICLE SAFETY CERTIFICATION LABEL A vehicle safety certification label is attached to the left side pillar post on the rearward-facing section of the left front door. This label indicates the month and year of manufacture as well as the **gross vehicle weight rating (GVWR)**, the **gross axle weight rating (GAWR)**, and the vehicle identification number.

VECI LABEL The **vehicle emissions control information (VECI)** label under the hood of the vehicle shows informative settings and emission hose routing information. ● SEE FIGURE 1–2.

The VECI label (sticker) can be located on the bottom side of the hood, the radiator fan shroud, the radiator core support, or on the strut towers. The VECI label usually includes the following information:

- Engine identification

- Emissions standard that the vehicle meets

- Vacuum hose routing diagram

FIGURE 1–2 The vehicle emissions control information (VECI) sticker is placed under the hood.

- Base ignition timing (if adjustable)
- Spark plug type and gap
- Valve lash
- Emission calibration code

CALIBRATION CODES **Calibration codes** are usually located on Powertrain Control Modules (PCMs) or other controllers. Whenever diagnosing an engine operating fault, it is often necessary to use the calibration code to be sure that the vehicle is the subject of a technical service bulletin or other service procedure. ● **SEE FIGURE 1–3.**

CASTING NUMBERS When an engine part such as a block is cast, a number is put into the mold to identify the casting. ● **SEE FIGURE 1–4.** These **casting numbers** can be used to identify the part and check dimensions such as the cubic inch displacement and other information, such as the year of manufacture. Sometimes changes are made to the mold, yet the casting number is not changed. Most often the casting number is the best piece of identifying information that the service technician can use for identifying an engine.

SERVICE INFORMATION

SERVICE MANUALS Service information is used by the service technician to determine specifications and service procedures, and any needed special tools.

Factory and aftermarket service manuals contain specifications and service procedures. While factory service manuals cover just one year and one or more models of the same vehicle, most aftermarket service manufacturers cover

FIGURE 1–3 A typical calibration code sticker on the case of a controller. The information on the sticker is often needed when ordering parts or a replacement controller.

FIGURE 1–4 Casting numbers on major components can be either cast or stamped.

multiple years and/or models in one manual. Included in most service manuals are the following:

- Capacities and recommended specifications for all fluids
- Specifications including engine and routine maintenance items
- Testing procedures
- Service procedures including the use of special tools when needed

ELECTRONIC SERVICE INFORMATION Electronic service information is available mostly by subscription and provides access to an Internet site where service manual–type information is available. ● **SEE FIGURE 1–5.** Most vehicle manufacturers also offer electronic service information to their dealers and to most schools and colleges that offer corporate training programs.

FIGURE 1–5 Electronic service information is available from aftermarket sources such as ALLDATA and Mitchell On Demand, as well as on websites hosted by vehicle manufacturers.

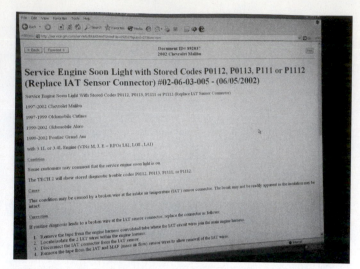

FIGURE 1–6 Technical service bulletins (TSBs) are issued by vehicle manufacturers when a fault occurs that affects many vehicles with the same problem. The TSB then provides the fix for the problem including any parts needed and detailed instructions.

TECHNICAL SERVICE BULLETINS

Technical service bulletins, often abbreviated **TSBs**, sometimes called *technical service information bulletins (TSIB)*, are issued by the vehicle manufacturer to notify service technicians of a problem and include the necessary corrective action. Technical service bulletins are designed for dealership technicians but are republished by aftermarket companies and made available along with other service information to shops and vehicle repair facilities. ● **SEE FIGURE 1–6.**

INTERNET

The Internet has opened the field for information exchange and access to technical advice. One of the most useful websites is the International Automotive Technician's Network at **www.iatn.net**. This is a free site but service technicians must register to join. If a small monthly sponsor fee is paid, the shop or service technician can gain access to the archives, which include thousands of successful repairs in the searchable database.

RECALLS AND CAMPAIGNS

A **recall** or **campaign** is issued by a vehicle manufacturer and a notice is sent to all owners in the event of a safety-related fault or concern. While these faults may be repaired by shops, it is generally handled by a local dealer. Items that have created recalls in the past have included potential fuel system leakage problems, exhaust leakage, or electrical malfunctions that could cause a possible fire or the engine to stall. Unlike technical service bulletins whose cost is only covered when the vehicle is within the warranty period, a recall or campaign is always done at no cost to the vehicle owner.

THREADED FASTENERS

BOLTS AND THREADS

Most of the threaded fasteners used on vehicles are **bolts**. Bolts are called *cap screws* when they are threaded into a casting. Automotive service technicians usually refer to these fasteners as *bolts*, regardless of how they are used. In this chapter, they are called bolts. Sometimes, studs are used for threaded fasteners. A **stud** is a short rod with threads on both ends. Often, a stud will have coarse threads on one end and fine threads on the other end. The end of the stud with coarse threads is screwed into the casting. A nut is used on the opposite end to hold the parts together.

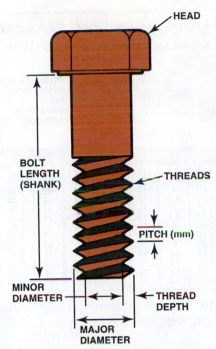

FIGURE 1–7 The dimensions of a typical bolt showing where sizes are measured.

FIGURE 1–8 Thread pitch gauge used to measure the pitch of the thread. This bolt has 13 threads to the inch.

The fastener threads *must* match the threads in the casting or nut. The threads may be measured either in fractions of an inch (called fractional) or in metric units. The size is measured across the outside of the threads, called the *crest* of the thread. ●**SEE FIGURE 1–7**.

FRACTIONAL BOLTS Fractional threads are either coarse or fine. The coarse threads are called **unified national coarse** (**UNC**), and the fine threads are called **unified national fine** (**UNF**). Standard combinations of sizes and number of threads per inch (called **pitch**) are used. Pitch can be measured with a thread pitch gauge as shown in ●**SEE FIGURE 1–8**. Bolts are identified by their diameter and length as measured from below the head, and not by the size of the head or the size of the wrench used to remove or install the bolt.

| SIZE | THREADS PER INCH | | OUTSIDE DIAMETER INCHES |
	NC UNC	NF UNF	
0	..	80	0.0600
1	64	..	0.0730
1	..	72	0.0730
2	56	..	0.0860
2	..	64	0.0860
3	48	..	0.0990
3	..	56	0.0990
4	40	..	0.1120
4	..	48	0.1120
5	40	..	0.1250
5	..	44	0.1250
6	32	..	0.1380
6	..	40	0.1380
8	32	..	0.1640
8	..	36	0.1640
10	24	..	0.1900
10	..	32	0.1900
12	24	..	0.2160
12	..	28	0.2160
1/4	20	..	0.2500
1/4	..	28	0.2500
5/16	18	..	0.3125
5/16	..	24	0.3125
3/8	16	..	0.3750
3/8	..	24	0.3750
7/16	14	..	0.4375
7/16	..	20	0.4375
1/2	13	..	0.5000
1/2	..	20	0.5000
9/16	12	..	0.5625
9/16	..	18	0.5625
5/8	11	..	0.6250
5/8	..	18	0.6250
3/4	10	..	0.7500
3/4	..	16	0.7500
7/8	9	..	0.8750
7/8	..	14	0.8750

CHART 1–3

American standard is one method of sizing fasteners.

Fractional thread sizes are specified by the diameter in fractions of an inch and the number of threads per inch. Typical UNC thread sizes would be 5/16–18 and 1/2–13. Similar UNF thread sizes would be 5/16–24 and 1/2–20. ●**SEE CHART 1–3**.

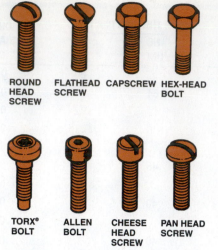

FLATHEAD SCREW | CAPSCREW | HEX-HEAD BOLT

ROUND HEAD SCREW

TORX® BOLT | ALLEN BOLT | CHEESE HEAD SCREW | PAN HEAD SCREW

FIGURE 1–9 Bolts and screws have many different heads which determine what tool is needed.

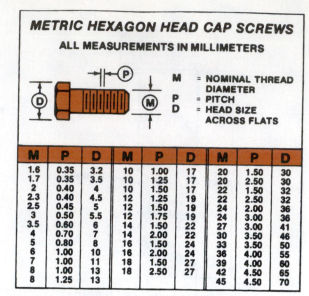

FIGURE 1–10 The metric system specifies fasteners by diameter, length, and pitch.

METRIC HEXAGON HEAD CAP SCREWS

ALL MEASUREMENTS IN MILLIMETERS

M = NOMINAL THREAD DIAMETER
P = PITCH
D = HEAD SIZE ACROSS FLATS

M	P	D	M	P	D	M	P	D
1.6	0.35	3.2	10	1.00	17	20	1.50	30
1.7	0.35	3.5	10	1.25	17	20	2.50	30
2	0.40	4	10	1.50	17	22	1.50	32
2.3	0.40	4.5	12	1.25	19	22	2.50	32
2.5	0.45	5	12	1.50	19	24	2.00	36
3	0.50	5.5	12	1.75	19	24	3.00	36
3.5	0.60	6	14	1.50	22	27	3.00	41
4	0.70	7	14	2.00	22	30	3.50	46
5	0.80	8	16	1.50	24	33	3.50	50
6	1.00	10	16	2.00	24	36	4.00	55
7	1.00	11	18	1.50	27	39	4.00	60
8	1.00	13	18	2.50	27	42	4.50	65
8	1.25	13				45	4.50	70

? FREQUENTLY ASKED QUESTION

How Many Types of Screw Heads Are Used in Automotive Applications?

There are many, including Torx, hex (also called Allen), plus many others used in custom vans and motor homes. ● **SEE FIGURE 1–9.**

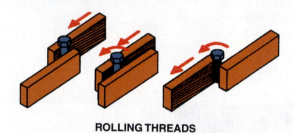

ROLLING THREADS

FIGURE 1–11 Stronger threads are created by cold-rolling a heat-treated bolt blank instead of cutting the threads, using a die.

METRIC BOLTS The size of a **metric bolt** is specified by the letter *M* followed by the diameter in millimeters (mm) across the outside (crest) of the threads. Typical metric sizes would be M8 and M12. metric threads are specified by the thread diameter followed by X and the distance between the threads measured in millimeters (M8 X 1.5). ● **SEE FIGURE 1–10.**

GRADES OF BOLTS Bolts are made from many different types of steel, and for this reason some are stronger than others. The strength or classification of a bolt is called the **grade**. The bolt heads are marked to indicate their grade strength.

The actual grade of bolts is two more than the number of lines on the bolt head. Metric bolts have a decimal number to indicate the grade. More lines or a higher grade number indicate a stronger bolt. In some cases, nuts and machine screws have similar grade markings. Higher grade bolts usually have threads that are rolled rather than cut, which also makes them stronger. ● **SEE FIGURE 1–11.**

CAUTION: *Never* use hardware store (nongraded) bolts, studs, or nuts on any vehicle steering, suspension, or brake component. Always use the exact size and grade of hardware that is specified and used by the vehicle manufacturer.

TENSILE STRENGTH OF FASTENERS Graded fasteners have a higher tensile strength than nongraded fasteners. **Tensile strength** is the maximum stress used under tension (lengthwise force) without causing failure of the fastener. Tensile strength is specified in pounds per square inch (psi).

The strength and type of steel used in a bolt is supposed to be indicated by a raised mark on the head of the bolt. The type of mark depends on the standard to which the bolt was manufactured. Most often, bolts used in machinery are made to SAE Standard J429. ● **SEE CHART 1–4** that shows the grade and specified tensile strength.

SAE BOLT DESIGNATIONS

SAE GRADE NO.	SIZE RANGE	TENSILE STRENGTH, PSI	MATERIAL	HEAD MARKING
1	1/4 through 1 1/2	60,000	Low or medium carbon steel	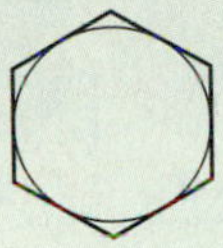
2	1/4 through 3/4	74,000		
	7/8 through 1 1/2	60,000		
5	1/4 through 1	120,000	Medium carbon steel, quenched and tempered	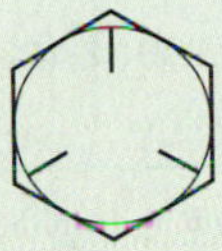
	1 1/8 through 1 1/2	105,000		
5.2	1/4 through 1	120,000	Low carbon martensite steel,* quenched and tempered	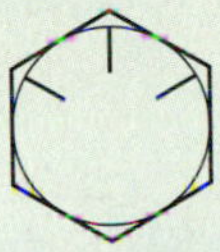
7	1/4 through 1 1/2	133,000	Medium carbon alloy steel, quenched and tempered	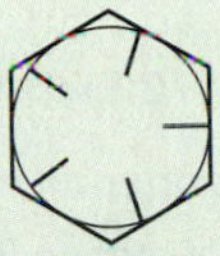
8	1/4 through 1 1/2	150,000	Medium carbon alloy steel, quenched and tempered	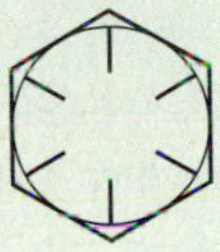
8.2	1/4 through 1	150,000	Low carbon martensite steel,* quenched and tempered	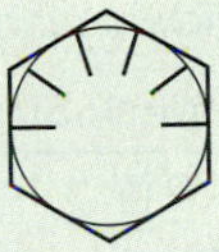

CHART 1–4

*Martensite steel is a specific type of steel that can be cooled rapidly, thereby increasing its hardness. It is named after a German metallurgist, Adolf Martens.
The tensile strength rating system as specified by the Society of Automotive Engineers (SAE).

Metric bolt tensile strength property class is shown on the head of the bolt as a number, such as 4.6, 8.8, 9.8, and 10.9; the higher the number, the stronger the bolt. ● SEE FIGURE 1–12.

NUTS Nuts are the female part of a threaded fastener. Most nuts used on cap screws have the same hex size as the cap screw head. Some inexpensive nuts use a hex size larger than the cap screw head. Metric nuts are often marked with dimples to show their strength. More dimples indicate stronger nuts. Some nuts and cap screws use interference fit threads to keep them from accidentally loosening. This means that the shape of the nut is slightly distorted or that a section of the threads is deformed. Nuts can also be kept from loosening with a nylon washer fastened in the nut or with a nylon patch or strip on the threads. ● SEE FIGURE 1–13.

NOTE: Most of these "locking nuts" are grouped together and are commonly referred to as *prevailing torque nuts.* This means that the nut will hold its tightness or torque and not loosen with movement or vibration. Most prevailing torque nuts should be replaced whenever removed to ensure that the nut will not loosen during service. Always follow the manufacturer's recommendations. Anaerobic sealers, such as Loctite, are used on the threads where the nut or cap screw must be both locked and sealed.

WASHERS Washers are often used under cap screw heads and under nuts. ● SEE FIGURE 1–14. Plain flat washers are used to provide an even clamping load around the fastener. Lock washers are added to prevent accidental loosening. In some accessories, the washers are locked onto the nut to provide easy assembly.

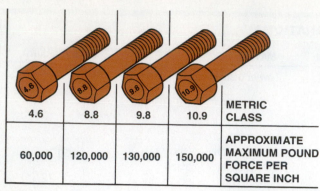

				METRIC CLASS
4.6	8.8	9.8	10.9	
60,000	120,000	130,000	150,000	APPROXIMATE MAXIMUM POUND FORCE PER SQUARE INCH

FIGURE 1–12 Metric bolt (cap screw) grade markings and approximate tensile strength.

FIGURE 1–13 Nuts come in a variety of styles, including locking (prevailing torque) types, such as the distorted thread and nylon insert type.

FIGURE 1–14 Washers come in a variety of styles, including flat and serrated used to help prevent a fastener from loosening.

🔧 **TECH TIP**

A 1/2 Inch Wrench Does Not Fit a 1/2 Inch Bolt

A common mistake made by persons new to the automotive field is to think that the size of a bolt or nut is the size of the head. The size of the bolt or nut (outside diameter of the threads) is usually smaller than the size of the wrench or socket that fits the head of the bolt or nut. Examples are given in the following table:

Wrench Size	Thread Size
7/16 inch	1/4 inch
1/2 inch	5/16 inch
9/16 inch	3/8 inch
5/8 inch	7/16 inch
3/4 inch	1/2 inch
10 mm	6 mm
12 or 13 mm*	8 mm
14 or 17 mm*	10 mm

* European (Système International d'Unités-SI) metric.

🔧 **TECH TIP**

It Just Takes a Second

Whenever removing any automotive component, it is wise to screw the bolts back into the holes a couple of threads by hand. This ensures that the right bolt will be used in its original location when the component or part is put back on the vehicle. Often, the same diameter of fastener is used on a component, but the length of the bolt may vary. Spending just a couple of seconds to put the bolts and nuts back where they belong when the part is removed can save a lot of time when the part is being reinstalled. Besides making certain that the right fastener is being installed in the right place, this method helps prevent bolts and nuts from getting lost or kicked away. How much time have you wasted looking for that lost bolt or nut?

HAND TOOLS

WRENCHES Wrenches are the most used hand tool by service technicians. **Wrenches** are used to grasp and rotate threaded fasteners. Most wrenches are constructed of forged alloy steel, usually chrome-vanadium steel. ● **SEE FIGURE 1–15.**

After the wrench is formed, it is hardened, and then tempered to reduce brittleness, and then chrome plated. There are several types of wrenches.

OPEN-END WRENCH. An open-end wrench is usually used to loosen or tighten bolts or nuts that do not require a lot of torque. Because of the *open* end, this type of wrench can be easily placed on a bolt or nut with an angle of 15 degrees, which allows the wrench to be flipped over and used again to continue to rotate the fastener. The major disadvantage of an open-end wrench is the lack of torque that can be applied due to the fact that the open jaws of the wrench only contact two flat surfaces of the fastener. An open-end wrench has two different sizes, one at each end. ● **SEE FIGURE 1–16.**

FIGURE 1–15 A wrench after it has been forged but before the flashing, extra material around the wrench, has been removed.

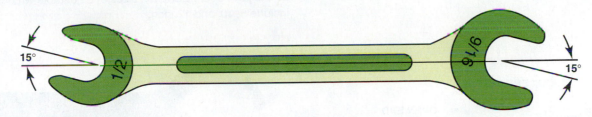

FIGURE 1–16 A typical open-end wrench. The size is different on each end and notice that the head is angled 15 degrees at the end.

BOX-END WRENCH. A *box-end wrench*, also called a *closed-end wrench*, is placed over the top of the fastener and grips the points of the fastener. A box-end wrench is angled 15 degrees to allow it to clear nearby objects.

Therefore, a box-end wrench should be used to loosen or to tighten fasteners because it grasps around the entire head of the fastener. A box-end wrench has two different sizes, one at each end. ● SEE FIGURE 1–17.

Most service technicians purchase *combination wrenches*, which have the open end at one end and the same size box end on the other end. ● SEE FIGURE 1–18.

A combination wrench allows the technician to loosen or tighten a fastener using the box end of the wrench, turn it around, and use the open end to increase the speed of rotating the fastener.

ADJUSTABLE WRENCH. An *adjustable wrench* is often used where the exact size wrench is not available or when a large nut, such as a wheel spindle nut, needs to be rotated but not tightened. An adjustable wrench should not be used to loosen or tighten fasteners because the torque applied to the wrench can cause the movable jaws to loosen their grip on the fastener, causing it to become rounded. ● SEE FIGURE 1–19.

LINE WRENCHES. Line wrenches are also called *flare-nut wrenches*, *fitting wrenches*, or *tube-nut wrenches* and are designed to grip almost all the way around a nut used to retain a fuel or refrigerant line, and yet, be able to be installed over the line. ● SEE FIGURE 1–20.

 **TECH TIP**

Hide Those from the Boss

An apprentice technician started working for a shop and put his top tool box on a workbench. Another technician observed that, along with a complete set of good-quality tools, the box contained several adjustable wrenches. The more experienced technician said, "Hide those from the boss." The boss does not want any service technician to use adjustable wrenches. If any adjustable wrench is used on a bolt or nut, the movable jaw often moves or loosens and starts to round the head of the fastener. If the head of the bolt or nut becomes rounded, it becomes that much more difficult to remove.

SAFE USE OF WRENCHES Wrenches should be inspected before use to be sure they are not cracked, bent, or damaged. All wrenches should be cleaned after use before being returned to the tool box. Always use the correct size of wrench for the fastener being loosened or tightened to help prevent the rounding of the flats of the fastener. When attempting to loosen a fastener, pull a wrench—do not push a wrench. If a wrench is pushed, your knuckles can be hurt when forced into another object if the fastener breaks loose or

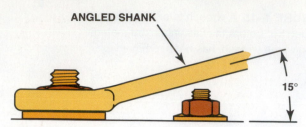

FIGURE 1–17 The end of a box-end wrench is angled 15 degrees to allow clearance for nearby objects or other fasteners.

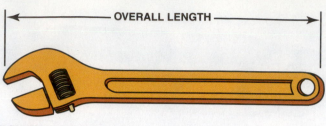

FIGURE 1–19 An adjustable wrench. Adjustable wrenches are sized by the overall length of the wrench and not by how far the jaws open. Common sizes of adjustable wrenches include 8, 10, and 12 inch.

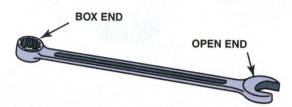

FIGURE 1–18 A combination wrench has an open end at one end and a box end at the other end.

FIGURE 1–20 The end of a typical line wrench, which shows that it is capable of grasping most of the head of the fitting.

if the wrench slips. Always keep wrenches and all hand tools clean to help prevent rust and to allow for a better, firmer grip. Never expose any tool to excessive heat. High temperatures can reduce the strength ("draw the temper") of metal tools.

Never use a hammer on any wrench unless you are using a special "staking face" wrench designed to be used with a hammer. Replace any tools that are damaged or worn.

RATCHETS, SOCKETS, AND EXTENSIONS
A **socket** fits over the fastener and grips the points and/or flats of the bolt or nut. The socket is rotated (driven) using either a long bar called a **breaker bar** (flex handle) or a ratchet. ● SEE **FIGURES 1–21 AND 1–22.**

A **ratchet** is a tool that turns the socket in only one direction and allows the rotating of the ratchet handle back and forth in a narrow space. Socket **extensions** and **universal joints** are also used with sockets to allow access to fasteners in restricted locations.

DRIVE SIZE. Sockets are available in various **drive sizes**, including 1/4, 3/8, and 1/2 inch sizes for most automotive use. ● **SEE FIGURES 1–23 AND 1–24.**

Many heavy-duty truck and/or industrial applications use 3/4 and 1 inch sizes. The drive size is the distance of each side

of the square drive. Sockets and ratchets of the same size are designed to work together.

REGULAR AND DEEP WELL. Sockets are available in regular length for use in most applications or in a deep well design that allows for access to a fastener that uses a long stud or other similar conditions. ● **SEE FIGURE 1–25.**

TORQUE WRENCHES
Torque wrenches are socket turning handles that are designed to apply a known amount of force to the fastener. There are two basic types of torque wrenches:

1. **Clicker type.** This type of torque wrench is first set to the specified torque and then it "clicks" when the set torque value has been reached. When force is removed from the

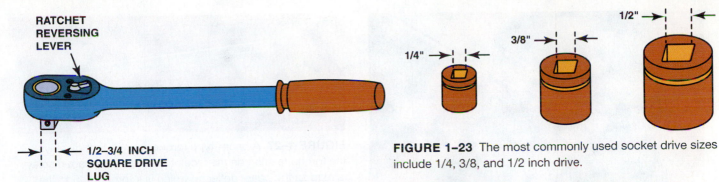

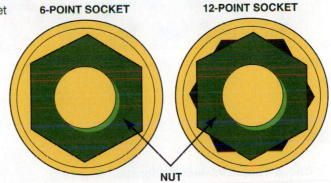

FIGURE 1–23 The most commonly used socket drive sizes include 1/4, 3/8, and 1/2 inch drive.

FIGURE 1–21 A typical ratchet used to rotate a socket. A ratchet makes a ratcheting noise when it is being rotated in the opposite direction from loosening or tightening. A knob or lever on the ratchet allows the user to switch directions.

FIGURE 1–22 A typical flex handle used to rotate a socket, also called a breaker bar because it usually has a longer handle than a ratchet and, therefore, can be used to apply more torque to a fastener than a ratchet.

FIGURE 1–24 A 6 point socket fits the head of a bolt or nut on all sides. A 12 point socket can round off the head of a bolt or nut if a lot of force is applied.

torque wrench handle, another click is heard. The setting on a clicker-type torque wrench should be set back to zero after use and checked for proper calibration regularly. ● **SEE FIGURE 1–26.**

2. **Beam-type.** This type of torque wrench is used to measure torque, but instead of presenting the value, the actual torque is displayed on the dial of the wrench as the fastener is being tightened. Beam-type torque wrenches are available in 1/4, 3/8, and 1/2 inch drives and both English and metric units. ● **SEE FIGURE 1–27.**

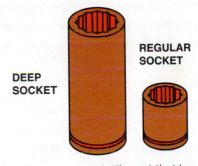

FIGURE 1–25 Allows access to the nut that has a stud plus other locations needing great depth, such as spark plugs.

SAFE USE OF SOCKETS AND RATCHETS Always use the proper size socket that correctly fits the bolt or nut. All sockets and ratchets should be cleaned after use before being placed back into the tool box. Sockets are available in short and deep well designs. Never expose any tool to excessive heat. High temperatures can reduce the strength ("draw the temper") of metal tools.

Never use a hammer on a socket handle unless you are using a special "staking face" wrench designed to be used with a hammer. Replace any tools that are damaged or worn.

Also select the appropriate drive size. For example, for small work, such as on the dash, select a 1/4 inch drive. For most general service work, use a 3/8 inch drive and for suspension and steering and other large fasteners, select a 1/2 inch drive. When loosening a fastener, always pull the ratchet toward you rather than push it outward.

SCREWDRIVERS

STRAIGHT-BLADE SCREWDRIVER. Many smaller fasteners are removed and installed by using a **screwdriver**. Screwdrivers are available in many sizes and tip shapes. The most commonly used screwdriver is called a *straight blade* or *flat tip*.

FIGURE 1–26 Using a clicker-type torque wrench to tighten connecting rod nuts on an engine.

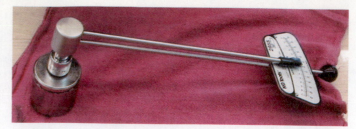

FIGURE 1–27 A beam-type torque wrench that displays the torque reading on the face of the dial. The beam display is read as the beam deflects, which is in proportion to the amount of torque applied to the fastener.

 **TECH TIP**

Check Torque Wrench Calibration Regularly

Torque wrenches should be checked regularly. For example, Honda has a torque wrench calibration setup at each of its training centers. It is expected that a torque wrench be checked for accuracy before every use. Most experts recommend that torque wrenches be checked and adjusted as needed at least every year and more often if possible. ●**SEE FIGURE 1–28.**

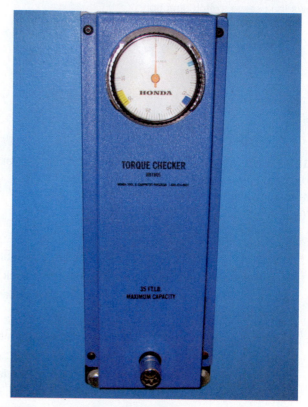

FIGURE 1–28 Torque wrench calibration checker.

Flat-tip screwdrivers are sized by the width of the blade and this width should match the width of the slot in the screw. ●**SEE FIGURE 1–29.**

CAUTION: Do not use a screwdriver as a pry tool or as a chisel. Screwdrivers are hardened steel only at the tip and are not designed to be pounded on or used for prying because they could bend easily. Always use the proper tool for each application.

PHILLIPS SCREWDRIVER. Another type of commonly used screwdriver is called a Phillips screwdriver, named for Henry F. Phillips, who invented the crosshead screw in 1934. Due to the shape of the crosshead screw and screwdriver, a Phillips screw can be driven with more torque than can be achieved with a slotted screw.

A Phillips head screwdriver is specified by the length of the handle and the size of the point at the tip. A #1 tip has a sharp point, a #2 tip is the most commonly used, and a #3 tip is blunt and is only used for larger sizes of Phillips head fasteners. For example, a #2 × 3 inch Phillips screwdriver would typically measure 6 inch from the tip of the blade to the end of the handle (3 inch long handle and 3 inch long blade) with a #2 tip.

Both straight-blade and Phillips screwdrivers are available with a short blade and handle for access to fasteners with limited room. ●**SEE FIGURE 1–30.**

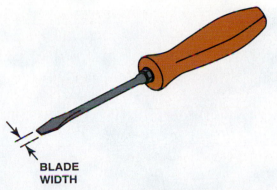

BLADE WIDTH

FIGURE 1–29 A flat-tip (straight-blade) screwdriver. The width of the blade should match the width of the slot in the fastener being loosened or tightened.

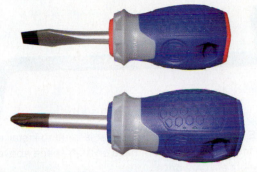

FIGURE 1–30 Two stubby screwdrivers that are used to access screws that have limited space above. A straight blade is on top and a #2 Phillips screwdriver is on the bottom.

TECH TIP

Use Socket Adapters with Caution

A **socket adapter** allows the use of one size of socket and another drive size ratchet or breaker bar. Socket adapters are available and can be used for different drive size sockets on a ratchet. Combinations include:

- 1/4 inch drive—3/8 inch sockets
- 3/8 inch drive—1/4 inch sockets
- 3/8 inch drive—1/2 inch sockets
- 1/2 inch drive—3/8 inch sockets

Using a larger drive ratchet or breaker bar on a smaller size socket can cause the application of too much force to the socket, which could crack or shatter. Using a smaller size drive tool on a larger socket will usually not cause any harm, but would greatly reduce the amount of torque that can be applied to the bolt or nut.

TECH TIP

Avoid Using "Cheater Bars"

Whenever a fastener is difficult to remove, some technicians will insert the handle of a ratchet or a breaker bar into a length of steel pipe sometimes called a **cheater bar**. The extra length of the pipe allows the technician to exert more torque than can be applied using the drive handle alone. However, the extra torque can easily overload the socket and ratchet, causing them to break or shatter, which could cause personal injury.

SAFE USE OF SCREWDRIVERS Always use the proper type and size screwdriver that matches the fastener. Try to avoid pressing down on a screwdriver because if it slips, the screwdriver tip could go into your hand, causing serious personal injury. All screwdrivers should be cleaned after use. Do not use a screwdriver as a prybar; always use the correct tool for the job.

HAMMERS AND MALLETS Hammers and mallets are used to force objects together or apart. The shape of the back part of the hammer head (called the *peen*) usually determines the name. For example, a ball-peen hammer has a rounded end like a ball and it is used to straighten oil pans and valve covers, using the hammer head, and for shaping metal, using the ball peen. ● SEE FIGURE 1–33.

NOTE: A claw hammer has a claw used to remove nails and is not used for automotive service.

A hammer is usually sized by the weight of the head of the hammer and the length of the handle. For example,

OFFSET SCREWDRIVERS. Offset screwdrivers are used in places where a conventional screwdriver cannot fit. An offset screwdriver is bent at the ends and is used similar to a wrench. Most offset screwdrivers have a straight blade at one end and a Phillips end at the opposite end. ● SEE FIGURE 1–31.

IMPACT SCREWDRIVER. An *impact screwdriver* is used to break loose or tighten a screw. A hammer is used to strike the end after the screwdriver holder is placed in the head of the screw and rotated in the desired direction. The force from the hammer blow does two things: It applies a force downward holding the tip of the screwdriver in the slot and then applies a twisting force to loosen (or tighten) the screw. ● SEE FIGURE 1–32.

FIGURE 1–31 An offset screwdriver is used to install or remove fasteners that do not have enough space above to use a conventional screwdriver.

 FREQUENTLY ASKED QUESTION

What Is a Torx?

A Torx is a six-pointed star-shaped tip that was developed by Camcar (formerly Textron) to offer higher loosening and tightening torque than is possible with a straight blade (flat tip) or Phillips. Torx is very commonly used in the automotive field for many components. Commonly used Torx sizes from small to large include:

T15, T20, T25, and T30. Some Torx fasteners include a round projection in the center requiring that a special version of a Torx bit be used. These are called security Torx bits, which have a hole in the center to be used on these fasteners. External Torx fasteners are also used as engine fasteners and are labeled E instead of T, plus the size, such as E45.

FIGURE 1–32 An impact screwdriver used to remove slotted or Phillips head fasteners that cannot be broken loose using a standard screwdriver.

FIGURE 1–33 A typical ball-peen hammer.

a commonly used ball-peen hammer has an 8 ounce head with an 11 inch handle.

MALLETS. *Mallets* are a type of hammer with a large striking surface, which allows the technician to exert force over a larger area than a hammer, so as not to harm the part or component. Mallets are made from a variety of materials including rubber, plastic, or wood. ● **SEE FIGURE 1–34**.

DEAD-BLOW HAMMER. A shot-filled plastic hammer is called a *dead-blow hammer*. The small lead balls (shot) inside a plastic head prevent the hammer from bouncing off of the object when struck. ● **SEE FIGURE 1–35**.

SAFE USE OF HAMMERS AND MALLETS

All mallets and hammers should be cleaned after use and not exposed to extreme temperatures. Never use a hammer or mallet that is damaged in any way and always use caution to avoid doing damage to the components and the surrounding area. Always follow the hammer manufacturer's recommended procedures and practices.

PLIERS

SLIP-JOINT PLIERS. A **pliers** is capable of holding, twisting, bending, and cutting objects and is an extremely useful classification of tools. The common household type of pliers is called the *slip-joint pliers*. There are two different positions where the junction of the handles meets to achieve a wide range of sizes of objects that can be gripped. ● **SEE FIGURE 1–36**.

MULTIGROOVE ADJUSTABLE PLIERS. For gripping larger objects, a set of *multigroove adjustable pliers* is a commonly used tool of choice by many service technicians. Originally designed to remove the various size nuts holding rope seals used in water pumps, the name *water pump pliers* is also used.

FIGURE 1–34 A rubber mallet used to deliver a force to an object without harming the surface.

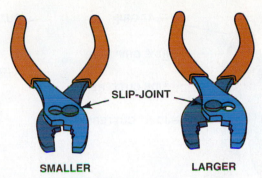

SLIP-JOINT

SMALLER   LARGER

FIGURE 1–36 Typical slip-joint pliers is a common household pliers. The slip joint allows the jaws to be opened to two different settings.

FIGURE 1–35 A dead-blow hammer that was left outside in freezing weather. The plastic covering was damaged, which destroyed this hammer. The lead shot is encased in the metal housing and then covered.

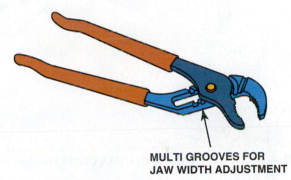

MULTI GROOVES FOR
JAW WIDTH ADJUSTMENT

FIGURE 1–37 Multigroove adjustable pliers is known by many names, including the trade name "Channel Locks®."

These types of pliers are commonly called by their trade name *Channel Locks®*. ● SEE FIGURE 1–37.

LINESMAN'S PLIERS. *Linesman's pliers* is a hand tool specifically designed for cutting, bending, and twisting wire. While commonly used by construction workers and electricians, linesman's pliers is a very useful tool for the service technician who deals with wiring. The center parts of the jaws are designed to grasp round objects such as pipe or tubing without slipping. ● SEE FIGURE 1–38.

DIAGONAL PLIERS. *Diagonal pliers* is designed to cut only. The cutting jaws are set at an angle to make it easier to cut wires. Diagonal pliers are also called *side cuts* or *dikes*. These pliers are constructed of hardened steel and they are used mostly for cutting wire. ● SEE FIGURE 1–39.

NEEDLE-NOSE PLIERS. *Needle-nose pliers* are designed to grip small objects or objects in tight locations. Needle-nose pliers

  TECH TIP

  Pound with Something Softer

  If you must pound on something, be sure to use a tool that is softer than what you are about to pound on to avoid damage. Examples are given in the following table.

The Material Being Pounded	What to Pound with
Steel or cast iron	Brass or aluminum hammer or punch
Aluminum	Plastic or rawhide mallet or plastic-covered dead-blow hammer
Plastic	Rawhide mallet or plastic dead-blow hammer

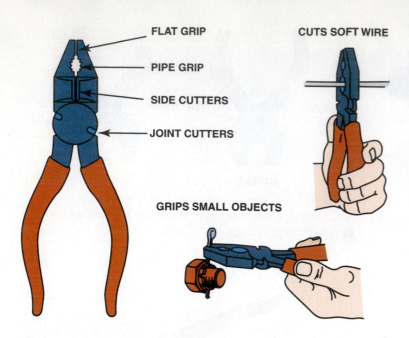

FLAT GRIP

PIPE GRIP

SIDE CUTTERS

JOINT CUTTERS

CUTS SOFT WIRE

GRIPS SMALL OBJECTS

FIGURE 1–38 Linesman's pliers are very useful because it can help perform many automotive service jobs.

CUTTING WIRES CLOSE TO TERMINALS

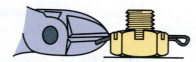

PULLING OUT AND SPREADING COTTER PIN

FIGURE 1–39 Diagonal-cut pliers is another common tool that has many names.

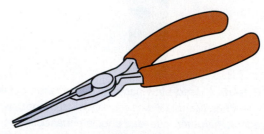

FIGURE 1–40 Needle-nose pliers are used where there is limited access to a wire or pin that needs to be installed or removed.

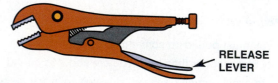

RELEASE LEVER

FIGURE 1–41 Locking pliers are best known by their trade name Vise Grips®.

have long, pointed jaws, which allow the tips to reach into narrow openings or groups of small objects. ● **SEE FIGURE 1–40.**

Most needle-nose pliers have a wire cutter located at the base of the jaws near the pivot. There are several variations of needle nose pliers, including right angle jaws or slightly angled to allow access to certain cramped areas.

LOCKING PLIERS. *Locking pliers* are adjustable pliers that can be locked to hold objects from moving. Most locking pliers also have wire cutters built into the jaws near the pivot point. Locking pliers come in a variety of styles and sizes and are commonly referred to by the trade name *Vise Grips®.* The size is the length of the pliers, not how far the jaws open. ● **SEE FIGURE 1–41.**

SNAP-RING PLIERS. *Snap-ring pliers* is used to remove and install snap-rings. Many snap-ring pliers are designed to be able to remove and install both inward, as well as outward, expanding snap rings. Some snap-ring pliers can be equipped with serrated-tipped jaws for grasping the opening in the snap ring, while others are equipped with points, which are inserted into the holes in the snap ring. ● **SEE FIGURE 1–42.**

SAFE USE OF PLIERS Pliers should not be used to remove any bolt or other fastener. Pliers should only be used when specified for use by the vehicle manufacturer.

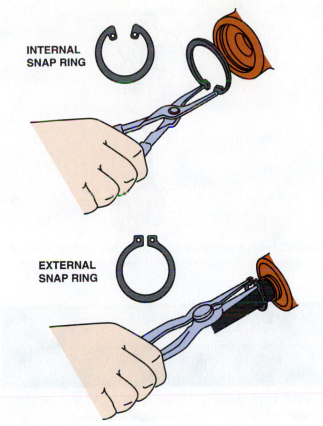

INTERNAL
SNAP RING

EXTERNAL
SNAP RING

FIGURE 1–42 Snap-ring pliers are also called lock ring pliers and most are designed to remove internal and external snap rings (lock rings).

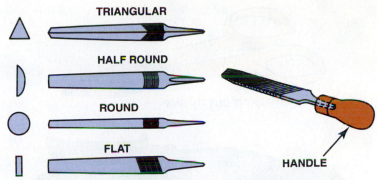

TRIANGULAR

HALF ROUND

ROUND

FLAT

HANDLE

FIGURE 1–43 Files come in many different shapes and sizes. Never use a file without a handle.

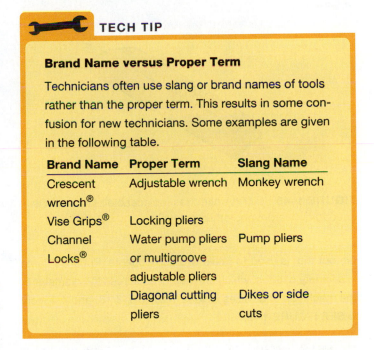

TECH TIP

Brand Name versus Proper Term

Technicians often use slang or brand names of tools rather than the proper term. This results in some confusion for new technicians. Some examples are given in the following table.

Brand Name	Proper Term	Slang Name
Crescent wrench®	Adjustable wrench	Monkey wrench
Vise Grips®	Locking pliers	
Channel Locks®	Water pump pliers or multigroove adjustable pliers	Pump pliers
	Diagonal cutting pliers	Dikes or side cuts

FILES Files are used to smooth metal and are constructed of hardened steel with diagonal rows of teeth. Files are available with a single row of teeth called a *single cut file*, as well as two rows of teeth cut at an opposite angle called a *double cut file*. Files are available in a variety of shapes and sizes from small flat files, half-round files, and triangular files. ● **SEE FIGURE 1–43.**

SAFE USE OF FILES Always use a file with a handle. Because files only cut when moved forward, a handle must be attached to prevent possible personal injury. After making a forward strike, lift the file and return the file to the starting position; avoid dragging the file backward.

SNIPS Service technicians are often asked to fabricate sheet metal brackets or heat shields and need to use one or more types of cutters available called **snips**. *Tin snips* are the simplest and are designed to make straight cuts in a variety of materials, such as sheet steel, aluminum, or even fabric. A variation of the tin snips is called *aviation tin snips*. There are three designs of aviation snips including one designed to cut straight (called a *straight cut aviation snip*), one

designed to cut left (called an *offset left aviation snip*), and one designed to cut right (called an *offset right aviation snip*). ● **SEE FIGURE 1–44.**

UTILITY KNIFE A *utility knife* uses a replaceable blade and is used to cut a variety of materials such as carpet, plastic, wood, and paper products, such as cardboard. ● **SEE FIGURE 1–45.**

SAFE USE OF CUTTERS Whenever using cutters, always wear eye protection or a face shield to guard against the possibility of metal pieces being ejected during the cut. Always follow recommended procedures.

PUNCHES A **punch** is a small diameter steel rod that has a smaller diameter ground at one end. A punch is used to drive a

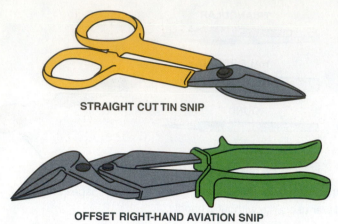

STRAIGHT CUT TIN SNIP

OFFSET RIGHT-HAND AVIATION SNIP

FIGURE 1–44 Tin snips are used to cut thin sheets of metal or carpet.

FIGURE 1–45 A utility knife uses replaceable blades and is used to cut carpet and other materials.

pin out that is used to retain two components. Punches come in a variety of sizes, which are measured across the diameter of the machined end. Sizes include 1/16, 1/8, 3/16, and 1/4 inch. ● **SEE FIGURE 1–46.**

CHISELS A **chisel** has a straight, sharp cutting end that is used for cutting off rivets or to separate two pieces of an assembly. The most common design of chisel used for automotive service work is called a *cold chisel*.

SAFE USE OF PUNCHES AND CHISELS Always wear eye protection when using a punch or a chisel because the hardened steel is brittle and parts of the punch could fly off and cause serious personal injury. See the warning stamped on the side of this automotive punch in ● **FIGURE 1–47**.

The tops of punches and chisels can become rounded off from use, which is called "mushroomed." This material must be ground off to help avoid the possibility of the overhanging material being loosened and becoming airborne during use. ● **SEE FIGURE 1–48.**

HACKSAWS A **hacksaw** is used to cut metals, such as steel, aluminum, brass, or copper. The cutting blade of a hacksaw

PIN

FIGURE 1–46 A punch used to drive pins from assembled components. This type of punch is also called a pin punch.

WEAR SAFETY GOGGLES

FIGURE 1–47 Warning stamped on the side of a punch warning that goggles should be worn when using this tool. Always follow safety warnings.

is replaceable and the sharpness and number of teeth can be varied to meet the needs of the job. Use 14 or 18 teeth per inch (TPI) for cutting plaster or soft metals, such as aluminum and copper. Use 24 or 32 teeth per inch for steel or pipe. Hacksaw blades should be installed with the teeth pointing away from the handle. This means that a hacksaw only cuts while the blade is pushed in the forward direction. ● **SEE FIGURE 1–49.**

SAFE USE OF HACKSAWS Check that the hacksaw is equipped with the correct blade for the job and that the teeth are pointed away from the handle. When using a hacksaw, move the hacksaw slowly away from you, then lift slightly and return for another cut.

BASIC HAND TOOL LIST

The following is a typical list of hand tools every automotive technician should possess. Specialty tools are not included.

Safety glasses

Tool chest

1/4 inch drive socket set (1/4 to 9/16 inch standard and deep sockets; 6 to 15 mm standard and deep sockets)

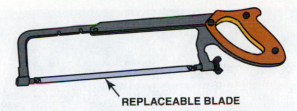

REPLACEABLE BLADE

FIGURE 1–49 A typical hacksaw that is used to cut metal. If cutting sheet metal or thin objects, a blade with more teeth should be used.

RIGHT   **WRONG**

FIGURE 1–48 Use a grinder or a file to remove the mushroom material on the end of a punch or chisel.

1/4 inch drive ratchet

1/4 inch drive 2 inch extension

1/4 inch drive 6 inch extension

1/4 inch drive handle

3/8 inch drive socket set (3/8 to 7/8 inch standard and deep sockets; 10 to 19 mm standard and deep sockets)

3/8 inch drive Torx set (T40, T45, T50, and T55)

3/8 inch drive 13/16 inch plug socket

3/8 inch drive 5/8 inch plug socket

3/8 inch drive ratchet

3/8 inch drive 1 1/2 inch extension

3/8 inch drive 3 inch extension

3/8 inch drive 6 inch extension

3/8 inch drive 18 inch extension

3/8 inch drive universal

1/2 inch drive socket set (1/2 to 1 inch standard and deep sockets)

1/2 inch drive ratchet

1/2 inch drive breaker bar

1/2 inch drive 5 inch extension

1/2 inch drive 10 inch extension

3/8 to 1/4 inch adapter

1/2 to 3/8 inch adapter

3/8 to 1/2 inch adapter

Crowfoot set (fractional inch)

Crowfoot set (metric)

3/8 through 1 inch combination wrench set

10 through 19 mm combination wrench set

1/16 through 1/4 inch hex wrench set

2 through 12 mm hex wrench set

3/8 inch hex socket

13 to 14 mm flare-nut wrench

15 to 17 mm flare-nut wrench

5/16 to 3/8 inch flare-nut wrench

7/16 to 1/2 inch flare-nut wrench

1/2 to 9/16 inch flare-nut wrench

Diagonal pliers

Needle pliers

Adjustable-jaw pliers

Locking pliers

Snap-ring pliers

Stripping or crimping pliers

Ball-peen hammer

Rubber hammer

Dead-blow hammer

Five-piece standard screwdriver set

Four-piece Phillips screwdriver set

#15 Torx screwdriver

#20 Torx screwdriver

Center punch

Pin punches (assorted sizes)

Chisel

Utility knife

Valve core tool

Filter wrench (large filters)

Filter wrench (smaller filters)

Test light

Feeler gauge

Scraper

Pinch bar

Magnet

FIGURE 1–50 A typical beginning technician tool set that includes the basic tools to get started.

FIGURE 1–51 A typical large tool box, showing just one of many drawers.

FIGURE 1–52 A typical 12 volt test light.

TOOL SETS AND ACCESSORIES

A beginning service technician may wish to start with a small set of tools before purchasing an expensive tool set. ● **SEE FIGURES 1–50 AND 1–51.**

ELECTRICAL HAND TOOLS

TEST LIGHT A test light is used to test for electricity. A typical automotive test light consists of a clear plastic screwdriver-like handle that contains a lightbulb. A wire is attached to one terminal of the bulb, which the technician connects to a clean metal part of the vehicle. The other end of the bulb is attached to a point that can be used to test for electricity at a connector or wire. When there is power at the point and a good connection at the other end, the lightbulb lights. ● **SEE FIGURE 1–52.**

SOLDERING GUNS

ELECTRIC SOLDERING GUN. This type of soldering gun is usually powered by 110 volt AC and often has two power settings expressed in watts. A typical electric soldering gun will produce from 85 to 300 watts of heat at the tip, which is more than adequate for soldering.

ELECTRIC SOLDERING PENCIL. This type of soldering iron is less expensive and creates less heat than an electric soldering gun. A typical electric soldering pencil (iron) creates 30 to 60 watts of heat and is suitable for soldering smaller wires and connections.

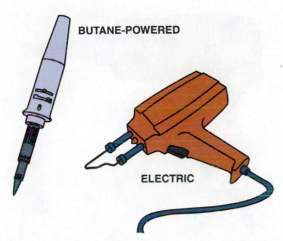

BUTANE-POWERED

ELECTRIC

FIGURE 1–53 Electric and butane-powered soldering guns used to make electrical repairs. Soldering guns are sold by the wattage rating. The higher the wattage, the greater amount of heat created. Most solder guns used for automotive electrical work usually fall within the 60 to 160 watt range.

BUTANE-POWERED SOLDERING IRON. A butane-powered soldering iron is portable and very useful for automotive service work because an electrical cord is not needed. Most butane-powered soldering irons produce about 60 watts of heat, which is enough for most automotive soldering. ● SEE FIGURE 1–53.

ELECTRICAL WORK HAND TOOLS In addition to a soldering iron, most service technicians who do electrical-related work should have the following:

- Wire cutters
- Wire strippers
- Wire crimpers
- Heat gun for heat shrink tubing

DIGITAL METER A digital meter is a necessary tool for any electrical diagnosis and troubleshooting. A digital multimeter, abbreviated DMM, is usually capable of measuring the following units of electricity:

- DC volts
- AC volts
- Ohms
- Amperes

HAND TOOL MAINTENANCE

Most hand tools are constructed of rust-resistant metals but they can still rust or corrode if not properly maintained. For best results and long tool life, the following steps should be taken:

? **FREQUENTLY ASKED QUESTION**

What Is an "SST"?

Vehicle manufacturers often specify a **special service tool (SST)** to properly disassemble and assemble components, such as transmissions and other components. These tools are also called special tools and are available from the vehicle manufacturer or their tool supplier, such as Kent-Moore and Miller tools. Many service technicians do not have access to special service tools so they use generic versions that are available from aftermarket sources.

- Clean each tool before placing it back into the tool box.
- Keep tools separated. Moisture on metal tools will start to rust more readily if the tools are in contact with another metal tool.
- Line the drawers of the tool box with a material that will prevent the tools from moving as the drawers are opened and closed. This helps to quickly locate the proper tool and size.
- Release the tension on all "clicker-type" torque wrenches.
- Keep the tool box secure.

TROUBLE LIGHTS

INCANDESCENT *Incandescent lights* use a filament that produces light when electric current flows through the bulb. This was the standard **trouble light**, also called a *work light* for many years until safety issues caused most shops to switch to safer fluorescent or LED lights. If incandescent lightbulbs are used, try to locate bulbs that are rated "rough service," which is designed to withstand shock and vibration more than conventional lightbulbs.

 WARNING

Do not use incandescent trouble lights around gasoline or other flammable liquids. The liquids can cause the bulb to break and the hot filament can ignite the flammable liquid, which can cause personal injury or even death.

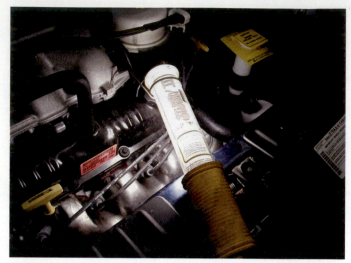

FIGURE 1–54 A fluorescent trouble light operates cooler and is safer to use in the shop because it is protected against accidental breakage where gasoline or other flammable liquids would happen to come in contact with the light.

FIGURE 1–55 A typical 1/2 inch drive air impact wrench. The direction of rotation can be changed to loosen or tighten a fastener.

FLUORESCENT A trouble light is an essential piece of shop equipment, and for safety, should be fluorescent rather than incandescent. Incandescent lightbulbs can scatter or break if gasoline were to be splashed onto the bulb creating a serious fire hazard. Fluorescent light tubes are not as likely to be broken and are usually protected by a clear plastic enclosure. Trouble lights are usually attached to a retractor, which can hold 20 to 50 feet of electrical cord. ● **SEE FIGURE 1–54.**

LED TROUBLE LIGHT Light-emitting diode (**LED**) trouble lights are excellent to use because they are shock resistant, are long lasting, and do not represent a fire hazard. Some trouble lights are battery powered and therefore can be used in places where an attached electrical cord could present problems.

FIGURE 1–56 A typical battery-powered 3/8 inch drive impact wrench.

AIR AND ELECTRICALLY OPERATED TOOLS

IMPACT WRENCH An impact wrench, either air or electrically powered, is a tool that is used to remove and install fasteners. The air-operated 1/2 inch drive impact wrench is the most commonly used unit. ● **SEE FIGURE 1–55.**

Electrically powered impact wrenches commonly include:

- Battery-powered units. ● **SEE FIGURE 1–56.**
- 110 volt AC-powered units. This type of impact is very useful, especially if compressed air is not readily available.

> ☠ **WARNING**
>
> Always use impact sockets with impact wrenches, and always wear eye protection in case the socket or fastener shatters. Impact sockets are thicker walled and constructed with premium alloy steel. They are hardened with a black oxide finish to help prevent corrosion and distinguish them from regular sockets. ● SEE FIGURE 1–57.

FIGURE 1–57 A black impact socket. Always use an impact-type socket whenever using an impact wrench to avoid the possibility of shattering the socket, which could cause personal injury. If a socket is chrome plated, it is not to be used with an impact wrench.

AIR RATCHET An air ratchet is used to remove and install fasteners that would normally be removed or installed using a ratchet and a socket. ● **SEE FIGURE 1–58.**

DIE GRINDER A die grinder is a commonly used air-powered tool which can also be used to sand or remove gaskets and rust. ● **SEE FIGURE 1–59.**

BENCH- OR PEDESTAL-MOUNTED GRINDER These high-powered grinders can be equipped with a wire brush wheel and/or a stone wheel.

- **Wire brush wheel**—This type is used to clean threads of bolts as well as to remove gaskets from sheet metal engine parts.
- **Stone wheel**—This type is used to grind metal or to remove the mushroom from the top of punches or chisels. ● **SEE FIGURE 1–60.**

Most **bench grinders** are equipped with a grinder wheel (stone) on one end and a wire brush wheel on the other end. A bench grinder is a very useful piece of shop equipment and the wire wheel end can be used for the following:

- Cleaning threads of bolts
- Cleaning gaskets from sheet metal parts, such as steel valve covers

CAUTION: Only use a steel wire brush on steel or iron components. If a steel wire brush is used on aluminum or copper-based metal parts, it can remove metal from the part.

FIGURE 1–58 An air ratchet is a very useful tool that allows fast removal and installation of fasteners, especially in areas that are difficult to reach or do not have room enough to move a hand ratchet or wrench.

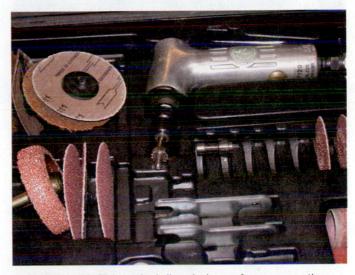

FIGURE 1–59 This typical die grinder surface preparation kit includes the air-operated die grinder as well as a variety of sanding disks for smoothing surfaces or removing rust.

FIGURE 1–60 A typical pedestal grinder with a wire wheel on the left side and a stone wheel on the right side. Even though this machine is equipped with guards, safety glasses or a face shield should always be worn whenever using a grinder or wire wheel.

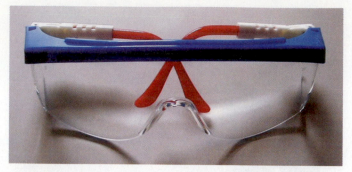

FIGURE 1–61 Safety glasses should be worn at all times when working on or around any vehicle or servicing any components.

The grinding stone end of the bench grinder can be used for the following:

- Sharpening blades and drill bits
- Grinding off the heads of rivets or parts
- Sharpening sheet metal parts for custom fitting

PERSONAL PROTECTIVE EQUIPMENT

Service technicians should wear **personal protective equipment (PPE)** to prevent personal injury. The personal protection devices include the following:

SAFETY GLASSES Wear safety glasses at all times while servicing any vehicle and be sure that they meet standard ANSI Z87.1. ● **SEE FIGURE 1–61.**

STEEL-TOED SAFETY SHOES ● **SEE FIGURE 1–62.** If steel-toed safety shoes are not available, then leather-topped shoes offer more protection than canvas or cloth covered shoes.

BUMP CAP Service technicians working under a vehicle should wear a **bump cap** to protect the head against under-vehicle objects and the pads of the lift. ● **SEE FIGURE 1–63.**

HEARING PROTECTION Hearing protection should be worn if the sound around you requires that you raise your voice (sound level higher than 90 dB). For example, a typical

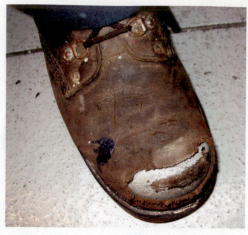

FIGURE 1–62 Steel-toed shoes are a worthwhile investment to help prevent foot injury due to falling objects. Even these well-worn shoes can protect the feet of this service technician.

FIGURE 1–63 One version of a bump cap is a molded plastic insert that is worn inside a regular cloth cap.

lawnmower produces noise at a level of about 110 dB. This means that everyone who uses a lawnmower or other lawn or garden equipment should wear ear protection.

GLOVES Many technicians wear gloves not only to help keep their hands clean but also to help protect their skin from the effects of dirty engine oil and other possibly hazardous materials.

Several types of gloves and their characteristics include:

- **Latex surgical gloves.** These gloves are relatively inexpensive, but tend to stretch, swell, and weaken when exposed to gas, oil, or solvents.
- **Vinyl gloves.** These gloves are also inexpensive and are not affected by gas, oil, or solvents.
- **Polyurethane gloves.** These gloves are more expensive, yet very strong. Even though these gloves are also not affected by gas, oil, or solvents, they do tend to be slippery.

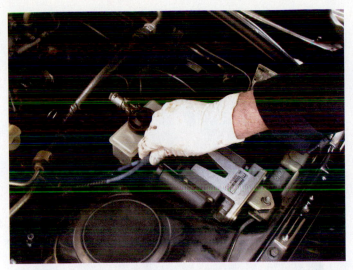

FIGURE 1–64 Protective gloves are available in several sizes and materials.

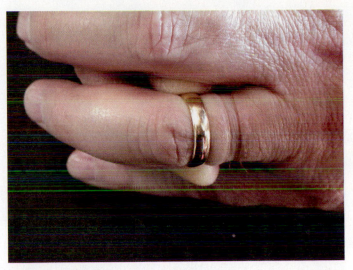

FIGURE 1–65 Remove all jewelry before performing service work on any vehicle.

- **Nitrile gloves.** These gloves are exactly like latex gloves, but are not affected by gas, oil, or solvents, yet they tend to be expensive.
- **Mechanic's gloves.** These gloves are usually made of synthetic leather and spandex and provide thermo protection, as well as protection from dirt and grime.

● **SEE FIGURE 1–64.**

SAFETY PRECAUTIONS

Besides wearing personal safety equipment, there are also many actions that should be performed to keep safe in the shop. These actions include:

- Remove jewelry that may get caught on something or act as a conductor to an exposed electrical circuit. ● **SEE FIGURE 1–65.**
- Take care of your hands. Keep your hands clean by washing with soap and hot water that is at least 110°F (43°C).
- Avoid loose or dangling clothing.
- When lifting any object, get a secure grip with solid footing. Keep the load close to your body to minimize the strain. Lift with your legs and arms, not your back.
- Do not twist your body when carrying a load. Instead, pivot your feet to help prevent strain on the spine.
- Ask for help when moving or lifting heavy objects.

FIGURE 1–66 Always connect an exhaust hose to the tailpipe of a vehicle to be run inside a building.

- Push a heavy object rather than pull it. (This is opposite to the way you should work with tools—never push a wrench! If you do and a bolt or nut loosens, your entire weight is used to propel your hand(s) forward. This usually results in cuts, bruises, or other painful injury.)
- Always connect an exhaust hose to the tailpipe of any running vehicle to help prevent the buildup of carbon monoxide inside a closed garage space. ● **SEE FIGURE 1–66.**
- When standing, keep objects, parts, and tools with which you are working between chest height and waist height. If seated, work at tasks that are at elbow height.
- Always be sure the hood is securely held open.

FIGURE 1–67 A binder clip being used to keep a fender cover from falling off.

FIGURE 1–68 Covering the interior as soon as the vehicle comes in for service helps improve customer satisfaction.

VEHICLE PROTECTION

FENDER COVERS Whenever working under the hood of any vehicle, be sure to use fender covers. They not only help protect the vehicle from possible damage but they also provide a clean surface to place parts and tools. The major problem with using fender covers is that they tend to move and often fall off the vehicle. To help prevent the fender covers from falling off secure them to a lip of the fender using a *binder clip* available at most office supply stores. ● **SEE FIGURE 1–67.**

INTERIOR PROTECTION Always protect the interior of the vehicle from accidental damage or dirt and grease by covering the seat, steering wheel, and floor with a protective covering. ● **SEE FIGURE 1–68.**

SAFETY LIFTING (HOISTING) A VEHICLE

Many chassis and underbody service procedures require that the vehicle be hoisted or lifted off the ground. The simplest methods involve the use of drive-on ramps or a floor jack and safety (jack) stands, whereas in-ground or surface-mounted lifts provide greater access.

✚ **SAFETY TIP**

Shop Cloth Disposal

Always dispose of oily shop cloths in an enclosed container to prevent a fire. ● **SEE FIGURE 1–69.** Whenever oily cloths are thrown together on the floor or workbench, a chemical reaction can occur, which can ignite the cloth even without an open flame. This process of ignition without an open flame is called **spontaneous combustion**.

Setting the pads is a critical part of this hoisting procedure. All vehicle service information, including service, shop, and owner's manuals, include recommended locations to be used when hoisting (lifting) a vehicle. Newer vehicles have a triangle decal on the driver's door indicating the recommended lift points. The recommended standards for the lift points and lifting procedures are found in SAE Standard JRP-2184. ● **SEE FIGURE 1–70.**

FIGURE 1–69 All oily shop cloths should be stored in a metal container equipped with a lid to help prevent spontaneous combustion.

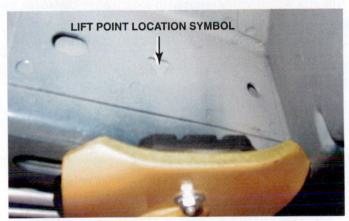

LIFT POINT LOCATION SYMBOL

FIGURE 1–70 Most newer vehicles have a triangle symbol indicating the recommended hoisting lift location.

These recommendations typically include the following points:

1. The vehicle should be centered on the lift or hoist so as not to overload one side or put too much force either forward or rearward. ● **SEE FIGURE 1–71.**

2. The pads of the lift should be spread as far apart as possible to provide a stable platform.

3. Each pad should be placed under a portion of the vehicle that is strong and capable of supporting the weight of the vehicle.

   a. Pinch welds at the bottom edge of the body are generally considered to be strong.

CAUTION: Even though pinch weld seams are the recommended location for hoisting many vehicles with unitized

(a)

(b)

FIGURE 1–71 (a) Tall safety stands can be used to provide additional support for the vehicle while on the hoist. (b) A block of wood should be used to avoid the possibility of doing damage to components supported by the stand.

bodies (unit-body), care should be taken not to place the pad(s) too far forward or rearward. Incorrect placement of the vehicle on the lift could cause the vehicle to be imbalanced, and the vehicle could fall. This is exactly what happened to the vehicle in ● **FIGURE 1–72.**

   b. Boxed areas of the body are the best places to position the pads on a vehicle without a frame. Be careful to note whether the arms of the lift might come into

FIGURE 1–72 This training vehicle fell from the hoist because the pads were not set correctly. No one was hurt but the vehicle was damaged.

contact with other parts of the vehicle before the pad touches the intended location. Commonly damaged areas include the following:

(1) Rocker panel moldings

(2) Exhaust system (including catalytic converter)

(3) Tires or body panels (● **SEE FIGURES 1–73 AND 1–74.**)

4. The vehicle should be raised about a foot (30 centimeters [cm]) off the floor, then stopped and shaken to check for stability. If the vehicle seems to be stable when checked at a short distance from the floor, continue raising the vehicle and continue to view the vehicle until it has reached the desired height. The hoist should be lowered onto the mechanical locks, and then raised off of the locks before lowering.

CAUTION: Do not look away from the vehicle while it is being raised (or lowered) on a hoist. Often one side or one end of the hoist can stop or fail, resulting in the vehicle being slanted enough to slip or fall, creating physical damage not only to the vehicle and/or hoist but also to the technician or others who may be nearby.

HINT: Most hoists can be safely placed at any desired height. For ease while working, the area in which you are working should be at chest level. When working on brakes or suspension components, it is not necessary to work on them down near the floor or over your head. Raise the hoist so that the components are at chest level.

5. Before lowering the hoist, the safety latch(es) must be released and the direction of the controls reversed. The speed downward is often adjusted to be as slow as possible for additional safety.

JACKS AND SAFETY STANDS

Floor jacks properly rated for the weight of the vehicle being raised are a common vehicle lifting tool. Floor jacks are portable and relatively inexpensive and must be used with safety (jack) stands. The floor jack is used to raise the vehicle off the ground and safety stands should be placed under the frame on the body of the vehicle. The weight of the vehicle should never be kept on the hydraulic floor jack because a failure of the jack could cause the vehicle to fall. ● **SEE FIGURE 1–75.** The jack is then slowly released to allow the vehicle weight to be supported on the safety stands. If the front or rear of the vehicle is being raised, the opposite end of the vehicle must be blocked.

CAUTION: Safety stands should be rated higher than the weight they support.

DRIVE-ON RAMPS

Ramps are an inexpensive way to raise the front or rear of a vehicle. ● **SEE FIGURE 1–76.** Ramps are easy to store, but they can be dangerous because they can "kick out" when driving the vehicle onto the ramps.

CAUTION: Professional repair shops do not use ramps because they are dangerous to use. Use only with extreme care.

ELECTRICAL CORD SAFETY

Use correctly grounded three-prong sockets and extension cords to operate power tools. Some tools use only two-prong plugs. Make sure these are double insulated and repair or replace any electrical cords that are cut or damaged to prevent the possibility of an electrical shock. When not in use, keep electrical cords off the floor to prevent tripping over them. Tape the cords down if they are placed in high foot traffic areas.

(a)

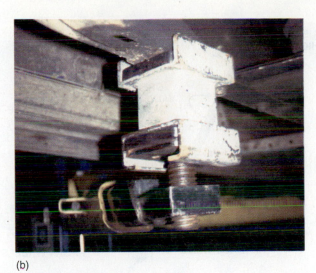
(b)

FIGURE 1–73 (a) An assortment of hoist pad adapters that are often needed to safely hoist many pickup trucks, vans, and sport utility vehicles (SUVs). (b) A view from underneath a Chevrolet pickup truck showing how the pad extensions are used to attach the hoist lifting pad to contact the frame.

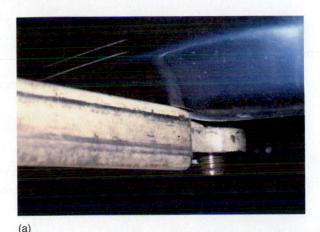
(a)

(b)

FIGURE 1–74 (a) The pad arm is just contacting the rocker panel of the vehicle. (b) The pad arm has dented the rocker panel on this vehicle because the pad was set too far inward underneath the vehicle.

JUMP STARTING AND BATTERY SAFETY

To jump start another vehicle with a dead battery, connect good-quality copper jumper cables as indicated in ● **SEE FIGURE 1–77** or a jump box. The last connection made should always be on the engine block or an engine bracket as far from the battery as possible. It is normal for a spark to be created when the jumper cables finally complete the jumper cable connections, and this spark could cause an explosion of the gases around the battery. Many newer vehicles have special ground connections built away from the battery just for the purpose of jump starting. Check the owner's manual or service information for the exact location.

Batteries contain acid and should be handled with care to avoid tipping them greater than a 45-degree angle. Always remove jewelry when working around a battery to avoid the possibility of electrical shock or burns, which can occur when the metal comes in contact with a 12 volt circuit and ground, such as the body of the vehicle.

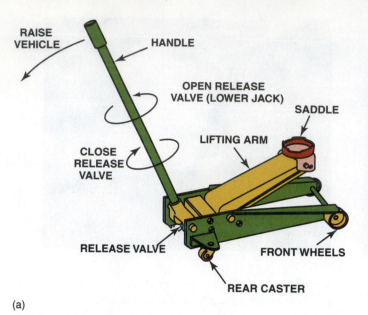

(a)

(b)

FIGURE 1–75 (a) A hydraulic hand-operated floor jack. (b) Whenever a vehicle is raised off the ground, a safety stand should be placed under the frame, axle, or body to support the weight of the vehicle.

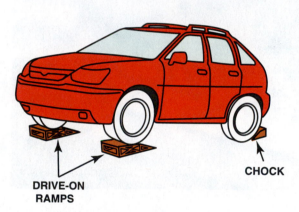

FIGURE 1–76 Drive-on-type ramps are dangerous to use. The wheels on the ground level must be chocked (blocked) to prevent accidental movement down the ramp.

SAFETY TIP

Air Hose Safety

Improper use of an air nozzle can cause blindness or deafness. Compressed air must be reduced to less than 30 psi (206 kPa). ● **SEE FIGURE 1–78.** If an air nozzle is used to dry and clean parts, make sure the airstream is directed away from anyone else in the immediate area. Coil and store air hoses when they are not in use.

FIRE EXTINGUISHERS

There are four **fire extinguisher classes**. Each class should be used on specific fires only:

- **Class A** is designed for use on general combustibles, such as cloth, paper, and wood.
- **Class B** is designed for use on flammable liquids and greases, including gasoline, oil, thinners, and solvents.
- **Class C** is used only on electrical fires.
- **Class D** is effective only on combustible metals such as powdered aluminum, sodium, or magnesium.

The class rating is clearly marked on the side of every fire extinguisher. Many extinguishers are good for multiple types of fires. ● **SEE FIGURE 1–79.**

When using a fire extinguisher, remember the word "PASS."

P = Pull the safety pin.

A = Aim the nozzle of the extinguisher at the base of the fire.

S = Squeeze the lever to actuate the extinguisher.

S = Sweep the nozzle from side-to-side.

● **SEE FIGURE 1–80.**

TYPES OF FIRE EXTINGUISHERS Types of fire extinguishers include the following:

- **Water.** A water fire extinguisher, usually in a pressurized container, is good to use on Class A fires by reducing

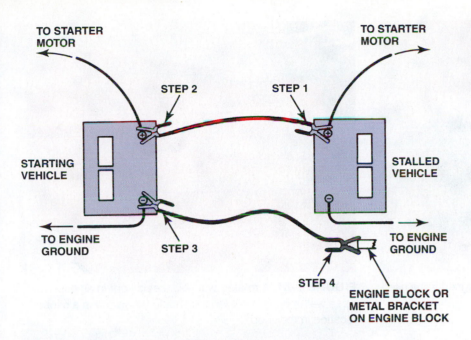

FIGURE 1–77 Jumper cable usage guide. Follow the same connections if using a portable jump box.

TO STARTER MOTOR

TO STARTER MOTOR

STEP 2

STEP 1

STARTING VEHICLE

STALLED VEHICLE

TO ENGINE GROUND

STEP 3

STEP 4

TO ENGINE GROUND

ENGINE BLOCK OR METAL BRACKET ON ENGINE BLOCK

FIGURE 1–78 The air pressure going to the nozzle should be reduced to 30 psi or less to help prevent personal injury.

the temperature to the point where a fire cannot be sustained.

- **Carbon dioxide (CO₂).** A carbon dioxide fire extinguisher is good for almost any type of fire, especially Class B and Class C materials. A CO_2 fire extinguisher works by removing the oxygen from the fire and the cold CO_2 also helps reduce the temperature of the fire.

- **Dry chemical (yellow).** A dry chemical fire extinguisher is good for Class A, B, and C fires. It acts by coating the flammable materials, which eliminates the oxygen from the fire. A dry chemical fire extinguisher tends to be very corrosive and will cause damage to electronic devices.

FIRE BLANKETS

Fire blankets are required to be available in the shop areas. If a person is on fire, a fire blanket should be removed from its storage bag and thrown over and around the victim to smother the fire. ● **SEE FIGURE 1–81** showing a typical fire blanket.

FIRST AID AND EYE WASH STATIONS

All shop areas must be equipped with a first aid kit and an eye wash station centrally located and kept stocked with emergency supplies. ● **SEE FIGURE 1–82.**

FIGURE 1–79 A typical fire extinguisher designed to be used on type A, B, or C fires.

FIGURE 1–81 A treated wool blanket is kept in an easy-to-open wall-mounted holder and should be placed in a central location in the shop.

FIGURE 1–80 A CO_2 fire extinguisher being used on a fire set in an open drum during a demonstration at a fire training center.

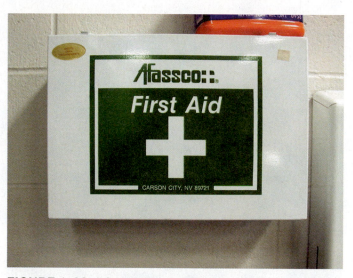

FIGURE 1–82 A first aid box should be centrally located in the shop and kept stocked with the recommended supplies.

FIRST AID KIT   A first aid kit should include:

- Bandages (variety)
- Gauze pads
- Roll gauze
- Iodine swab sticks
- Antibiotic ointment
- Hydrocortisone cream
- Burn gel packets
- Eye wash solution
- Scissors
- Tweezers
- Gloves
- First aid guide

Every shop should have a person trained in first aid. If there is an accident, call for help immediately.

EYE WASH STATION   An **eye wash station** should be centrally located and used whenever any liquid or chemical gets into the eyes. If such an emergency does occur, keep eyes in a constant stream of water and call for professional assistance. ● **SEE FIGURE 1–83.**

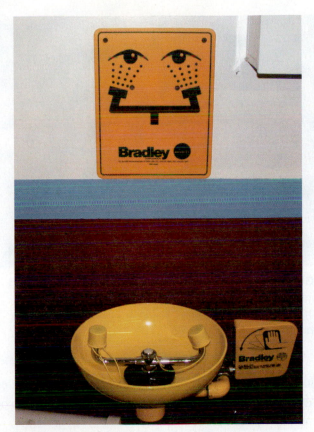

FIGURE 1–83 A typical eye wash station. Often a thorough flushing of the eyes with water is the first and often the best treatment in the event of eye contamination.

HYBRID ELECTRIC VEHICLE SAFETY ISSUES

Hybrid electric vehicles (HEVs) use a high-voltage battery pack and an electric motor(s) to help propel the vehicle. ● **SEE FIGURE 1–84** for an example of a typical warning label on a hybrid electric vehicle. The gasoline or diesel engine also is equipped with a generator or a combination starter and an integrated starter generator (ISG) or integrated starter alternator (ISA). To safely work around a hybrid electric vehicle, the high-voltage (HV) battery and circuits should be shut off following these steps:

☠ **WARNING**

Some vehicle manufacturers specify that insulated rubber *lineman's gloves* be used whenever working around the high-voltage circuits to prevent the danger of electrical shock.

FIGURE 1–84 A warning label on a Honda hybrid warns that a person can be killed due to the high-voltage circuits under the cover.

✚ **SAFETY TIP**

Infection Control Precautions

Working on a vehicle can result in personal injury including the possibility of being cut or hurt enough to cause bleeding. Some infections such as hepatitis B, HIV (which can cause acquired immunodeficiency syndrome, or AIDS), and hepatitis C virus are transmitted through blood. These infections are commonly called blood-borne pathogens. Report any injury that involves blood to your supervisor and take the necessary precautions to avoid coming in contact with blood from another person.

STEP 1 Turn off the ignition key (if equipped) and remove the key from the ignition switch. (This will shut off all high-voltage circuits if the relay[s] is [are] working correctly.)

STEP 2 Disconnect the high-voltage circuits.

TOYOTA PRIUS The cutoff switch is located in the trunk. To gain access, remove three clips holding the upper left portion of the trunk side cover. To disconnect the high-voltage system, pull the orange handled plug while wearing insulated rubber lineman's gloves. ● **SEE FIGURE 1–85.**

FORD ESCAPE/MERCURY MARINER Ford and Mercury specify that the following steps should be included when working with the high-voltage (HV) systems of a hybrid vehicle:

FIGURE 1–85 The high-voltage disconnect switch is in the trunk area on a Toyota Prius. Insulated rubber lineman's gloves should be worn when removing this plug.

FIGURE 1–87 The shut-off switch on a GM parallel hybrid truck is green because this system uses 42 volts instead of higher, and possibly fatal, voltages used in other hybrid vehicles.

FIGURE 1–86 The high-voltage shut-off switch on a Ford Escape hybrid. The switch is located under the carpet at the rear of the vehicle.

- Four orange cones are to be placed at the four corners of the vehicle to create a buffer zone.
- High-voltage insulated gloves are to be worn with an outer leather glove to protect the inner rubber glove from possible damage.
- The service technician should also wear a face shield and a fiberglass hook should be in the area and used to move a technician in the event of electrocution.

The high-voltage shut-off switch is located in the rear of the vehicle under the right side carpet. ● SEE FIGURE 1–86.

Rotate the handle to the "service shipping" position, lift it out to disable the high-voltage circuit, and wait five minutes before removing high-voltage cables.

HONDA CIVIC   To totally disable the high-voltage system on a Honda Civic, remove the main fuse (labeled number 1) from the driver's side underhood fuse panel. This should be all that is necessary to shut off the high-voltage circuit. If this is not possible, then remove the rear seat cushion and seat back. Remove the metal switch cover labeled "up" and remove the red locking cover. Move the "battery module switch" down to disable the high-voltage system.

CHEVROLET SILVERADO/GMC SIERRA PICKUP TRUCK   The high-voltage shut-off switch is located under the rear passenger seat. Remove the cover marked "energy storage box" and turn the green service disconnect switch to the horizontal position to turn off the high-voltage circuits. ● SEE FIGURE 1–87.

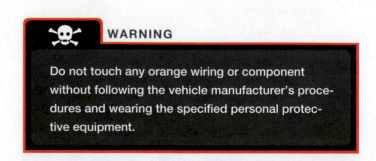

☠ **WARNING**

Do not touch any orange wiring or component without following the vehicle manufacturer's procedures and wearing the specified personal protective equipment.

1 The first step in hoisting a vehicle is to properly align the vehicle in the center of the stall.

2 Most vehicles will be correctly positioned when the left front tire is centered on the tire pad.

3 The arms can be moved in and out and most pads can be rotated to allow for many different types of vehicle construction.

4 Most lifts are equipped with short pad extensions that are often necessary to use to allow the pad to contact the frame of a vehicle without causing the arm of the lift to hit and damage parts of the body.

5 Tall pad extensions can also be used to gain access to the frame of a vehicle. This position is needed to safely hoist many pickup trucks, vans, and sport utility vehicles.

6 An additional extension may be necessary to hoist a truck or van equipped with running boards to give the necessary clearance.

CONTINUED ▶

7 Position the pads under the vehicle under the recommended locations.

8 After being sure all pads are correctly positioned, use the electromechanical controls to raise the vehicle.

9 With the vehicle raised one foot (30 cm) off the ground, push down on the vehicle to check to see if it is stable on the pads. If the vehicle rocks, lower the vehicle and reset the pads. The vehicle can be raised to any desired working level. Be sure the safety is engaged before working on or under the vehicle.

10 If raising a vehicle without a frame, place the flat pads under the pinch weld seam to spread the load. If additional clearance is necessary, the pads can be raised as shown.

11 When the service work is completed, the hoist should be raised slightly and the safety released before using the hydraulic lever to lower the vehicle.

12 After lowering the vehicle, be sure all arms of the lift are moved out of the way before driving the vehicle out of the work stall.

1. Bolts, studs, and nuts are commonly used as fasteners in the chassis. The sizes for fractional and metric threads are different and are not interchangeable. The grade is the rating of the strength of a fastener.

2. Whenever a vehicle is raised above the ground, it must be supported at a substantial section of the body or frame.

3. Wrenches are available in open end, box end, and combination open and box end.

4. An adjustable wrench should only be used where the proper size is not available.

5. Line wrenches are also called flare-nut wrenches, fitting wrenches, or tube-nut wrenches and are used to remove fuel or refrigerant lines.

6. Sockets are rotated by a ratchet or breaker bar, also called a flex handle.

7. Torque wrenches measure the amount of torque applied to a fastener.

8. Screwdriver types include straight blade (flat tip) and Phillips.

9. Hammers and mallets come in a variety of sizes and weights.

10. Pliers are a useful tool and are available in many different types, including slip-joint, multigroove, linesman's, diagonal, needle-nose, and locking pliers.

11. Other common hand tools include snap-ring pliers, files, cutters, punches, chisels, and hacksaws.

12. Hybrid electric vehicles should be de-powered if any of the high-voltage components are going to be serviced.

REVIEW QUESTIONS

1. List three precautions that must be taken whenever hoisting (lifting) a vehicle.

2. Describe how to determine the grade of a fastener, including how the markings differ between fractional and metric bolts.

3. List four items that are personal protective equipment (PPE).

4. List the types of fire extinguishers and their usage.

5. Why are wrenches offset 15 degrees?

6. What are the other names for a line wrench?

7. What are the standard automotive drive sizes for sockets?

8. Which type of screwdriver requires the use of a hammer or mallet?

9. What is inside a dead-blow hammer?

10. What type of cutter is available in left and right cutters?

CHAPTER QUIZ

1. The correct location for the pads when hoisting or jacking the vehicle can often be found in the _____.
   a. Service manual
   b. Shop manual
   c. Owner's manual
   d. All of the above

2. For the best working position, the work should be _____.
   a. At neck or head level
   b. At knee or ankle level
   c. Overhead by about 1 foot
   d. At chest or elbow level

3. A high-strength bolt is identified by _____.
   a. A UNC symbol
   b. Lines on the head
   c. Strength letter codes
   d. The coarse threads

4. A fastener that uses threads on both ends is called a _____.
   a. Cap screw
   b. Stud
   c. Machine screw
   d. Crest fastener

5. When working with hand tools, always _____.
   a. Push the wrench—don't pull toward you
   b. Pull a wrench—don't push a wrench away from you

6. The proper term for Channel Locks is _____.
   a. Vise Grips
   b. Crescent wrench
   c. Locking pliers
   d. Multigroove adjustable pliers

7. The proper term for Vise Grips is _____.
   a. Locking pliers
   b. Slip-joint pliers
   c. Side cuts
   d. Multigroove adjustable pliers

8. Two technicians are discussing torque wrenches. Technician A says that a torque wrench is capable of tightening a fastener with more torque than a conventional breaker bar or ratchet. Technician B says that a torque wrench should be calibrated regularly for the most accurate results. Which technician is correct?
   a. Technician A only
   b. Technician B only
   c. Both Technicians A and B
   d. Neither Technician A nor B

9. What type of screwdriver should be used if there is very limited space above the head of the fastener?
   a. Offset screwdriver
   b. Standard screwdriver
   c. Impact screwdriver
   d. Robertson screwdriver

10. What type of hammer is plastic coated, has a metal casing inside, and is filled with small lead balls?
    a. Dead-blow hammer
    b. Soft-blow hammer
    c. Sledgehammer
    d. Plastic hammer

LEARNING OBJECTIVES

After studying this chapter, the reader will be able to:

1. Identify hazardous waste materials in accordance with state and federal regulations and follow proper safety precautions while handling hazardous materials.

2. Define the Occupational Safety and Health Act (OSHA).

3. Explain the term material safety data sheets (MSDS).

4. Define the steps required to safely handle and store automotive chemicals and waste.

This chapter will help you prepare for the ASE assumed knowledge content required by all service technicians to adhere to environmentally appropriate actions and behavior.

KEY TERMS

HAZARDOUS WASTE

DEFINITION OF HAZARDOUS WASTE **Hazardous waste materials** are chemicals, or components, that the shop no longer needs and that pose a danger to the environment and people if they are disposed of in ordinary garbage cans or sewers. However, no material is considered hazardous waste until the shop has finished using it and is ready to dispose of it.

PERSONAL PROTECTIVE EQUIPMENT (PPE) When handling hazardous waste material, one must always wear the proper protective clothing and equipment detailed in the right-to-know laws. This includes respirator equipment. All recommended procedures must be followed accurately. Personal injury may result from improper clothing, equipment, and procedures when handling hazardous materials.

FEDERAL AND STATE LAWS

OCCUPATIONAL SAFETY AND HEALTH ACT The U.S. Congress passed the **Occupational Safety and Health Act (OSHA)** in 1970. This legislation was designed to assist and encourage the citizens of the United States in their efforts to assure:

- Safe and healthful working conditions by providing research, information, education, and training in the field of occupational safety and health.
- Safe and healthful working conditions for working men and women by authorizing enforcement of the standards developed under the act.

Because about 25% of workers are exposed to health and safety hazards on the job, OSHA standards are necessary to monitor, control, and educate workers regarding health and safety in the workplace.

EPA The **Environmental Protection Agency (EPA)** publishes a list of hazardous materials that is included in the **Code of Federal Regulations (CFR)**. The EPA considers waste hazardous if it is included on the EPA list of hazardous materials, or it has one or more of the following characteristics:

- **Reactive**—Any material that reacts violently with water or other chemicals is considered hazardous.
- **Corrosive**—If a material burns the skin, or dissolves metals and other materials, a technician should consider

it hazardous. A pH scale is used, with number 7 indicating neutral. Pure water has a pH of 7. Lower numbers indicate an acidic solution and higher numbers indicate a caustic solution. If a material releases cyanide gas, hydrogen sulfide gas, or similar gases when exposed to low pH acid solutions, it is considered hazardous.

- **Toxic**—Materials are hazardous if they leak one or more of eight different heavy metals in concentrations greater than 100 times the primary drinking water standard.
- **Ignitable**—A liquid is hazardous if it has a flash point below 140°F (60°C), and a solid is hazardous if it ignites spontaneously.
- **Radioactive**—Any substance that emits measurable levels of radiation is radioactive. When individuals bring containers of a highly radioactive substance into the shop environment, qualified personnel with the appropriate equipment must test them.

 WARNING

Hazardous waste disposal laws include serious penalties for anyone responsible for breaking these laws.

RIGHT-TO-KNOW LAWS The **right-to-know laws** state that employees have a right to know when the materials they use at work are hazardous. The right-to-know laws started with the Hazard Communication Standard published by the Occupational Safety and Health Administration (OSHA) in 1983. Originally, this document was intended for chemical companies and manufacturers that required employees to handle hazardous materials in their work situation but the federal courts have decided to apply these laws to all companies, including automotive service shops. Under the right-to-know laws, the employer has responsibilities regarding the handling of hazardous materials by their employees. All employees must be trained about the types of hazardous materials they will encounter in the workplace. The employees must be informed about their rights under legislation regarding the handling of hazardous materials.

MATERIAL SAFETY DATA SHEETS. All hazardous materials must be properly labeled, and information about each hazardous material must be posted on **material safety data sheets (MSDS)**, now called simply *safety data sheets (SDS),* available from the manufacturer. In Canada, MSDS information is called **Workplace Hazardous Materials Information Systems (WHMIS)**.

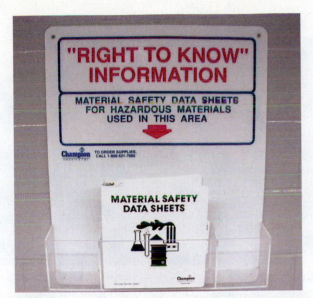

FIGURE 2–1 Safety data sheets (SDS), formerly known as material safety data sheets (MSDS) should be readily available for use by anyone in the area who may come into contact with hazardous materials.

The employer has a responsibility to place MSDS information where they are easily accessible by all employees. The data sheets provide the following information about the hazardous material: chemical name, physical characteristics, protective handling equipment, explosion/fire hazards, incompatible materials, health hazards, medical conditions aggravated by exposure, emergency and first-aid procedures, safe handling, and spill/leak procedures.

The employer also has a responsibility to make sure that all hazardous materials are properly labeled. The label information must include health, fire, and reactivity hazards posed by the material, as well as the protective equipment necessary to handle the material. The manufacturer must supply all warning and precautionary information about hazardous materials. This information must be read and understood by the employee before handling the material. ● SEE FIGURE 2–1.

RESOURCE CONSERVATION AND RECOVERY ACT

Federal and state laws control the disposal of hazardous waste materials and every shop employee must be familiar with these laws. Hazardous waste disposal laws include the **Resource Conservation and Recovery Act (RCRA)**. This law states that hazardous material users are responsible for hazardous materials from the time they become a waste until the proper disposal is completed. Many shops hire an independent hazardous waste hauler to dispose of hazardous waste material. The shop owner, or manager, should have a written contract with the hazardous waste hauler. Rather than have hazardous waste material hauled to an approved hazardous

FIGURE 2–2 Tag identify that the power has been removed and service work is being done.

waste disposal site, a shop may choose to recycle the material in the shop. Therefore, the user must store hazardous waste material properly and safely, and be responsible for the transportation of this material until it arrives at an approved hazardous waste disposal site, where it can be processed according to the law. The RCRA controls the following types of automotive waste:

- Paint and body repair products waste
- Solvents for parts and equipment cleaning
- Batteries and battery acid
- Mild acids used for metal cleaning and preparation
- Waste oil and engine coolants or antifreeze
- Air-conditioning refrigerants and oils
- Engine oil filters

LOCKOUT/TAGOUT According to OSHA Title 29, code of Federal Regulations (CPR), part 1910.147, machinery must be locked out to prevent injury to employees when maintenance or repair work is being performed. Any piece of equipment that should not be used must be tagged and the electrical power disconnected to prevent it from being used. Always read, understand, and follow all safety warning tags. ● SEE FIGURE 2–2.

CLEAN AIR ACT Air-conditioning (A/C) systems and refrigerant are regulated by the **Clean Air Act (CAA)**, Title VI, Section 609. Technician certification and service equipment is also regulated. Any technician working on automotive A/C systems must be certified. A/C refrigerants must not be released or vented into the atmosphere, and used refrigerants must be recovered.

ASBESTOS HAZARDS

Friction materials such as brake and clutch linings often contain asbestos. While asbestos has been eliminated from most original equipment friction materials, the automotive service technician cannot know whether or not the vehicle being serviced is or is not equipped with friction materials containing asbestos. It is important that all friction materials be handled as if they do contain asbestos.

Asbestos exposure can cause scar tissue to form in the lungs. This condition is called **asbestosis**. It gradually causes increasing shortness of breath, and the scarring to the lungs is permanent.

Even low exposures to asbestos can cause *mesothelioma*, a type of fatal cancer of the lining of the chest or abdominal cavity. Asbestos exposure can also increase the risk of *lung cancer* as well as cancer of the voice box, stomach, and large intestine. It usually takes 15 to 30 years or more for cancer or asbestos lung scarring to show up after exposure. Scientists call this the *latency period*.

Government agencies recommend that asbestos exposure should be eliminated or controlled to the lowest level possible. These agencies have developed recommendations and standards that the automotive service technician and equipment manufacturer should follow. These U.S. federal agencies include the National Institute for Occupational Safety and Health (NIOSH), Occupational Safety and Health Administration (OSHA), and Environmental Protection Agency (EPA).

ASBESTOS OSHA STANDARDS The Occupational Safety and Health Administration has established three levels of asbestos exposure. Any vehicle service establishment that does either brake or clutch work must limit employee exposure to asbestos to less than 0.2 fibers per cubic centimeter (cc) as determined by an air sample.

If the level of exposure to employees is greater than specified, corrective measures must be performed and a large fine may be imposed.

NOTE: Research has found that worn asbestos fibers such as those from automotive brakes or clutches may not be as hazardous as first believed. Worn asbestos fibers do not have sharp flared ends that can latch onto tissue, but rather are worn down to a dust form that resembles talc. Grinding or sawing operations on unworn brake shoes or clutch discs *will* contain *harmful* asbestos fibers. To limit health damage, always use proper handling procedures while working around any component that may contain asbestos.

FIGURE 2–3 All brakes should be moistened with water or solvent to help prevent brake dust from becoming airborne.

ASBESTOS EPA REGULATIONS The federal Environmental Protection Agency has established procedures for the removal and disposal of asbestos. The EPA procedures require that products containing asbestos be "wetted" to prevent the asbestos fibers from becoming airborne. According to the EPA, asbestos-containing materials can be disposed of as regular waste. Only when asbestos becomes airborne is it considered to be hazardous.

ASBESTOS HANDLING GUIDELINES The air in the shop area can be tested by a testing laboratory, but this can be expensive. Tests have determined that asbestos levels can easily be kept below the recommended levels by using a liquid, like water, or a special vacuum.

NOTE: Even though asbestos is being removed from brake and clutch lining materials, the service technician cannot tell whether or not the old brake pads, shoes, or clutch discs contain asbestos. Therefore, to be safe, the technician should assume that all brake pads, shoes, or clutch discs contain asbestos.

HEPA VACUUM. A special **high-efficiency particulate air (HEPA) vacuum** system has been proven to be effective in keeping asbestos exposure levels below 0.1 fibers per cubic centimeter.

SOLVENT SPRAY. Many technicians use an aerosol can of brake cleaning solvent to wet the brake dust and prevent it from becoming airborne. A **solvent** is a liquid that is used to dissolve dirt, grime, or solid particles. Commercial brake cleaners are available that use a concentrated cleaner that is mixed with water. ● **SEE FIGURE 2–3**. The waste liquid is filtered, and when dry, the filter can be disposed of as solid waste.

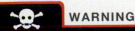

WARNING

Never use compressed air to blow brake dust. The fine talclike brake dust can create a health hazard even if asbestos is not present or is present in dust rather than fiber form.

DISPOSAL OF BRAKE DUST AND BRAKE SHOES. The hazard of asbestos occurs when asbestos fibers are airborne. Once the asbestos has been wetted down, it is then considered to be solid waste, rather than hazardous waste. Old brake shoes and pads should be enclosed, preferably in a plastic bag, to help prevent any of the brake material from becoming airborne. *Always follow current federal and local laws concerning disposal of all waste.*

USED BRAKE FLUID

Most brake fluid is made from polyglycol, is water soluble, and can be considered hazardous if it has absorbed metals from the brake system.

STORAGE AND DISPOSAL OF BRAKE FLUID

- Collect brake fluid in a container clearly marked to indicate that it is designated for that purpose.
- If the waste brake fluid is hazardous, be sure to manage it appropriately and use only an authorized waste receiver for its disposal.
- If the waste brake fluid is nonhazardous (such as old, but unused), determine from your local solid waste collection provider what should be done for its proper disposal.
- Do not mix brake fluid with used engine oil.
- Do not pour brake fluid down drains or onto the ground.
- Recycle brake fluid through a registered recycler.

USED OIL

Used oil is any petroleum-based or synthetic oil that has been used. During normal use, impurities such as dirt, metal scrapings, water, or chemicals can get mixed in with the oil. Eventually, this used oil must be replaced with virgin or re-refined oil. The EPA's used oil management standards include a three-pronged approach to determine if a substance meets the definition of *used oil*. To meet the EPA's definition of used oil, a substance must meet each of the following three criteria.

- **Origin.** The first criterion for identifying used oil is based on the oil's origin. Used oil must have been refined from crude oil or made from synthetic materials. Animal and vegetable oils are excluded from the EPA's definition of used oil.
- **Use.** The second criterion is based on whether and how the oil is used. Oils used as lubricants, hydraulic fluids, heat transfer fluids, and for other similar purposes are considered used oil. The EPA's definition also excludes products used as cleaning agents, as well as certain petroleum-derived products like antifreeze and kerosene.
- **Contaminants.** The third criterion is based on whether or not the oil is contaminated with either physical or chemical impurities. In other words, to meet the EPA's definition, used oil must become contaminated as a result of being used. This aspect of the EPA's definition includes residues and contaminants generated from handling, storing, and processing used oil.

NOTE: The release of only one gallon of used oil (a typical oil change) can make a million gallons of fresh water undrinkable.

If used oil is dumped down the drain and enters a sewage treatment plant, concentrations as small as 50 to 100 PPM (parts per million) in the waste water can foul sewage treatment processes. Never mix a listed hazardous waste, gasoline, waste water, halogenated solvent, antifreeze, or an unknown waste material with used oil. Adding any of these substances will cause the used oil to become contaminated, which classifies it as hazardous waste.

STORAGE AND DISPOSAL OF USED OIL

Once oil has been used, it can be collected, recycled, and used over and over again. An estimated 380 million gallons of used oil are recycled each year. Recycled used oil can sometimes be used again for the same job or can take on a completely different task. For example, used engine oil can be re-refined and sold at some discount stores as engine oil or processed for furnace fuel oil. After collecting used oil in an appropriate container such as a 55-gallon steel drum, the material must be disposed of in one of two ways:

- Shipped offsite for recycling
- Burned in an onsite or offsite EPA-approved heater for energy recovery

Used oil must be stored in compliance with an existing **underground storage tank (UST)** or an **aboveground**

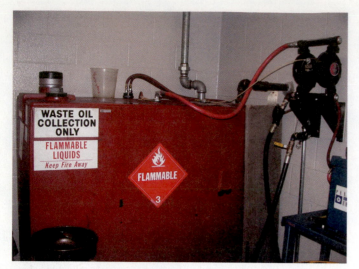

FIGURE 2–4 A typical aboveground oil storage tank.

storage tank (AGST) standard, or kept in separate containers. ●**SEE FIGURE 2–4.** Containers are portable receptacles, such as a 55-gallon steel drum.

KEEP USED OIL STORAGE DRUMS IN GOOD CONDITION. This means that they should be covered, secured from vandals, properly labeled, and maintained in compliance with local fire codes. Frequent inspections for leaks, corrosion, and spillage are an essential part of container maintenance.

NEVER STORE USED OIL IN ANYTHING OTHER THAN TANKS AND STORAGE CONTAINERS. Used oil may also be stored in units that are permitted to store regulated hazardous waste.

USED OIL FILTER DISPOSAL REGULATIONS. Used oil filters contain used engine oil that may be hazardous. Before an oil filter is placed into the trash or sent to be recycled, it must be drained using one of the following hot-draining methods approved by the EPA.

- Puncture the filter antidrainback valve or filter dome end and hot-drain for at least 12 hours
- Hot-drain and crushing
- Dismantling and hot draining
- Any other hot-draining method, which will remove all the used oil from the filter

After the oil has been drained from the oil filter, the filter housing can be disposed of in any of the following ways:

- Sent for recycling
- Picked up by a service contract company
- Disposed of in regular trash

SOLVENTS

The major sources of chemical danger are liquid and aerosol brake cleaning fluids that contain chlorinated hydrocarbon solvents. Several other chemicals that do not deplete the ozone, such as heptane, hexane, and xylene, are now being used in nonchlorinated brake cleaning solvents. Some manufacturers are also producing solvents they describe as environmentally responsible, which are biodegradable and noncarcinogenic (non-cancer-causing).

There is no specific standard for physical contact with chlorinated hydrocarbon solvents or the chemicals replacing them. All contact should be avoided whenever possible. The law requires an employer to provide appropriate protective equipment and ensure proper work practices by an employee handling these chemicals.

 SAFETY TIP

Hand Safety

Service technicians should wash their hands with soap and water after handling engine oil, differential oil, or transmission fluids or wear protective rubber gloves. Another safety tip is that the service technician should not wear watches, rings, or other jewelry that could come in contact with electrical or moving parts of a vehicle. ●**SEE FIGURE 2–5.**

EFFECTS OF CHEMICAL POISONING The effects of exposure to chlorinated hydrocarbon and other types of solvents can take many forms. Short-term exposure at low levels can cause symptoms such as:

- Headache
- Nausea
- Drowsiness
- Dizziness
- Lack of coordination
- Unconsciousness

It may also cause irritation of the eyes, nose, and throat, and flushing of the face and neck. Short-term exposure to higher concentrations can cause liver damage with symptoms such as yellow jaundice or dark urine. Liver damage may not become evident until several weeks after the exposure.

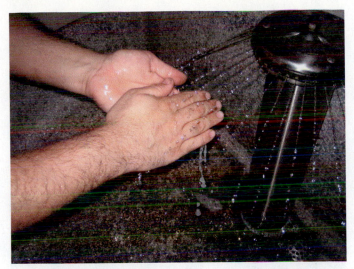

FIGURE 2–5 Washing hands and removing jewelry are two important safety habits all service technicians should practice.

FIGURE 2–6 Typical fireproof flammable storage cabinet.

 FREQUENTLY ASKED QUESTION

How Can You Tell If a Solvent Is Hazardous?

If a solvent or any of the ingredients of a product contains "fluor" or "chlor," then it is likely to be hazardous. Check the instructions on the label for proper use and disposal procedures.

HAZARDOUS SOLVENTS AND REGULATORY STATUS

Most solvents are classified as hazardous wastes. Other characteristics of solvents include the following:

- Solvents with flash points below 60°C are considered flammable and, like gasoline, are federally regulated by the Department of Transportation (DOT).

- Solvents and oils with flash points above 60°C are considered combustible and, like engine oil, are also regulated by the DOT. All flammable items must be stored in a fireproof container. ● SEE FIGURE 2–6.

It is the responsibility of the repair shop to determine if its spent solvent is hazardous waste. Solvent reclaimers are available that clean and restore the solvent so it lasts indefinitely.

USED SOLVENTS Used or spent solvents are liquid materials that have been generated as waste and may contain xylene, methanol, ethyl ether, and methyl isobutyl ketone (MIBK). These materials must be stored in OSHA-approved safety containers with the lids or caps closed tightly. Additional requirements include the following:

- Containers should be clearly labeled "Hazardous Waste" and the date the material was first placed into the storage receptacle should be noted.

- Labeling is not required for solvents being used in a parts washer.

- Used solvents will not be counted toward a facility's monthly output of hazardous waste if the vendor under contract removes the material.

- Used solvents may be disposed of by recycling with a local vendor, like SafetyKleen®, to have the used solvent removed according to specific terms in the vendor agreement.

- Use aqueous-based (nonsolvent) cleaning systems to help avoid the problems associated with chemical solvents. ● SEE FIGURE 2–7.

COOLANT DISPOSAL

Coolant is a mixture of antifreeze and water. New antifreeze is not considered to be hazardous even though it can cause death if ingested. Used antifreeze may be hazardous due to dissolved metals from the engine and other components of the cooling system. These metals can include iron, steel, aluminum, copper, brass, and lead (from older radiators and

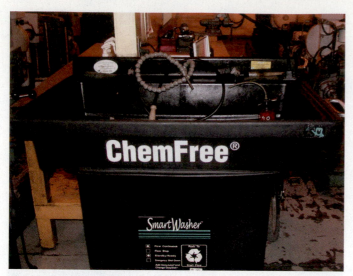

FIGURE 2–7 Using a water-based cleaning system helps reduce the hazards from using strong chemicals.

FIGURE 2–8 Used antifreeze coolant should be kept separate and stored in a leakproof container until it can be recycled or disposed of according to federal, state, and local laws. Note that the storage barrel is placed inside another container to catch any coolant that may spill out of the inside barrel.

heater cores). Coolant should be disposed of in one of the following ways:

- Coolant should be recycled either onsite or offsite.
- Used coolant should be stored in a sealed and labeled container. ● SEE FIGURE 2–8.
- Used coolant can often be disposed of into municipal sewers with a permit. Check with local authorities and obtain a permit before discharging used coolant into sanitary sewers.

LEAD-ACID BATTERY WASTE

About 70 million spent lead-acid batteries are generated each year in the United States alone. Lead is classified as a toxic metal, and the acid used in lead-acid batteries is highly corrosive. The vast majority (95% to 98%) of these batteries are recycled through lead reclamation operations and secondary lead smelters for use in the manufacture of new batteries.

BATTERY DISPOSAL Used lead-acid batteries must be reclaimed or recycled in order to be exempt from hazardous waste regulations. Leaking batteries must be stored and transported as hazardous waste. Some states have more strict regulations, which require special handling procedures and

transportation. According to the **Battery Council International (BCI)**, battery laws usually include the following rules:

1. Lead-acid battery disposal is prohibited in landfills or incinerators. Batteries are required to be delivered to a battery retailer, wholesaler, recycling center, or lead smelter.

2. All retailers of automotive batteries are required to post a sign that displays the universal recycling symbol and indicates the retailer's specific requirements for accepting used batteries.

3. Battery electrolyte contains sulfuric acid, which is a very corrosive substance capable of causing serious personal injury, such as skin burns and eye damage. In addition, the battery plates contain lead, which is highly poisonous. For this reason, disposing of batteries improperly can cause environmental contamination and lead to severe health problems.

BATTERY HANDLING AND STORAGE Batteries, whether new or used, should be kept indoors if possible. The storage location should be an area specifically designated for battery storage and must be well ventilated (to the outside). If outdoor storage is the only alternative, a sheltered and secured area with acid-resistant secondary containment is strongly recommended. It is also advisable that acid-resistant secondary containment be used for indoor storage. In addition, batteries should be placed on acid-resistant pallets and never stacked.

FIGURE 2–9 This red gasoline container holds about 30 gallons of gasoline and is used to fill vehicles used for training.

FUEL SAFETY AND STORAGE

Gasoline is a very explosive liquid. The expanding vapors that come from gasoline are extremely dangerous. These vapors are present even in cold temperatures. Vapors formed in gasoline tanks on many vehicles are controlled, but vapors from gasoline storage may escape from the can, resulting in a hazardous situation. Therefore, place gasoline storage containers in a well-ventilated space. Although diesel fuel is not as volatile as gasoline, the same basic rules apply to diesel fuel and gasoline storage. These rules include the following:

1. Use storage cans that have a flash-arresting screen at the outlet. These screens prevent external ignition sources from igniting the gasoline within the can when someone pours the gasoline or diesel fuel.

2. Use only a red approved gasoline container to allow for proper hazardous substance identification. ● **SEE FIGURE 2–9.**

3. Do not fill gasoline containers completely full. Always leave the level of gasoline at least one inch from the top of the container. This action allows expansion of the gasoline at higher temperatures. If gasoline containers are completely full, the gasoline will expand when the temperature increases. This expansion forces gasoline from the can and creates a dangerous spill. If gasoline or diesel fuel containers must be stored, place them in a designated storage locker or facility.

4. Never leave gasoline containers open, except while filling or pouring gasoline from the container.

5. Never use gasoline as a cleaning agent.

6. Always connect a ground strap to containers when filling or transferring fuel or other flammable products from one container to another to prevent static electricity that could result in explosion and fire. These ground wires prevent the buildup of a static electric charge, which could result in a spark and disastrous explosion.

AIRBAG HANDLING

Airbag modules are pyrotechnic devices that can be ignited if exposed to an electrical charge or if the body of the vehicle is subjected to a shock. Airbag safety should include the following precautions:

1. Disarm the airbag(s) if you will be working in the area where a discharged bag could make contact with any part of your body. Consult service information for the exact procedure to follow for the vehicle being serviced. The usual procedure is to deploy the airbag using a 12 volt power supply, such as a jump start box, using long wires to connect to the module to ensure a safe deployment.

2. Do not expose an airbag to extreme heat or fire.

3. Always carry an airbag pointing away from your body.

4. Place an airbag module facing upward.

5. Always follow the manufacturer's recommended procedure for airbag disposal or recycling, including the proper packaging to use during shipment.

6. Wear protective gloves if handling a deployed airbag.

7. Always wash your hands or body well if exposed to a deployed airbag. The chemicals involved can cause skin irritation and possible rash development.

FIGURE 2–10 Air-conditioning refrigerant oil must be kept separated from other oils because it contains traces of refrigerant and must be treated as hazardous waste.

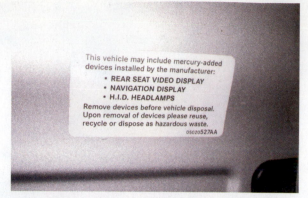

FIGURE 2–11 Placard near driver's door, including what devices in the vehicle contain mercury.

USED TIRE DISPOSAL

Used tires are an environmental concern because of several reasons, including the following:

1. In a landfill, they tend to "float" up through the other trash and rise to the surface.

2. The inside of tires traps and holds rainwater, which is a breeding ground for mosquitoes. Mosquito-borne diseases include encephalitis and dengue fever.

3. Used tires present a fire hazard and, when burned, create a large amount of black smoke that contaminates the air.

Used tires should be disposed of in one of the following ways:

1. Used tires can be reused until the end of their useful life.

2. Tires can be retreaded.

3. Tires can be recycled or shredded for use in asphalt.

4. Derimmed tires can be sent to a landfill (most landfill operators will shred the tires because it is illegal in many states to landfill whole tires).

5. Tires can be burned in cement kilns or other power plants where the smoke can be controlled.

6. A registered scrap tire handler should be used to transport tires for disposal or recycling.

AIR-CONDITIONING REFRIGERANT OIL DISPOSAL

Air-conditioning refrigerant oil contains dissolved refrigerant and is therefore considered to be hazardous waste. This oil must be kept separated from other waste oil or the entire amount of oil must be treated as hazardous. Used refrigerant oil must be sent to a licensed hazardous waste disposal company for recycling or disposal. ● **SEE FIGURE 2–10**.

WASTE CHART All automotive service facilities create some waste and while most of it is handled properly, it is important that all hazardous and nonhazardous waste be accounted for and properly disposed. ● **SEE CHART 2–1** for a list of typical wastes generated at automotive shops, plus a checklist for keeping track of how these wastes are handled.

TECH TIP

Remove Components that Contain Mercury

Some vehicles have a placard near the driver's side door that lists the components that contain the heavy metal, mercury. **Mercury** can be absorbed through the skin and is a heavy metal that once absorbed by the body does not leave. ● **SEE FIGURE 2–11**.

These components should be removed from the vehicle before the rest of the body is sent to be recycled to help prevent releasing mercury into the environment.

WASTE STREAM	TYPICAL CATEGORY IF NOT MIXED WITH OTHER HAZARDOUS WASTE	IF DISPOSED IN LANDFILL AND NOT MIXED WITH A HAZARDOUS WASTE	IF RECYCLED
Used oil	Used oil	Hazardous waste	Used oil
Used oil filters	Nonhazardous solid waste, if completely drained	Nonhazardous solid waste, if completely drained	Used oil, if not drained
Used transmission fluid	Used oil	Hazardous waste	Used oil
Used brake fluid	Used oil	Hazardous waste	Used oil
Used antifreeze	Depends on characterization	Depends on characterization	Depends on characterization
Used solvents	Hazardous waste	Hazardous waste	Hazardous waste
Used citric solvents	Nonhazardous solid waste	Nonhazardous solid waste	Hazardous waste
Lead-acid automotive batteries	Not a solid waste if returned to supplier	Hazardous waste	Hazardous waste
Shop rags used for oil	Used oil	Depends on used oil characterization	Used oil
Shop rags used for solvent or gasoline spills	Hazardous waste	Hazardous waste	Hazardous waste
Oil spill absorbent material	Used oil	Depends on used oil characterization	Used oil
Spill material for solvent and gasoline	Hazardous waste	Hazardous waste	Hazardous waste
Catalytic converter	Not a solid waste if returned to supplier	Nonhazardous solid waste	Nonhazardous solid waste
Spilled or unused fuels	Hazardous waste	Hazardous waste	Hazardous waste
Spilled or unusable paints and thinners	Hazardous waste	Hazardous waste	Hazardous waste
Used tires	Nonhazardous solid waste	Nonhazardous solid waste	Nonhazardous solid waste

CHART 2–1

Typical wastes generated at auto repair shops and typical category (hazardous or nonhazardous) by disposal method.

TECH TIP

What Every Technician Should Know

OSHA has adopted new hazardous chemical labeling requirements making it agree with global labeling standards established by the United Nations. As a result, workers will have better information available on the safe handling and use of hazardous chemicals, allowing them to avoid injuries and possible illnesses related to exposures to hazardous chemicals. ● SEE FIGURE 2–12.

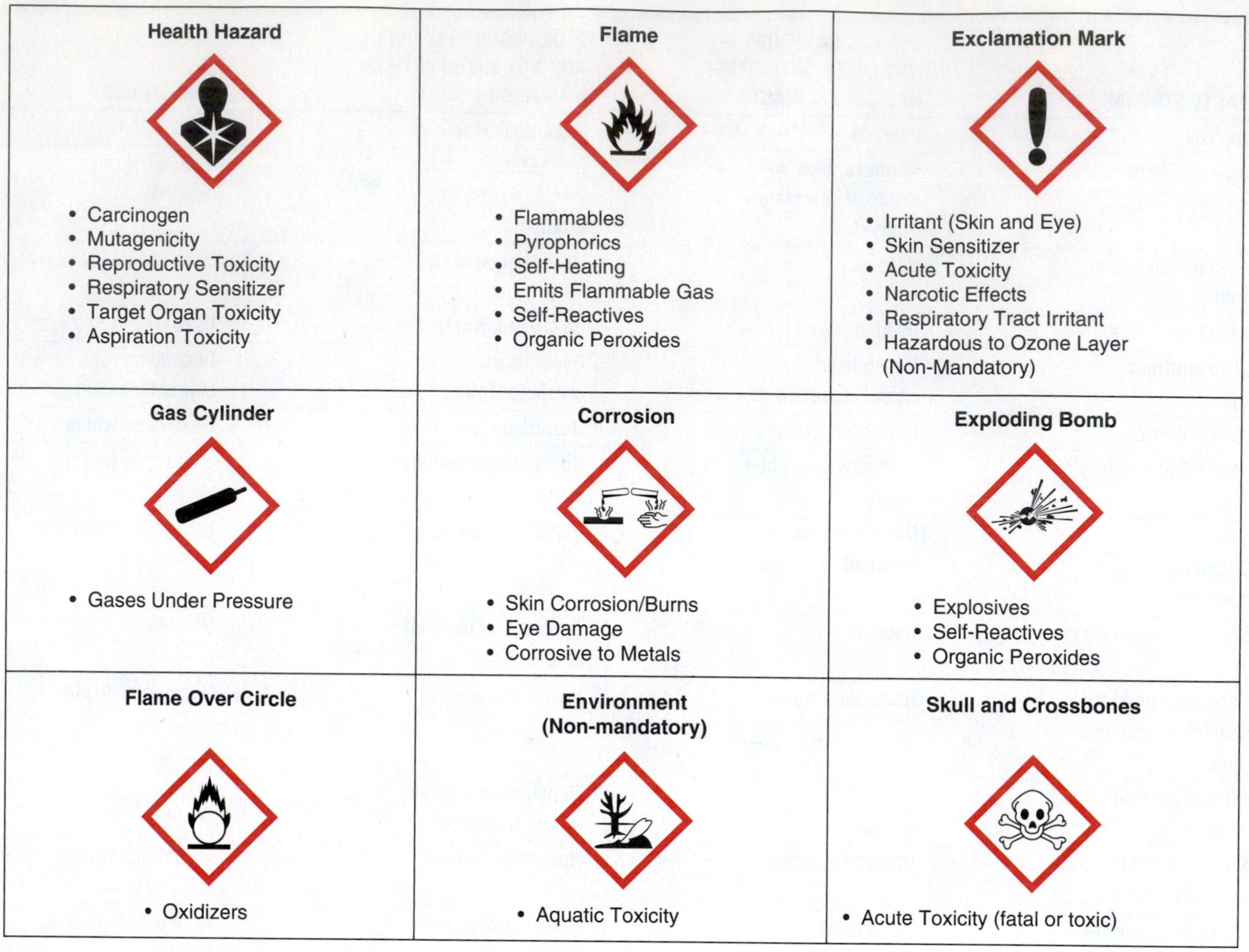

Health Hazard	Flame	Exclamation Mark
• Carcinogen • Mutagenicity • Reproductive Toxicity • Respiratory Sensitizer • Target Organ Toxicity • Aspiration Toxicity	• Flammables • Pyrophorics • Self-Heating • Emits Flammable Gas • Self-Reactives • Organic Peroxides	• Irritant (Skin and Eye) • Skin Sensitizer • Acute Toxicity • Narcotic Effects • Respiratory Tract Irritant • Hazardous to Ozone Layer (Non-Mandatory)
Gas Cylinder	**Corrosion**	**Exploding Bomb**
• Gases Under Pressure	• Skin Corrosion/Burns • Eye Damage • Corrosive to Metals	• Explosives • Self-Reactives • Organic Peroxides
Flame Over Circle	**Environment** **(Non-mandatory)**	**Skull and Crossbones**
• Oxidizers	• Aquatic Toxicity	• Acute Toxicity (fatal or toxic)

FIGURE 2–12 The OSHA global hazardous materials labels.

SUMMARY

1. Hazardous materials include common automotive chemicals, liquids, and lubricants, especially those whose ingredients contain *chlor* or *fluor* in their name.

2. Right-to-know laws require that all workers have access to material safety data sheets (MSDS).

3. Asbestos fibers should be avoided and removed according to current laws and regulations.

4. Used engine oil contains metals worn from parts and should be handled and disposed of properly.

5. Solvents represent a serious health risk and should be avoided as much as possible.

6. Coolant should be disposed of properly or recycled.

7. Batteries are considered to be hazardous waste and should be discarded to a recycling facility.

REVIEW QUESTIONS

1. List five common automotive chemicals or products that may be considered hazardous.

2. Describe the labels used to identify flammables and explosive materials used by OSHA.

1. Hazardous materials include all of the following *except* _____.
   a. Engine oil
   b. Asbestos
   c. Water
   d. Brake cleaner

2. To determine if a product or substance being used is hazardous, consult _____.
   a. A dictionary
   b. An MSDS
   c. SAE standards
   d. EPA guidelines

3. Exposure to asbestos dust can cause what condition?
   a. Asbestosis
   b. Mesothelioma
   c. Lung cancer
   d. All of the above

4. Wetted asbestos dust is considered to be _____.
   a. Solid waste
   b. Hazardous waste
   c. Toxic
   d. Poisonous

5. An oil filter should be hot drained for how long before disposing of the filter?
   a. 30 to 60 minutes
   b. 4 hours
   c. 8 hours
   d. 12 hours

6. Used engine oil should be disposed of by all *except* the following methods.
   a. Disposed of in regular trash
   b. Shipped offsite for recycling
   c. Burned onsite in a waste oil-approved heater
   d. Burned offsite in a waste oil-approved heater

7. All of the following are the proper ways to dispose of a drained oil filter *except* _____.
   a. Sent for recycling
   b. Picked up by a service contract company
   c. Disposed of in regular trash
   d. Considered to be hazardous waste and disposed of accordingly

8. Which act or organization regulates air-conditioning refrigerant?
   a. Clean Air Act (CAA)
   b. MSDS
   c. WHMIS
   d. Code of Federal Regulations (CFR)

9. Gasoline should be stored in approved containers that include what color(s)?
   a. A red container with yellow lettering
   b. A red container
   c. A yellow container
   d. A yellow container with red lettering

10. What automotive devices may contain mercury?
    a. Rear seat video displays
    b. Navigation displays
    c. HID headlights
    d. All of the above

After studying this chapter, the reader should be able to:

1. Define torque, and explain the relationship between torque and horsepower.
2. Describe the various gear types and their effect on speed, torque, and direction of rotation.
3. Explain gear ratios and their effect on vehicle operation.
4. Discuss the types of manual transmissions and transaxles that are currently in use.
5. Discuss automatic transmissions and the planetary gear sets used for automatic transmissions.
6. Compare rear-wheel drive, front-wheel drive, four-wheel drive, and all-wheel drive.
7. Explain the characteristics of driveshafts and drive axle assemblies.

All-wheel drive (AWD) 67
Automatic transmission 60
Bevel gear 57
Clutch 59
Constant-velocity (CV) joint 65
Differential 65
Dynamometer 55
Drive axle 65
Driveshaft 65
Final drive 64
Four-wheel drive (4WD) 67
Front-wheel drive (FWD) 64
Gear ratio 58
Half shaft 64
Helical gear 56
Horsepower 55
Hypoid gear 57

Manual transmission 59
Overdrive 58
Pinion gear 59
Pitch diameter 55
Planet carrier 62
Planetary gear set 62
Power transfer unit 67
Rear-wheel drive (RWD) 64
Ring gear 62
Spiral bevel gear 57
Spur gear 56
Sun gear 62
Torque 53
Torque converter 62
Transaxle 64
Transfer case 67
Transmission 59
Universal joint (U-joint) 65
Worm gear 57

DRIVETRAINS

PURPOSE AND FUNCTION The purpose of a vehicle drivetrain is to transfer power from the engine to the drive wheels. The drivetrain, also called a powertrain, serves the following functions:

- It allows the driver to control the power flow.
- It multiplies the engine torque.
- It controls the engine speed.

TORQUE

DEFINITION *Torque* is a rotating or twisting force that may or may not result in motion. A vehicle moves because of the torque the drive axle exerts on the wheels and tires to make them rotate. Being a form of mechanical energy, torque cannot be created or destroyed—it is converted from one form of energy to another form of energy.

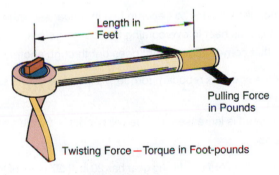

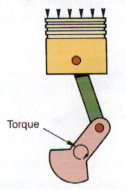

FIGURE 3–1 Torque, a twisting force, is produced when you pull on a wrench. An engine produces torque at the crankshaft as combustion pressure pushes the piston downward.

? FREQUENTLY ASKED QUESTION

Is It Lb-Ft or Ft-Lb of Torque?
The unit for torque is expressed as a force times the distance (leverage) from the object. Therefore, the official unit for torque is lb-ft (pound-feet) or Newton-meters (a force times a distance). However, it is commonly expressed in ft-lb and most torque wrenches are labeled with this unit.

UNITS OF TORQUE Engine torque is developed when combustion pressure pushes a piston downward to rotate the crankshaft. ● **SEE FIGURE 3–1.**

The amount of torque produced will vary depending on the size and design of the engine and the throttle opening. Torque is measured in pounds-feet (lb-ft) or Newton-meters (N-m). One Newton-meter of torque is equal to 0.737 lb-ft. A factor that greatly affects drivetrain design is that very little or no torque is developed at engine speeds below 1000 RPM (revolutions per minute). An engine begins producing usable torque at about 1200 RPM and peak torque at about 2500 to 4000 RPM, with an upper usable speed limit of 5000 to 7000 RPM. The gear ratios in the transmission and drive axle are used to match the engine speed and torque output to the vehicle speed and torque requirements. ● **SEE FIGURE 3–2.**

DRIVE VS. DRIVEN GEARS The *drive* gear is the gear that is the source of the engine torque and rotation. The *driven* gear is the gear that is driven or rotated by the drive gear. Two gears meshed together are used to transmit torque and rotational motion. The driven gear can then rotate yet another gear. In this case, the second gear becomes the drive gear and the third gear is the driven gear.

TORQUE MULTIPLICATION The gear teeth are cut proportional to the diameter of the gear. If one of two mating gears were twice as large as the other, it would have twice as many teeth. For example, if the smaller gear has 10 teeth, a gear twice as large will have 20 teeth. If the teeth of these gears are intermeshed, 10 teeth of each gear will come into contact when the smaller gear rotates one revolution. This will require one revolution of the small gear and one-half revolution of the larger gear. It will take two revolutions of the small gear to produce one revolution of the larger gear. This is a gear ratio of 2:1, assuming that the small gear is the drive gear. To determine a gear ratio, divide the driven gear by the driving gear. ● **SEE FIGURE 3–3.**

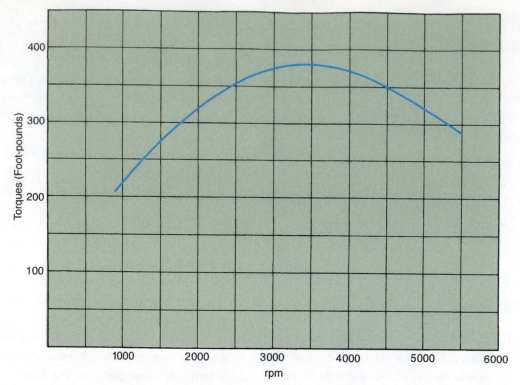

FIGURE 3–2 The torque produced by a 5.7 L engine as plotted on a graph. Note that the engine begins producing usable torque at 1000 to 1200 RPM and a maximum torque (381 ft-lb) at 3500 RPM. The torque produced by the engine decreases at higher RPM due to a decrease in volumetric efficiency.

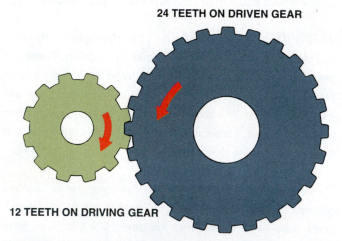

24 TEETH ON DRIVEN GEAR

12 TEETH ON DRIVING GEAR

FIGURE 3–3 Gear ratio is determined by dividing the number of teeth of the driven (output) gear (24 teeth) by the number of teeth on the driving (input) gear (12 teeth). The ratio illustrated is 2:1.

GEARS ARE LEVERS Torque is increased because of the length of the gear lever, as measured from the center of the gear. Think of each tooth as a lever, with the fulcrum being the center of the gear. The lever lengths of the two gears can provide leverage much like that of a simple lever. Physics does not allow energy to become lost in a gear set, other than what is lost as heat in overcoming friction. Therefore, whatever power that comes in one shaft, goes out through another.

- If the speed is reduced, torque will increase by the same amount.
- If speed is increased, torque will decrease by the same amount.

For example, if the driving gear has 20 lb-ft (27 N-m) of torque at 500 RPM and the ratio is 2:1, the driven gear will have 40 lb-ft (54 N-m) of torque (twice as much) at 250 RPM (half the speed).

HORSEPOWER

DEFINITION The term power means the rate of doing work. Power equals work divided by time.

- Work is done when a certain amount of mass (weight) is moved a certain distance by a force. If the object is moved in 10 seconds or 10 minutes does not make a difference in the amount of work accomplished, but it does affect the amount of power needed. ● **SEE FIGURE 3–4.**

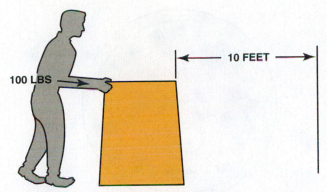

FIGURE 3–4 Work is calculated by multiplying force times distance. If you push 100 pounds 10 feet, you have done 1,000 foot-pounds of work.

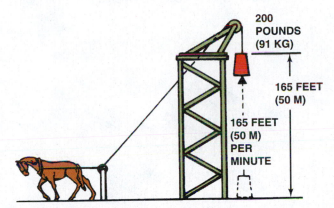

FIGURE 3–5 One horsepower is equal to 33,000 foot-pounds (200 lbs × 165 ft) of work per minute.

- Power is expressed in units of foot-pounds per minute. One **horsepower** is the power required to move 550 pounds one foot in one second, or 33,000 pounds one foot in one minute (550 lb × 60 sec = 33,000 lb). This is expressed as 550 foot-pounds (ft-lb) per second or 33,000 foot-pounds per minute. ● **SEE FIGURE 3–5**.

HORSEPOWER AND TORQUE RELATIONSHIP

To determine horsepower, a **dynamometer** is used to measure the amount the torque an engine can produce at various points through its operating range. The formula used to convert torque at a certain revolution per minute (RPM) into a horsepower reading is

$$\text{Horsepower} = \text{Torque} \times \text{RPM}/5{,}252$$

The various readings are then plotted into a curve. A typical horsepower and torque curve shows us that an engine does not produce very much torque at low RPM. The most usable torque is produced in the mid-RPM range. Torque decreases with an increase in horsepower at a higher RPM.

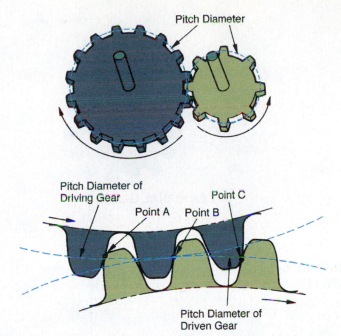

FIGURE 3–6 The pitch diameter is the effective diameter of the gear. Note how the contact points slide on the gear teeth as they move in and out of contact.

🔧 **TECH TIP**

How to Explain the Difference between Horsepower and Torque

As Carroll Shelby, the well-known racer and business owner, said "Horsepower sells cars, but torque wins races." Torque determines how fast the vehicle will accelerate, and horsepower determines how fast the vehicle will go.

The torque from an engine can be increased or decreased through the use of gears, belts, and chains. Gears, belts, or chains cannot increase horsepower; they can only modify its effect. A gear set can increase torque, but it will decrease speed by the same amount.

GEARS

TERMINOLOGY The effective diameter of a gear is the **pitch diameter** (or *pitch line*). ● **SEE FIGURE 3–6**.

The pitch diameter is the diameter of the gear at the point where the teeth of the two gears meet and transfer power. The gear teeth are shaped to be able to slide in and out of mesh with a minimum amount of friction and wear. Major points include:

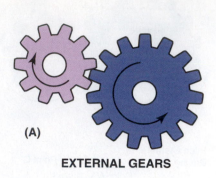

(A)

EXTERNAL GEARS

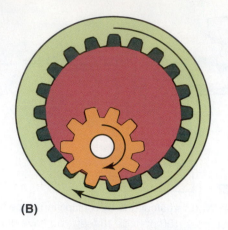

(B)

INTERNAL AND EXTERNAL GEARS

FIGURE 3–7 (a) When one external gear drives another, the direction of rotation is always reversed. (b) When an external gear drives an internal gear, the two gears will rotate in the same direction.

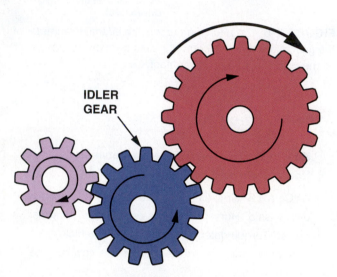

IDLER GEAR

EXTERNAL GEARS

FIGURE 3–8 An idler gear reverses the direction of rotation so that the driving and driven gears rotate in the same direction.

- Driven and driving gears will rotate in opposite directions.
- External gears will always reverse shaft motion.
- If same-direction motion is required, the power will be routed through two gear sets.
- When power goes through a series of gears, an even number of gears (2, 4, 6, and 8) will cause a reversal in direction and an odd number of gears (3, 5, 7, and 9) will produce same-direction of rotation. ● **SEE FIGURE 3–7.**

REVERSING DIRECTION OF ROTATION External gears reverse the direction of rotation when the drive gear transfers power to the driven gear. When it is necessary to change the

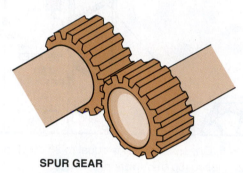

SPUR GEAR

FIGURE 3–9 The teeth of a spur gear are cut parallel to the shaft, and this produces a straight pressure between the driving and the driven gear teeth.

ratio without changing the direction of power flow, an idler gear is added. An idler gear changes the rotational direction but does not affect the ratio. ● **SEE FIGURE 3–8.**

GEAR TYPES Gears come in different types depending on the cut and relationship of the teeth to the shafts.

- **Spur gears** Spur gears, the simplest gears, are on parallel shafts with teeth cut straight or parallel to the shaft. ● **SEE FIGURE 3–9.**
- **Helical gear** Helical gears are the most used of all gears used in transmissions. These gears have teeth cut in a spiral or helix shape. ● **SEE FIGURE 3–10.**

Helical gears are quieter than spur gears, but generate axial or end thrust under a load. A helical gear is stronger than a comparable-sized spur gear and has an almost continuous power flow because of the angled teeth. ● **SEE FIGURE 3–10.**

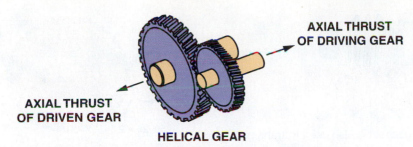

AXIAL THRUST OF DRIVING GEAR

AXIAL THRUST OF DRIVEN GEAR

HELICAL GEAR

FIGURE 3–10 The teeth of a helical gear are cut on a slant, and this produces an axial or side thrust.

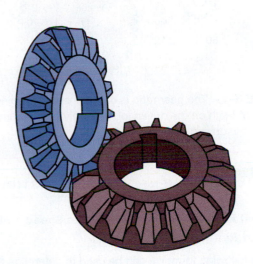

FIGURE 3–11 Bevel gears are commonly used in differentials.

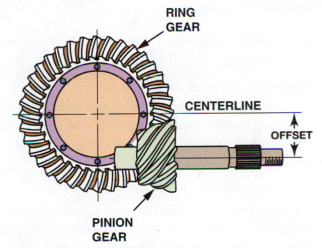

RING GEAR

CENTERLINE

OFFSET

PINION GEAR

FIGURE 3–12 A hypoid gear set uses a pinion gear that is located below the centerline of the ring gear and is commonly used in drive axles.

NOTE: When discussing gears, a pinion gear is the smaller gear of a pair.

- **Bevel gears**—Bevel gears are used on nonparallel shafts. The outer edge of the gear must be cut on the angle that bisects the angle of the two shafts. In other words, if the two shafts meet at an angle of 90° and the two gears are the same size, the outer edge of the gears will be cut at 45°. The simplest bevel gears have teeth cut straight and are called spur bevel gears. They are inexpensive but noisy. ● **SEE FIGURE 3–11.**

- **Spiral bevel gears**—Spiral bevel gears, like helical gears, have curved teeth for quieter operation.

- **Hypoid gear**—A variation of the spiral bevel gear is the hypoid gear, also called an *offset-bevel gear*. Hypoid gears are used in most drive axles and transaxles that have longitudinal mounted engines. The hypoid gear

design places the drive pinion gear lower in the housing (below the centerline) of the ring gear and axle shafts. ● **SEE FIGURE 3–12**

- **Worm gear**—A gear set used with shafts that cross each other but do not intersect is the worm gear. The worm gear or drive pinion is cut in a rather severe helix, much like a bolt thread, and the ring gear or wheel is cut almost like a spur gear. Worm gears are used in vehicle speed sensor drives. To determine the ratio of a worm gear, divide the number of teeth on the wheel by the pitch of the worm gear. For example, a single-pitch worm gear tooth driving a 20-tooth ring gear will have a ratio of 20:1, a very low ratio, and the wheel does not have to be 20 times larger than the worm gear. A 20:1 ratio in most gear sets requires the driven gear to be 20 times larger than the driving gear. ● **SEE FIGURE 3–13.**

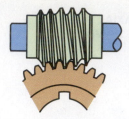

FIGURE 3–13 A worm gear set is also used to transmit power between angled shafts.

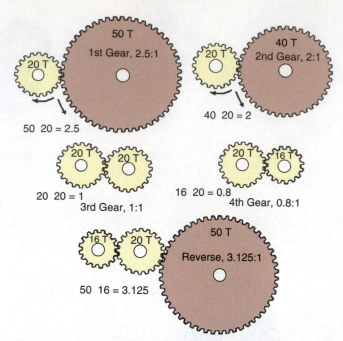

FIGURE 3–14 The gear ratio is determined by dividing the number of teeth on the driven (output) gear by the number of teeth on the driving (input) gear.

GEAR RATIOS

TERMINOLOGY **Gear ratios** are determined by the following methods:

- Dividing the number of teeth on the driven gear (output) by the number of teeth on the driving gear (input). Most of the time, this means dividing a larger number, such as 20, by a smaller number, such as 5. In this case, $20 \div 5 = 4$, so the ratio will be 4:1.

- Gear ratio = driven gear/drive gear

- The driving gear will turn four times for each revolution of the driven gear. This results in a speed reduction and a torque increase. The speed of the output will be 4 times slower than the input speed but, the output torque will be four times more than the input torque. The higher the ratio number, the lower the gear ratio. A 5:1 ratio is higher numerically, but, in terms of speed of the driven gear, it is a lower ratio than 4:1. ● **SEE FIGURE 3–14.**

Most of the time, the ratio will not end up as whole numbers. It will be something like an 11-tooth driving gear and a 19-tooth driven gear, which results in a ratio of 19 divided by 11, which equals 1.7272727 and can be rounded off to 1.73.

COMMONLY USED RATIOS The automotive industry commonly rounds off gear ratios to two decimal points. Drivetrain engineers usually do not use even ratios like 3:1 or 4:1 but instead use ratios that are at least 10 percent greater or less than even numbers. An even ratio, like 3:1, repeats the same gear tooth contacts every third revolution. If there is a damaged tooth, a noise will be repeated continuously, and most drivers will not like the noise. A gear set with a ratio such as 3.23:1 is called a hunting gear set, and a tooth of one gear contacts all of the other gear teeth, which produces quieter operation.

? **FREQUENTLY ASKED QUESTION**

What is the Relationship between Speed and Gear Ratio?

The following formulas can be used to determine the vehicle speed based on the gear ratio and engine speed, or the engine speed based on the gear ratio and MPH:

- MPH = (RPM × tire diameter) ÷ (gear ratio × 336)
- Engine RPM = (MPH × gear ratio × 336) ÷ tire diameter

NOTE: Use the loaded tire radius times two for the tire diameter.

OVERDRIVE If the driving gear has more teeth (20) than the driven gear (5), there will be an increase in speed and a reduction in torque. This is called an **overdrive**. The ratio is computed by dividing 5 by 20, $5 \div 20 = 0.25$, so the ratio would be expressed as 0.25:1. The driving gear will turn 0.25 or one-fourth of a revolution for each turn of the driven gear. Note that a gear ratio is always written with the number 1 to the right of the colon. This represents one turn of the output gear, while the number to the left represents the revolutions of the input gear.

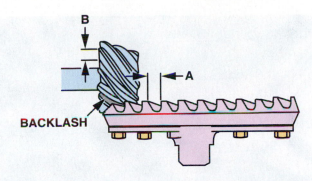

A - B = BACKLASH

FIGURE 3–15 Backlash is the clearance between the teeth of two meshing gears. There has to be some clearance (backlash) to prevent the gears from getting into a bind condition when they are transmitting torque.

CALCULATING OVERALL RATIOS
When power goes through more than one gear set, two or more ratios are involved. In most cases, the simplest way to handle this is to figure the ratio of each set and then multiply the ratios. An example of this is a vehicle with a first-gear ratio of 2.68:1 and a rear axle ratio of 3.45:1. The overall ratio in first gear is 2.68×3.45 or 9.246:1.

- At the same time there will be 9.246 times as much torque at the rear wheels than the engine produced.
- The engine will rotate at a speed that is 9.246 times faster than the rear axle shafts. The overall ratios for the other transmission gears would be figured in the same manner.

GEAR SET SUMMARY
Typical rules about gear sets include the following:

- Two mated external gears will always rotate in opposite directions.
- Gear sets will multiply torque but at a reduced speed.
- An idler gear allows the drive and driven gears to rotate in the same direction.
- To find the ratio, divide the driven gear by the drive gear.
- When power transfers through an even number (two or four) of gears, the input and out-put gears will rotate in opposite directions.
- When power transfers through an uneven number (one, three, or five) of gears, the input and output gears will rotate in the same direction.
- To find the overall ratio of multiple gear sets, multiply the ratios of the gear sets.

- Two gears transferring power push away from each other in an action called *gear separation*. The gear separation force (thrust) is proportional to the torque being transferred.
- The smaller gear(s) in a gear set may also be called a **pinion gear**.
- All gear sets *must* have backlash to prevent binding.
  ● **SEE FIGURE 3–15.**

TRANSMISSIONS

PURPOSE AND FUNCTION   The purpose and function of gears in a **transmission** include the following:

- Low/first gear must provide enough torque to get the vehicle moving.
- High gear should provide an engine speed for fuel-efficient operation at highway speeds.
- The intermediate ratios should be spaced to provide adequate acceleration while minimizing the potential of overrevving the engine before the shift or lugging the engine after the shift.

TRENDS   The majority of vehicles up to the 1970s used three-speed transmissions while some added an overdrive unit for a fourth gear ratio to lower engine RPM at cruise speeds. As the need to improve fuel economy and reduce exhaust emissions has improved, four-, five-, and six-speed transmissions have been introduced to provide lower first gears, overdrive, and/or smaller steps between gear ratios.

MANUAL TRANSMISSIONS

PURPOSE AND FUNCTION   A **manual transmission**, also called a *standard transmission*, is constructed with a group of paths through which power can flow with each path used being a different gear ratio. ● **SEE FIGURE 3–16.**

Synchronizer assemblies or sliding gears and the shift linkage are used to control or engage the power paths.

CLUTCH   Engine power must be stopped when making a shift in a manual transmission. The **clutch** is used to stop the power flow to allow the transmission to be shifted. It is also

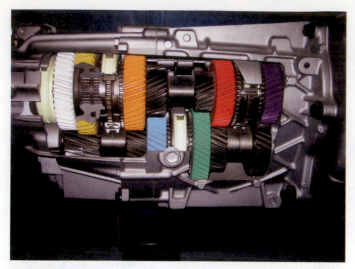

FIGURE 3–16 A manual transmission provides several gear ratios and a method to shift them.

FIGURE 3–17 A Muncie four-speed manual transmission on a restored muscle car.

? **FREQUENTLY ASKED QUESTION**

What is a "Close-Ratio" Transmission?

Gear ratio spread (GRS), is the difference between the lowest and highest ratios or, in other words, the overall range of a transmission gear ratios. In transmissions, it is fairly easy to visualize the difference between a 3.59:1 first gear and a 0.83:1 fifth gear. Gear ratio spread is determined by dividing the low gear ratio by the high gear ratio. The GRS for the gear transmission is $3.59 \div 0.83 = 4.33$.
RPM change/drop is fairly easy to determine:

- Subtract the higher ratio from the lower ratio and divide the product by the lower ratio
- A close-ratio Muncie four-speed has ratios spaced fairly close together (25% or less), closer than the wide-ratio version. ● **SEE FIGURE 3–17.**

? **FREQUENTLY ASKED QUESTION**

What is an Automated Manual Transmission?

An automated manual transmission is a type of automatic transmission/transaxle that uses two clutches and a manual transmission-type gears and shifted hydraulically by computer-controlled solenoids. This type of transmission is commonly called a *dual clutch* or an *electronically controlled manual transmission*.

used to ease the engagement of the power flow when the vehicle starts from a standstill. The slight slippage as the clutch engages allows the engine speed to stay up where it produces usable torque as the vehicle begins moving.

Most vehicles use a foot-pedal-operated single-plate clutch assembly that is mounted on the engine flywheel. When the pedal is pushed down, the power flow is disengaged and when the pedal is released, power can flow from the engine to the transmission through the engaged clutch. ● **SEE FIGURE 3–18**

AUTOMATIC TRANSMISSIONS

PURPOSE AND FUNCTION The purpose and function of an **automatic transmission** is to provide the forward and reverse gear ratios needed without requiring the driver to make the change in gearing as with a manual transmission. An automatic transmission has various gear ratios, but the paths of power flow are different from those of a manual transmission.

SHIFT MODES The transmission provides the various gear ratios for forward and reverse operations as well as two methods for the engine to run without moving the vehicle. Most automatic transmissions and transaxles include the following shift modes. ● **SEE FIGURE 13–19.**

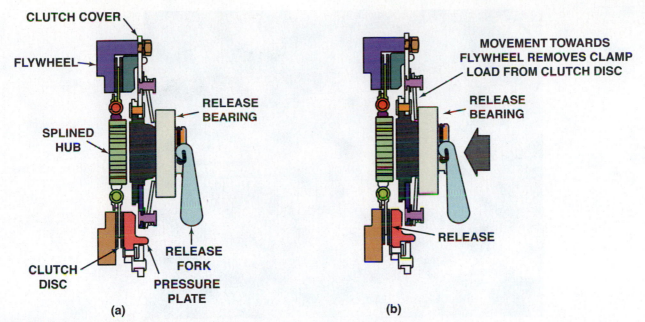

FIGURE 3–18 (a) A clutch cover (pressure plate assembly) is bolted onto the flywheel with the clutch disc between them. The release bearing and fork provide a method to release (disengage) the clutch. (b) When the clutch is engaged, the disc is squeezed against the flywheel by the pressure plate. Releasing the clutch separates the disc from the flywheel and pressure plate.

FIGURE 3–19 The gear selector is often called the "PRNDL," pronounced "prindle," regardless of the actual letters or numbers used.

- **Park.** In the park position, the output shaft is locked to the case of the transmission/transaxle which keeps the vehicle from moving. No power is transmitted through the unit so the engine can remain running while the vehicle is held stationary. In the park position
  1. The engine can be started by the driver.
  2. To move the shifter out of the park position on a late model vehicle, the brake pedal must be depressed to release the transmission shift interlock.

- **Reverse.** The reverse gear selector position is used to move the vehicle in reverse. Reverse usually uses a gear ratio similar to first gear.

- **Neutral.** In the neutral position no torque is being transmitted through the automatic transmission/transaxle. In this position the engine can be started by the driver.

CAUTION: The vehicle is free to roll when the gear selector is placed in the neutral position unless the brake pedal is depressed to prevent the vehicle from moving.

- **Overdrive (OD).** The OD is the normal position for the shift selector for most driving conditions. This position allows the transmission or transaxle to shift through all forward gears as needed for the best fuel economy and lowest exhaust emissions.

NOTE: The overdrive button on many automatic transmissions is used to turn off overdrive and is used while towing or when in driving in city traffic to prevent the transmission from shifting in and out of overdrive.

- **Drive (D).** The D position includes the overdrive ratios in most vehicles. If there is an overdrive shift mode, however, then D is used to provide all forward gears except overdrive. Use this position when driving on the highway.

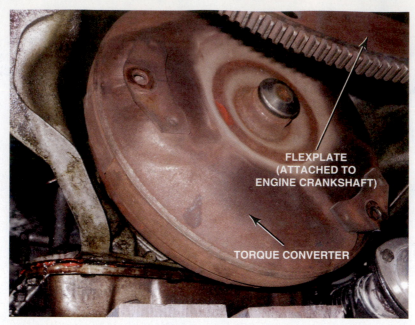

FIGURE 3–20 A torque converter is attached to the engine crankshaft and the other end is splined to the input shaft of the automatic transmission. The torque converter is used to transmit engine torque to the transmission yet slip when the engine is at idle speed.

- **Third (3).** In third position the transmission/transaxle will upshift normally to third gear but will not upshift to a higher gear. When the third (3) position is selected while driving in a higher gear, the transmission will downshift into third if the vehicle speed is low enough to prevent the engine from being overrevved. This gear selection is used for the gentle grades at a moderate vehicle speed when compression braking is needed.

- **Second (2).** The second position is used for slowing the vehicle while descending long grades. In this gear selection, the vehicle speed is controlled and the engine speed is increased to provide engine compression braking. This gear selection is used for the gentle grades at a moderate vehicle speed.

- **First (1 or Low).** The first (or low) position is used for slowing the vehicle while descending steep grades. In this gear selection, the vehicle speed is controlled and engine compression braking is used to slow the vehicle. This gear selection is used for the steepest grades at the lowest possible speed.

TORQUE CONVERTERS A **torque converter** replaces the manual transmission clutch. It is a type of fluid coupling that can release the power flow at slow engine speeds and also multiply the engine torque during acceleration. Torque converters in newer vehicles include a friction clutch that locks up to eliminate slippage at cruising speeds, improving fuel economy and reducing exhaust emissions. ● SEE FIGURE 3–20.

PLANETARY GEAR SETS Most automatic transmissions use **planetary gear sets**, which are a combination of gears. When the gear set is assembled, the sun gear is in the center and meshed with the planet gears, which are located around it, somewhat like the planets in our solar system. The ring gear is meshed around the outside of the planet gears. The three main members of the planetary gear set include the following:

1. **Sun gear** It is the gear in the center.
2. **Ring gear** It is also called an *annulus gear* or *internal gear*.
3. **Planet carrier** It holds the planet gears (also called *pinions*) in position. ● SEE FIGURE 3–21.

Each of these gears can have two possible actions: They can rotate or stand still.

The planet gears/pinions have the following three possible actions.

1. They can rotate on their shafts in a stationary carrier and act like idler gears.
2. They can rotate on their shafts in a rotating carrier; the planet gears are walking.
3. They can stand still on their shafts and rotate with the carrier.

Planetary gear sets are used and combined in a complex manner so that transmissions with seven or eight speeds forward plus reverse are possible. Shifts are made by engaging or releasing one or more internal clutches that drive a gear set member, or by engaging or releasing other clutches or bands that hold a gear set member stationary. An automatic transmission might have as many as seven of these power control units

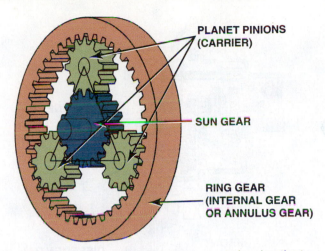

FIGURE 3–21 A typical planetary gear set showing the terms that are used to describe each member.

(clutches or bands). One-way clutches are also used that self-release and overrun when the next gear is engaged. The control units can operate without the interruption of the power flow.

PLANETARY GEAR SET OPERATION
Planetary gear sets are so arranged that power enters through one of the members and leaves through one of the other members while the third member is held stationary in reaction. Power flow through a planetary gear set is controlled by clutches, bands, and one-way clutches. One or more clutches will control the power coming to a planetary member and one or more reaction members can hold a gear set member stationary. The third planetary member will be the output. ● SEE FIGURE 3–22.

PLANETARY GEAR SET RATIOS
A simple planetary gear set can produce one of the following:

- A neutral if either the input clutch or reaction member is not applied
- Two reduction ratios
- Two overdrive ratios
- Two reverse ratios, one a reduction and one an overdrive
- The reduction, overdrive, and reverse ratios will require one driving member, one output member, and one reaction member in the gear set.

NOTE: A 1:1, direct-drive ratio is achieved if two gear set members are driven.

ADVANTAGES OF PLANETARY GEAR SETS
Planetary gear sets offer several advantages over conventional gear sets.

1. Because there is more than one gear transferring power, the torque load is spread over several gear teeth.

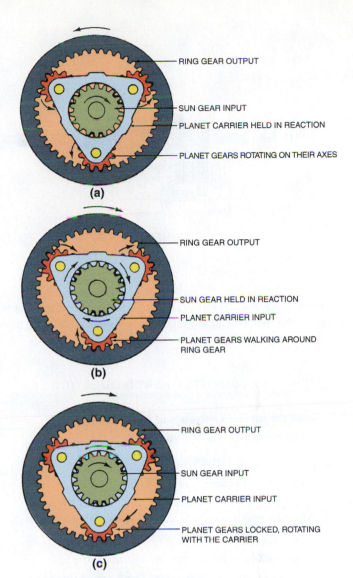

(a)

(b)

(c)

FIGURE 3–22 (a) If the planet carrier is held with the sun gear rotating, the planet gears simply rotate in the carrier and act as idler gears between the sun and ring gears. (b) If the sun or ring is held, the planet gears will walk around that stationary gear; they rotate on their shafts as the carrier rotates. (c) If two parts are driven and no parts are held, the planet gears are stationary on their shafts, and the whole assembly rotates as a unit.

2. Also, any gear separation forces (as gears transfer power, they tend to push away from each other) are contained within the planetary gear set, preventing this load from being transmitted to the transmission case.

3. Another advantage is the small relative size of the planetary gear set. Conventional gears are normally side by side, and for a 2:1 gear ratio, one gear has to be twice the size of the other. A planetary gear set can easily produce this same ratio in a smaller package.

4. Also, planetary gear sets are in constant mesh and no coupling or uncoupling of the gears is required.

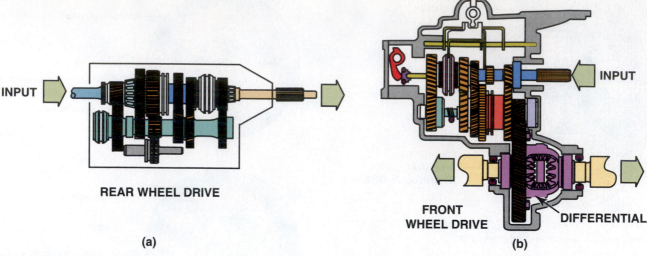

REAR WHEEL DRIVE

(a)

FRONT WHEEL DRIVE **DIFFERENTIAL**

(b)

FIGURE 3–23 A RWD drivetrain uses a transmission to provide the necessary gear ratio and a single driveshaft to transfer power to the rear axle (a). A FWD drivetrain uses a transaxle that combines the transmissions final drive, and differential (b). A driveshaft is used for each front drive wheel.

 ? FREQUENTLY ASKED QUESTION

What Do All the Letters and Numbers Mean in Transmission Designations?

The numbers and letters usually mean the following:

- **Number of forward speeds.** The number of forward speeds may include four, five, or six such as the GM 4T60-E four-speed unit and the ZF 5HP24 five-speed unit.
- **Front-wheel drive or rear-wheel drive.** The letter **T** usually means *transverse* (front-wheel-drive transaxle) such as the Chrysler 41-TE; the **L** means *longitudinal* (rear-wheel-drive transmission) such as the General Motors 6L80; and the **R** means *rear-wheel drive* such as the Ford 5R55E.
- **Electronically controlled.** The letter **E** is often used to indicate that the unit is electronically controlled, and **M** or **H** is used to designate older mechanically (hydraulically) controlled units. Most automatic transmissions built since the early 1990s are electronically controlled and therefore the **E** is often included in the designation of newer designs of transmission or transaxles.
- **Torque rating.** The torque rating is usually designated by a number where the higher the number, the higher the amount of torque load the unit is designed to handle. In a GM 6L80-E, the torque rating is 80. Always check service information for the exact transmission designation for the vehicle being studied.

REAR-WHEEL DRIVE VS. FRONT-WHEEL DRIVE

At one time, most vehicles had the transmission mounted behind the engine and used a driveshaft to transfer power to the rear axle and driving wheels. This drivetrain is called **rear-wheel drive (RWD)**.

Many vehicles use a transaxle to drive the front wheels, called **front-wheel drive (FWD)**. Most FWD vehicles have the engine mounted in a transverse position, crosswise in the vehicle. Some are longitudinally mounted, in a lengthwise position as in RWD vehicles.

Two short driveshafts, called **half shafts**, are used to connect the transaxle to the front wheels. Driving only two wheels is adequate for most driving conditions. When the roads are slippery and driving off road, driving all four wheels provides better vehicle control. ● **SEE FIGURE 3–23.**

TRANSAXLES

TERMINOLOGY A **transaxle** is a compact combination of a transmission, the **final drive** gear reduction, and the differential. It can be either a manual, automatic, or continuously variable transaxle. Transaxles are used in nearly all front-wheel-drive vehicles, some mid-engine vehicles, rear engine, and even a few rear-wheel-drive vehicles. ● **SEE FIGURE 3–24.**

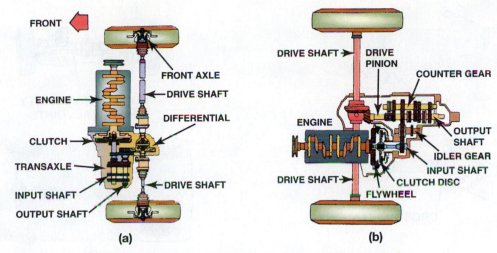

FIGURE 3–24 Transverse (a) and longitudinal (b) mounted front-wheel-drive (FWD) drivetrains.

OPERATION A transmission normally has one output shaft that couples to the rear axle through the driveshaft. A transaxle has two output shafts that couple to the two front wheels through a pair of driveshafts. The **differential** used in transaxles or drive axles is a torque-splitting device that allows the two axle shafts to operate at different speeds so that a vehicle can turn corners. When a vehicle turns a corner, the wheel on the outer side of the turning radius must travel farther than the inner wheel, but it must do this in the same period of time. Therefore, it must rotate faster while turning. Most differentials are composed of a group of four or more gears. One gear is coupled to each axle and two are mounted on the differential pinion shaft.

DRIVESHAFTS

TERMINOLOGY Driveshafts, also called a *propeller shaft* or *prop shaft*, transfer power from one component to another. Rear-wheel-drive vehicle driveshafts are usually made from steel tubing, and normally have either a **universal joint (U-joint)** or a **constant-velocity (CV) joint** at each end. Most front-wheel-drive vehicles use driveshafts that are a solid shaft or hollow steel tubing. A U-joint allows the shaft to change angle as the drive axle moves up and down when the wheels travel over bumps. Speed fluctuations occur in the driveshaft as the U-joints transfer power at an angle, but these fluctuations are

canceled out or eliminated by the position of the U-joint at the other end of the driveshaft.

A front-wheel-drive vehicle driveshaft must use a CV joint at its ends because the front wheels must be steered at sharp angles. The short driveshafts used with transaxles and independent rear suspension drive axles are often called half shafts. ● **SEE FIGURE 3–25.**

DRIVE AXLE ASSEMBLIES

TERMINOLOGY Rear-wheel-drive vehicles use a drive axle assembly at the rear. A **drive axle** performs four functions:

1. It supports the weight of the rear of the vehicle.

2. It contains the final drive reduction gears.

3. It contains the differential, which transfers torque to both drive wheels and allows the wheels to rotate at different speeds when cornering.

4. It allows the power to turn 90 degrees.

Most axle assemblies use strong axle shafts to transfer the torque from the differential gears to the wheels and tires. A bearing at the outer end of the axle housing serves to transfer vehicle weight to the axle and then to the wheels and tires while allowing the shaft to rotate.

The term final drive refers to the last set of reduction gears in a gear train. The torque that is applied to the drive wheels, and cruising speed engine RPM, is determined by the reduction gears and the drive wheel diameter. ● **SEE FIGURE 3–26.**

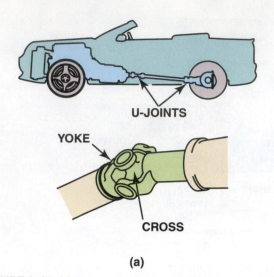

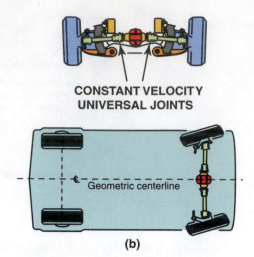

FIGURE 3–25 (a) A rear-wheel-drive (RWD) driveshaft uses a pair of universal joints to allow the rear axle to move up and down. (b) A front-wheel-drive (FWD) driveshaft uses a pair of constant-velocity joints to allow the front wheels to move up and down and steer.

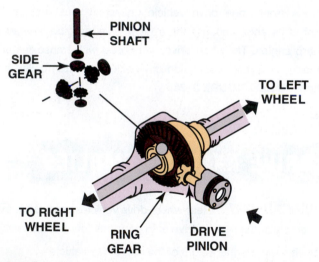

FIGURE 3–26 A drive axle includes a ring and pinion gear to produce a lower gear ratio as it turns the power flow 90° and a differential (differential pinion and side gears) to allow the drive wheels to rotate at different speeds.

? FREQUENTLY ASKED QUESTION

What Must the Powertrain Overcome to Move the Vehicle?

To propel the vehicle, the engine and drivetrain must overcome the following:

- Rolling friction, which is the drag of the tires on the road, and bearing friction. These frictions increase at a constant rate, doubling as the speed is doubled.
- Aerodynamic drag, which is the wind resistance of air moving over the size and shape of the vehicle. It increases at a rapid rate, roughly four times as the speed is doubled (actually, velocity squared).
- Grade resistance, which is equal to 0.01 times the vehicle weight times the angle of the grade in percent.

TOWING CAPABILITY

DRIVETRAIN REQUIREMENTS Trucks are often used to tow trailers or heavy loads. In order for a vehicle to tow a heavy load, the vehicle must have the following features:

- An engine that can produce the needed torque and horsepower.
- A strong frame to withstand the forces involved.
- A strong trailer hitch properly installed and attached to the frame of the vehicle.

- A strong drivetrain (transmission, driveshaft, and drive axle(s)) that can transmit the engine torque to the drive wheels.
- Heavy-duty brakes so that the heavy load can be slowed and stopped safely.

SAE J2807 STANDARD Starting in 2013, the Society of Automotive Engineers (SAE) established a standardized test procedure to determine the tow rating for vehicles. The standard includes three vehicle performance standards including:

1. **Climbing test** During the climbing test, the vehicle with the loaded trailer (at the specified rating that the vehicle

manufacture states is the capacity of the vehicle) has 12 seconds to climb a hill that rises 3,000 feet (900 m) over a length of 11.4 miles (18 km) without dropping below 40 MPH (64 km/h). This test is based on a stretch of interstate I-15 between Los Angeles and Las Vegas.

2. **Acceleration test** During this test, the vehicle with loaded trailer must accelerate from 0 to 30 MPH (48 km/h) in 12 seconds and less than 30 seconds to reach 60 MPH (100 km/h).

3. **Launching** This test is used to test the vehicle and loaded trailer in both forward and reverse. The test places the vehicle at the base of a long hill with a 12% grade. The vehicle must be able to climb the grade 16 feet (5 m) from a stop five times within five minutes.

These tests not only test the power of the vehicle but also that the engine and transmission can be kept at the proper temperature meaning that the engine and transmission (if automatic) be equipped with a cooler.

NOTE: Not all vehicle manufactures adhere to the SAE standard when reporting their recommended tow rating because while standardized, the use of the SAE J2807 is voluntary.

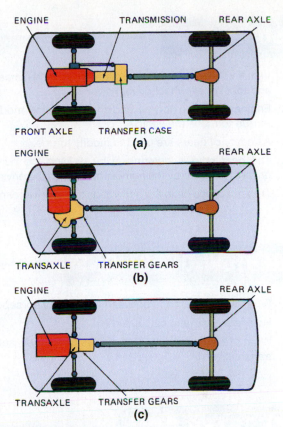

FIGURE 3–27 Three major 4WD configurations. The traditional form (a) uses a transfer case to split the torque for the front and rear drive axles. Both (b) and (c) are typical AWD configurations.

FOUR-WHEEL DRIVE

TERMINOLOGY **Four-wheel drive (4WD)** is often designated as "4 × 4" and refers to a vehicle that has four driven wheels.

- The first 4 indicates that the vehicle has four wheels.
- The second 4 indicates that all four wheels are driven

A vehicle will have more pulling power and traction if all of its wheels are driven. This requires a drive axle at each end of the vehicle, another driveshaft, and a **transfer case** or **power transfer unit** to drive the additional driveshaft and drive axle. The transfer case is normally attached to the rear of the transmission. It has a single input shaft from the transmission and two output shafts, one to the front drive axle and one to the rear drive axle. Some transfer cases are two-speed and include a set of reduction gears for lower-speed, higher-torque operation.

Four-wheel drive can be built into

- A front-engine rear-wheel drive
- A front-engine front-wheel drive
- A rear-engine rear-wheel drive

● **SEE FIGURE 3–27.**

ALL-WHEEL DRIVE **All-wheel-drive (AWD),** also called full-time four-wheel drive, vehicles are four-wheel-drive vehicles equipped with a center (inner-axle) differential so they can be operated on pavement in four-wheel drive. Full-time four-wheel drive is another name for all-wheel drive. All-wheel-drive vehicles are designed for improved on-road handling. There will be one differential in each drive axle assembly plus a differential between the two drive axles. The inter-axle differential allows the front-to-rear wheel speed differential. Because all wheels are driven, these vehicles are excellent for use in rain and snow where added control is needed.

1. Vehicles are built as rear-wheel drive, front-wheel drive, and four- or all-wheel drive.

2. Engines develop torque and the drivetrains modify that torque to move the vehicle.

3. A variety of gears are used to modify torque.

4. The gear ratio is determined by dividing the number of driven gear teeth by the number of teeth on the driving gear.

5. Transmissions have the gear ratios that a driver can select.

6. Manual transmissions use a clutch and automatic transmissions use a torque converter.

7. Transaxles combine the final drive gears and differential with the transmission.

8. Driveshafts and the drive axle complete the drivetrain.

9. Four-wheel-drive and all-wheel-drive vehicles have a transfer case or transfer gears and a second drive axle.

REVIEW QUESTIONS

1. What is the difference between torque and horsepower?

2. How is a gear ratio calculated?

3. What are the common shift modes used in an automatic transmission?

4. What is an inter-axle differential?

CHAPTER QUIZ

1. Torque is _____.
   a. A twisting force
   b. The rate of doing work
   c. Results in motion
   d. The gear ratio

2. Gears can be used to _____.
   a. Increase speed
   b. Increase torque
   c. Reverse direction
   d. All of the above

3. If a gear with 20 teeth is driving a gear with 60 teeth, the gear ratio is _____.
   a. 2:6
   b. 3:1
   c. 1:3
   d. 0.33:1

4. Technician A says a helical gear is stronger than a spur gear. Technician B says a helical gear is noisier than a spur gear. Which technician is correct?
   a. Technician A only
   b. Technician B only
   c. Both Technicians A and B
   d. Neither Technician A nor B

5. Which type of gear may be found in a rear-wheel-drive axle?
   a. Hypoid
   b. Spiral Bevel
   c. Spur
   d. Helical

6. The transmission is in first gear, which has a 2.5:1 ratio, and the rear axle has a ratio of 2:1. What is the overall ratio?
   a. 2:1
   b. 2.5:1
   c. 4.5:1
   d. 5:1

7. The type of gear set used in most automatic transmission is _____.
   a. Spur gears
   b. Planetary gears
   c. Helical gears
   d. Any of the above

8. What shift mode should be used when descending a steep hill?
   a. Drive (D)
   b. Second (2)
   c. Neutral (N)
   d. Low (L)

9. Full-time four-wheel-drive vehicles use _____.
   a. Transfer case
   b. Spiral bevel drive axles
   c. Three differentials
   d. Both a and c

10. What is used to transfer engine torque to all four wheels?
    a. Four driveshafts
    b. A transfer case or power transfer unit
    c. Four differentials
    d. All of the above

chapter 4

CLUTCH PARTS AND OPERATION

After studying this chapter, the reader will be able to:

1. Prepare for ASE Manual Drive Train and Axles (A3) certification test content area "A" (Clutch Diagnosis and Repair).
2. List the major parts that are included in the clutch system and describe how the clutch works.
3. Discuss the purpose and function of clutch discs.
4. Discuss the purpose and function of pressure plates.
5. State the characteristics of a flywheel and explain how a dual-mass flywheel works.
6. Describe how a clutch pedal linkage and a clutch pedal switch works.
7. Describe the operation of the release bearing and state the types of release bearings.

Belleville spring 74
Clutch disc 70
Coefficient of friction (COF) 72
Coil spring style 74
Cushion spring 73
Diaphragm spring style 74
Dual-mass flywheel 77
Front bearing retainer 72
Inertia 76
Marcel spring 73
Pilot bearing 78
Pressure plate 70
Release bearing 70
Slave cylinder 79
Torsional dampers 73
Throwout bearing 70

CLUTCHES

PURPOSE AND FUNCTION The clutch assembly is located between the engine and the transmission/transaxle. The purpose and function of a clutch include the following:

- To disconnect engine power from the transmission/transaxle to permit the engine to remain running when the vehicle is stopped and to permit the transmission/transaxle to be shifted into different gears including reverse.

- To connect and transmit engine torque to the transmission/transaxle.

- To dampen and absorb engine power impulses and drivetrain vibration.

- To provide a smooth engagement and disengagement of torque between the engine and the transmission/transaxle.

PARTS INVOLVED A clutch assembly consists of a **clutch disc** that is splined to the input shaft of the transmission/transaxle. When the driver depresses the clutch pedal, a **release bearing**, also called a **throwout bearing**, is forced against the release levers (fingers) of the **pressure plate**. The pressure plate is bolted to and rotates with the flywheel. ● **SEE FIGURE 4–1.**

CLUTCH OPERATION When force is exerted on the center of the pressure plate by the release bearing, the applied force is released from the clutch disc that had been squeezed between the engine flywheel and the pressure plate. With the pressure removed from the clutch disc, the engine can be operated without transferring torque to the transmission/transaxle. Using a clutch also permits the transmission/transaxle to be shifted easily because a shift cannot be made easily if the transmission/transaxle is transferring engine torque. When the driver releases force on the clutch pedal, the pedal return

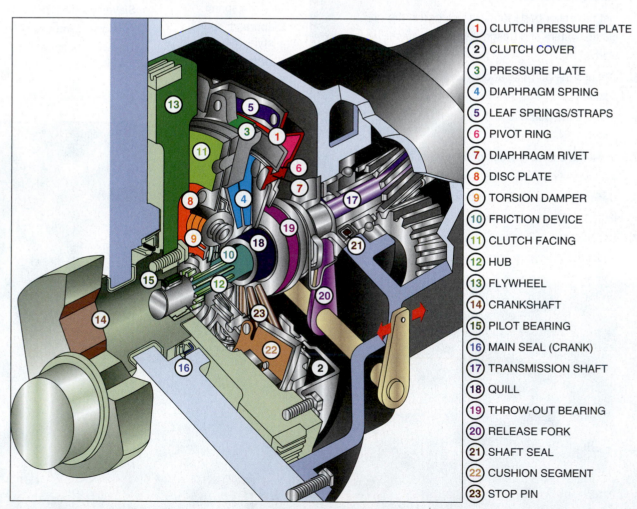

1. CLUTCH PRESSURE PLATE
2. CLUTCH COVER
3. PRESSURE PLATE
4. DIAPHRAGM SPRING
5. LEAF SPRINGS/STRAPS
6. PIVOT RING
7. DIAPHRAGM RIVET
8. DISC PLATE
9. TORSION DAMPER
10. FRICTION DEVICE
11. CLUTCH FACING
12. HUB
13. FLYWHEEL
14. CRANKSHAFT
15. PILOT BEARING
16. MAIN SEAL (CRANK)
17. TRANSMISSION SHAFT
18. QUILL
19. THROW-OUT BEARING
20. RELEASE FORK
21. SHAFT SEAL
22. CUSHION SEGMENT
23. STOP PIN

FIGURE 4–1 Typical automotive clutch assembly showing all related parts.

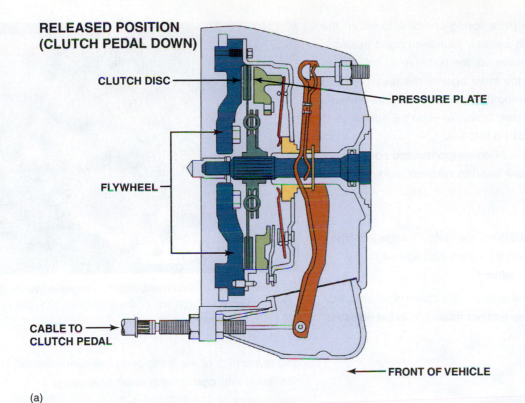

RELEASED POSITION (CLUTCH PEDAL DOWN)

CLUTCH DISC

PRESSURE PLATE

FLYWHEEL

CABLE TO CLUTCH PEDAL

← FRONT OF VEHICLE

(a)

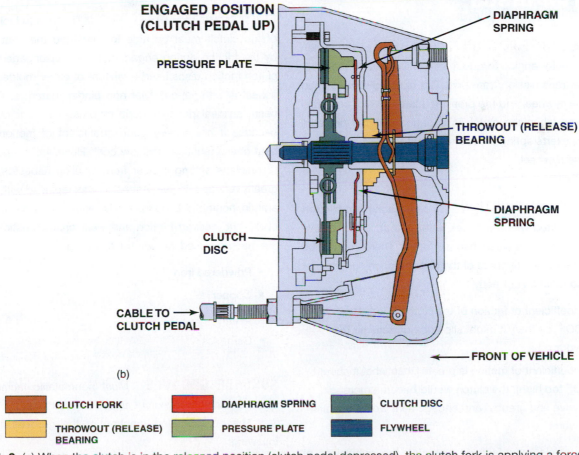

ENGAGED POSITION (CLUTCH PEDAL UP)

DIAPHRAGM SPRING

PRESSURE PLATE

THROWOUT (RELEASE) BEARING

DIAPHRAGM SPRING

CLUTCH DISC

CABLE TO CLUTCH PEDAL

← FRONT OF VEHICLE

(b)

CLUTCH FORK DIAPHRAGM SPRING CLUTCH DISC

THROWOUT (RELEASE) BEARING PRESSURE PLATE FLYWHEEL

FIGURE 4–2 (a) When the clutch is in the released position (clutch pedal depressed), the clutch fork is applying a force to the throwout (release) bearing, which pushes on the diaphragm spring, releasing the pressure on the friction disc. (b) When the clutch is in the engaged position (clutch pedal up), the diaphragm spring exerts force on the clutch disc, holding it between the flywheel and the pressure plate.

spring and the pressure plate spring combine to return the clutch pedal to its at-rest position (clutch-engaged position). When the clutch pedal moves up, the pressure on the release bearing is released and the force against the pressure plate spring(s) is released, allowing the spring force of the pressure plate to clamp the clutch disc tightly between the flywheel and the pressure plate. ● **SEE FIGURE 4–2.**

The release bearing is often supported and rides on the transmission/transaxle **front bearing retainer** (also called the *quill*).

To summarize:

- When the clutch pedal is up, the clutch is *engaged*. (The pressure plate pressing the clutch disc against the flywheel and rotating together.)

- When the clutch pedal is down, the clutch is *disengaged*. (The clutch disc is free and not rotating with the pressure plate.)

FIGURE 4–3 A replacement clutch is designed to meet the same friction specifications of the original so the new clutch will operate like new.

disc is installed or the lining becomes contaminated, then the coefficient can change and result in slippage or harsh clutch engagement. ● **SEE FIGURE 4–3.**

CLUTCH DISCS

PURPOSE AND FUNCTION   The purpose of the clutch disc is to transfer engine torque from the flywheel to the input shaft of the transmission/transaxle. The clutch disc is located between the flywheel and the pressure plate where it connects the two parts when the clutch is engaged and the pressure plate spring exerts spring pressure against the disc and forces it against the flywheel.

COEFFICIENT OF FRICTION   The **coefficient of friction (COF)**, abbreviated with the Greek letter μ (mu), is the relative amount of friction between two surfaces. There has to be friction between the members of the clutch friction surfaces for the clutch to function correctly.

- If the coefficient of friction of the clutch is less than correct (COF too low), it might slip and not transmit the required torque.

- If the coefficient of friction is greater than what it should be (COF too high), the clutch would become more aggressive and grabby, and engagement would be harsh and severe.

Each vehicle manufacturer specifies the coefficient of friction for each vehicle. The desired coefficient of friction is obtained by using a combination of different friction materials in the manufacture of the clutch disc. If a different clutch friction

CLUTCH FACING MATERIAL   The friction facing material of the clutch must be able to withstand the heat generated by the friction during engagement and disengagement. Older clutch friction discs used a mixture of either molded or woven asbestos with various filler and binder materials. Asbestos is nearly an ideal friction material for brake lining and clutch facing because it has a very good coefficient of friction, excellent heat characteristics, and low cost. However, the possibility of technicians getting cancer from inhaling asbestos fibers has greatly reduced its use. Asbestos was replaced with fiberglass, aramid nonmetallic compounds, and/or metallic materials to obtain the desired friction and wear characteristics. Some of the materials used include the following:

- Powdered iron
- Copper
- Graphite
- Ceramics

SURFACE GROOVES   Most nonmetallic facings have a series of radial grooves cut across their surface.

The purpose and function of the grooves include the following:

- Wipe dust and dirt from the surfaces of the flywheel and pressure plate.

- Allow airflow to help cool the friction surfaces.

- Prevent a vacuum that might cause the friction surfaces to stick together during release. Sticking during release will cause clutch drag.
- Some metallic discs have a series of radial slots cut across the facing which allows the disc to expand without warping when it gets hot.

RIVETS The facing of the clutch disc is attached to the steel cushioning spring by a series of rivets installed in counterbored holes or by bonding which involves attaching the lining to the steel spring by using adhesives (gluing). Some metallic facings are formed directly onto a steel backing. If there is less than 0.015 inch (0.38 mm) of facing above the rivets or backing, a disc is considered worn out.

HUB AND DAMPENER ASSEMBLY An engine produces uneven power impulses that cause torsional vibration. The damper reduces the torsional vibrations that result from the uneven engine power impulses from the rest of the drivetrain.

- As an engine goes through its power cycle, the crankshaft will speed up and slow down during each revolution.
- If these slight speed fluctuations are not removed by the damper, they could cause "gear rattle," vibration, noise, and increased wear.

The clutch hub has internal splines (from 10 to 26 teeth) that slide on the external splines of the transmission input/clutch shaft. Each time the clutch is applied, the disc must slide forward slightly to contact the flywheel, and it must slide back to prevent drag on the flywheel when the clutch is released.

The damper assembly is composed of the hub with four to eight openings or fingerlike extensions, one or more springs for each extension, a spring washer, and a friction washer. These parts are fitted between the web of the disc and a metal retainer and are held together by a series of rivets called stop pins, which also keep the hub from revolving too far. The damper springs, called **torsional dampers**, are positioned by a series of windows in the web and retainer. The torque must pass through the damper springs on its way from the engine to the transmission, and any power impulses that tend to speed up the clutch hub will compress the springs and help dampen engine firing pulses being transmitted into and through the transmission/transaxle. ● **SEE FIGURE 4-4.**

In the space between the friction surfaces is a wavy spring steel material called a **cushion spring** or **marcel spring**. The marcel spring helps to absorb the initial shock of rapid

FIGURE 4-4 A typical stock clutch friction disc that uses coil spring torsional dampers.

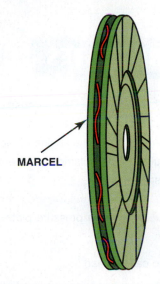

FIGURE 4-5 A marcel is a wavy spring that is placed between the two friction surfaces to cushion the clutch engagement.

engagement and allows for a smooth engagement of the clutch. ● **SEE FIGURE 4-5.**

HIGH-PERFORMANCE CLUTCH DISC Another type of friction material is a ceramic and metallic mixture. This creates a hard, long-lasting lining, but is more expensive and does not cushion clutch engagement as much as a softer lining. Instead of a full circle of softer friction material, the disc may have only a few segments or buttons of this ceramic-metallic material. Clutches that use these discs, which are sometimes called "button clutches," are found in racing applications where strength and durability are a greater concern than smooth engagement. ● **SEE FIGURE 4-6.**

FIGURE 4–6 A racing or high-performance clutch disc lacks the features of a stock clutch disc that help provide smooth engagement.

PRESSURE PLATES

PURPOSE AND FUNCTION The purpose of the pressure plate is to exert a force on the clutch disc so that engine torque can be transmitted from the engine to the transmission/transaxle. The required strong clamping force is provided by the pressure plate spring(s).

COMPONENT PARTS The pressure plate assembly is a combination of

- The *cover* (also called a *hat*)
- The *pressure springs* and *release levers* (also called *fingers*)
- The cast iron *pressure ring* (*driving plate*) that contacts the friction disc

The strong pressure plate spring force must be released by the force of the driver's foot to engage the clutch. Most pressure plates are made of stamped steel with a nodular cast iron pressure ring, also called a driving plate. A smooth, machined area on one side forms the friction disc contact surface. When the clutch engages, spring force pushes the pressure plate toward the flywheel so the friction disc is clamped between the flywheel and the pressure plate.

STYLES OF PRESSURE PLATES Several styles of pressure plates have been used, including

- **Coil spring style**. This style of pressure plate uses coil springs and three or four release levers. A coil

FIGURE 4–7 A coil spring (lever style) clutch pressure plate.

spring-style pressure plate is also called the *lever style* because it uses levers to compress the coil springs. This type of pressure plate is often called a "three finger" pressure plate. ● **SEE FIGURE 4–7.**

Two types of coil spring style include

1. *Borg and Beck:* This style uses a round closed cover with three wide stamped-steel release levers and up to 12 springs with six evenly spaced mounting holes.

2. *Long:* This style uses a triangular-shaped cover with three narrow, forged-steel release levers, which extend through the cover and often have weights on them. This style also usually uses nine springs and has mounting bolt holes in three groups of two.

- **Diaphragm spring style**. This style is the most commonly used pressure plate design. It uses one large, round, steel spring, called a **Belleville spring** to apply even force on the clutch disc. **SEE FIGURE 4–8.**

ADVANTAGES OF A DIAPHRAGM-TYPE CLUTCH
Diaphragm-type pressure plates have several advantages over the other types including

1. Diaphragm-type clutch pressure plates tend to be smaller assemblies, weigh less, and have fewer parts than coil spring assemblies. The one-piece diaphragm spring does the job of all the release levers and coil springs in a coil spring clutch.

2. The driver pedal effort required for a diaphragm-type plate is less than that required in a coil spring type. The typical diaphragm-type clutch requires just 35 pounds of force (156 Newtons) to depress the clutch pedal compared

FIGURE 4–8 Typical diaphragm-style pressure plate that uses a Belleville spring.

to 60 pounds of force (267 Newtons) for a typical coil spring–type clutch. The pedal effort for a coil spring clutch increases the farther down the pedal is pushed.

3. The pedal effort for a diaphragm spring clutch decreases during the second half of pedal travel. As the friction disc wears, coil springs expand and lose some of their clamping force. In contrast, the design of the diaphragm spring tends to increase its clamping force as the friction disc wears to half its original thickness. Then, as the friction disc continues to wear, the clamping force of the spring gradually returns to its original level. This happens without any obvious change in clutch pedal effort.

4. The relatively low height of the diaphragm design is highly favored for transverse engine vehicles where engine and transaxle lengths are critical.

PRESSURE PLATE RING Pressure plate diameter is measured at the outside diameter of the *pressure plate ring*. It should always be the same size or slightly larger than the disc diameter. A pressure ring is simply a flat, fairly heavy ring usually made from nodular cast iron. The heavy weight is necessary to dissipate heat and provides a heat sink so as not to warp. It also provides sufficient strength so it will spread the spring force evenly onto the disc. For high RPM use, the ring is made from cast steel because centrifugal force can cause a cast iron ring to fail.

- When a clutch slips, heat is generated at the friction surfaces, and this heat will warm the facing, the pressure ring, and the flywheel.

- Excess heat will cause the pressure ring to expand to the point of warpage, destroying its flatness and causing poor ring-to-disc facing contact.

- The greater the mass of the pressure ring, the less the temperature will rise because the heat will spread through more metal which will hold the heat longer.

Torque enters the pressure ring from the cover, either through a drive strap or a boss where the release levers extend through openings in the cover. Torque passes out through the friction contact with the facing on the disc.

COVER (HAT) The cover (hat) is the stamped-steel housing that transmits the torque from the flywheel to the pressure ring. It also provides a mounting place for the springs and release levers and, it must be strong enough to contain the various forces without distorting.

RELEASE LEVERS The release levers provide a means of compressing the spring(s) and pulling the pressure ring away from the disc. This movement is called *plate lift*. Along with the leverage of the clutch linkage, release levers provide a lever that will produce the necessary 500 to 1,500 pounds (230 to 700 kg) of force needed at the pressure plate from the 20 pounds (9 kg) or so used to push the clutch pedal.

DOUBLE DISC CLUTCHES A relatively inexpensive method of increasing clutch torque capacity is to use two or more clutch discs. All that is required is another disc (much like the first) and a floater plate, located between the two friction

TECH TIP

Use a "Bent Finger" Pressure Plate

Centrifugal force can affect a diaphragm clutch. During a very high RPM disengagement, the fingers can be moved far enough forward by centrifugal force so that they pass over center (beyond flat). Some people have experienced this during a shift at high RPM when the pedal stays on the floor while the engine overrevs. To prevent this, "bent finger" diaphragms are used for installations where high RPM shifts might occur. The shape of the fingers keeps them from traveling over center. ● **SEE FIGURE 4–9.**

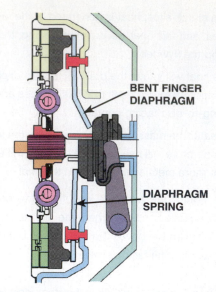

FIGURE 4–9 A bent finger diaphragm clutch. The shape of the fingers keeps the fingers and release bearing from going past center during clutch release.

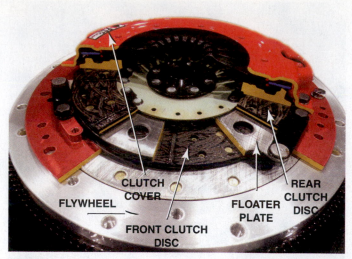

FIGURE 4–10 A double disc clutch that uses a floater plate between the two discs. The second disc doubles the clutch torque capacity.

FIGURE 4–11 The ring gear, which is attached to the outer rim of the flywheel, provides the teeth needed to mesh with the starter pinion gear.

discs and a lengthened pressure plate cover with provision for the floater plate. ● **SEE FIGURE 4–10.**

The floater plate must be able to move forward to squeeze the front disc against the flywheel and rearward during release to provide air gaps. The pressure plate provides the clamping force for both discs, and has enough movement to provide air gaps at both discs when released.

FLYWHEELS

PURPOSE AND FUNCTION   The engine flywheel serves four basic purposes:

1. Smooth out or dampens engine power pulses.
2. Absorbs some of the heat created by clutch operation.
3. Provides the connection point for the starter motor to rotate the engine.
4. Provides the friction surface for the clutch friction disc.

INERTIA   A flywheel is heavy, or has a large mass, which creates **inertia**. Inertia is the tendency of a moving object to remain in motion, because of its weight, unless forced to slow. This inertia acts upon crankshaft rotation to smooth out or dampen engine power pulses. On a running engine, the crankshaft speeds up as a cylinder fires, then slows due to internal engine friction until the next cylinder fires. The inertia provided by the flywheel mass tends to keep crankshaft speed

more constant. The flywheel also absorbs some of the heat created by clutch operation by acting as a heat sink for the clutch friction disc.

STARTER RING GEAR   An external ring gear is commonly cast and machined as part of the flywheel or pressed or welded onto the flywheel along its outer circumference. The starter-drive gear meshes with the flywheel ring gear. Through gear reduction, the flywheel transfers starter motor rotation to the crankshaft to crank the engine. When the starter motor is engaged the starter motor will spin but the engine will not crank if the ring gear on the flywheel is broken. Often the ring gear can be replaced separately without having to replace the flywheel in the event of a failure. ● **SEE FIGURE 4–11.**

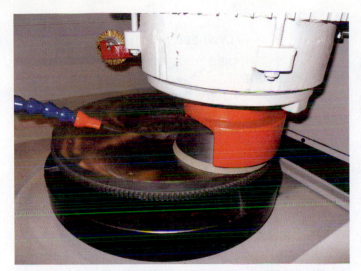

FIGURE 4–12 A flywheel being machined (ground) to provide the correct surface finish for the replacement clutch disc.

FIGURE 4–13 A stepped flywheel has more mass on the outer edge which helps smooth out the impulses from a four-cylinder engine especially at idle speed.

CONSTRUCTION   The flywheel is constructed of cast iron and attaches to the end of the engine crankshaft. The carbon content of the cast iron (about 3%) provides a suitable surface for the clutch disc.

The carbon, in the form of graphite, acts as a lubricant to help provide a smooth engagement of the clutch. The face on the transmission side of the flywheel has a smooth, machined area that creates the application surface for the clutch friction disc. This surface must be properly finished to allow adequate slippage as the clutch engages and disengages, and to prevent slippage when the clutch is engaged. Being made from cast iron makes resurfacing easy. ● **SEE FIGURE 4–12.**

STEPPED FLYWHEELS   Some manufacturers use a stepped flywheel. These are combined with a pressure plate that has either a flat or almost flat cover. Stepped flywheels have more of the mass at the outer edge, which increases the rotational inertia. ● **SEE FIGURE 4–13.**

DUAL-MASS FLYWHEELS

PURPOSE AND FUNCTION   Some vehicles, especially high-performance vehicles and vehicles equipped with diesel engines use a dual-mass flywheel. The purpose of a **dual-mass flywheel** is to dampen engine vibrations and keep them

from being transmitted to the passenger compartment through the transmission and shift linkage.

PARTS AND OPERATION   A dual-mass flywheel consists of two separate flywheels attached with damper springs, friction material, and ball bearings to allow some movement between the primary and secondary flywheel. By allowing a slight amount of movement between the two flywheels, the damper springs absorb engine torque peaks and normal vibration to provide smoother drivetrain operation. The damper assembly is completely sealed, because it also contains a fluid or lubricant, typically silicone based, which also helps absorb vibration and transmit torque. Typically, the two flywheels twist out of phase with each other by up to about 60 degrees to absorb torsional oscillations.

- The starter ring gear mounts on the primary flywheel. Power from the starter motor does not have to flow through the damper assembly to reach the engine crankshaft.

- The pilot bearing is also attached to the primary flywheel.

- The clutch friction surface is usually on the secondary flywheel. ● **SEE FIGURE 4–14.**

NOTE: If the dual-mass flywheel fails, the symptom is the same as a slipping clutch. The torque-limiting friction material connecting the primary and secondary flywheels can fail. This failure requires the replacement of the flywheel assembly.

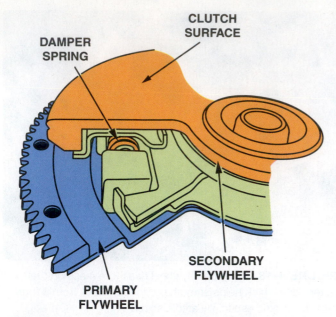

FIGURE 4–14 A dual-mass wheel consists of two flywheels connected between with a spring to help absorb engine pulsations.

FIGURE 4–15 A pilot bearing or bushing, such as one being used on the rear-wheel-drive pickup truck, is pressed into the end of the engine crankshaft and supports the input shaft of the transmission.

PILOT BEARINGS

PURPOSE AND FUNCTION The engine end of a transmission input (clutch) shaft is supported by a **pilot bearing** that is pressed into the end of the crankshaft. ● **SEE FIGURE 4–15.**

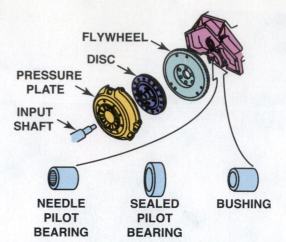

FIGURE 4–16 Pilot bearings (bushings) are made in several different designs depending on the application.

NEED FOR A PILOT BEARING The transmission input shaft goes all the way from the transmission, through the clutch assembly, to the engine. Transmission bearings support the transmission end of the shaft. The pilot bearing or bushing supports it at the engine end. A front-wheel-drive vehicle has a transaxle with an input shaft supported by a pair of bearings and a short input shaft which may not reach all the way to the flywheel. This design does not need a pilot bushing or bearing to support the engine end of the input shaft.

Other designs, such as a rear-wheel-drive vehicle with a flat flywheel, have a much longer transmission input shaft and require the use of a pilot bearing to support the end of the shaft.

CONSTRUCTION Pilot bearings can be constructed using

- Sintered bronze Oilite® bushing, which is impregnated with oil to lubricate it
- Needle bearing
- Sealed ball bearing

● **SEE FIGURE 4–16.**

OPERATION At the engine, the transmission input shaft rests inside a small bore in the flywheel or crankshaft flange. The pilot bearing or bushing supports the engine end of the input shaft and provides a low-friction surface for the shaft to ride on. This keeps the shaft and friction disc perfectly aligned with the flywheel and pressure plate. The pilot bearing or bushing rotates with the crankshaft while the engine is running. When the clutch is released, the input shaft does not rotate when the engine is running. The pilot bearing or bushing lowers the friction between these two moving parts.

CLUTCH PEDAL LINKAGE

PURPOSE AND FUNCTION The purpose and function of the clutch pedal linkage is to transfer the force the driver exerts on the clutch pedal to the release bearing.

TYPES OF CLUTCH LINKAGE There are three methods of transferring the force of the driver's foot on the clutch pedal to the release (throwout) bearing, including

- **Levers and rods.** Mechanical linkages use a series of levers and rods to move the release fork against the throw-out bearing. This method was commonly used on many older vehicles. If a change in direction is needed, *bell cranks* are mounted on pivot shafts to reverse the direction of the force. This type of linkage ends at the clutch fork after it passes through an equalizer shaft that pivots from both the engine/bell housing and the vehicle body. Clutch assembly and engine are on rubber mounts, the engine can move relative to the body and clutch pedal, and any movement during clutch operation can cause an unwanted apply, release, or chatter. The clutch pedal used with this linkage usually includes an overcenter, or assist spring. This spring is mounted to pull the pedal upward during the first half of pedal travel and downward during the second half. This last action reduces pedal effort and helps release the clutch. This can be demonstrated by carefully pushing on the clutch pedal with the linkage disconnected.

CAUTION: In most cases, the pedal will move downward rather violently as the spring passes over center.

Mechanical linkage includes an adjustment at some point so that *free travel* can be adjusted. Free travel, also called *free play,* is the slight clearance (about 1 inch [25 mm]) measured at the pedal, or is measured at the clutch fork between the throwout bearing and the pressure plate (about 1/16 inch [2 mm]).

- **Cable operation.** A cable is used similar to a brake cable used on a bicycle. Cable linkage consists of a steel cable attached to the clutch pedal. The clutch cable is routed to the engine/bell housing, where it can pull on the clutch fork/lever. Much of the cable is enclosed in a housing or conduit so that it can be routed around corners or obstacles. Although simple and inexpensive, cables have a drawback in that they develop internal friction through time, which makes them harder to operate.

Many vehicles include a *self-adjuster mechanism* at the clutch pedal. Older vehicles include a method of manual adjustment, at the end of either the cable or cable housing. The self-adjuster is usually a spring-loaded cam that is mounted onto the pedal when a spring-loaded pawl engages it. The pawl is lifted each time the clutch is released so that the cam spring can rotate and remove any slack or clearance in the cable. When the pedal is applied, the pawl's spring returns it to lock the cam to the pedal. ● **SEE FIGURE 4–17.**

- **Hydraulic** A small master cylinder is located on the bulkhead and operated by the clutch pedal and a **slave cylinder** located near the release (throwout) bearing. This is the most common method of connecting the clutch pedal to the release fork on vehicles equipped with a manual transmission. ● **SEE FIGURE 4–18.**

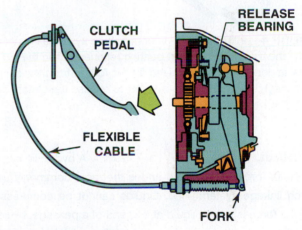

FIGURE 4–17 A typical cable clutch linkage uses a cable to transmit motion from the pedal to the release bearing.

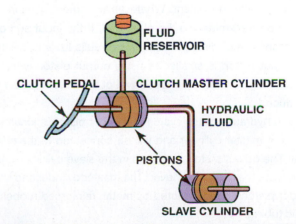

FIGURE 4–18 Simple hydraulic clutch system. The hydraulic fluid will transmit force and motion from the clutch pedal to the slave cylinder.

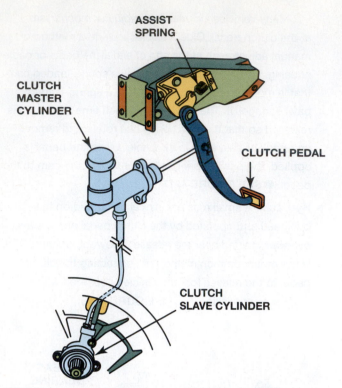

ASSIST SPRING

CLUTCH MASTER CYLINDER

CLUTCH PEDAL

CLUTCH SLAVE CYLINDER

FIGURE 4–19 The slave cylinder of some systems is concentric to the transmission input bearing retainer. When the clutch pedal is depressed, pressurized fluid is forced from the clutch master cylinder to the slave cylinder to release the clutch.

HYDRAULIC CLUTCH OPERATION A hydraulic system transmits force using a fluid and is the most commonly used clutch linkage system used. Liquids cannot be compressed, and if a force is put on liquid at one end of a passage, liquid at the other end of the passage will exert the same force.

In a simple foot-operated system, force is exerted on a piston in the input cylinder, or pump, and leaves at the output cylinder. If these pistons are the same size, they will have equal force and movement. Whatever movement goes in one end will be transmitted to the other end. If the input and output pistons are of different sizes, a hydraulic lever is created. If the input piston is smaller than the output piston (which is normal), force will increase, but travel of the output piston will be reduced.

In a hydraulic clutch system, the input piston is located in the clutch master cylinder and will be connected to the clutch pedal. The output piston is located in the slave cylinder, and it will operate the clutch fork/lever. The master cylinder and slave cylinder pistons are connected by metal, reinforced rubber, or plastic tubing.

- When the clutch pedal is depressed, the master cylinder piston forces fluid through the tubing to the slave

cylinder, where the pressure forces the slave cylinder piston to move the clutch fork/lever.

- When the pedal is released, the pressure plate forces the slave cylinder piston to return the fluid to the master cylinder.

- When the master cylinder is released, a compensating port is opened up between the cylinder bore and the fluid reservoir. This port allows for fluid expansion or contraction due to temperature changes, for any air to leave the fluid, and in many cases, for self-adjustment for disc wear.

- Because air can be compressed, any air trapped in a hydraulic system will cause a mushy, spongy pedal, or incomplete operation. DOT 3 brake fluid is generally used in clutch hydraulic systems.

The slave cylinder is usually mounted on the exterior of the bell housing. Some systems use a slave cylinder that is concentric to the bearing retainer and has the release bearing connected directly to it. ● SEE FIGURE 4–19.

RELEASE (THROWOUT) BEARING

PURPOSE AND FUNCTION The release bearing, also called a *throwout bearing*, rides on the transmission front bearing retainer and when the clutch pedal is pushed down, it pushes against the fingers of the pressure plate. The clutch operating system moves the clutch release bearing when the driver presses or releases the clutch pedal.

OPERATION The release bearing presses against the diaphragm spring fingers or coil spring levers. This takes spring force off the pressure plate so that it no longer clamps the friction disc against the flywheel. The diaphragm spring fingers or coil spring levers rotate at crankshaft speed, but the clutch operating system is a part of the vehicle chassis and does not rotate. The release bearing is the point where the fixed, stationary clutch operating system meets the rapidly spinning clutch assembly. ● SEE FIGURE 4–20.

RELEASE BEARING CONSTRUCTION Most clutch release bearings are ball bearings. The bearing absorbs a thrust load when its outer race presses against the diaphragm spring fingers or coil spring levers. When the outer race contacts the spring fingers or levers, it must rotate with them at engine crankshaft speed. The inner bearing race is pressed onto an

(a)

(b)

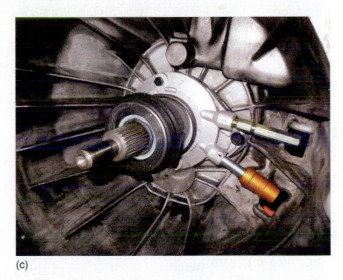

(c)

FIGURE 4–20 (a) A release (throwout) bearing on a transmission that uses a clutch fork and a mechanical or cable-operated linkage. (b) A style of release bearing that includes the slave cylinder, sometimes called a *concentric slave cylinder.* (c) A combination release bearing and slave cylinder showing the two hydraulic lines. The lower line is from the master clutch cylinder and the upper line is used to bleed air from the hydraulic system.

iron hub, or sleeve. In some designs, the inner bearing race and sleeve are machined as one piece. The inner bearing race and sleeve are stationary and do not spin when the outer race spins.

RELEASE BEARING LOCATION   The transmission front bearing retainer has a long, hollow tube extending toward the engine.

The release bearing sleeve slides on the outer surface of this tube, which is also commonly called (slang)

- *Quill*
- *Quill shaft*
- *Candlestick*

In a typical system, the outside of the release bearing sleeve has grooves or raised flat surfaces that fit into the clutch release fork. A snap ring, spring clips, or lock pins secure the release bearing to the release fork. The clutch operating system pivots the release fork back and forth when the driver presses and releases the clutch pedal. The pivoting motion of the fork slides the release bearing away from or toward the engine to engage or disengage the clutch.

TYPES OF RELEASE BEARINGS
If the clutch operating system self-adjusts, then there is no clearance between the release bearing outer race and the diaphragm spring fingers or coil spring levers.

- The release bearing outer race constantly turns at engine crankshaft speed. This is called a *constant-running release bearing*. In some self-adjusting systems, a snap ring holds the outer race to the spring fingers. This design is typical of pull-type clutch operating systems that move away from the flywheel to disengage the clutch.

- If the clutch operating system does not self-adjust, then there must be some clearance between the release bearing outer race and the spring fingers when the clutch is engaged. The outer race does not contact the spring fingers and so it does not turn. As the driver depresses the clutch pedal, the release bearing moves into contact with the fingers and the outer race begins to rotate with them. This type of release bearing is not designed to rotate constantly. If the clutch is not adjusted properly and there is no clearance, the release bearing spins constantly and wears out quickly.

RELEASE BEARING LUBRICATION
The ball bearing portion of the release bearing is usually permanently lubricated and sealed during manufacture. This part of the bearing should not be lubricated during service. The sleeve, or quill shaft, often needs lubrication during clutch service. Typically, a thin film of high-temperature grease coats the sliding surfaces. Always follow the vehicle manufacturer's recommendations for release bearing lubrication, and avoid overlubricating.

CLUTCH PEDAL SWITCH

PURPOSE AND FUNCTION
A clutch pedal position switch is used to signal the starter circuit that the clutch is released which prevents starter operation unless the clutch pedal is depressed.

OPERATION
The switch is normally electrically open, and it closes when the pedal is completely depressed. This completes the circuit from the ignition switch to the starter relay, and when the circuit is completed, the starter relay energizes the starter, cranking the engine. This safety feature prevents the vehicle from moving accidentally when the starter is engaged.

CAUTION: Not all vehicles are equipped with a clutch safety switch, so it is very important that the transmission be placed in neutral and/or the clutch fully depressed before starting the engine. ● SEE FIGURE 4–21.

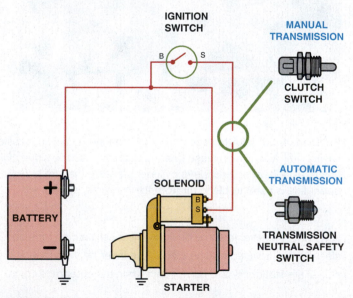

FIGURE 4–21 To prevent the engine from cranking, an electrical switch is usually installed to open the circuit between the ignition switch and the starter solenoid. When the clutch pedal is depressed, the switch closes and completes the circuit to the starter.

? **FREQUENTLY ASKED QUESTION**

What Is a Pull-Type Release Bearing?

The pressure plate used on a few FWD vehicles is bolted directly onto the engine's crankshaft, and the flywheel is bolted onto the pressure plate. This allows the release bearing to be placed inside the pressure plate and operated by a pull rod through the transmission input shaft. It is often called a *pull-type clutch*. The mounting of the diaphragm spring is moved in the cover and at the pressure ring so a pulling force is used to release the clutch instead of the normal pushing force. This change produces an improvement in clutch system efficiency and a lower clutch pedal effort.

SUMMARY

1. The purpose and function of a clutch include the following:
   - To disconnect the engine torque from the transmission/transaxle to permit the engine to remain running when the vehicle is stopped and to permit the transmission/transaxle to be shifted.
   - To connect and transmit engine torque to the transmission/transaxle.
   - To dampen and absorb engine power impulses and drivetrain vibration.
   - To provide a smooth engagement and disengagement of torque between the engine and the transmission/transaxle.

2. The clutch assembly includes the flywheel, clutch disc, release (throwout) bearing, and pressure plate.

3. The purpose of the clutch disc is to transfer engine torque from the flywheel to the input shaft of the transmission/transaxle.

4. The engine flywheel serves four basic purposes:
   - Smooth out or dampens engine power pulses.
   - Absorbs some of the heat created by clutch operation.
   - Provides the connection point for the starter motor to rotate the engine.
   - Provides the application surface for the clutch friction disc.

5. The engine end of a transmission input (clutch) shaft is supported by a pilot bearing that is pressed into the end of the crankshaft.

6. The purpose and function of the clutch pedal linkage is to transfer the force the driver exerts on the clutch pedal to the release bearing.

REVIEW QUESTIONS

1. List the parts of a typical clutch assembly.

2. Describe the sequence of events that happen in the clutch system when the driver depresses the clutch pedal.

3. Explain why a dual-mass flywheel is used on some vehicles.

CHAPTER QUIZ

1. Which part does *not* rotate when the engine is running and the clutch is depressed?
   - a. Pilot bearing (bushing)
   - b. Pressure plate
   - c. Input shaft
   - d. Flywheel

2. What part is often *not* used on a front-wheel-drive vehicle with a manual transaxle?
   - a. Flywheel
   - b. Clutch fork
   - c. Release (throwout) bearing
   - d. Pilot bearing

3. A dual-mass flywheel is used to_____
   - a. Reduce clutch effort
   - b. Reduce vibration
   - c. Increase torque holding ability of a clutch
   - d. Decrease vehicle weight

4. Most hydraulic clutch systems use what hydraulic fluid?
   - a. DOT 3 Brake fluid
   - b. Mineral (hydraulic) oil
   - c. SAE 80W-90 Gear oil
   - d. ATF

5. Flywheels are constructed of cast iron because _____.
   - a. They contain about 3% carbon which acts as a lubricant for the clutch
   - b. They have a lot of inertia
   - c. Can be resurfaced
   - d. All of the above

6. The most commonly used clutch linkage is_____.
   - a. Mechanical (rods and levers)
   - b. Hydraulic
   - c. Cable
   - d. Electrically controlled

7. The release bearing sleeve slides on the outer surface of a tube, which is commonly called the_____.
   - a. Quill
   - b Front bearing retainer
   - c. Candlestick
   - d. Any of the above

8. A clutch switch is used to_____.
   - a. Disengage the clutch
   - b. Engage the clutch
   - c. Prevent the engine from starting unless the clutch pedal is depressed
   - d. Provide an input signal for the PCM to disengage the clutch

9. Springs are mounted at the center of a clutch disc. Technician A says they help cushion clutch engagement. Technician B says they absorb engine torsional vibrations. Which technician is correct?
   a. Technician A only
   b. Technician B only
   c. Both technicians A and B
   d. Neither technician A nor B

10. When the clutch is released (clutch pedal down) _____.
    a. Springs force the pressure ring toward the clutch cover.
    b. Springs force the pressure ring toward the flywheel.
    c. The release (throwout) bearing is used to move the pressure ring toward the clutch cover
    d. The pilot bearing is pressed toward the engine

CLUTCH DIAGNOSIS AND SERVICE

INTRODUCTION

Most automotive technicians perform three different levels of clutch service.

1. **Preventive maintenance:** Check pedal free travel and fluid levels and make the necessary inspections and adjustments to ensure proper operation.

2. **Troubleshooting and diagnosis:** Determine the cause of a clutch concern and make recommendations for repair.

3. **Replacement:** Replace the clutch components to get the vehicle back in proper operation.

CLUTCH INSPECTION

CLUTCH PEDAL FREE TRAVEL The typical maintenance and service items for a clutch includes the following:

1. Checking clutch *pedal free travel*, or *free play* (older vehicles).

2. Inspecting mechanical linkage systems (older vehicles).

3. Checking the fluid level in hydraulic systems.

These operations are normally performed along with the other routine service checks. When diagnosing a clutch or transmission concern, the first step is always a clutch pedal free travel check.

- Excessive free travel will cause the clutch to not release completely.

- Too little free travel will not allow the clutch to engage completely, which is more common because clutch pedal free travel will decrease as the clutch disc facing wears.

Note: Not all vehicle clutch systems use free pedal. Always check with service information for the exact procedures to follow on the vehicle being checked.

CLUTCH PEDAL FREE TRAVEL TEST PROCEDURE To check and adjust clutch pedal free travel, perform the following steps:

STEP 1 Push the clutch pedal downward by hand. As the pedal moves, there should be a light resistance from the clutch pedal return spring. A much greater resistance is felt as the release bearing contacts the release levers of the pressure plate assembly. The free travel is the distance the pedal moves before the greater resistance of the release levers is felt. Some manufacturers recommend checking and measuring free travel

The Tape Measure Trick

To easily make a free clutch pedal travel measurements try this

1. Hook the end of a tape measure onto the pedal, and run it through the steering wheel. Note the reading at the steering wheel as the pedal is depressed through its travel.

2. Clutches that use hydraulic or cable linkage should have a small amount of free travel, whereas rod and lever linkage clutches should have about one inch (25 mm) free travel.

at the clutch fork or lever. In this case, push on the end of the fork in the direction of release. Some resistance should be felt for a short distance, which is the free travel.

STEP 2 Measure the free travel with a ruler or tape. Compare the distance measured with the specifications. Free travel that is more or less than the specifications indicates the need for a clutch adjustment. It should be noted that some manufacturers recommend measuring free travel with the engine running. If no specifications are available, many technicians will use 3/4 to 1 inch (20 to 25 mm) at the clutch pedal and 1/8 to 1/4 inch (3 to 6 mm) at the clutch fork as a rule-of-thumb. ● **SEE FIGURE 5–1.**

STEP 3 If an adjustment is necessary, locate the adjuster and shorten or lengthen the linkage as necessary to correct the free travel. As a final check, operate the clutch pedal through its full range of travel. It should operate smoothly without any unusual lags, skips, binding, roughness, or noise.

Note: On most non-self-adjusting clutch systems, as the clutch disc wears, the free-pedal distance will decrease.

CLUTCH FLUID LEVEL Clutch hydraulic fluid level is checked by looking at the fluid level at the clutch master cylinder reservoir. Many reservoirs will be marked to indicate the correct fluid level. If there are no markings, assume that the fluid level should be between 1/4 and 1/2 inch (6 and 13 mm) from the top. Normally, the fluid level will rise slightly as the clutch facing wears. A low fluid level usually indicates a leak in the system. ● **SEE FIGURE 5–2.**

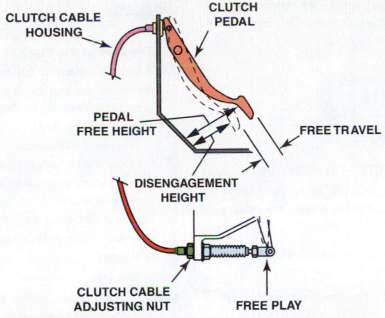

FIGURE 5–1 A typical cable operated clutch adjustment location.

FIGURE 5–2 A typical clutch master cylinder and reservoir mounted on the bulkhead on the driver's side of the vehicle. Brake fluid is used in the hydraulic system to operate the slave cylinder located on the bell housing.

TYPES OF HYDRAULIC BRAKE FLUID Brake fluid meeting the DOT 3 designated specification is the most commonly used fluid used in hydraulic clutch systems.

FIGURE 5–3 Clutch fluid is similar brake fluid.

However, there are several fluids that may be specified depending on vehicle manufacturer, model, and year. The fluids that may be specified include the following types:

- DOT 3 brake fluid (Clear; amber)
- DOT 4 brake fluid (Clear; amber)
- DOT 4+ brake fluid (Clear; amber) (European vehicles)
- Brake hydraulic fluid (clear/amber) ● **SEE FIGURE 5–3.**

Clutch hydraulic fluid is *hygroscopic,* and absorbs water directly from the moisture in the air. This means that the hydraulic system may need to be drained, and refilled with new fluid to prevent corrosion and increase the service life of the components. Always follow the vehicle manufacturers' recommend procedures and service intervals.

CLUTCH PROBLEM DIAGNOSIS

SYMPTOMS OF A DEFECTIVE CLUTCH The following symptoms will occur if there is a fault in the clutch or in the linkage or hydraulic system that could prevent the clutch from being fully disengaged:

- The transmission will be difficult (or impossible) to shift into reverse.
- The transmission will be difficult (or impossible) to shift between forward gears.

LEAK DETECTION A drop in fluid level at the reservoir indicates a fluid leak. Normally, facing wear will cause an increase, or rise, in the fluid level, so topping off the reservoir is not necessary or recommended. The cause of a fluid leak is usually found through visual inspection of the cylinders and lines to locate the wetness. Fluid leak repair is done by correcting the fault which could include

- Tightening a loose line fitting.
- Replacing an O-ring, fluid line or hose.
- Replacing the clutch master cylinder or slave cylinder.

SLAVE CYLINDER TRAVEL Inability to release the clutch completely can be checked by observing slave cylinder travel as the clutch pedal is depressed. The slave cylinder should begin moving immediately and travel in a smooth, steady manner. Some manufacturers provide slave cylinder travel or extension specifications. For example, one manufacturer specifies 0.5 inch (13 mm) of slave cylinder motion for one complete stroke of the clutch pedal. Insufficient slave cylinder travel indicates air in the system or a faulty slave or master cylinder.

CLUTCH SLIPPAGE DIAGNOSIS Clutch slippage can be checked easily in a shop, however, a more thorough check can be made during a road test.

To check for slippage in a shop, perform the following steps:

STEP 1 Check and adjust clutch pedal free travel.

STEP 2 Warm up the engine to operating temperature, block the wheels, and apply the parking brake completely.

 REAL WORLD FIX

The Case of the Stuck in Gear Jeep
A Jeep Wrangler (120,000 mi) sometimes got stuck in first or reverse, and the only way to get it out of gear is to shut the engine off. The transmission shifted okay most of the time.

Thinking that clutch or related components were the most likely cause, the transmission was removed, and an inspection revealed a seizing pilot bushing. Replacement of the bushing fixed this problem. The pilot bushing did not allow the input shaft to move independently of the flywheel when the clutch was depressed.

STEP 3 Shift the transmission into high gear and let out the clutch pedal smoothly. The engine should stall immediately. A delay indicates slow engagement and slipping.

To check for slippage on a road test, perform the following steps:

STEP 1 Check and adjust clutch pedal free travel.

STEP 2 Drive to an area with very little traffic. Accelerate slowly and drive at 15 to 20 mph (24 to 32 km/h) in the highest transmission gear. Use the lowest speed at which the vehicle will operate smoothly.

STEP 3 Depress the accelerator completely to wide-open throttle and listen to the engine RPM or watch the tachometer. The engine speed should increase steadily as the vehicle accelerates. If the engine speed flares upward, the clutch is slipping and needs service. Slipping becomes even more evident if this test is made while driving up a hill.

CLUTCH SPIN-DOWN TEST Hard shifting into gear from neutral, sometimes accompanied by gear clash, can be caused by a clutch that is not releasing completely. This is called drag and is easily checked by a spin-down test. **Clutch spin-down** is the time it takes for the clutch disc and transmission gears to spin to a stop when the clutch is released. This time will vary depending on clutch disc diameter and transmission drag.

To check clutch spin-down, perform the following steps:

STEP 1 Check and adjust clutch pedal free travel.

STEP 2 Warm up the engine and transmission to operating temperatures.

STEP 3 With the engine running at idle speed and the transmission in neutral, push in the clutch pedal, wait 9 seconds, and shift the transmission into reverse

The Case of the Stretched Shift Cable

The clutch on a Dodge Ram pickup (260,000 km) did not release completely. Adjusting the cable helped, but the end of the adjustment was reached. The transmission and clutch were removed. The clutch was carefully inspected, and it showed little wear and no damage.

After reading some similar cases on www.iatn.net a new cable was purchased, and it was determined that the old cable had stretched. Installation of the new cable repaired this problem.

The Case of the Broken Chevrolet Clutch

The clutch in a Chevrolet HHR (119,000 mi) would not disengage. A broken pressure plate or clutch disc was suspected, so the transaxle was removed. Inspection showed normal clutch wear, nothing to prevent disengagement. A new pressure plate, disc, and throwout bearing were installed, and the flywheel was machined. The clutch still would not disengage. A small leak was found at the slave cylinder, so the entire hydraulic system was replaced with an OEM assembly. The new assembly was full of fluid, so bleeding was not necessary. The slave cylinder push rod travel has normal movement during clutch pedal travel application. At the suggestion of the parts supplier, a flywheel shim was installed to compensate for the thinner machined flywheel, but this did not help.

Close inspection revealed that the release fork was bent and worn. Replacement of the fork and its bushings fixed this problem. It is important to spend a few minutes inspecting all of the clutch components to ensure a complete and proper repair.

(a nonsynchronized gear). The shift should occur silently. Gear clash or grinding indicates a dragging clutch that has not released completely. The 9-second time period is very long. Some vehicles that will shift quietly and cleanly into reverse in 3 or 4 seconds. If a clutch fails the spin-down check, it likely needs to be replaced.

CLUTCH SYMPTOM GUIDE

CLUTCH SLIPS   Possible causes include the following:

1. Clutch is worn or out-of-adjustment.
2. Clutch disc has oil on the surface.
3. Flywheel height is out-of-specifications.

CLUTCH GRABS   Possible causes include the following:

1. Clutch disc has oil on the surface.
2. Clutch linkage is binding.

CLUTCH NOISES   Possible causes include the following:

1. Pilot bearing is defective or worn.
2. Release bearing is defective or worn.

NOTE: A squeal that begins as the clutch pedal is depressed about 1 inch (25 mm) is probably caused by a defective or worn release (throwout) bearing.

CLUTCH REPLACEMENT

PARTS INVOLVED   Clutch replacement, commonly called a *clutch job*, is a fairly expensive and labor intensive repair. During disassembly, each part should be checked to determine if it

is the cause of the failure and if it is suitable for reuse. During reassembly, each phase is normally accompanied by checks for proper clearances or operation so that any faulty parts or assemblies can be corrected as early in the assembly as possible.

Clutch replacement normally involves replacing four items:

1. Pressure plate assembly
2. Clutch disc
3. Release bearing
4. Pilot bearing ● **SEE FIGURE 5–4.**

CLUTCH REMOVAL   The clutch replacement for a typical rear-wheel-drive vehicle includes the following steps.

1. Hoist the vehicle safely and mark and remove the driveshaft. This step ensures that the driveshaft will be reinstalled correctly and in phase.
2. Disconnect the shift linkage, speedometer connections, and reverse light switch connection as well as the clutch linkage or cable or slave cylinder.
3. Support the transmission with a transmission jack and then remove the rear cross member and bell housing bolts.

FIGURE 5–4 A typical clutch kit, which includes the clutch disc, pressure plate, and release (throwout) bearing as well as grease for the spline and a clutch disc alignment tool.

4. Carefully move the transmission toward the rear. Try to keep the transmission level to avoid causing damage to the pilot bearing or clutch components. A slight wiggling of the transmission is usually necessary to allow the input shaft to slide over the spline of the clutch disc.

5. After the transmission has cleared the clutch, it can be lowered and inspected before being reinstalled after the clutch assembly has been replaced.

6. Mark the pressure plate and flywheel if they are to be reused to allow them to be reinstalled in the same location to maintain assembly balance.

7. Remove the clutch pressure plate retaining bolts, and remove the clutch assembly including the release bearing, pressure plate, and clutch disc.

> ☠ **WARNING**
>
> The clutch driven disc may contain asbestos, which is known to be a cancer causing agent. Never clean clutch surfaces with compressed air. Avoid inhaling any dust from any clutch surface. When cleaning the clutch surfaces, use a commercially available brake cleaning fluid.

PILOT BEARING A commonly used pilot bushing removal method is to thread a coarse bolt into the bushing so it bottoms against the crankshaft. Further tightening will move the bushing outward. Some vehicle manufactures recommend the use

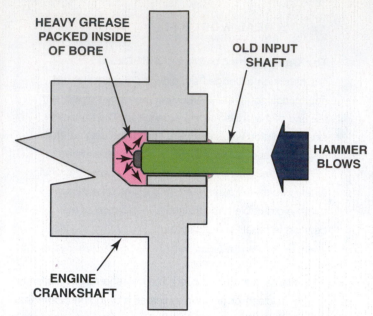

FIGURE 5–5 An old input shaft obtained from a disassembled transmission can be used to force the old pilot bushing out.

of a special puller. A somewhat messy alternative method to remove a pilot bearing is to fill the cavity behind the bearing with chassis grease and drive a close-fitting round rod or dowel into the grease. This will create a hydraulic force behind the bearing, forcing it outward. Soap or wet tissue can also be used. ● **SEE FIGURE 5–5.**

CLUTCH COMPONENT INSPECTION

IMPORTANCE OF INSPECTION Technicians should check each part as it is disassembled to determine if it is reusable or why it failed. This identifies any condition that needs special attention before the clutch is reassembled. If the clutch is slipping, the disc and the pressure plate should be replaced. The following sections explain the normal checks to be made during a clutch job.

FLYWHEEL INSPECTION The friction surface of the flywheel should be checked for

- Grooves
- Nicks
- Heat damage (discoloration or cracks caused by excessive heat)

Any of these indicates that the flywheel needs to be resurfaced or replaced.

FIGURE 5–6 Using an abrasive disc to remove the glaze and to restore the proper surface finish to a flywheel.

FLYWHEEL RESURFACING

Blanchard grinding moves a spinning grinding stone around the flywheel surface. This is the recommended method of resurfacing because it leaves a truly flat surface with a circular, nondirectional pattern. A nondirectional finish promotes rapid disc facing-to-flywheel break-in.

If the friction surface is flat and smooth but highly polished or glazed, some technicians will sand the friction surface using a disc sander with 80- to 120-grit paper. When doing this, the sander is kept in motion while attempting to duplicate the ground finish of a new unit without cutting grooves. ● SEE FIGURE 5–6.

FLYWHEEL AXIAL RUNOUT

Many flywheels are forged steel, which tends to warp (potato chip shape) or dish if overheated. This is checked by placing a straightedge across the flywheel in several locations. Over 0.0005 inch (0.013 mm) of warpage per inch of diameter is considered excessive. This means that a 12-inch-diameter flywheel can have 0.006 inch (12 × 0.0005) of warpage error.

If there is a vibration concern or an odd wear pattern at the hub of the disc or pressure plate release levers, the flywheel should be checked for excessive runout. Face or axial runout is checked by positioning a dial indicator with the indicating stylus at the outer edge of the flywheel face. ● SEE FIGURE 5–7.

To measure flywheel axial runout, perform the following steps:

STEP 1 Mount the dial indicator so the measuring stem is parallel to the crankshaft and pointing directly toward the flywheel contacting the disc friction area, and adjust the indicator to read zero.

STEP 2 Rotate the flywheel while watching the dial indicator. Maintain an even pressure, either inward or outward, to maintain zero crankshaft end play. The variation in reading is the amount of axial runout.

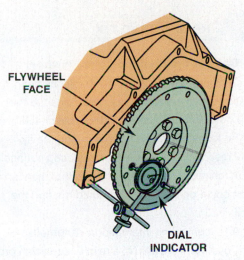

FIGURE 5–7 A dial indicator set up to measure flywheel face or axial runout.

STEP 3 Set up the dial indicator to measure lengthwise flywheel/crankshaft motion, and push and pull on the flywheel and crankshaft in a direction that is parallel to the crankshaft. The dial indicator is measuring crankshaft end play. Normal crankshaft end play should be about 0.002 to 0.010 inch (0.05 to 0.25 mm). Movement greater than specified indicates worn engine crankshaft thrust bearings.

To measure flywheel radial runout, perform the following steps:

STEP 1 Mount the dial indicator so it is at the edge of the flywheel, pointing directly toward the center of the flywheel.

STEP 2 Adjust the dial indicator to read zero.

STEP 3 Rotate the flywheel while watching the dial indicator.

STEP 4 The variation in reading is the amount of radial runout.

Radial runout has a greater effect on balance and vibration than on clutch operation. Runout in either direction greater than 0.010 inch (0.25 mm) is considered excessive axial runout, as little as 0.005 inch (0.1 mm) can cause chatter. If the flywheel is to be removed, place index marks at the crankshaft flange for faster alignment during reassembly. Also inspect the starter ring gear teeth. If they are damaged, replace either the starter gear or the flywheel.

PRESSURE PLATE ASSEMBLY INSPECTION

A used pressure plate assembly should be inspected visually for all of the following.

- Friction surface damage
- Release lever wear
- Lever pivot wear
- Cover distortion

The Case of the Stepped-Type Flywheel

The clutch in a 2005 VW (107,000 mi) has been replaced and the flywheel was resurfaced at the same time. But now there is noticeable clutch chatter. The technician was told that during the flywheel resurfacing, only the clutch mating surface was machined. The technician feels that the step height could be incorrect, but could not find the specification.

After contacting international Automotive Technician Network (iATN), a fellow technician provided the step-height specification. A check of the flywheel showed that its step was at the limit, but the clutch surface also had 0.003 inch of runout. Machining the flywheel fixed this problem.

Like the flywheel, the friction surface will tend to polish or glaze from normal use. If there is excessive slippage, grooves, heat checks, and warping can occur. Warpage can be checked by placing a straightedge across the friction surface and will show up as a gap between the straightedge and the inner portion of the pressure plate ring. Set the pressure plate on the flywheel without the clutch disc in place. All of the mounting points should meet the flywheel evenly and completely. Any air gaps indicate a distorted clutch cover. Release lever wear occurs at the contact surface with the release bearing and this area should appear smooth and polished with no metal removed. Release lever height should be checked after the pressure plate and disc are bolted to the flywheel. Soft reddish-brown rust and highly polished or shiny rough areas around the lever pivots are indications of wear at these points. If any problems are noticed, the pressure plate assembly should be replaced.

CLUTCH DISC INSPECTION If installing a used disc, it should be checked for all of the following:

- Facing thickness
- Damper spring condition
- Wear of the hub splines
- Contaminated or oil soaked facing material (oil or grease on the friction surface can cause clutch grab or chatter)
- Warpage or axial runout

The thickness of the facing can be checked by two different methods.

FIGURE 5–8 The thickness of the clutch disc facing can be measured using a vernier caliper.

Method 1 The first method is to place cardboard or a shop cloth over the facing to keep it clean and squeeze the facings together to compress the marcel spring. If specifications are not available, the minimum thickness of the compressed disc should be 0.280 inch (7.1 mm).
● **SEE FIGURE 5–8.**

Method 2 The most popular method is to measure the height of the facing surface above the rivets which is also called *rivet head depth*. With a new disc, rivet head depth will be about 0.050 inch (1.2 mm). A disc with less than 0.015 to 0.020 inch (0.38 to 0.5 mm) should be replaced. ● **SEE FIGURE 5–9.**

The damper springs and hub splines are checked visually for reddish rust, often called "rust dust" and shiny worn areas as well as loose, broken, or missing springs. Disc runout warpage is checked by making an axial runout check. This usually requires a pair of tapered centers or an expanding arbor at true center to the hub splines. The disc is rotated while watching for runout or wobbling of the facing surfaces. More than 0.020 inch (0.5 mm) is excessive, and the disc should be replaced.

A quick check for warpage is to set the disc against the flywheel. The facing should contact the flywheel evenly all around the disc.

CLUTCH/BELL HOUSING INSPECTION There should not be any oil or grease residue inside the bell housing. If oil is present, check for a leaking front bearing retainer seal or oil galleys plugs or back of the intake manifold. If there has been early failure of the pilot or release bearings, clutch pedal vibration, or the transmission is jumping out of gear, the face and bore surfaces of the bell housing should be checked for excessive runout.

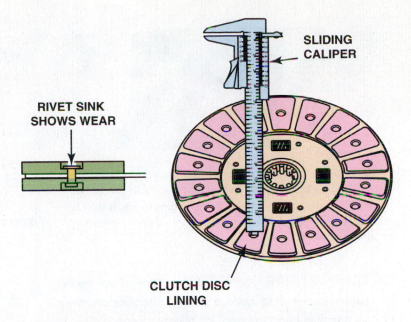

SLIDING CALIPER

RIVET SINK SHOWS WEAR

CLUTCH DISC LINING

FIGURE 5–9 The overall disc thickness can be measured using a vernier caliper by first compressing the marcel spring using pliers.

FIGURE 5–10 The active radius determines the torque capacity of a clutch disc. Therefore, a narrower band of friction material at a further distance from the center may have improved torque capacity over a clutch disc that has a wider band but has a shorter active radius.

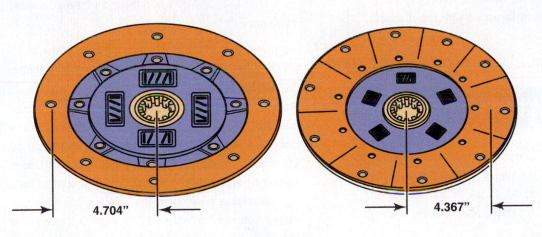

4.704"

4.367"

? **FREQUENTLY ASKED QUESTION**

Why Is the New Clutch Disc Use a Thinner Band of Friction Material?

Sometimes a replacement clutch disc looks totally wrong compared to the original. The wise technician always checks that the new part is the correct part before installing it. By using a thinner band of friction material, the centerline of the disc is further from the center. This distance is called the **active radius**. The more the distance between the centerline of the friction material and the centerline of the clutch disc, the higher the torque capacity of the clutch disc. Therefore, some replacement clutch discs may have a different appearance compared to the original. Double check with the supplier that the replacement clutch disc is designed for the vehicle being serviced before installing the new part. ● **SEE FIGURE 5–10.**

Check for excessive runout with a dial indicator attached to the crankshaft, flywheel, pressure plate, or disc, depending on the equipment available and how far the clutch is disassembled.

HOUSING BORE RUNOUT To check clutch housing bore runout, perform the following steps:

STEP 1 Reposition the dial indicator so the measuring stem is inside the bore and pointing outward.

STEP 2 Adjust the dial indicator to read zero.

STEP 3 Rotate the crankshaft while watching the indicator reading.

STEP 4 Any variation in reading is the amount of bore runout.

If the runout cannot be corrected, the bell housing is usually replaced, but it is possible to put shims between the bell housing and the engine block to correct excessive runout. The limit for bore runout is about 0.010 inch (0.25 mm). Bore runout can be corrected by using eccentric dowel pins to reposition the bell housing. These are available in different sizes. Position the bell housing so it is centered with the crankshaft. ● **SEE FIGURE 5–11.**

FIGURE 5–11 The dial indicator has a lever added to check clutch housing bore runout. Excessive runout can be caused by damaged or missing dowels in the engine block. If the dowels are okay, excessive runout can be corrected by installing eccentric dowels.

RELEASE BEARING INSPECTION Other than feeling for roughness or seeing obvious wear or discoloration, there are no effective bench checks for release bearings. This is one reason why they are normally replaced with the disc and pressure plate.

CLUTCH INSTALLATION

PRECAUTIONS During replacement, the clutch components must be kept clean and dry. All grease and oil that contacts the friction surfaces must be cleaned off. Small amounts of oil on the clutch facing will cause the clutch to grab or chatter.

CLUTCH ASSEMBLY REPLACEMENT To replace a clutch assembly perform the following steps:

STEP 1 Check the flywheel bolts to make sure that they are tight and torqued to specifications.

STEP 2 Check the pilot bearing recess to ensure that it is clean, and drive the new pilot bearing into place. The best tool for this is a commercial or shop-made driver with a stem the same size as the bearing bore and a face that is larger than the diameter of the bearing. The new pilot bearing is driven in until it is fully seated or has entered completely into the crankshaft. Most pilot bearings do not require lubrication. Roller bearings with exposed rollers should be lubricated with a thin film of grease or a few drops of engine oil is all that is needed on a sintered bushing.

STEP 3 Place the new clutch disc over the transmission clutch shaft and make sure that it slides freely over the splines. Determine which side of the disc goes against the flywheel which will often be marked *flywheel side*.

If not marked, the damper assembly normally faces the pressure plate.

Note: To determine the correct clutch disc position, place each side of the disc against the flywheel and rotate it. The side that contacts the flywheel bolts or does not let the clutch facing contact the flywheel is the wrong side.

STEP 4 Position the *disc alignment tool* or an old transmission shaft or a plastic dummy transmission shaft through the disc and into the pilot bearing to center the disc.

STEP 5 Install the pressure plate over the disc, making sure that it is properly aligned with the dowel pins and mounting bolt holes, and install the mounting bolts.

CAUTION: Use only the bolts that were used originally or if replacement bolts are used, be sure that they are grade 8 (high tensile strength) fasteners.

STEP 6 Tighten the mounting bolts two turns at a time alternating back and forth across the pressure plate. Tighten the bolts to the correct torque.

STEP 7 Remove the alignment device and check to make sure that the pilot bearing is in the exact center of the disc. The height variation of the release levers can be checked after the pressure plate is installed. Use a vernier or dial caliper, measure from the contact face for the release bearing to the clutch disc. All of the heights should be within 0.020 inch (0.5 mm). The readings will be more accurate after the clutch has been applied a few times.

STEP 8 Check the clutch linkage to make sure that it operates smoothly. On cable-operated clutches, this is a good time to remove, clean, and lubricate the cable.

STEP 9 Fill the groove inside the bore of the release bearing with grease, apply a thin film of the specified high-temperature grease on the fork contact areas, and slide the release bearing onto the transmission quill, making sure that the bearing collar slides smoothly. The quill portion of the transmission bearing retainer should be smooth and unworn. On clutch forks that use pivot balls, a thin film of grease should be put on the ball. On forks mounted on pivot shafts, the pivot bushings should be lubricated.

STEP 10 Replace the transmission/transaxle, being sure to observe the following:

- Place a very thin film of grease on the clutch splines.
- Never let the transmission hang on the clutch disc splines.

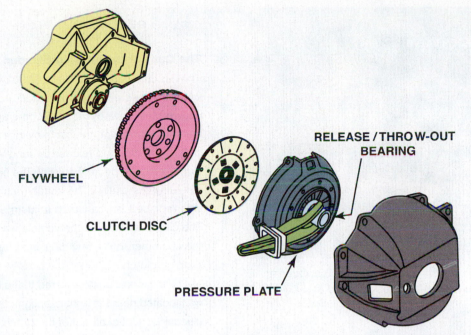

FLYWHEEL

CLUTCH DISC

RELEASE / THROW-OUT BEARING

PRESSURE PLATE

FIGURE 5–12 A summary of the entire rear-wheel-drive clutch replacement procedure.

- The transmission should be completely seated against the clutch housing or engine before the mounting bolts are tightened.
- Tighten the transmission mounting bolts two turns at a time, working back and forth across the transmission until they are tightened to the correct torque. It should not be necessary to force the transmission into place.
- Adjust the free travel before operating the clutch.

CLUTCH SERVICE SUMMARY To summarize the clutch replacement procedure, check or service the flywheel, clutch disc, pressure plate, release (throwout) bearing, and check the spines of the input shaft. ● **SEE FIGURE 5–12.**

HYDRAULIC CLUTCH SERVICE

PRECAUTIONS Fluid leaks or failure to release completely indicate the need for hydraulic system service. Clutch hydraulic systems have evolved from the early systems that had free travel adjustment and required clearance at the release bearing to newer systems that maintain a slight preload. Older systems used steel and reinforced rubber lines with threaded fittings, whereas the newer systems use plastic tubing sealed by O-rings and held together by locking pins at the connections.

 REAL WORLD FIX

The Case of the Clogged Hose

A Chevrolet K30 pickup (157,000 mi) came in with no clutch operation. The hydraulic system was bled, and the clutch tested. But during a road test, the clutch would no longer release. The clutch master cylinder, slave cylinder, and connecting hose were replaced, but the problem was still there.

The technician blocked the outlet line of the master cylinder, and a solid clutch pedal proved that the master cylinder worked properly. Closer inspection showed that there was no fluid movement at the reservoir when the clutch pedal was applied. Replacement of the hose between the reservoir and the master cylinder fixed this problem.

HYDRAULIC CLUTCH BLEEDING In many cases, a clutch hydraulic system can be bled by **gravity bleeding** while in others, a helper may be needed. To bleed a clutch hydraulic system using the gravity method, perform the following steps:

STEP 1 Clean the bleeder valve at the slave cylinder and place a shop cloth under it to catch escaping fluid. ● **SEE FIGURE 5–13.**

STEP 2 Open the bleeder valve by loosening the bleeder screw and observe the flow. If no flow occurs, have a helper

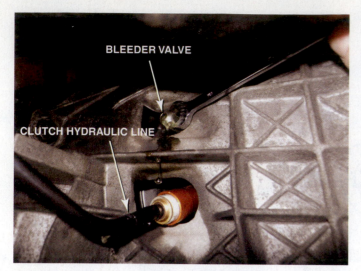

BLEEDER VALVE

CLUTCH HYDRAULIC LINE

FIGURE 5–13 Gravity bleeding a hydraulic clutch. Opening the bleeder valve should allow air to escape and then fluid should flow.

depress the clutch pedal in a smooth, slow manner. Air bubbles coming from the bleed valve indicate that the system needed bleeding. After the air bubbles stop and a constant flow of fluid occurs, close the bleed valve. An alternative method is reverse, or back-bleeding. This is done by forcing fluid through the slave cylinder bleed valve and upward to the reservoir.

STEP 3   Check the fluid level and correct it, if necessary.

Some master and slave cylinders are mounted so that the cylinder portion is above the line connection, which makes it extremely difficult to bleed air from them.

- In some cases, it is possible to bench bleed them to remove all the air before installing on the vehicle. An alternative bleeding method is to have a helper partially

 REAL WORLD FIX

The Case of the Missing Bleeder

The clutch failed in the Nissan 300ZX (181,000 mi) because the clutch arm pivot ball broke, which allowed the slave cylinder to come apart. The broken part along with the slave cylinder, clutch disc, pressure plate, and release bearing were replaced. But, the clutch pedal would go the floor without releasing the clutch. The clutch master cylinder was replaced, and a clutch adjustment was made. The clutch worked so the vehicle was returned to the customer, but a few days later it returned with a slipping clutch.

The technician discovered that a bleeder screw was located near the right headlight. Opening this bleeder let a lot of air out of the clutch line. Completely bleeding the clutch along with a free travel readjustment fixed this comeback.

apply the clutch while reverse bleeding using pressure surges from the fluid injector.

- Some clutch hydraulic systems will partially self-bleed if the clutch pedal is held completely depressed overnight using a brake pedal depressing tool.

- Another bleeding method is to construct an adapter to the fluid reservoir so a vacuum can be applied to the fluid using a hand, electric, or air-powered vacuum pump. Reducing the air pressure on the fluid will cause the air bubble to expand and move upward to the reservoir.

1 The first step in the process of replacing the clutch on this Chevrolet S-10 pickup truck is to remove the negative battery cable.

2 Remove the shifter mechanism inside the vehicle. This step may involve removing the center console and other components.

3 Mark and then remove the driveshaft.

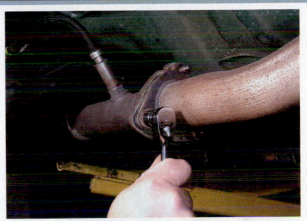

4 Remove the exhaust pipe if needed. It was needed in this case, according to service information.

5 Remove the transmission mount fasteners.

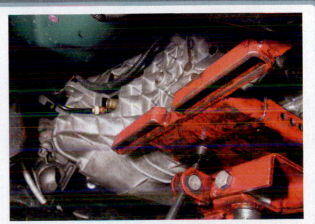

6 Using a transmission jack, support the transmission and remove the bell housing bolts.

CONTINUED ▶

7 A view of the bell housing and throwout bearing as the transmission assembly is removed from the engine.

8 Removing the fasteners holding the pressure plate to the flywheel.

9 Removing the pressure plate and clutch disc.

10 Using a special puller, remove the pilot bearing.

11 The flywheel is being removed to be refinished or replaced as needed.

12 With the flywheel removed, check to see if the rear main seal is leaking and replace if needed.

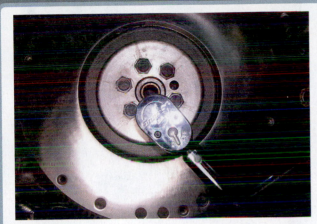

13 Installing a reconditioned flywheel and torquing new bolts to factory specifications.

14 Installing a new pilot bearing and lubricate as per instructions in service information.

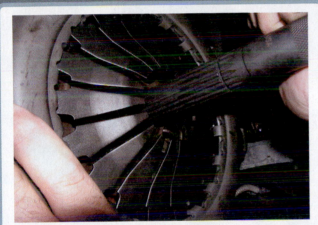

15 Using a pilot tool to align the clutch disc with the pilot bearing through the center opening of the pressure plate.

16 Installing the transmission assembly with a new throwout bearing.

17 Bleeding the air from the hydraulic clutch circuit.

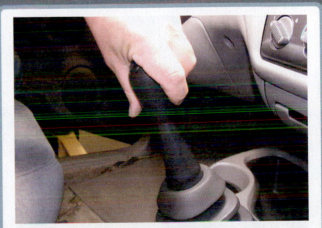

18 Finish the clutch replacement by reinstalling all components removed and check for proper operation.

CLUTCH REPLACEMENT—FRONT-WHEEL DRIVE

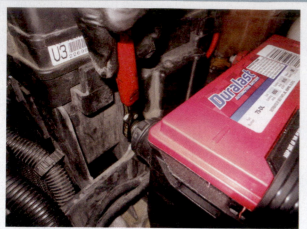

1 The first step in almost all major service work is to disconnect the negative battery cable from the battery.

2 A new clutch kit, including the pressure plate, release bearing, and clutch disc, was purchased making sure that all of the needed information was compiled before ordering to help insure that the correct parts were purchased.

3 A holding fixture was attached to support the engine when the transaxle was removed from underneath the vehicle.

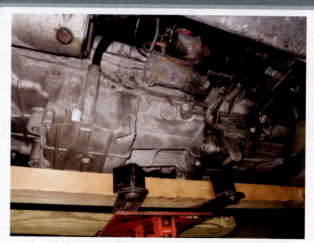

4 The "K" (lower support) member was removed to get access to the transaxle.

5 Both drive axle shafts (half shafts) were removed.

6 The transaxle is supported by a transmission jack as it is being removed from underneath the vehicle.

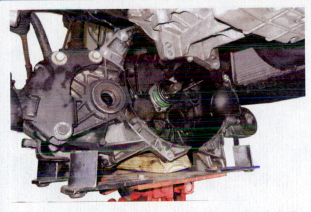

7 The transaxle assembly is lowered from underneath the vehicle.

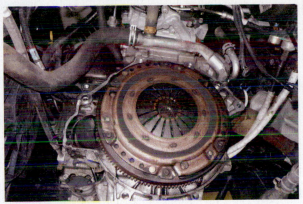

8 The original pressure plate shows normal wear. The problem with this clutch was a leaking slave cylinder/ release bearing assembly.

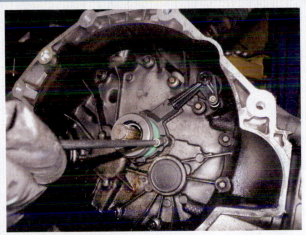

9 The new slave cylinder/release bearing assembly is being installed.

10 The pressure plate is being removed from the flywheel.

11 The flywheel is cleaned using an abrasive pad to remove the glaze on the surface.

12 The flywheel was thoroughly cleaned after being cleaned.

CONTINUED ▶

13 The spline grease that was included with the clutch kit is being applied to the splines of the clutch disc.

14 The pressure plate retaining bolts are torqued to factory specification while an assistant uses a pry bar to keep the flywheel from turning.

15 The transaxle is then reinstalled from underneath the vehicle.

16 The engine and transaxle mounts are reattached and the half shafts reinstalled.

17 The hydraulic clutch master cylinder is filled with DOT3 brake fluid and allowed to gravity bleed.

18 All fasteners were torqued to factory specification and the vehicle was test driven to confirm proper operation.

SUMMARY

1. Clutch system preventive maintenance ensures proper clutch pedal free travel and/or proper master cylinder fluid level.

2. Excessive slippage, grab, chatter, and unusual noise are common indications of clutch problems.

3. A clutch job requires transmission/transaxle removal to replace the pressure plate, disc, release bearing, and pilot bearing.

4. The flywheel as well as the bell housing should be checked whenever replacing a clutch.

5. Abnormal clutch failure requires additional checks to locate the root cause of the failure.

6. The clutch disc must be kept clean and centered to the pilot bearing during installation.

7. Newer hydraulic systems are replaced as an assembly. They are prefilled with fluid, eliminating the need for system bleeding.

REVIEW QUESTIONS

1. How is clutch pedal free travel measured?

2. How is a clutch spin-down test performed?

3. What parts are normally replaced as part of a clutch job?

4. What should be lubricated during clutch replacement?

CHAPTER QUIZ

1. A cable-operated clutch is being adjusted. Technician A says that free travel is measured at the clutch pedal and should be between 3/4 and 1 inch (19 and 25 mm). Technician B says that the clutch spin-down time should be less than two seconds. Which technician is correct?
   a. Technician A only
   b. Technician B only
   c. Both technicians A and B
   d. Neither technician A nor B

2. A vehicle has a slipping clutch. Technician A says slippage will be most noticeable when accelerating in first gear. Technician B says a clutch slip test can be performed in the shop. Which technician is correct?
   a. Technician A only
   b. Technician B only
   c. Both technicians A and B
   d. Neither technician A nor B

3. Clutch chatter can be caused by_____.
   a. Grease or oil on the clutch friction material
   b. Broken engine mount(s)
   c. Low hydraulic clutch fluid level
   d. Too little free play in the clutch pedal

4. Technician A says that clutch slipping can be caused by a warped clutch disc. Technician B says that slippage is the result of too little free travel. Which technician is correct?
   a. Technician A only
   b. Technician B only
   c. Both technicians A and B
   d. Neither technician A nor B

5. A squeal begins as the clutch pedal is depressed about 1 inch (25 mm). This is probably caused by a _____.
   a. Defective or worn release (throwout) bearing
   b. Worn clutch disc
   c. Weak pressure plate
   d. Worn pilot bearing

6. What should be lubricated when replacing a clutch assembly?
   a. Disc splines
   b. Pivot bushings (if equipped)
   c. Pilot bearing
   d. All of the above

7. A clutch disc is being installed. Technician A says the damper assembly of the clutch disc normally faces the pressure plate. Technician B says that the disc splines should be lightly lubricated. Which technician is correct?
   a. Technician A only
   b. Technician B only
   c. Both technicians A and B
   d. Neither technician A nor B

8. Technician A says that a pilot bearing can be removed using chassis grease and a round rod. Technician B says that some pilot bearings may need a thin coating of grease after installation. Which technician is correct?
   a. Technician A only
   b. Technician B only
   c. Both technicians A and B
   d. Neither technician A nor B

9. During clutch installation, the clutch disc can be aligned to the pilot bearing using _____.
   a. A commercial clutch disc alignment tool
   b. An old transmission shaft
   c. A plastic dummy transmission shaft
   d. Any of the above

10. While discussing the installation of a pressure plate, Technician A says that grade 8 bolts be used for the mounting bolts. Technician B says to move from bolt to bolt at least a two times while tightening the bolts. Which technician is correct?
   a. Technician A only
   b. Technician B only
   c. Both technicians A and B
   d. Neither technician A nor B

MANUAL TRANSMISSIONS PARTS AND OPERATION

LEARNING OBJECTIVES

After studying this chapter, the reader should be able to:

1. Prepare for ASE Manual Drive Train and Axles (A3) certification test content area "B" (Transmission Diagnosis and Repair).

2. Explain the construction of a manual transmission.

3. Discuss synchronizer operation.

4. Explain five-speed transmission torque flow.

5. Discuss shifter operation.

6. Explain the construction of manual transmission gears.

7. Discuss the purpose of transmission case and bearings.

KEY TERMS

Blocker ring   108, 110
Clutch shaft   106
Constant mesh gears   107
Detent   116
Double cone   112
Hub   108
Idler gear   107
Input shaft   106
Interlock   108
Main drive gear   106
Main shaft   106

Manual transmission fluid (MTF)   120
Output shaft   106
Reverse idler shaft   106
Shift fork   116
Sliding Sleeve   108
Speed gears   107
Struts   110
Synchronizer Keys   110
Synchronizer rings   108
Viscosity   120

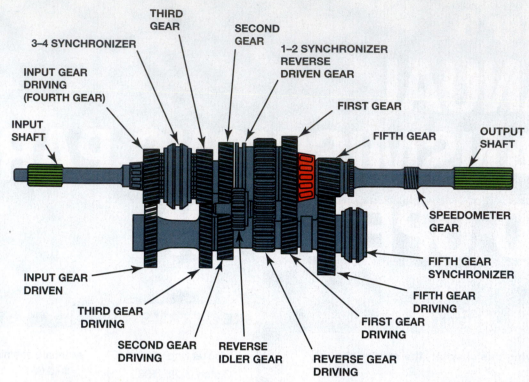

FIGURE 6–1 A five-speed transmission gear train. Power enters through the input shaft and leaves through the transmission output shaft.

PURPOSE OF MANUAL TRANSMISSONS

The purpose of the transmission is to provide neutral, forward gear speeds or ranges, and reverse. It must be able to provide a gear ratio that is low enough, when multiplied by the final drive ratio, to increase the engine's torque sufficiently to accelerate the vehicle at the desired rate. The highest gear ratio should allow the vehicle to cruise at an engine speed that is low enough to conserve fuel and decrease noise. There also needs to be intermediate ratios that are spaced so that the engine will not overrev before a shift or lug after a shift. Reverse must be roughly the same ratio as first since the vehicle will be starting from a stop in both cases.

CONSTRUCTION

POWER PATHS A transmission has several different paths through which power can flow. These paths provide the required forward gear ranges and a reverse. In a rear-wheel-drive (RWD) transmission, power enters the input shaft and passes through at least two gear sets before transferring to the main shaft. The power will exit through the main shaft and will then pass on to the driveshaft. The transmission main shaft, the output shaft, is directly in line with the input shaft. ● SEE FIGURE 6–1.

PARTS INVOLVED A rear-wheel-drive (RWD) manual transmission includes the following four shafts:

1. A cluster gear, countershaft gear or *layshaft* (a British term).

2. The **input shaft**, also called a **main drive gear** or **clutch shaft**.

3. The **output shaft**, also called a **main shaft**.

4. The **reverse idler shaft**.

The main shaft is piloted into the rear of the input shaft gear with a bearing. It is also supported at the rear of the transmission case by another large bearing, and by the universal joint slip yoke, which in turn is supported by a bushing at the rear of the extension housing. The input shaft gear is supported by a bearing at the front of the transmission case and the pilot bearing at the end of the crankshaft. Most transmissions support the cluster gear directly by a bearing set. Some transmissions with very long cluster gears and main shaft gear groups use a support in the middle of the transmission with bearings for the cluster gear and main shaft. ● SEE FIGURE 6–2.

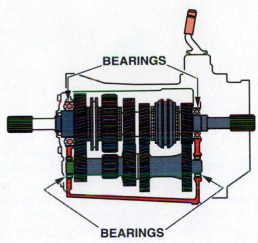

FIGURE 6–2 Bearings support the input shaft, countershaft, main shaft, and speed gears.

SHIFTING GEARS   **Constant mesh gears** are always engaged with their mating gear and are mounted so that one of them, called a **speed gear**, can freewheel on its shaft. The gears are shifted by connecting the freewheeling gear to its shaft. This is done through a synchronizer assembly. The synchronizer is splined to the shaft and has a sleeve that can be slid into place to engage the gear to the synchronizer. The power will then be able to flow from the gear to the synchronizer and then to the shaft. The advantage of constant mesh gears is that the synchronizer will allow shifts to be made while the vehicle is moving and without the driver doing any extra clutching.

GEAR RATIOS   In all gear speeds but one, the power flows from the main drive gear (input) to the cluster gear and then from the cluster gear to the main shaft (output).

The power passes through two gear sets. The exception is a 1:1 ratio, where the power flows directly from the main drive gear to the main shaft.

- All the forward gears are normally in constant mesh so they always rotate at their designed speed relative to engine speed.
- The gears of the cluster gear rotate as an assembly.
- The output (speed) gears usually are mounted on the main shaft so they float or rotate freely.
- The speed gears complete the ratio for each gear speed when they become coupled to the main shaft.
- The main shaft includes synchronizer assemblies for each pair of gear speeds and can lock the individual speed gears to the main shaft. This is done for each shift.

Because the gears in most transmissions are in constant mesh, they will always rotate at their gear ratio speed relative to the input shaft gear.

TORQUE CAPACITY   A transmission is designed to be strong enough to handle the torque output of the engine. High torque requires large input shafts, even larger output shafts, wide gears, and large bearings. This increases the weight of the transmission and also increases the drag and power loss. Smaller transmissions improve fuel mileage, but they can break under load. Using an engine that has a higher torque output than the transmission is designed to handle will cause failure of the transmission. To handle more torque, the following two factors are designed into the transmission:

> **Factor 1** The diameters of the input and output shafts of a transmission are enlarged.
>
> **Factor 2** The distance between the main shaft and the countershaft is increased. This is needed to allow the space in the case for the larger gears and shafts.
> ● **SEE FIGURE 6–3.**

REVERSE

PRINCIPLES   Because the engine is not able to operate backward, the transmission has to reverse the direction of rotation, requiring one more gear in the gear train. When one external gear drives another, they will rotate in opposite directions. In a transmission

- The input shaft gear rotates in a clockwise direction the same as the engine as viewed from the front of the engine (accessory drive belt end).
- The cluster gear rotates in a counter clockwise direction.
- The main shaft rotates clockwise when driven either through the gear train or by the direct coupling.

REVERSE IDLER NEEDED   To make the vehicle back up, the main shaft must rotate counter clockwise. To accomplish this, an **idler gear** is meshed between the cluster gear and the reverse gear on the main shaft. ● **SEE FIGURE 6–4** on page 106.

A simple idler will not change the ratio, but it will cause a reversal of rotation. The idler gears used in some transmissions are long, with a gear of one size meshed with the cluster gear and a different-sized gear to mesh with the reverse gear. This idler gear will affect the ratio.

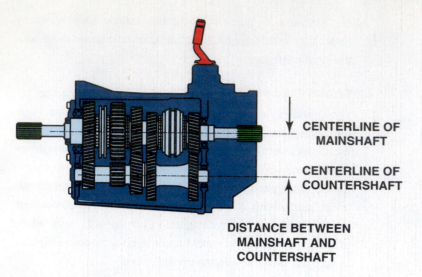

CENTERLINE OF
MAINSHAFT

CENTERLINE OF
COUNTERSHAFT

DISTANCE BETWEEN
MAINSHAFT AND
COUNTERSHAFT

FIGURE 6–3 The torque capacity of a transmission is determined by the size of the gear and bearings used. The greater the distance, usually measured in millimeters such as 77 mm, between the main shaft and the countershaft, the greater the torque capacity.

SPEED GEARS

All gears on the countershaft are permanently attached to the shaft. When the countershaft rotates, all gears on the countershaft rotate. The input shaft gear is also part of the input shaft. However, the gears on the main shaft are free to move on the shaft and are connected to the main shaft through the synchronizer hub when a shift is made. The gears that rotate on the main shaft are called speed gears and are free to rotate on a film of oil or on bearings.

SYNCHRONIZERS

PURPOSE AND FUNCTION Synchronizers are used in manual transmissions/transaxles to make shifting easier. To synchronize means to make two or more events occur at the same time. When the driver depresses the clutch pedal, torque is no longer being transmitted to the input shaft and the drive wheels are "driving" the main shaft of the transmission/transaxle. To achieve a clash-free (no grinding sound) shift, the two gears to be meshed must be rotating at the same speed.

PARTS AND OPERATION Most vehicles today in a manually shifted transmission use a floor-mounted shifter to change gears. The shifting lever either moves cables that transfer the shifting motion to the transmission or transaxle or move the shift forks directly. Inside the transmission/transaxle are shift forks that control shifts between two gears, such as first and second or second and third. **Interlocks** either in the

shifter linkage itself or inside the transmission/transaxle prevent the accidental selection of reverse except when shifting from neutral and also prevent selecting two gears at the same time. ● SEE FIGURE 6–5.

The detents and interlocks hold the shift mechanism in position. The real "shifting" in a synchromesh transmission takes place in the synchronizer assemblies, not the gears. Most synchronizer assemblies ride on the output shaft between two gears. A synchronizer assembly is named for the gears on either side of it, which are the two speeds that it engages. For example, a five-speed transmission with constant-mesh reverse uses a 1–2 synchronizer, a 3–4 synchronizer, and a 5-reverse synchronizer.

SYNCHRONIZER CONSTRUCTION Although there are number of design variations, all are similar and include the following:

- a **hub**
- a **sliding sleeve**
- a **blocker ring**, also called *stop ring* or **synchronizer ring**
- **keys**
- **springs**

In addition, the tapered cone and coupling teeth machined on the speed gear are part of the synchronizer assembly. ● SEE FIGURE 6–6.

In a typical synchronizer

- Splines attach the center hub of the synchronizer to the output shaft, so the hub and output shaft rotate together. There are also splines machined on the outer circumference of the hub.

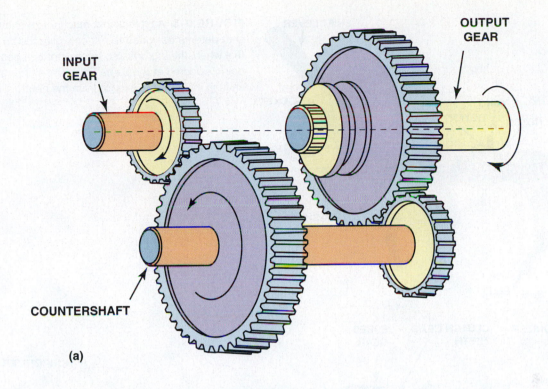

(a)

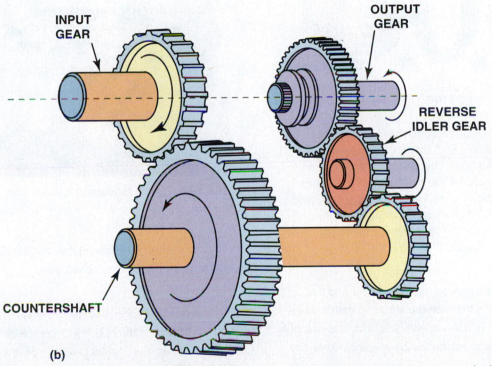

(b)

FIGURE 6–4 (a) The input shaft rotates in a clockwise direction; the countershaft rotates in a counter clockwise direction and the first–reverse gear drives the output shaft in a clockwise direction. (b) When meshed with the idler gear, the first–reverse gear will be driven in a counter clockwise direction. A simple (single) idler is shown.

- An outer sliding sleeve rides on the external hub splines with enough clearance so that it slides freely. The splines on the sleeve also match the small coupling teeth of the stop ring and speed gear. Coupling teeth are also called engagement or clutch teeth. The sleeve is splined to the hub, so it rotates with the output shaft.

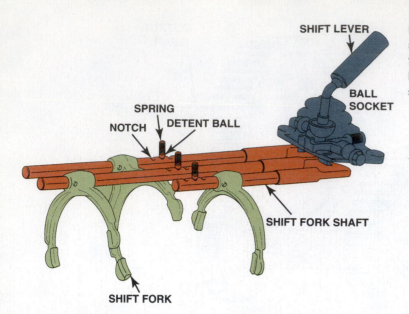

SHIFT LEVER

BALL SOCKET

SPRING

NOTCH   DETENT BALL

SHIFT FORK SHAFT

SHIFT FORK

FIGURE 6–5 A typical shift mechanism showing the shift detents designed to not only give the driver a solid feel when shifting but also to prevent two gears from being selected at the same time. The shifter also prevents shifting into reverse except from the neutral position.

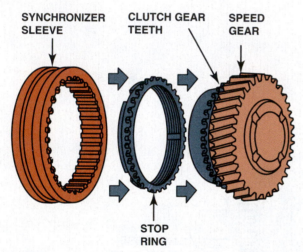

SYNCHRONIZER SLEEVE

CLUTCH GEAR TEETH

SPEED GEAR

STOP RING

FIGURE 6–6 The shifter fork fits into the groove of the synchronizer sleeve. When a shift is made, the sleeve is moved toward the speed gear. The sleeve presses the stop ring (synchronizer ring) against the cone area of the speed gear. The friction between the stop ring and the speed gear causes the speed of the two to become equal, permitting the sleeve to engage the gear clutch teeth of the speed gear. When this engagement occurs, the shift is complete.

- A **blocker ring** sits between the speed gear and the sleeve. The coupling teeth on the stop ring match those on both the sleeve and the speed gear. The stop ring also has a tapered cone to match the cone machined on the speed gear.

- Small, spring-loaded detent keys, also called **synchronizer keys** or **struts**, ride in slots on the outer sleeve. The stop ring has slots to match these keys. This allows the stop ring to rotate slightly, relative to the sleeve, before the keys hit the sides of their slots and stop the stop ring. As the sleeve moves, the synchronizer

SYNCHRONIZER SLEEVE

BLOCKER RING (STOP RING)

GEAR CLUTCH TEETH

SPEED GEAR

FIGURE 6–7 Typical synchronizer assembly.

keys move with it, which pushes the blocking ring onto the tapered cone of the speed gear.

SYNCHRONIZER OPERATION When the synchronizer sleeve is centered on the hub, the synchronizer is in its neutral position—it does not contact either of the speed gears. ● **SEE FIGURE 6–7.**

To shift into gear, the driver disengages the clutch and moves the shift linkage. The shift linkage, which is described later in this chapter, pushes the sleeve toward one of the speed gears. As the sleeve moves, the detent keys help guide the stop ring toward the speed gear. This causes the ring cone to slide onto the tapered cone of the speed gear.

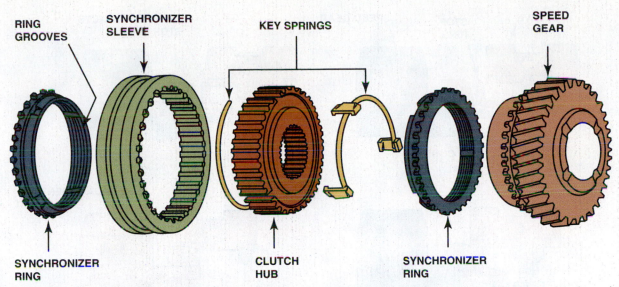

RING GROOVES   SYNCHRONIZER SLEEVE   KEY SPRINGS   SPEED GEAR

SYNCHRONIZER RING   CLUTCH HUB   SYNCHRONIZER RING

FIGURE 6–8 Synchronizer keys are attached to the clutch hub and push against the synchronizer ring when the sleeve is being moved during a shift. Notice the grooves on the synchronizer ring. These grooves prevent lubricating oil from becoming trapped between the ring and the cone surface of the speed gear. The grooves also help the ring release from the cone surface when a shift is made out of a gear.

The speed gear is turning because it is in constant mesh with a countershaft gear. However, the gear may not be turning at the same speed as the synchronizer assembly even though both are on the same shaft. When the clutch is disengaged, the engine is no longer driving the transmission, so there is no torque applied to the input shaft, and the countershaft, or cluster gear, simply freewheels. As the shift is made, the stop ring acts as a brake to slow down the gear so that its speed matches the speed of the synchronizer assembly. That is, it synchronizes the shift. This matched speed allows the internal hub splines to easily engage the coupling teeth on the stop ring and speed gear. When the clutch disengages, the crankshaft drives the input shaft, which drives the countershaft, which in turn drives the output shaft through the selected gear.

The synchronizer goes through three stages during a shift:

1. As the shift is selected, the synchronizer sleeve moves toward the speed gear. If the speeds of the sliding sleeve (main shaft) and the speed gear (counter shaft) are not identical, the speed difference will cause the tapered cone to "misalign" the teeth of the sleeve, the stop ring, and the speed gear. This "blocks" the shift. Now, the tapered teeth of the sliding sleeve push against the teeth of the stop ring, which in turn pushes the stop ring tapered surface up against the tapered surface of the speed gear. This causes the speed gear to either speed up or slow down based on the difference between the main shaft speed (hub) and the counter gear speed (speed gear). When the speeds are equal, the thrust is released on the tapered surface, which now allows the "alignment" of the sliding sleeve teeth, the

stop ring teeth, and the speed gear teeth, which allows the shift to be completed. ● **SEE FIGURE 6–8.**

2. The sleeve overcomes the force of the detent key springs as the shift linkage continues to move it toward the gear. This allows the stop ring to relax and move slightly so that the sleeve splines begin to engage the coupling teeth on the stop ring. At this point, the coupling teeth on the stop ring and the speed gear may not line up with each other. However, friction continues to build between the ring and the cone, so the gear continues to slow down.

3. Once the sleeve, stop ring, and gear are all turning at the same speed, it takes just a small movement between the stop ring and gear to align the coupling teeth and allow the sleeve to slip completely over both sets. The speed gear is now locked to the output shaft through the synchronizer stop ring and sleeve. ● **SEE FIGURE 6–9.**

Synchronizer stop rings are a simple type of clutch, called a cone clutch for the shape of the mating surfaces. Some manufacturers refer to the synchronizer action as "clutching." Synchronizer sleeves and hubs are gear-quality steel. Stop rings are a softer metal—usually brass, copper, or a sintered metal—to absorb the friction of synchronizer operation. The tapered cone is relieved; that is, grooves are machined into its contact surface. These grooves serve two purposes:

1. They channel excess lubricant out from between the two pieces for better contact.

2. Retain a small amount of lubricant. This decreases wear when the cone clutch must slip slightly during coupling tooth alignment.

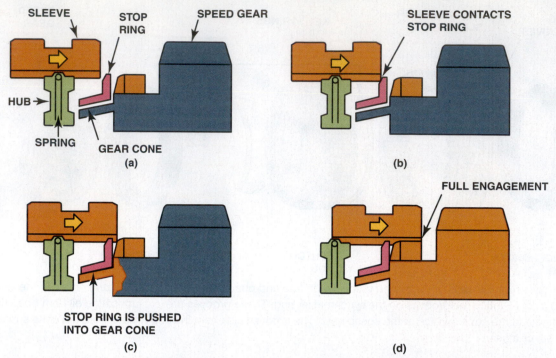

FIGURE 6–9 A shift sequence starts when the shift fork is moved by the driver. (a) Applying a force on the sleeve that moves it toward the speed gear. (b) The sleeve and the inserts contact the stop ring (blocking ring). (c) The synchronizer ring (stop ring) engages the cone on the speed gear, causing both assemblies to reach the same speed. (d) The shift is completed when the internal teeth of the sleeve mesh with the gear clutch teeth of the speed gear.

The internal splines on the synchronizer sleeve and the coupling gear teeth on stop rings and speed gears have a special shape that works to hold the gear engaged once the driver releases the shift lever. The ends of the gear teeth are chamfered, giving them a triangular shape. These pointed ends allow easier sleeve-to-gear alignment as the angles tend to center the splines between the teeth. Once aligned, a back taper machined behind the chamfered end of the teeth and splines tends to keep the sleeve in place until the linkage pushes the sleeve away for another shift. Back taper is an angle cut opposite to the chamfer so that spline or tooth narrows just behind the chamfered end. ● **SEE FIGURE 6–10.**

The back taper creates resistance to motion to keep the splines from sliding off the coupling teeth. This is especially important when there is no torque load, such as coasting, to help keep the parts meshed. Worn back taper may cause the transmission to jump out of gear, usually when the throttle is released. Some synchronizer stop rings have friction material on the cone surface. This paper friction material is the same as used on automatic transmission clutch plates, and provides a smoother synchronizing action than metal-to-metal contact. A manual transmission with paper stop rings

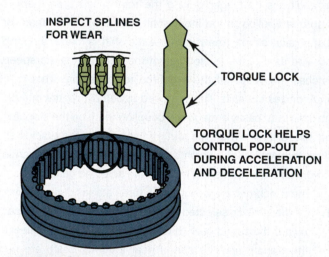

FIGURE 6–10 The shape of the splines helps prevent the transmission/transaxle from jumping out of gear during acceleration and deceleration.

must use automatic transmission fluid (ATF). Other lubricants damage the paper ring surface. Some synchronizers use a **double cone**, with an outer cone and an inner cone along with the blocker ring. The multiple cones provide more surface area for better synchronization and longer service life. ● **SEE FIGURE 6–11.**

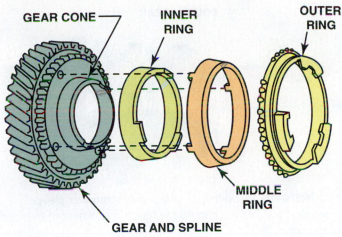

FIGURE 6–11 Exploded view of a triple-cone synchronizer. The inner and outer rings rotate with the synchronizer sleeve while the middle ring rotates with the speed gear.

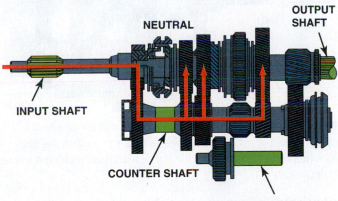

FIGURE 6–12 In neutral, the input shaft and the countershaft are rotating if the clutch is engaged (clutch pedal up), but no torque is being transmitted through the transmission.

FIVE-SPEED TRANSMISSION TORQUE FLOW

BORG-WARNER FIVE-SPEED A five-speed transmission has six gear sets that provide five forward speeds and one reverse speed. Either a sliding gear or constant-mesh gears may be used for reverse. All forward gears are the constant-mesh type. The Borg-Warner T5 manual transmission serves as an example of a contemporary five-speed design. In addition to reverse, the T5 provides three gear reduction ratios (first, second, and third), direct drive (fourth), and an overdriven ratio (fifth). A sliding idler gear is used to change output shaft direction and provide reverse.

NEUTRAL. In neutral, all of the synchronizer sleeves are centered on their hubs. ● **SEE FIGURE 6–12.**

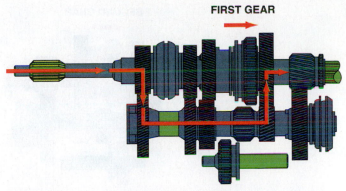

FIGURE 6–13 In first gear, the 1–2 synchronizer sleeve is moved rearward, locking the first speed gear to the output shaft. Torque is transmitted from the input shaft to the countershaft and then to the output shaft.

Note that in this and the following illustrations, the reverse idler shaft and sliding gear have been repositioned for clarity. In actuality, the assembly is positioned so it meshes with the reverse gears of the countershaft and output shaft simultaneously. With the clutch engaged, the drive gear of the input shaft turns the cluster gear, or countershaft. The speed gears are driven by the cluster gears, but rotate freely, on the output shaft. The output shaft may turn if the vehicle is moving or coasting, but no engine torque being transferred through the transmission.

FIRST GEAR. In first gear, the shift linkage slides the 1–2 synchronizer sleeve rearward toward the first speed gear. ● **SEE FIGURE 6–13.**

The synchronizer assembly locks the speed gear to the output shaft. With the clutch engaged, the input shaft drives the countershaft, delivering engine torque to the gearbox. Torque transfers from the first counter gear to the first speed gear, which drives the output shaft through the 1–2 synchronizer hub splines. Torque flows through the transmission in gear reduction at the first gear ratio.

SECOND GEAR. In second gear, the shift linkage slides the 1–2 synchronizer sleeve forward, away from the first speed gear and toward the second speed gear. ● **SEE FIGURE 6–14.**

The synchronizer assembly releases first gear, then locks the second speed gear to the output shaft. With the clutch engaged, the input shaft is driven at crankshaft speed and turns the countershaft. Engine torque transfers from the second counter gear to the second speed gear, which drives the output shaft through the 1–2 synchronizer hub splines. Torque flows through the transmission in gear reduction at the second gear ratio.

THIRD GEAR. In third gear, the shift linkage centers the 1–2 synchronizer sleeve and moves the 3–4 synchronizer sleeve back toward the third speed gear. ● **SEE FIGURE 6–15.**

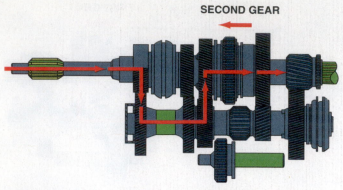

SECOND GEAR

FIGURE 6–14 In second gear, the 1–2 synchronizer sleeve is moved forward, which locks the second speed gear to the output shaft.

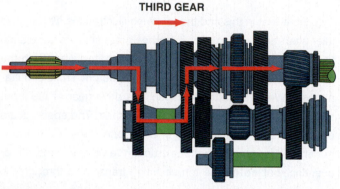

THIRD GEAR

FIGURE 6–15 To achieve third gear, the shaft linkage first centers the 1–2 synchronizer sleeve and then moves the 3–4 synchronizer sleeve rearward, locking third speed gear to the output shaft.

The synchronizer assembly locks the third speed gear to the output shaft. With the clutch engaged and the input shaft driving the countershaft, the third counter gear transfers torque to the third speed gear. The speed gear drives the output shaft through the 3–4 synchronizer hub splines. Torque flows through the transmission in gear reduction at the third gear ratio.

FOURTH GEAR. In fourth gear, the shift linkage moves the 3–4 synchronizer sleeve forward, away from the third speed gear and toward the input shaft drive gear. ● **SEE FIGURE 6–16.**

The synchronizer assembly locks the input shaft drive gear to the output shaft. With the clutch engaged, the input shaft drives the output shaft through the 3–4 synchronizer hub splines and both shafts rotate at crankshaft speed. Torque flows straight through the transmission at a 1:1 ratio, delivering engine torque to the drive shaft. This is called *direct drive* because there is no gear reduction through the transmission. The counter gears also turn because they are in constant mesh, but they do not affect torque flow because all of the speed gears are freewheeling on the output shaft.

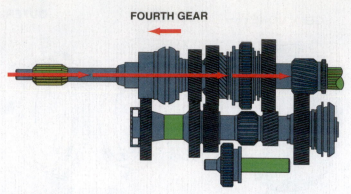

FOURTH GEAR

FIGURE 6–16 In fourth gear, the 3–4 synchronizer sleeve is moved forward, which locks the fourth speed gear to the output shaft.

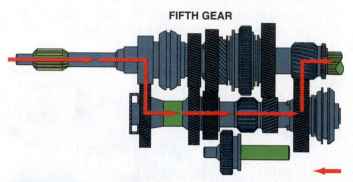

FIFTH GEAR

FIGURE 6–17 To achieve fifth gear, the shift linkage first centers the 3–4 synchronizer sleeve and then moves the fifth synchronizer sleeve toward the fifth speed gear, locking it to the output shaft.

FIFTH GEAR. In fifth gear, the shift linkage centers the 3–4 synchronizer sleeve and moves the fifth synchronizer sleeve toward the fifth speed gear. ● **SEE FIGURE 6–17.**

Note that on the T5 transmission the synchronizer assembly locks the fifth speed gear to the countershaft. The speed gear drives a fixed gear on the output shaft. With the clutch engaged, the input shaft drives the countershaft. The fifth synchronizer hub is splined to the countershaft, so it is driven and driving the fifth speed gear when fifth gear is engaged. This transfers engine torque to the output shaft through the fixed fifth gear. Note the countershaft gear is larger than the output shaft gear. Therefore, fifth gear is overdriven. Torque flows through the transmission at the fifth gear, or overdrive, ratio. Typical overdrive gear ratios are between 0.6:1 and 0.8:1. This lowers engine speed for economical highway cruising.

On some five-speed transmissions, the fifth speed gear is on the output shaft with the other speed gears. This type of arrangement is typically used with constant-mesh reverse gears. In these designs, fifth and reverse gears share a synchronizer assembly. The fixed countershaft gear drives the speed gear, which drives the output shaft through the

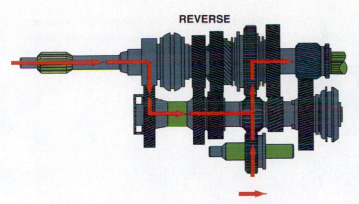

REVERSE

FIGURE 6–18 Torque flows through the transmission in reverse gear. Note that the idler gear drives the 1–2 synchronizer sleeve gear, which is splined to the output shaft.

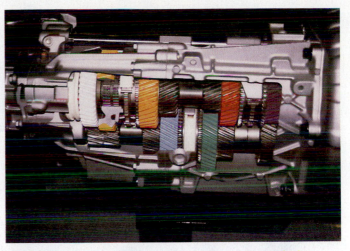

FIGURE 6–19 Cutaway of a T56 six-speed transmission showing all of its internal parts.

hub splines when the sliding sleeve is engaged. Torque flow through the transmission is similar to any of the gear reduction forward speeds but the fifth speed gear is generally overdriven.

REVERSE. There are two common reverse gear designs used on transmissions:

1. Sliding gear.
2. Constant-mesh gear.

With a sliding reverse gear design, such as on the Borg-Warner T5, the shift linkage slides the reverse idler gear on its shaft until it engages the reverse gears on the countershaft and output shaft gear. Both gears are fixed to their respective shafts. This design uses spur gears for reverse, not helical gears, because the gear teeth must move into and out of mesh. On some gearboxes, the sliding gear splines to the output shaft. The linkage moves the gear along the output shaft splines to engage the reverse idler gear. An unusual feature of the Borg-Warner T5 is that it does not have a separate reverse output shaft gear. ● **SEE FIGURE 6–18.**

Instead, spur teeth machined around the outside of the 1–2 synchronizer sleeve act as the reverse output gear. When the T5 is shifted into reverse, the linkage moves the reverse idler gear rearward so it simultaneously meshes with the countershaft reverse gear and the gear on the synchronizer sleeve. When the clutch is engaged, the countershaft is driven and the reverse gear drives the idler gear, which rotates in the opposite direction of the countershaft. The idler gear drives the 1–2 synchronizer sleeve, so there is another directional change in rotation. Although the sleeve is not engaged to a speed gear, it remains splined to the output shaft, so the sleeve drives the output shaft when the idler gear is engaged. The output shaft rotates in the opposite direction of the input shaft because the idler gear is between them. With constant-mesh gears, the shift linkage moves the 5-reverse synchronizer sleeve away from the fifth speed gear and toward the reverse speed gear when reverse is selected.

Typically, no stop ring is used between the synchronizer sleeve and the reverse gear, so the output shaft must be stopped to engage reverse without grinding the sleeve splines against the coupling teeth of the reverse gear. The synchronizer assembly locks the reverse speed gear to the output shaft.

With the clutch engaged, the input shaft drives the countershaft. The reverse counter gear drives the reverse idler gear, which drives the reverse speed gear in the direction opposite normal rotation. The reverse speed gear drives the output shaft through the 5-reverse synchronizer hub splines. Torque flows through the transmission in gear reduction at the reverse gear ratio. The output shaft turns opposite its normal direction of rotation, so the vehicle moves to the rear.

SIX-SPEED TRANSMISSIONS A six-speed transmission requires one more gear on the cluster, an additional speed gear, and one-half of a synchronizer assembly. This increases the weight, length, and cost of the unit. The additional gear is usually another overdrive ratio. Some six-speeds have low and high gear ratios similar to those of a five-speed, with the ratios closer together. ● **SEE FIGURE 6–19.**

SHIFT MECHANISMS

PURPOSE AND FUNCTION The purpose and function of shift mechanisms is to transfer the action of the driver to the shifting forks inside the transmission or transaxle.

SHIFTER OPERATION As the gearshift lever moves, the shifter mechanism moves one or two synchronizer sleeves or gears to engage the desired gear speed. The standard

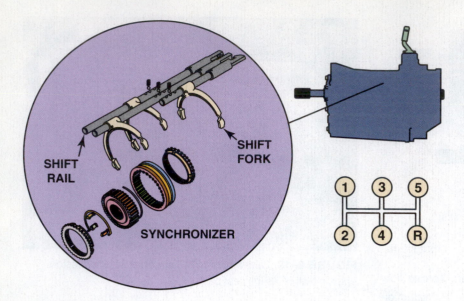

FIGURE 6–20 When the gearshift lever is moved, the internal linkage (shift rails) moves the shift fork and synchronizer sleeve to shift gear speeds.

shift lever moves in an H pattern for a four-speed or a double H pattern for a five-speed. As the lever is moved across the H, the transmission is in neutral and a shift lever is being selected. Moving the shifter into one of the arms of the H moves a shift fork to engage a gear. ● **SEE FIGURE 6–20.**

During upshift or downshift, one synchronizer sleeve is moved to neutral before the sleeve of the desired gear is moved to engage the desired gear.

Transmissions use two basic types of linkages:

1. Internal linkage (most commonly used).

2. External linkage, where the shift motion is transmitted from the shift lever to the transmission by a group of two or three metal rods mount on the side of the transmission.

INTERLOCK
A shift mechanism must include two features:

1. An interlock system

2. A series of detents

Some transmissions also include a reverse lockout. The interlock prevents engagement of more than one gear at a time. It is impossible for the transmission to transmit power through two different ratios and have two different output shaft speeds at the same time. If two gears are engaged, the transmission will lock up, and both the input and output shafts will become stationary.

SHIFT FORKS
As a shift of gears is made, the action of the detents can be felt as they engage and disengage the shift rails or cams. The synchronizer sleeve is moved by a **shift fork** that is mounted on either a rail or a cam. A rail is a metal rod that slides lengthwise. A cam usually pivots on its shaft, which extends out the side of the case or side cover. Since it must contact and move the spinning synchronizer sleeve,

the contact surfaces of the fork are made of hardened steel, bronze, or a low-friction plastic/nylon pad attached to the fork. After the sleeve/gear has been positioned, there should be little contact between the fork and the sleeve/gear. At this time, the fork is located by the detent. The sleeve is located by the synchronizer keys when in neutral and by the dog clutch teeth on the mating gear when it is shifted. The detents, shift rails, and forks are not designed to hold the gear or sleeve into mesh, only to position it completely into mesh. The cut of the sleeve or gear is what actually keeps it into mesh during the different driving situations. Holding a gear into mesh with the fork will cause rather rapid wear of the fork and fork groove.

The detents are used to locate the internal shift forks in one of their three positions—neutral plus a gear to each side. A **detent** is usually a spring-loaded ball or bullet-shaped rod that is pushed into one of a series of three notches or a spring-loaded lever with three notches that drop over a cam. ● **SEE FIGURE 6–21.**

REVERSE LOCKOUT
A reverse lockout mechanism is used to prevent accidental engagement of reverse while making an upshift. This mechanism requires the driver to perform an additional operation to shift into reverse. This might require that the shift lever be pushed downward or lifted up, or there may be an additional lever or button to be pushed. Some transmissions use a stronger shift lever centering spring so it takes extra effort to move the shifter to select the reverse shift rail. ● **SEE FIGURE 6–22.**

Some six-speed transmissions include a reverse lockout to prevent shifting into reverse gear while the vehicle is moving forward. The six-speed shift pattern along with a synchronized reverse gear make a shift into reverse quite possible,

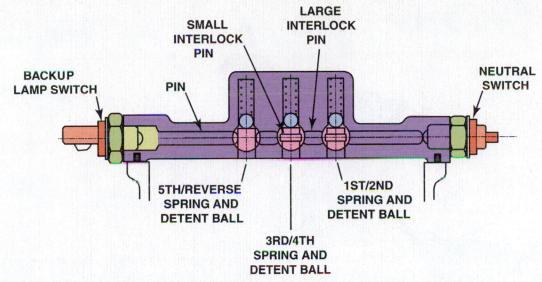

FIGURE 6–21 The internal shift mechanism includes the shift detents and the interlock to keep the shifter from selecting two gear ratios at the same time.

FIGURE 6–22 Getting into reverse requires extra effort to overcome a strong centering spring.

and powertrain damage could easily occur. This mechanism uses an electric solenoid that is electronically controlled by the Powertrain Control Module (PCM).

MANUAL TRANSMISSION GEARS

TYPES USED   All forward gears in a transmission are helical gears with spur gears sometimes used for reverse. When driving in reverse, a whine or light growl from transmissions that use spur gears can often be heard. Spur gears are used for reverse because they are

? **FREQUENTLY ASKED QUESTION**

What Is a Remote Shifter?

Some rear-wheel-drive manual transmissions such as the Getrag MT-82 used in newer Ford Mustangs use a remote-type shifter. ● **SEE FIGURE 6–23.**

The use of a remote shifter allows the shifter to be placed in the same location as other types of manual transmissions such as the Tremec TR-6060 (lower unit) used in the Shelby Mustang. Using a remote shifter allows the engineers to isolate road noise for a quieter cabin but at the expense of the direct feel that an internal shifter can provide.

- Less expensive
- Will easily shift into mesh
- Do not generate end thrust under load

The end thrust created by a helical gear requires a thrust surface on the side of the gear that is loaded. This is especially true at the side loaded during forward motion. During deceleration, the thrust direction will reverse, and a helical gear will thrust in the opposite direction. Gear side or end float should be limited to reduce noise or possible damage, especially in the gears used at cruising speeds where throttle change is normal.

A helical gear can also be made with the helix cut at different angles. As the angle is increased, the gear will run more quietly, but end thrust will increase. Some modern five-speeds use fine-pitched gears with a greater helix angle for the fifth

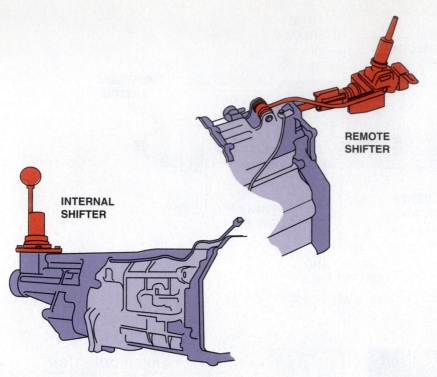

INTERNAL
SHIFTER

REMOTE
SHIFTER

FIGURE 6–23 A remote shifter (upper unit) is used to locate the shifter inside the vehicle in the same location of another type used in a similar vehicle.

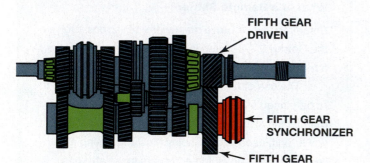

FIFTH GEAR
DRIVEN

FIFTH GEAR
SYNCHRONIZER

FIFTH GEAR
DRIVING

FIGURE 6–24 Notice the gear teeth in this transmission that those on the fifth gears have a finer pitch and a greater helix angle, to produce quieter operation while cruising.

gear. This produces quiet operation at cruising speeds where low torque loading is encountered. ● SEE FIGURE 6–24.

MAIN SHAFT Close inspection of a main shaft reveals specific areas that serve specific purposes. For example, the positioning of the snap ring grooves is very exacting to locate parts in precise locations. The snap rings may be available in different widths to adjust thrust clearance/gear end play. The main shaft itself is located by the rear bearing, bearing surface, and retaining ring. Each synchronizer assembly has a set of splines so that torque can transfer to the shaft. Each gear location has a bearing surface, or journal, which often has a special provision for lubricating the floating speed gear. A main shaft will have a surface for the pilot bearing to the main drive gear at the front and the splines to match the U-joint splines at

the rear. Close to the rear of the shaft, there will be provision for mounting a speedometer drive gear or vehicle speed sensor (VSS) or the worm teeth for the speedometer drive gear will be cut into the shaft.

COUNTERSHAFT AND CLUSTER GEAR The cluster gear is supported by the rod-like countershaft with a set of needle bearings at each end in older transmissions. The countershaft has a press fit into the case. Units with high torque loading use a double set of needle bearings at each end to support the cluster gear. A thrust washer is used between the gear and the case at each end to control end thrust. The thrust washer or a wear plate is keyed into the case so that it will not spin and wear into the case.

The fit between the countershaft and the case is tight enough to prevent lubricant leaks. At one end of the shaft there is normally a locating device to prevent shaft rotation.

Some newer transmissions support the countershaft assembly, which includes the cluster gear, with a pair of tapered roller bearings. Tapered bearing design is capable of absorbing thrust loads along with the normal side loads. Tapered roller bearings are normally adjusted during installation to obtain free running with a very slight clearance.

Most cluster gears are one-piece units, and if one of the gears is damaged, the entire unit must be replaced. The cluster gear used in the Tremec TR-3550 transmission is a three-piece unit ● SEE FIGURE 6–25.

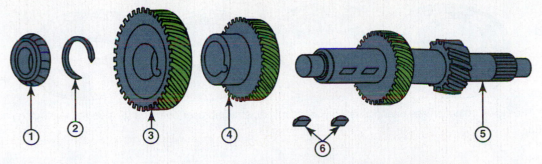

FIGURE 6–25 Two gears, (3) and (4), are press fit onto the cluster gear in a TR-3550 transmission.

The two gears at the front of the cluster gear have a press fit onto the main cluster gear. Woodruff keys help the assembly transfer torque. Another unusual cluster gear is used in the six-speed, T56 transmission. The cluster gear/countershaft fits in the main case and has the gears needed for first through fourth. A countershaft extension drives fifth, sixth, and reverse, and it fits in the extension housing. The back of the cluster gear and the front of the extension have matching splines to transfer torque.

TRANSMISSION CASE AND BEARINGS

TRANSMISSION CASE The main case and extension housing are usually made from aluminum castings, whereas older transmissions use cast iron cases. Most cases have openings for access to the gear train. The term *open case* is sometimes used for a case in which the side or top cover is removable and includes the shifting forks and other mechanisms. ● SEE FIGURE 6–26.

A cover that includes the shift mechanism is normally located by dowel pins so that the shift motions do not cause movement of the cover, which could cause incomplete gear engagement. Closed case refers to a case that might have access openings, but the shift mechanism is located entirely within the case. In a split case design, the case has two halves that are bolted together. Many five- and six-speed transmissions use a *center plate* design. The center plate has bearings that support the main shaft and cluster gear.

BEARINGS Transmissions use a variety of bearings, depending on the particular design. The types used can include the following:

- Needle bearings
- Ball bearings

FIGURE 6–26 A Borg-Warner T5 five-speed transmission shown with the shifter cover removed.

- Tapered roller bearings
- Bushings

● SEE FIGURE 6–27.

- Needle bearings, either caged or free, can carry large side loads but are unable to control end thrust loads. Free needle bearings are used to support the cluster gear in older transmissions. The speed gears in many transmissions are mounted over caged needle bearings.

- Ball bearings can carry moderate to high side loads and thrust loads. Therefore they are commonly used for the main drive gear and main shaft. A "maxi" version of the ball bearing can carry even greater side loads. A maxi bearing can be identified by the increased number of balls as well as loading notches at one side of the inner and outer races.

- Tapered roller bearings can carry large side and thrust loads and are generally used in pairs with the cones and cups facing in opposite directions. This bearing is normally installed with a method (usually shims) for adjusting end play or, in a few cases, preload. In some

FIGURE 6–27 The types of frictionless bearings are ball bearings (a), straight roller bearings (b), needle bearings (c) and tapered roller bearings (d).

transmissions, tapered roller bearings are used to support the main drive gear, the main shaft, and the countershaft.

- A bushing is used to support the driveshaft slip yoke in the extension housing. A bushing can support a large side load and allows free in-and-out movement.

MANUAL TRANSMISSION LUBRICATION

PURPOSE AND FUNCTION Manual transmissions, transfer cases, and drive axles must be lubricated to reduce heat and friction. Lubricants can be either refined petroleum or synthetic products. The job of the lubricant includes:

- Reduce friction
- Transfer heat away from the gears and bearings
- Reduce corrosion and rust
- Flush dirt and wear particles away from the moving parts

Two rating systems are used to select the proper lubricant:

1. Society of Automotive Engineers (SAE) viscosity rating
2. American Petroleum Institute (API) Service Classification

VISCOSITY **Viscosity** is a measurement of fluid thickness. Viscosity is determined by observing how fast the fluid runs through a precisely sized orifice at a particular temperature. All oils are thicker and flow slower when cold and thinner and flow faster when hot. The *viscosity index (VI)* is an indication of the flow difference between hot and cold. Viscosity index numbers are low, such as 80, if the lubricant is not able to maintain a consistent viscosity and high, such as 150, if the lubricant has a more stable viscosity throughout a wide temperature range.

- In a gearbox, a lubricant that is too thick will deliver poor lubrication when cold because the thick fluid will not flow

into smaller areas. Too-thick gear oil might channel which means that it flows in a rope-like pattern. It also increases drag between parts so they do not turn as easily, and shift collars will not slide as easily. Synchronizer cones will not work very well because they cannot break through the thick oil film. This can cause hard shifting until the fluid warms.

- A too-thin lubricant will not provide the lubricating film under hot conditions. Thin fluids also cause more gear noise. The viscosity numbers used for gear oils are higher than those for engine oils, but the actual viscosity is similar. ● **SEE FIGURE 6–28.**

GEAR OIL CLASSIFICATIONS The API gear oil classifications are as follows:

GL-1 Straight mineral oil and not suitable for current passenger car transmissions.

GL-2 A designation for worm gear drives used mostly in industrial applications.

GL-3 Contains mild extreme pressure (EP) additives and specified for use in manual transmissions and transaxles with spiral bevel final drives.

GL-4 Formulated for use in manual transmissions and transaxles with hypoid final drives and contains about half the additives used in GL-5.

GL-5 Enough EP additive to lubricate hypoid gears in drive axles.

GL-6 An obsolete designation.

An additional classification, GLS (Gear Lubricant Special), is sometimes used to indicate a proprietary set of specifications determined by the vehicle or gearbox manufacturer. **Manual transmission fluid (MTF)** usually is in this category. An MTF might contain a friction modifier to give proper synchronizer action and long life. ● **SEE FIGURE 6–29.**

SYNTHETIC LUBRICANTS Synthetic lubricants usually have a much higher viscosity index (VI) than conventional lubricants, which means that the viscosity stays more stable with temperature changes. Stable viscosity provides better

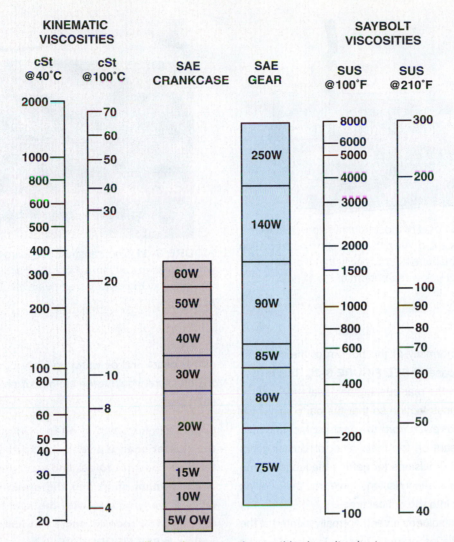

FIGURE 6–28 Gear oil and crankcase (engine oil) are shown together on this viscosity chart.

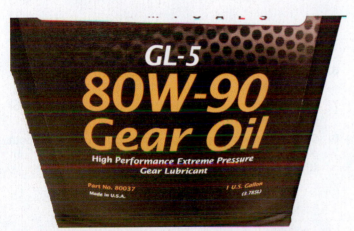

GL-5
80W-90
Gear Oil
High Performance Extreme Pressure
Gear Lubricant

Part No. 80037   1 U.S. Gallon
Made in U.S.A.   (3.785L)

FIGURE 6–29 When selecting the specified lubricant to be used in a manual transmission, always check that the viscosity and the rating match factory specifications.

lubrication and this allows more efficiency, less cold-operation drag, and better high-temperature lubrication. A synthetic lubricant also offers better resistance to oxidation, so the fluid will normally have a longer life span.

LUBRICATION INSIDE THE TRANSMISSION The transmission cluster gears run in a bath of lubricant, and as they spin, their motion will throw the lubricant throughout the case. The lubricant can be any of the following depending on vehicle manufacturer, model, and year:

- Gear oil such as SAE 80W-90
- Engine oil such as SAE 5W-30
- ATF such as Dexron III/VI
- Manual transmission fluid

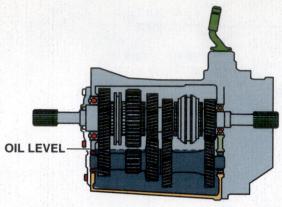

FIGURE 6–30 The fluid level of most transmissions is at the bottom of the fill plug opening. Always check service information because some vehicle manufacturers specify that the correct full level is one inch (25 mm) below the bottom of the fill hole.

FIGURE 6–31 The transmission gears rotating in the case is what forces the oil throughout the transmission as shown in this cutaway that is powered by an electric motor to show the action.

The fluid level is normally at the bottom of the check/fill plug in the side of the case. ● **SEE FIGURE 6–30.** This is usually at a level just below the rear bushing and seal.

The lubricant reduces friction so that the parts spin more easily and transfers heat away from the gear contact and rubbing parts. Floating gears on the main shaft or cluster gears have special paths and provisions for getting the lubricant into their bearings, and some transmissions have troughs or oiling funnels to get lubricant into the critical areas.

Each transmission includes a vent, normally located at the top of the case. This relieves internal pressure that would occur as the gears and oil warm up while operating. If not relieved, the pressure would force the oil out past the input and output shaft seals.

CAUTION: A transmission is lubricated by oil thrown off the cluster gear. If a vehicle is towed in neutral, the cluster gear does not rotate and wear can occur between the rotating main shaft and the stationary gears that float on it. A transmission with the synchronizer on the cluster gear will receive some lubrication through its gear action. ● SEE FIGURE 6–31.

SUMMARY

1. Transmissions provide gear sets for forward speeds and reverse as well as neutral.
2. Transmissions normally have four shafts: cluster gear (countershaft), input shaft, output shaft and reverse idler shaft.
3. Synchronizer assemblies normally have a hub, sleeve, a set of keys, two blocker rings, and a speed gear on each side.
4. Early blocker rings were a single, brass ring, whereas newer blocker rings are double, paper-lined rings.
5. Transmissions torque capacity is determined by the size of the gears and shafts.
6. Transmissions shifts use external or internal linkages that include detents, interlocks, and shift forks.
7. Transmissions are lubricated with gear oil, engine oil, or manual transmission fluid (MTF).
8. Special transmission design features include gear tooth pitch and helix angle, cluster gear variations, case construction, and bearing type.

REVIEW QUESTIONS

1. What are the two types of gear sets used in standard transmissions?
2. Synchronizer assembly includes what parts?
3. How does a synchronizer work?
4. What does a detent do?

1. The input and output shafts of a rear-wheel-drive transmission are called _____ and _____.
   a. Input and output
   b. countershaft and main shaft
   c. Clutch shaft and main shaft
   d. Both a and c are correct

2. What is designed into a transmission so that it can handle more engine torque?
   a. Longer length
   b. Input and output shafts are larger
   c. The case is made from cast steel
   d. Needle bearings are used in all locations

3. Which gear is most likely to use a spur gear?
   a. First
   b. Second
   c. Fourth
   d. Reverse

4. To achieve a clash-free (no grinding sound) shift, what is used in a manual transmission?
   a. Large diameter gears
   b. Synchronizers
   c. Roller bearings
   d. Internal shift linkage

5. A _____ is used to prevent accidental engagement of reverse while making an upshift.
   a. Reverse lockout
   b. Internal shift linkage
   c. External shift linkage
   d. Detent

6. Most manual transmissions use a case made from _____.
   a. Cast steel
   b. Cast aluminum
   c. Pressed steel
   d. Cast iron

7. The idler gear is used for which gear?
   a. First gear
   b. Second gear
   c. Third gear
   d. Reverse

8. The types of bearing used in a manual transmission is _____
   a. Needle bearing
   b. Ball bearing
   c. Tapered roller bearing
   d. Any of the above

9. The lubricant used in a manual transmission is _____
   a. Gear oil
   b. ATF
   c. Manual transmission fluid
   d. Any of the above depending on the make and model of vehicle

10. The detent mechanism inside a transmission is used to _____.
    a. Locate the synchronizer sleeves in the correct position
    b. Prevent more than one shift fork from moving at one time
    c. Hold a gear into mesh
    d. All of these

MANUAL TRANSAXLE PARTS AND OPERATION

(a)

(b)

FIGURE 7–1 (a) The Cord was one of the first front-wheel-drive vehicles. (b) The Cord did not use a transaxle but instead drove the front wheels through a transmission and drive axle through constant velocity (CV) joints.

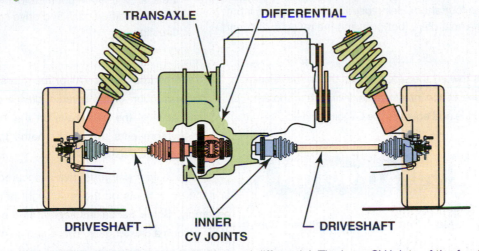

FIGURE 7–2 A transaxle is a transmission plus the final drive and differential. The inner CV joints of the front drive shafts connect to the side gears in the transaxle differential.

PURPOSE AND FUNCTION

BACKGROUND The development of the transaxle has, in part, made the modern, fuel-saving front-wheel-drive (FWD) vehicle possible. Early FWD vehicles included the American Cord of the 1930s ● **SEE FIGURE 7–1**.

A large majority of the vehicles sold today are front-wheel drive. The engine and transaxle are either transverse or longitudinally mounted.

- A **transverse engine** points across the vehicle also called *East-West* positioning.

- A **longitudinal engine** is commonly used in rear-wheel-drive vehicles and is often called *North-South* positioning.

Many features of the transmission part of a transaxle are similar to those of an rear-wheel-drive transmission. There

are differences, however, in the number of shafts and the power flow. There is also the addition of the final drive gears and the differential.

TRANSAXLES DESIGNS Most front-wheel-drive vehicles have transverse-mounted engines, and the engine-transmission package must fit in the vehicle between the suspension components. Many transaxles have the differential mounted off center which results in unequal-length drive shafts.
● **SEE FIGURE 7–2**.

Unequal-length drive shafts can cause the vehicle to pull to one side during acceleration, which is called **torque steer**. Torque steer is caused by

- Unequal CV joint angles
- Unequal length of the shafts
- The tendency for the longer drive shaft to twist

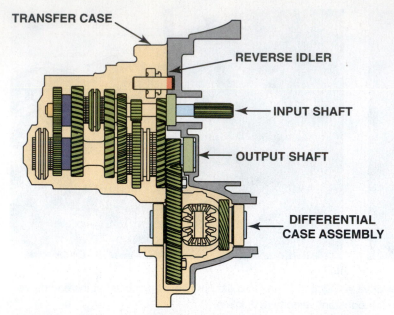

FIGURE 7–3 Note the four shafts being used in this transaxle; input shaft, output shaft, the final drive (bottom), and the reverse idle gear (top).

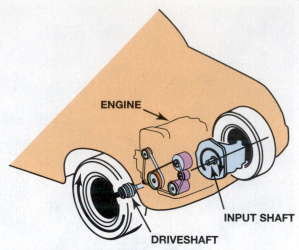

FIGURE 7–4 The engine and the transaxle input shaft rotate in a clockwise direction in most FWD vehicles (viewed from the right side). The intermediate shaft will rotate counterclockwise and drive the ring gear, differential, and drive shafts in a clockwise direction.

The vehicle turns toward the side that has the longer driveshaft. Some vehicles use a short intermediate driveshaft to shorten the length of the long axle and equalize the CV joint angles.

TRANSAXLE CONSTRUCTION

PARTS INVOLVED Most transaxles are made with four parallel shafts:

1. **Input shaft**—The input shaft is sometimes called the **clutch shaft** because it is splined to the clutch disc. The driving gears are positioned on the input shaft, and there is one for each forward speed.

2. **Main shaft**—The main shaft, also called a **countershaft** or an **intermediate shaft,** also includes a gear for each forward speed and these are the driven gears. The main shaft also includes the **drive pinion gear**. The drive pinion gear is the transmission output and the input for the final drive.

3. **Final drive ring gear**—The final drive ring gear is mounted on the differential case. The **differential** divides the power flow between the two CV joints coupled to the drive shafts and on to the wheels. The differential **pinion gears** and side (axle) gears in the differential allow for speed differences when the vehicle turns a corner. This gear arrangement also splits the power from a single source to two sources with, typically, 50/50 torque distribution.

4. **Reverse idler shaft**—All of the gears in a transaxle, with the exception of the reverse idler, are in constant mesh, and each of the gear pairs on the input shaft and main shaft represents the power paths for a particular gear ratio. ● SEE FIGURE 7–3.

At each gear pair, one gear is secured solidly to the shaft and the other floats on the shaft, right next to a synchronizer assembly. Some transaxles secure all the gears on the input shaft to form a cluster gear. These can be either a single cluster gear or a group of gears pressed onto a splined shaft. Other designs float all or some of the driving gears on the input shaft and secure the driven gears onto the main shaft.

Most engines rotate in a clockwise direction (viewing the drive rotation from the right, or passenger, side of the vehicle). The input shaft rotates clockwise, the main shaft rotates counterclockwise in forward gears, and the differential rotates clockwise to drive the wheels in a clockwise direction. ● SEE FIGURE 7–4.

TRANSAXLE OPERATION

POWER FLOW The power flow through the transmission section of a transaxle is essentially the same in all the forward gears. The power (torque) passes

- From the driving gear on the input shaft
- To the driven gear on the main shaft and then

- Through the synchronizer assembly to the main shaft itself

- The power leaves the transaxle main shaft through the drive pinion, which drives the final drive ring gear

Because the power passes through only one set of gears, the ratio for that gear speed is determined by that pair of gears. The smallest gear on the input shaft drives the largest gear on the main shaft for first gear, and the largest gear on the input shaft drives the smallest gear on the main shaft for highest gear. For example, the power flow through a commonly used five-speed transaxle is shown in ● FIGURE 7–5.

GEAR RATIOS The synchronizers are the same as those used in a rear-wheel-drive transmission and their parts and operation are identical.

The power flow for reverse gear is also similar to that of a rear-wheel-drive transmission. In most cases, the reverse idler is shifted into mesh with the reverse gear on the input shaft and the sleeve of the 1–2 synchronizer assembly, which has the spur gear teeth for reverse on the outer diameter. The idler gear will rotate in a counterclockwise direction viewed from the right side, the 1–2 synchronizer assembly will rotate clockwise, and the differential and drive wheels will rotate counterclockwise to drive the vehicle backward. ● SEE FIGURE 7–6.

FINAL DRIVE AND DIFFERENTIAL The power leaves the transaxle main shaft through the drive pinion, which drives the final drive ring gear. The drive pinion and ring gear are a pair of helical gears. This gear set operates rather quietly and does not require critical adjustments like a hypoid gear set. ● SEE FIGURE 7–7.

LONGITUDINAL TRANSAXLES A few front-wheel-drive vehicle manufacturers place the engine longitudinally (lengthwise) rather than placing transversally. This requires a major change in the transaxle. In these units, the power must turn 90° to align with the front drive. Some units use a hypoid gear set that mounts the drive pinion above or below the center of the ring gear. This gear set turns the power flow as it produces the necessary final drive reduction. The power flow from the ring gear through the differential to the CV joints is the same as described previously.

Hypoid gears require adjustments for proper ring and pinion gear positioning during assembly procedures. This transaxle lends itself to AWD or 4WD because of the longitudinal position of the main shaft. It is a fairly simple matter for the manufacturer to install a clutch at the rear end of the main shaft and extend an output shaft to connect to a driveshaft for the rear wheels. ● SEE FIGURE 7–8.

TRANSAXLE GEARS Like manual transmissions, manual transaxles use helical gears for all the forward speeds

and spur gears for reverse. To allow for engine length in the cramped width of the engine compartment, the speed gears, synchronizer assemblies, and bearings are kept as narrow and compact as practical. This design factor is much more critical with transaxles than with transmissions.

TRANSAXLE BEARINGS The bearing surfaces on many transaxles are made with lubrication slots to compensate for the reduced gear width, whereas on other units the speed gears are mounted on roller or needle bearings. These features also improve the efficiency of the transaxle and fuel economy. Some transaxles use a roller bearing at the engine end of the input shaft and main shaft and a ball bearing at the other end of the shaft.

The ball bearing supports one end and also positions the shaft to the case as the roller bearing supports the end with the greater side loading from the final drive. This feature makes for easy servicing, as the roller bearing can slide through the openings when the cover is removed or installed.

On transaxles that use tapered roller bearings, bearing clearance or preload is adjusted by selecting the correct size of shim to place at the bearing or bearing cup. The *selective shim* is positioned under the bearing cup in the case. A selective shim means that there are several different thickness shims available that can be inserted behind the bearing to provide the specified bearing preload. In loaded areas where shaft movement can create a problem, the bearings are adjusted to a slight preload. ● SEE FIGURE 7–9.

TRANSAXLE CASE DESIGN Transaxle cases are made from cast aluminum. Many cases use a two-part assembly with a right-hand case or cover that also forms the clutch housing and a left-hand or main case that contains the gears. Some units have a separate side case or side cover that encloses the fifth gear set and the synchronizer or just the left-side bearings. Some units have a bottom or differential cover that provides access to the differential assembly.

SPLASH LUBRICATION Like transmissions, transaxles use a supply of oil in the sump at the bottom of the case that is circulated by gear rotation. This type of lubrication is called *splash lubrication*. The oil is directed to critical areas by troughs and oiling funnels. The fluid level is normally checked at a fill-level plug or with a dipstick.

- Most transaxles have a common case, so the transmission and final drive share the same lubricant.

- Some units separate the two and different oils may be used for each gear set, and there will be two fluid-level plugs.

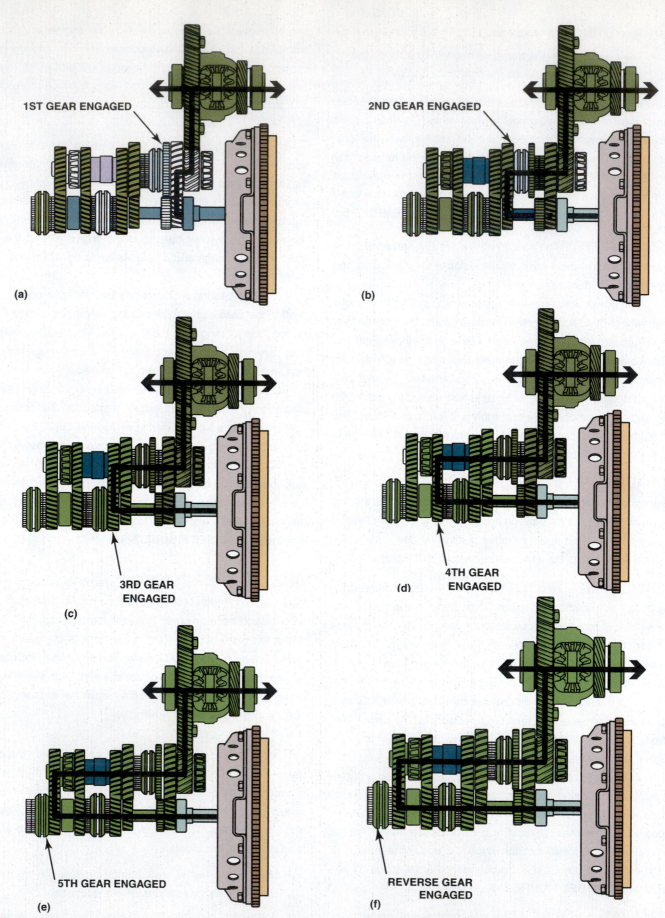

FIGURE 7–5 (a) First gear power flow through a Mitsubishi KM M5AF3 five-speed transaxle. (b) Second gear. (c) Third gear. (d) Fourth gear. (e) Fifth gear. (f) Reverse.

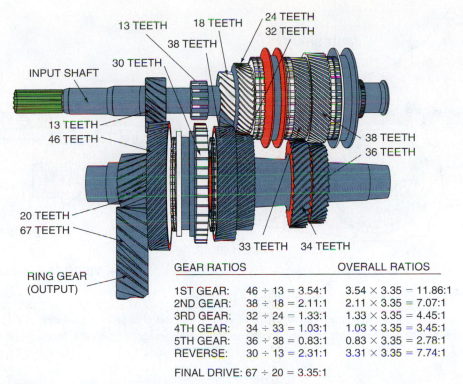

13 TEETH	18 TEETH	24 TEETH
		32 TEETH

INPUT SHAFT
38 TEETH
30 TEETH
13 TEETH
46 TEETH
38 TEETH
36 TEETH
20 TEETH
67 TEETH
33 TEETH   34 TEETH
RING GEAR
(OUTPUT)

GEAR RATIOS			OVERALL RATIOS
1ST GEAR:	46 ÷ 13 = 3.54:1		3.54 × 3.35 — 11.86:1
2ND GEAR:	38 ÷ 18 = 2.11:1		2.11 × 3.35 = 7.07:1
3RD GEAR:	32 ÷ 24 = 1.33:1		1.33 × 3.35 = 4.45:1
4TH GEAR:	34 ÷ 33 = 1.03:1		1.03 × 3.35 = 3.45:1
5TH GEAR:	36 ÷ 38 = 0.83:1		0.83 × 3.35 = 2.78:1
REVERSE:	30 ÷ 13 = 2.31:1		3.31 × 3.35 = 7.74:1

FINAL DRIVE: 67 ÷ 20 = 3.35:1

FIGURE 7–6 The gear ratios of a transaxle are determined by dividing the tooth count of the driven gear by that of the driving gear. Multiplying the transaxle gear ratio by the final drive ratio gives us the overall ratio.

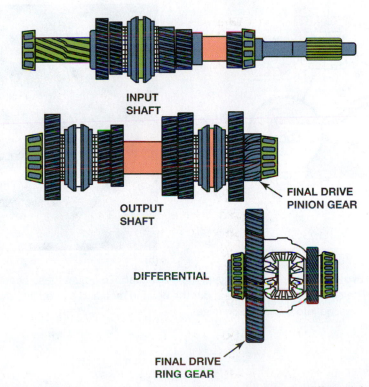

INPUT
SHAFT

OUTPUT
SHAFT

FINAL DRIVE
PINION GEAR

DIFFERENTIAL

FINAL DRIVE
RING GEAR

FIGURE 7–7 The final drive pinion gear drives the ring gear, which is mounted on the differential case.

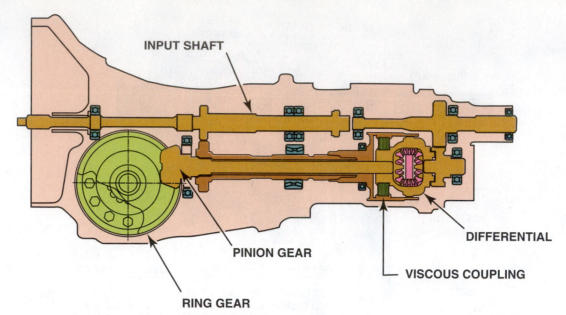

FIGURE 7–8 This Subaru transaxle is used with an engine that is mounted lengthwise in the vehicle. Note how the final drive is through a ring and pinion gear set. Also note the center differential and extension to drive the rear wheels of an all-wheel-drive vehicle.

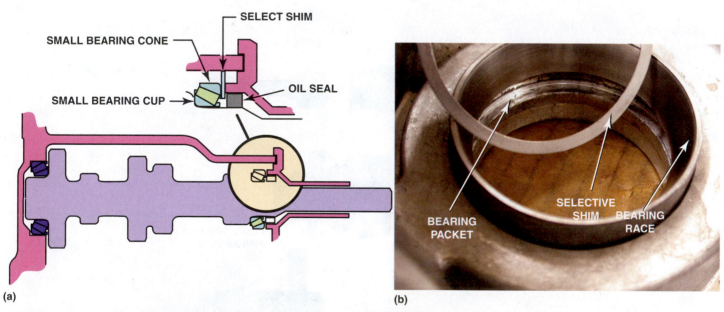

(a)

(b)

FIGURE 7–9 (a) This transaxle uses tapered roller bearings at the input shaft. To adjust these bearings, the selective shim is located at each bearing set. (b) The selective shim is used under the bearing race and placed into the bearing pocket (bearing counter-bore) before the race is pressed into the transaxle case.

SUMMARY

1. Transaxles combine a transmission with the final drive gear set and differential.

2. Some transaxles are mounted in a longitudinal position and use a hypoid final drive gear set.

3. Transaxles use helical cut gears except for reverse where straight cut spur gears are often used.

REVIEW QUESTIONS

1. What is the major difference between a rear-wheel-drive manual transmission and a front-wheel-drive manual transaxle?

2. The final drive gears of a typical transaxle use what type of gears?

3. What type of transaxle bearing requires selective shims to provide the proper preload?

CHAPTER QUIZ

1. An early front-wheel vehicle was a _____.
   a. Cord
   b. Ford Model T
   c. Cadillac
   d. Mercedes

2. The inboard CV joints on the driveshaft are splined to the _____.
   a. Differential pinion gears
   b. Differential case
   c. Differential side gears
   d. Output shaft

3. The main shaft is also called the _____.
   a. Counter shaft
   b. Intermediate shaft
   c. Clutch shaft
   d. Either a or b

4. Most transaxles use _____
   a. Spur gears except for reverse, which uses helical-cut gears
   b. Helical-cut gears except for reverse, which uses spur gears
   c. Spiral bevel gears except for reverse, which uses hypoid gears
   d. Hypoid gears except reverse, which uses spiral bevel gears

5. In a transaxle, what type of bearing is used?
   a. Roller
   b. Tapered roller
   c. Ball
   d. All of the above

6. The final drive ring and pinion gears in a typical transaxle are _____ type.
   a. Hypoid gears
   b. Helical gears
   c. Spiral bevel gears.
   d. Both b and c

7. A typical transaxle has how many shafts?
   a. Four
   b. Three
   c. Two
   d. One

8. Torque steer can be caused by _____.
   a. Unequal CV joint angles
   b. Unequal length of the shafts
   c. The tendency for the longer drive shaft to twist
   d. All of the above

9. The lubrication used in most transaxles uses _____.
   a. Engine-driven an oil pump
   b. Splash lubrication
   c. Oil from the engine to lubricate the gears and bearings
   d. Any of the above depending on make and model of the vehicle

10. Transaxle cases are made from _____.
    a. Cast aluminum
    b. Pressed steel
    c. Cast iron
    d. Either a or b

chapter 8

MANUAL TRANSMISSION/ TRANSAXLE DIAGNOSIS AND SERVICE

LEARNING OBJECTIVES

After studying this chapter, the reader should be able to:

1. Prepare for the Manual Drivelines and Axles (A2) ASE certification test content area "C" (Transmission/Transaxle Diagnosis and Repair).

2. Explain how to perform transaxle/transmission maintenance operations.

3. Explain manual transaxle/transmission diagnosis.

4. Discuss the procedure for transaxle/ transmission removal and replacement.

5. Discuss the procedure for transaxle/ transmission overhaul.

KEY TERMS

Anaerobic sealants 151
Blocker ring clearance 147
Brinelling 145
Contamination 145
Dynamic shift test 138
Electric arcing 145
End play 150
Formed-in-place gaskets (FIPG) 151
Fretting 145
Lubricant checks 133

Misalignment 145
Peeling 145
Preload 150
Room-temperature vulcanizing (RTV) 151
Rust dust 136
Seizing 145
Shim 150
Spalling 145
Static shift test 137
Visual inspection 136

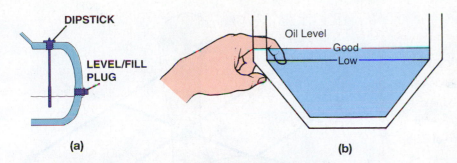

(a)

(b)

FIGURE 8-1 (a) Transaxles and transmissions use either a dipstick or level plug to check the oil level. (b) To determine the fluid level, insert a finger into the opening and feel for the fluid level. Some vehicle manufacturers specify that the fluid level be 1 inch (25 mm) below the fill plug opening.

PREVENTIVE MAINTENANCE

MAINTENANCE ITEMS In-vehicle service, also called *on-vehicle service*, in most cases is a normal maintenance operation and includes

- Periodic check of the lubricant level
- Linkage/shifter adjustment
- Mount inspection or replacement as needed
- Visual inspection for leaks and other abnormal conditions

When a problem such as hard shifting occurs, the shift linkage is also checked and readjusted, if necessary. If possible, service and repair operations are done with the transaxle/ transmission in the vehicle. Transmission removal and replacement (R&R) takes about 2.5 hours and transaxle removal and replacement may take up to 5 hours. This varies greatly depending on the vehicle and the experience of the technician, but in any case, transmission/transaxle removal and replacement is time consuming.

LUBRICANT CHECK Often, the **lubricant check** is a neglected operation. It is recommended to check the lubricant level at each engine oil change. When the fluid level is correct, most transaxle/transmissions will operate for the life of the vehicle. Gears and bearings can be damaged in just a few minutes if operated with low lubricant level. A transmission/ transaxle usually requires the vehicle be raised to gain access to the filler/level plug. The way the fluid level is checked depends on whether the unit has a dipstick (rare) or just a sight plug. Check service information for the exact procedure to follow.

- If equipped with a dipstick, remove the dipstick, wipe it clean, reinsert it making sure it goes completely into the opening, remove it again, and read both sides. The fluid level should be between the "full" and "low" marks.
- If equipped with a level plug, be sure the engine is off before removing the plug. Be prepared for a fluid spill due to a high fluid level. The fluid level should be even with

the bottom of the opening. If the fluid is not running out, carefully insert a finger into the opening to feel the level of the fluid. ● **SEE FIGURE 8–1.**

CAUTION: Always properly identify the drain/check plug as in the case of the Tremec 5-speed, a plug looks like a check plug. If this plug is removed, it will cause a shift lever to fall inside the transmission. Always check service information for the exact location of the drain and fill plugs of the vehicle being serviced.

If the fluid level is low, add the recommended fluid to bring it to the correct level. Also, check for leaks or the reason for the low fluid level. If the level is high, drain out the excess fluid.

While checking fluid level, the condition of the fluid should also be noted.

- Color and smell in case of manual transmission fluids should be like new fluid.
- Dirty fluid should be changed.
- Fluid with silver or gold metallic flakes indicates severe wear and repair is required.
- Also check that the vent for the transmission/transaxle is free and clear.

 REAL WORLD FIX

The Case of the Hard Shifting Acura

A 2006 Acura Civic (140,000 mi) came in with a hard shifting concern. A road test confirmed that the car shifted hard into every gear. There was no grinding that would indicate a clutch problem. The fluid level was good, and seemed to be SAE 5W-30 engine oil.

The technician drained, flushed, and filled the transaxle with Honda manual transmission fluid (MTF), and this fixed the hard shift problem. Always check service information to determine the specified fluid to use.

Double Check the Specified Fluid Is Being Used

Many transmissions and transaxles do *not* use SAE 80W-90 gear oil. If the wrong lubricant is used, it can soak into the composite blocker ring linings. Even if drained immediately and refilled with the correct fluid, noise or erratic shifts can result.

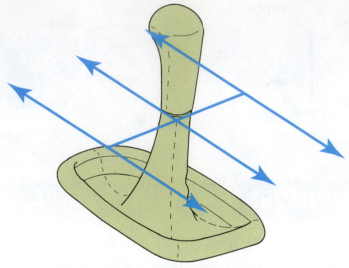

CHECK SHIFTER MOVEMENT

(a)

TRANSMISSION LUBRICANT REPLACEMENT

Some vehicle manufactures specify that the fluid be replaced at regular intervals. To change transaxle/transmission fluid, perform the following steps:

STEP 1 If possible, drive the vehicle to bring the lubricant up to operating temperature.

STEP 2 Raise and securely support the vehicle on a hoist or safety (jack) stands.

STEP 3 Check service information for the exact location of the fill and drain plugs. Then locate and loosen the fill plug to make sure that it can be removed before draining the fluid from the transmission or transaxle.

STEP 4 Locate the drain plug at the bottom of the transaxle/transmission, place a drain pan under it, and remove the drain plug.

> **NOTE: Some vehicles do not have a drain plug. The lower extension housing bolts are often drilled through to the inside of the case so these bolts can be removed to drain the case.**

STEP 5 Allow the lubricant to drain out completely before replacing the plug. Check for any steel particles on the magnetic drain plug, which could indicate serious internal problems.

STEP 6 Inspect the old lubricant for any contamination, and dispose of it in the proper manner.

STEP 7 Check the owner's manual or service information to determine the correct lubricant type and refill quantity.

STEP 8 Refill the transaxle/transmission to the correct level.

TRANSAXLE LINKAGE ADJUSTMENT

The exact method of adjusting transaxle shift linkage varies. Some have no adjustment, whereas others provide adjustments with gauging methods. Always follow the procedures found in service information for the vehicle being serviced.
● **SEE FIGURE 8–2.**

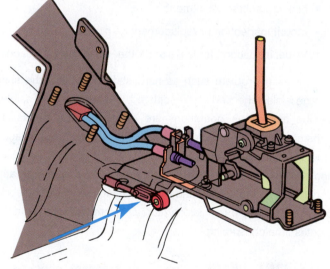

ADJUST SHIFTER LINKAGE

(b)

FIGURE 8–2 (a) Operate the shift levers through all of the gears with the engine off and again with it running. (b) If necessary, adjust the shift linkage following the vehicle manufacturer's specified procedure.

ALIGN TRANSMISSION/TRANSAXLE MOUNTS

Rear-wheel-drive transmission mounts are aligned by the mounting bolts. A front-wheel-drive transaxle must be aligned to the two front-drive shafts. The alignment check is accomplished by completely compressing both inboard CV joints and measuring the distance between the joint and the transaxle. The position of the transaxle is then adjusted so that both distances are equal. Adjustment is accomplished by loosening the mounts and sliding the engine and transaxle sideways.
● **SEE FIGURE 8–3.**

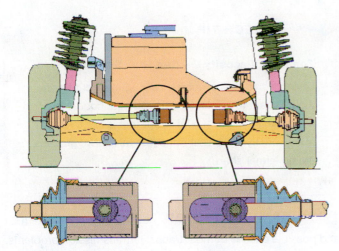

FIGURE 8–3 The enlarged views of the inner CV joints show that the engine and transaxle are misaligned; they should be moved toward the right.

MANUAL TRANSMISSION/ TRANSAXLE DIAGNOSIS

FIVE STEP DIAGNOSTIC PROCESS   The process of diagnosing manual transmission/transaxle faults or concerns involves the following eight steps:

STEP 1   Verify the customer concern by performing a road test.

STEP 2   Perform a visual inspection.

STEP 3   Follow service information and follow pinpoint tests to determine the root cause.

STEP 4   Perform the needed repair.

STEP 5   Verify the repair.

VERIFY CUSTOMER CONCERN   The first step is to verify the customer concern. The customer should be asked the following questions in an effort to determine as much about the problem as possible.

- What exactly seems to be the concern? (Ask the customer to be as detailed as possible.)
- When did the problem first appear?
- Is there a problem between forward gears and reverse?
- Under what conditions do the symptoms occur? (Do they occur first thing in the morning? After the vehicle has been driven for a while?) Describe under what driving conditions the problem is noticed, such as when accelerating or while coasting to a stop or some other condition. Has the vehicle been serviced recently, such as a fluid change?

TEST DRIVE   The vehicle should be test driven and the technician should check the following:

- The quality of the upshifts and downshifts.
- Listen for any unusual noises.
- Feel for any unusual movements or vibrations as the vehicle accelerates or decelerates in each gear.
- In cases where there is doubt about proper operation, the operation can be compared with that of a similar vehicle.

FIGURE 8–4 Check the clutch pedal for proper operation and be sure that the floor mat or carpet is not interfering with the operation of the clutch.

A typical test drive procedure includes the following operations:

- Check clutch pedal free play. ● **SEE FIGURE 8–4.**
- Warm up transmission before testing (drive aluminum case units for about 20 minutes).
- With vehicle stationary, engine idling, clutch depressed, and in neutral:
  a. Release clutch and listen for noise, depress pedal noting any noises.
  b. Release clutch, depress pedal, wait 3 seconds, and shift into reverse, then first gear, and then back to reverse. Repeat, but wait 20 seconds. Note any differences in noise or shifting ability.
  c. Shift into reverse, release pedal, and while carefully backing, increase engine speed to 2500 RPM, and note any noises.
- Drive vehicle on road with little traffic:

  a. Start in first, accelerate, and upshift at 4000 RPM (1–2, 2–3, and 3–4). Upshift 3–4 and 4–5 as possible depending on speed limits and driving conditions. Note shift quality and any noises.
  b. Decelerate using engine braking, downshifting in each gear at about 3000 RPM. Note shift quality and any noises.
  c. Drive in fourth gear at highway speed, accelerate (if speed limit allows), and shift to fifth gear.
  d. Drive in fifth gear for a moment, and downshift to fourth gear and note any problems.

Too High Viscosity Oil Can Hurt Shifting

During a shift, the synchronizer ring must cut through the lubricant to contact the speed gear cone. Hard shifts can result from a lubricant that is too thick or from worn synchronizer rings (the threadlike grooves are no longer sharp).

TYPICAL PROBLEM AREAS

● **SEE CHART 8–1** for a list and possible causes of most transaxle/transmission problems.

VISUAL INSPECTION

Hoist vehicle safely and perform a thorough **visual inspection** of the driveline including the following:

- Examine the driveshaft for damage or mud that could affect its balance.
- Examine U-joints for damage or looseness. Check for "**rust dust**," which is a reddish dust found around areas that have rusted and is a likely location where wear has occurred. ● **SEE FIGURE 8–5.**
- Examine engine and transmission mounts for damage.
- Check electrical and mechanical connections.
- Check for leaks at the transmission/transaxle.
- Clutch master cylinder fluid level or mechanical clutch linkage.
- Broken or damaged motor mounts.
- Transaxle/transmission and bell housing bolt tightness.
- Damage to the transaxle/transmission case, mounts, and support.
- Worn, bent, or sloppy shift linkage.
- Loose or missing transaxle/transmission or clutch housing mounting bolts.
- Fluid leaks from the transaxle/transmission or clutch area.

TRANSMISSION NOISE DIAGNOSIS

Manual transmission noises will vary greatly between makes and models. Some older transmission models normally were noisy, especially in reverse or first gear. The Muncie "Rock Crusher" four-speed transmission is an example where the transmission was very noisy because it used spur gears instead of the quieter helical-cut gears. The variations in noise levels are due to manufacturing variations, transmission type (heavy duty trucks are usually noisier), clutch disc damper, flywheel type, and

TRANSMISSION/ TRANSAXLE FAULT	DESCRIPTION OF FAULT	POSSIBLE CAUSE(S)
Leaks	Fluid escapes from the transaxle/ transmission	Leaking gaskets or seals
Hard shifts	Requires an abnormally high amount of force to shift into gear	Possible incorrect lubricant in the transmission and/or shifter/ linkage/shift fork problems
Shift block-out	Will not shift into one or more gears	Possible shift linkage and/or interlock concerns. Can be caused by the "shift skip" system which forces a shift to 4th instead of 2nd at lower vehicle speeds to improve fuel economy
Locked into gear	Transmission/transaxle will not shift out of a gear	Shifter/linkage/shift fork problems
Jumps out of gear	Will shift into neutral on its own	Often caused by worn synchronizer assemblies
Clash/grinding during a shift	Gear clash/grinding noise occurs as shift is made	Often caused by worn synchronizer assemblies
Noisy	A grinding, growling noise while in neutral	Worn or defective bearings
No gear at all	Sometimes the teeth are sheared and there is no gear at all (usually second gear)	Usually caused by driver abuse

CHART 8–1

Typical manual transmission/transaxles faults and some possible causes.

FIGURE 8–5 When performing a visual inspection, check for "rust dust," which is evidence of a worn components such as universal joints.

amount of vehicle noise insulation. Some transmission noises are caused by the uneven power flow pulses from the engine.

- A bearing noise problem while in neutral with the clutch disengaged is related to clutch bearing noises.
- Noises can travel. For example, the driveshaft can transmit rear drive axle noises so they seem to be coming from the transmission. A helpful diagnostic tool, called a "Chassis Ears," consists of a headset and six sensors

TECH TIP

How to Pin Down the Source of a Vibration

A noise concern that occurs with the vehicle at idle speed in neutral can be caused by harmonic vibrations. Slowly increase engine speed to about 2500 RPM. If the noise goes away, it is engine harmonics. The problem is not in the transmission and it could be caused by a faulty clutch disc damper, bad dual-mass flywheel, or an engine fault.

that can be attached to various locations under the vehicle. The vehicle is then driven for a road test while the technician listens to each of the six different locations. This should help locate the exact location of the noise.

● **SEE CHART** 8–2 for some of the more common noise problems to look for when the transmission/transaxle is disassembled.

ENGINE-OFF SHIFT TEST The engine-off shift test, also called a **static shift test** or a *shift effort test*, measures the effort required to move the synchronizer sleeve or gear, fork, and shift rail past the neutral detent and into mesh.

COMMONLY HEARD NOISES	USUALLY HEARD WHEN	POSSIBLE CAUSES
Gear rattle	Most noticeable while accelerating at low RPM and lugging the engine	Possible defective clutch disc (broken damper springs) or a defective dual mass flywheel, if equipped
Neutral rattle	Occurs with the engine running in neutral with the clutch engaged	These vibrations can occur in the engine with balance shafts and dual-mass flywheels, and proper clutch-disc hub damper springs
Backlash	Occurs when the driveline load or direction is changed, for example, when the throttle is changed abruptly or when the vehicle is brought to a stop and shifted into reverse	Often caused by worn U-joints or lack of lubrication on the splines on the output shaft of a rear-wheel-drive transmission
Gear clash	The grinding that occurs if the clutch is released too quickly while making a shift or a shift is made too quickly with nonsynchronized gears	Clash can be the result of improper shifts (rushed too quickly), wrong gear oil, worn synchronizers, or a misadjusted clutch

CHART 8–2

Typical noises and their causes plus possible items to look for to solve these noise concerns.

TECH TIP

Drips Run Downhill

If a leak is noted and the source cannot be seen, remember that a fluid normally runs downward and that the wind under the vehicle will move the fluid to the rear, so the point of leakage is normally above and forward of the fluid drips.

- The shift effort will vary with transmission and synchronizer design, and heavy-duty transmissions usually require greater shift effort. Shift effort also varies with temperature and is usually higher at cold temperature because the transmission fluid is thicker. It is also greater if the shifts are rushed and slower shift speeds usually require less effort.

- Try comparing the effort to shift into one gear with the effort to shift into the gears on a similar transaxle/transmission. As the test is made, listen for any unusual noises that might occur in the transaxle/transmission or linkage.

ENGINE-RUNNING SHIFT TEST The engine-running shift test, also called a **dynamic shift test**, is almost a repeat of the engine-off check except that it checks for clutch drag as well as transaxle/transmission problems. A dragging clutch will cause the gears to rotate, and the synchronizer action will block shifts until equal speeds occur.

TRANSAXLE/ TRANSMISSION REMOVAL

EQUIPMENT NEEDED Removal and replacement of a transaxle/transmission is required to repair internal transaxle/transmission problems or gain access to the clutch assembly. The exact operation varies somewhat between vehicle models, so it is highly recommended that service information covering the particular vehicle model be used when removing and replacing a transaxle/transmission. In some vehicles, the transmission or transaxle can only be removed along with the engine. With most four-wheel-drive vehicles, the transfer case is removed before or along with the transmission.

Some transaxles/transmissions are quite heavy and awkward to handle and therefore the shop should have available

- A transmission jack
- A tall safety stand to support the vehicle or the engine
- An engine support fixture must be used to support and move the unit in and out of the vehicle

TRANSAXLE REMOVAL To remove a transaxle, perform the following steps:

STEP 1 Disconnect the negative (–) battery cable.

STEP 2 Disconnect the following accessible parts: shift cables or rods, clutch linkage, backup light switch or wires,

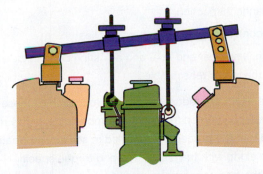

FIGURE 8–6 Most front-wheel-drive (FWD) vehicles require the use of a fixture to support the engine before removing the transaxle.

FIGURE 8–7 A transaxle being removed from underneath a vehicle and being supported by a transmission jack.

speedometer cable or speed sensor connections, and any hose or cable brackets with connections to the body or engine.

STEP 3 Many front-wheel-drive (FWD) vehicles require the installation of an *engine support tool* to keep the engine in the proper location as the transaxle and its mounts are removed. ● **SEE FIGURE 8–6.**

STEP 4 Remove the upper clutch housing bolts and install a guide pin into one or two of the bolt holes.

STEP 5 Raise and securely support the vehicle on a hoist or on jack stands.

STEP 6 If a drain opening is provided, drain the transaxle oil, be sure to check the condition and the amount of fluid that comes out.

STEP 7 Position a transmission jack to support the transaxle, remove any transaxle mounts or supports, remove the remaining clutch housing bolts, and install the second guide pin (if not already installed). Slide the transaxle away from the engine to clear the clutch and right driveshaft. Carefully lower it from the vehicle. ● **SEE FIGURE 8–7.**

CAUTION: Do not depress the clutch pedal while the transaxle is being removed.

TRANSAXLE INSTALLATION Replacement of the transaxle usually follows the procedure just described, only in reverse. The following points should be observed during transaxle installation:

- Use guide pins and/or a transmission jack to support the unit to eliminate the possibility of hanging the transaxle on the clutch shaft.
- Be sure that wires, cables, and hoses are positioned correctly as the transaxle is slid into place.

- Install the mounts, mounting bolts, and supports before removing the transmission jack.
- Tighten all nuts and bolts to the correct torque.
- If the front suspension mounting points were disturbed, perform a wheel alignment to ensure proper vehicle operation.
- Fill the transaxle to the correct level with the correct lubricant before starting the engine.
- If necessary, check and adjust clutch pedal free travel and the shift linkage.

REMOVAL OF A TRANSMISSION The procedure usually includes the following steps:

STEP 1 Disconnect the negative (–) battery cable.

STEP 2 Raise and securely support the vehicle.

STEP 3 Drain the fluid, noting the amount and condition of fluid that comes out. If the fluid is not drained, install a stop-off tool into the rear seal. This can be a commercial tool, an old driveshaft slip yoke, or a plastic bag secured by a rubber band. ● **SEE FIGURE 8–8.**

STEP 4 Remove the backup light wires, speedometer cable or speed sensor connections, any hose or cable brackets attached to the vehicle, and the shift linkage. Check under any switches for removable operating pins or balls. On transmissions with internal linkage, it is usually necessary to remove the boot and shift lever from inside the vehicle before it is lifted. On

FIGURE 8–8 A tail shaft housing plug is being used to help keep the transmission fluid from leaking as the transmission is being removed from the vehicle.

some vehicles it is necessary to remove part of the exhaust system.

STEP 5 Position a transmission jack to support the transmission. Remove the transmission support bolts, raise the transmission slightly, and remove the transmission support. In some cases, it may also be necessary to remove the cross-member.

STEP 6 Remove the transmission-to-clutch housing or transmission-to-engine bolts. On many vehicles the transmission can be lowered enough to gain access to the upper mounting bolts.

STEP 7 Move the transmission and jack to the rear to clear the clutch shaft, and lower the unit out of the vehicle.

TRANSMISSION INSTALLATION Transmission replacement usually follows the procedure just described, only in reverse.

TRANSAXLE/ TRANSMISSION OVERHAUL

TYPICAL PROCEDURE The overhaul operations for most transaxles/transmissions are very similar. The steps involved are as follows:

- Disassembly of the unit
- Clean and identify the unit so that the correct parts and specifications can be found.
- Gear inspection

- Bearing inspection
- Reconditioning of the subassemblies
- Checking gear end float and adjusting bearing clearances as the unit is reassembled

The exact procedure for carrying out each of these steps will vary depending on the make and model. It is highly recommended that the procedure specified in service information be followed along with the clearances and torque specifications.

As the transaxle/transmission is disassembled, the experienced technician will look for the possible causes of the problem. For example, if a transaxle/transmission jumps out of fifth gear, the technician would check for a worn internal shift linkage, fork, or synchronizer sleeve, burred fifth-gear clutching teeth, or excessive fifth-gear end float. Experienced technicians diagnose the problem and usually know what is wrong before the transmission is removed from the vehicle.

WEAR ITEMS TO BE CHECKED The following are normally checked during disassembly:

- The internal shift linkages for rough operation and wear
- Clearance between all shift forks and sleeves
- All shafts for excessive end play and rough operation
- All floating gears for excess end float or rough rotation
- All blocker rings for free motion and excessive or insufficient clearance or damaged lining
- All gears for chipped or broken teeth

PARTS NEEDED A transmission/transaxle kit is recommended for every transmission/transaxle overhaul. These kits contain most of the normal wear items but not any hard parts. A typical kit includes the following items:

- New snap rings
- Thrust washers
- Slingers
- Synchronizer rings
- Synchronizer springs
- Special clips
- Bushings
- Roller bearings
- Gaskets and seals
- Strut keys

Check local parts suppliers or do Internet searches for manual transmission repair kits. ● **SEE FIGURE 8–9.**

FIGURE 8–9 A service parts kit for a Borg-Warner T5 manual transmission which includes bearings, seals, and snap rings.

FIGURE 8–10 Using a holding fixture is a great way to support the transaxle during disassembly and reassembly.

What is required to remove a part is found in service information. A hydraulic press and special pullers may be required. Many bearings, synchronizer assemblies, and some counter-shafts will slide out of and into the proper location using only light force. For example, when a shift rail will not slide out of the case, it is usually held by a detent or interlock. If it is necessary to force parts, use a "soft" hammer (plastic, brass, or lead) or a soft punch made from either brass or aluminum.

Worn parts are normally replaced with new ones. When purchasing parts, sometimes upgraded parts, which are stronger than the original, should be purchased to solve problems with particular units.

TRANSAXLE DISASSEMBLY
To disassemble a transaxle, perform the following steps:

STEP 1 Install a holding fixture to support the unit during disassembly and reassembly, ● **SEE FIGURE 8–10.**

STEP 2 Remove the drain plug, and check the quantity and condition of the fluid. Also, remove the fill plug to ensure that it is not seized or has damaged threads.

STEP 3 On some transaxles, the differential bearing retainer, extension housing, and differential are removed first. On some transaxles, the disassembly begins with the removal of the left side case cover, fifth-gear synchronizer assembly, and the fifth counter gear. Sometimes service information specifies that the disassembly begin with the removal of the backup light switch, reverse idler shaft retaining bolt, detent plunger retaining screw, interlock sleeve retaining pin, and fill plug.

STEP 4 Remove the case-to-clutch housing or end-cover-to-case attachment bolts. As these bolts are removed,

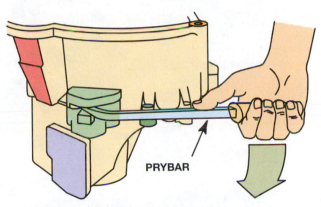

PRYBAR

FIGURE 8–11 Most transaxles use formed-in-place gaskets that tend to glue the case and covers together. This unit has a slot to allow prying without damaging the gasket surfaces.

note their length so that they can be replaced in the proper location. It will usually be necessary to tap the case with a plastic hammer or pry upward using a small prybar to break the seal between the two parts. If using a prying tool, try not to scratch the sealing surfaces. ● **SEE FIGURE 8–11.**

STEP 5 After removing the cover, remove the shift mechanism, the reverse idler gear, and its shaft, if necessary.

STEP 6 Remove the input and main shaft assemblies together, holding them so that the gears stay in mesh until the shafts leave their bearings.

STEP 7 Remove the ring gear and differential assembly. ● **SEE FIGURE 8–12.**

The side gears of some differentials have rounded thrust faces so that they will rotate easily to the windows of the differential case and fall out. These gears are normally held in place by a special tool or wooden or plastic plug inserted into them when the drive shafts are removed.

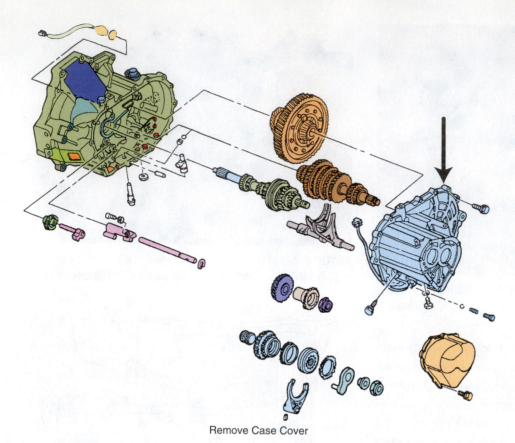

FIGURE 8–12 Removing the side cover allows access to the shift forks and differential assembly.

Remove Case Cover

TRANSMISSION DISASSEMBLY

TYPICAL PROCEDURE As with a transaxle, the procedure given here is general and intended to familiarize the service procedures and how they are performed. The exact procedure for disassembling a specific transmission is found in service information.

Synchronizer assemblies are normally left assembled until it is time to inspect the parts. Most sleeves and hubs are factory-matched sets and should be kept in their same position relative to each other. An experienced technician will use a permanent marker or small grinder to place index marks on both the sleeve and hub to speed up reassembly and prevent future problems. In most cases, if any part of this assembly is damaged, except for the blocker rings, replacement of the entire synchronizer assembly will be required.

To disassemble a typical transmission, perform the following steps:

STEP 1 Clean and identify the unit so that the correct parts and specifications can be found. ● **SEE FIGURE 8–13.**

FIGURE 8–13 The Borg-Warner T5 five-speed manual transmission is used in many makes and models of vehicles and they vary with the number of splines for either the input shaft or output shaft or both.

STEP 2 Remove the drain plug and check the quantity and condition of the fluid. ● **SEE FIGURE 8–14.**

STEP 3 Remove the case cover or case cover with shift mechanism. On some units, it is necessary to disconnect the shift shaft in the extension housing, remove the

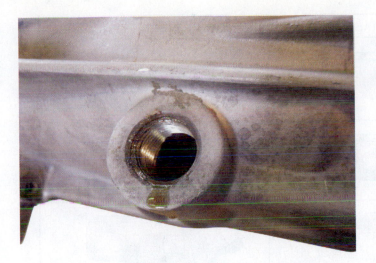

FIGURE 8–14 Drain the fluid into a suitable container and dispose of the old fluid accruing to local, state, and federal regulations.

FIGURE 8–15 A rear bearing being removed using a gear/bearing puller.

FIGURE 8–16 Visually check the condition of all gears and bearings.

extension housing, and then remove the case cover and shift mechanism.

STEP 4 On units that use tapered roller bearings, remove the shims and bearing cup. The input shaft/main drive gear can now be removed.

STEP 5 Remove the extension housing. The countershaft extension with the fifth and sixth drive gears and the synchronizer assembly along with the shift fork can now be removed.

STEP 6 Remove the rear bearing and then remove the main shaft assembly. This usually involves using a puller to remove a ball bearing or sliding the cup of a tapered roller bearing out of the case and then moving the main shaft forward, upward, and out of the case.

STEP 7 Remove the cluster gear and countershaft. On one-piece tapered roller bearing units, remove the rear bearing retainer and slide the countershaft to the rear of the case to remove the rear bearing cup, then move the shafts forward and upward for removal. ● **SEE FIGURE 8–15.**

STEP 8 Locate and remove the reverse idler gear shaft locking device, and remove the shaft, gear, and any thrust washers or O-rings. On some units, the idler gear shaft must be driven out using a long tapered punch. On other units, the idler gear shaft must be pressed out.

PARTS CLEANING The first step in cleaning is to check the debris attached to the magnet located in the bottom of the case.

This will provide an important clue to the internal damage that may be found. Large, irregular-shaped particles are probably chips from gear teeth. Small, fine, sand like or powder like particles indicate material worn off a bearing, gear, or synchronizer assembly.

CAUTION: Parts should *not* be wiped dry with shop towels because this could leave lint, which later could block an oiling funnel or passage.

The cleanup of most of the internal parts is done using safety solvent while scrubbing them with a cleaning brush or by running them through a hot-water washer. After cleaning, the parts are dried using compressed air and if necessary, then rewashed and redried until they are clean.

CAUTION: Do not allow the bearing to spin which will damage the bearing because it is being spun without any lubrication.

GEAR INSPECTION In some cases, gear damage is quite obvious and easy to locate. With other gears, however, a close inspection is necessary to determine if there is a problem with the teeth or thrust or bearing surfaces. ● **SEE FIGURE 8–16.**

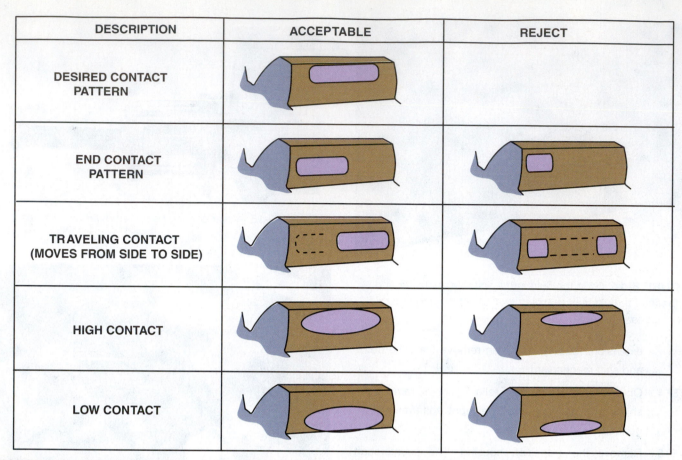

DESCRIPTION	ACCEPTABLE	REJECT
DESIRED CONTACT PATTERN		
END CONTACT PATTERN		
TRAVELING CONTACT (MOVES FROM SIDE TO SIDE)		
HIGH CONTACT		
LOW CONTACT		

FIGURE 8–17 Worn gears will often show a contact pattern on close inspection. Good and bad patterns are shown.

Each of the gears should be inspected for wear or damage. Close inspection of a gear tooth will often show a smooth metallic sheen with a duller, cleaner area and this indicates the gear contact with its mating gear. Many gear teeth will also show underlying machine marks from when the gear was originally made and these marks are normal. The contact area should occur in the vertical center of the tooth and be almost as long as the tooth. Improper contact patterns are especially important when checking for gear noise problems. ● **SEE FIGURE 8–17**.

NOTE: If one gear of a set has a broken tooth, be aware that a tooth on the mating gear encountered the same load and is probably damaged. The broken gear and its mate are replaced as a set.

BEARING INSPECTION Immediately after cleaning an antifriction (ball, roller, or needle) bearing, it should be dipped in a clean, lightweight lubricant and covered to keep it clean

TECH TIP

Reuse Old or Replace?

A technician often has to decide whether to reuse or replace slightly worn or damaged parts. Some cluster gears, for example, are very expensive, and replacement can raise the cost of a rebuild significantly. Normally, chips that do not extend into the contact area do not require gear replacement. They can, however, cause a slight noise or be the base of a stress crack or further chipping. Small burrs and chips can be removed or blended into the gear surface using a high-speed grinder with a small abrasive stone. Worn, rounded, or burred clutching teeth can also be corrected by grinding.

and dust free. Inspection of a bearing is normally done by sight, feel, and sound. Visual inspection of a worn bearing can reveal a broken cage or pitted races. ● **SEE FIGURE 8–18.**

FIGURE 8–18 Carefully inspect all bearings before reassembling the unit. If one is worn or damaged, then many experts recommend that all of the bearings be replaced because they all share the same lubricating oil and any wear metal will be thrown throughout the assembly.

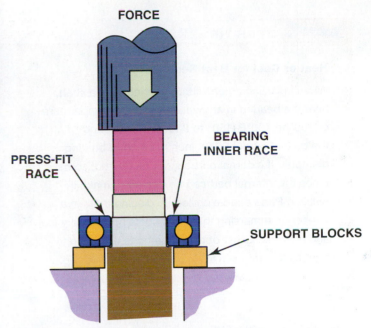

APPLY FORCE ONLY TO PRESS-FIT RACE

FIGURE 8–19 When a ball bearing is pressed off a shaft, the bearing should be supported by the inner race (if possible) so the force is not exerted on the outer race by the balls.

TECH TIP

Bearing Checks

Holding the bearing in a vertical position by the outer race while spinning the inner race by hand allows damage to be felt or heard. Many technicians place the shaft inside the inner race, giving it a slight load and a much better turning handle. The weight of the shaft also makes any bearing problem more evident.

Bearing damage occurs in many forms. The terms commonly used to describe bearing damage are as follows:

- **Brinelling:** a series of indentations pressed or worn into a race
- **Contamination:** scratches, pitting, or scoring in a scattered pattern on the ball or roller surfaces
- **Electric arcing:** a series of small burn marks or grooves across the raceways
- **Fretting:** small particles that decay and break off the bearing races
- **Misalignment:** a diagonal polish of the stationary race while excess wear occurs all over the rotating raceway from a bore and shaft that are not correctly aligned
- **Peeling:** a light scraping away of the surface of the bearing race

TECH TIP

Bearing Failure? Check the Body Grounds

Premature bearing failure that results in a pitted bearing can be caused by poor electrical grounds. The pits are often completely around the bearing races. Current flow for the electrical systems must return to battery ground. Poor engine ground straps will force this current to pass through the transmission and across the bearings, and this can cause an arc at the bearing races. If arcing of bearings is discovered, check and repair the factory ground wiring and connections at the body, engine block, and the transmission/transaxle itself.

- **Seizing:** caused when balls or rollers fail to roll and this causes damage to cage and end of rollers with evidence of excessive heat
- **Spalling:** an advanced stage of decay with flaking away of particles from the bearing race

BEARING REMOVAL AND INSTALLATION The inner races of bearing are often pressed onto the shaft and the pressing force should be transmitted only to the inner race. ● SEE FIGURE 8–19.

Heat or Cool for Best Results

When installing a tight-fitting bearing over a shaft, heat the bearing in an oven or hot oil. A temperature of 300° to 400°F (150° to 200° C) will expand the bearing about 0.001 inch per inch of bearing diameter. If external part cannot be heated, sometimes the internal part can be cooled to make it smaller. Parts can be chilled by placing them in a freezer or immersing them in a container with dry ice and acetone. Either of these methods can change a press fit into a slip fit.

Take a Photo Before Disassembling

Many technicians have learned that it is helpful to have a photo available of a part that is together before it is disassembled. Take a photo of the main shaft with a phone or camera to use just in case it is needed to insure proper assembly.

FIGURE 8–20 Use caution when pressing parts onto the main shaft. Always follow the specified assembly procedures as found in service information.

When pressing a bearing, an experienced technician will always place some form of a shield over the bearing to contain possible flying parts. It is often possible to remove a bearing with a gear so that the gear will press against the inner race, saving the bearing. Some shops make it a practice to heat any bearing that is pressed onto a shaft because the expansion makes installation easier, with less possibility of damage to the bearing.

MAIN SHAFT DISASSEMBLY

Transaxle/transmission main shafts are disassembled to allow a thorough inspection of the journals and bearings where the gears are mounted and for access to the synchronizer assemblies. In some cases, this is simply a matter of removing snap rings and sliding the various parts off the shaft but in most cases, the parts must be removed using a press or puller. All of these parts have a front and back and some technicians place a small index mark using a die grinder on the front of each part as it is removed. This mark will ensure that the part is positioned correctly during reassembly.

To disassemble a main shaft, a typical procedure includes the following steps:

STEP 1 In some cases, the end gear will simply slide off the shaft. In other cases, the end gear will be held in place by a bearing that must be pressed off the shaft. Use a bearing separator and press the shaft out of the gear and bearing. ● SEE FIGURE 8–20.

Because the gear will contact the inner bearing race, this should remove the bearing with no damage to it. A puller can also be used.

STEP 2 Remove the blocker ring and the synchronizer hub retaining ring and install a bearing separator onto the gear next to the synchronizer assembly then press the shaft out of the gear, blocker ring, and synchronizer assembly.

STEP 3 Continue this disassembly procedure to remove any remaining gears, thrust washers, synchronizer assembly, and bearings.

SYNCHRONIZER DISASSEMBLY, INSPECTION, AND REASSEMBLY

Synchronizer assemblies are disassembled for cleaning, inspection, and occasionally for deburring the ends of the splines in the sleeve.

NOTE: The sleeve and hub are matched at the factory and should be marked before it is disassembled.

Some synchronizer sleeves have notches for the inserts only in certain areas, and some assemblies include a detent ball and spring in addition to the inserts and energizer springs. Other assemblies use winged inserts or keys, which remain in place as the sleeve is removed. Most inserts have straight sides and pop out of place as the sleeve is slid off.

To disassemble a synchronizer assembly, remove the energizer springs and slide the sleeve off the hub. The inserts will either fall or slide out of their grooves.

Inspection includes checking the inserts for wear or breakage, checking the sleeve for burrs, and checking the fit of the sleeve to the hub. A hub should fall freely through the sleeve. A tight-fitting sleeve will cause hard shifts. Usually, a fault with any part of the assembly will require replacement with a new synchronizer assembly.

To reassemble a synchronizer assembly, usually includes the following steps:

STEP 1 Place the sleeve over the hub with the index marks aligned. If there are no index marks, locate the sleeve over the hub in a position where it moves freely and in the correct front-to-rear position. When aligned properly, the sleeve should free-fall over the hub. Many technicians set the sleeve and hub on the bench top with the front/engine ends upward.

STEP 2 Slide an insert into each of the grooves.

STEP 3 Set an energizer spring in place. A common spring style has a tang that enters one of the inserts and a tail that is placed under the other inserts in a clockwise direction. Other spring styles are positioned in a similar manner.

STEP 4 Turn the assembly over and place the tang of the second spring into the other end of the same insert, and place the spring under the other insert in a clockwise direction. In this way, the two springs are running in opposite directions. It should be noted that some manufacturers recommend placing the spring tangs into different inserts.

The purpose of the energizer spring placement is to obtain equal spring pressure under each of the inserts. When other spring styles are used, they are also positioned so as to distribute their force equally.

Although separate from the assembly, also check the blocker rings and cone clutch area of the gear. Blocker ring problems commonly encountered include the following:

- Burred clutching teeth
- Broken rings
- Worn insert grooves
- Wear on the inner cone surface

Then, place the ring over the gear's cone and measure the clearance. Some manufacturers specify a minimum clearance of about 0.020 inch (0.5 mm). **Blocker ring clearance** is also called *ride height* or *synchronizer reserve*. ● **SEE FIGURE 8–21.**

Each gear next to a synchronizer assembly has a center bearing and a thrust surface on each side of it. The center bearing is either the smooth bore of the gear, a sleeve, or a set of needle bearings and operates on the main shaft journals. The thrust surfaces are the smooth sides of the gears that can run

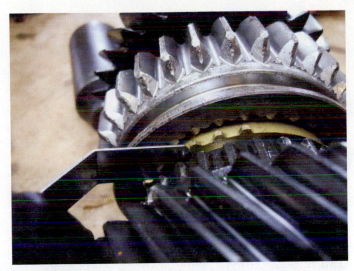

FIGURE 8–21 When the cone is pushed against the gear, there should be a minimum amount of clearance between the blocker ring and gear clutching teeth. Use a feeler gauge to determine this measurement.

🔧 **TECH TIP**

Blocker Ring Inspection Tips

1. A good metal blocker ring will have a thread-like inner surface with the threads coming to a sharp point; the edges will not reflect light. A worn blocker ring will have flattened rings around the inner surface. ● **SEE FIGURE 8–22.**

2. After a quick visual check for damage, a technician will drop a metal blocker ring onto a bench top from a short distance. A good blocker ring will make a bell-like ringing noise, whereas a cracked or broken ring will make a dull, flat sound.

Paper-lined and composite blocker rings should be checked for glazing of the friction surface and discoloration, which often indicates glazing.

---

against the smooth side of the synchronizer hub or a thrust washer. The parts should be washed in solvent and air dried.

BLOCKER RING INSPECTION There are several ways to check a blocker ring. If specifications are not available, measure the clearance using a new ring as a guide.

- The cone surface of the gear should be smooth and polished with no metal buildup (usually brass from the old ring). Metal buildup can be removed using fine emery cloth and polished using crocus cloth.
- Another check is to push the ring onto the cone as the gear is rotated. The ring should lock to the gear and rotate, but it should also pull right off the gear without sticking.

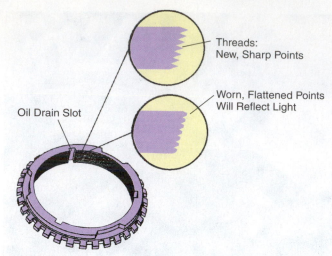

FIGURE 8–22 The thread-like grooves of a new blocker ring are sharp so that they cut through the lubrication film. They become flattened as they wear, and the flat edges will reflect light.

MAIN SHAFT REASSEMBLY
After the used parts are cleaned and checked and any new parts needed are made available, the main shaft is ready for reassembly.

To reassemble a main shaft, perform the following steps:

STEP 1 Place the first gear to be installed (with its sleeve, bushing, or bearing, if used) onto the main shaft along with its blocker ring. Set the synchronizer assembly in place, making sure that it is facing the proper direction. Turn the main shaft so that the gear is above the synchronizer, align the blocker ring so that its notches engage the inserts, and shift the synchronizer sleeve to engage the gear's clutching teeth to keep the blocker ring aligned. Some synchronizer hubs have oiling grooves that must be aligned with an oil hole in the shaft. ● **SEE FIGURE 8–23.**

STEP 2 Press the shaft into the synchronizer hub and install the snap ring to retain it. Place wooden blocks or a shop cloth onto the press plates to protect the hub from becoming burred.

STEP 3 Shift the synchronizer sleeve to neutral, and check the gear and blocker ring for *end float* and free movement. In some cases, *selective-fit* snap rings or thrust washers are available to adjust the clearance, if necessary.

STEP 4 Place the next blocker ring and gear in place, making sure the blocker ring notches engage the inserts, and shift the sleeve to keep them aligned. Depending on the main shaft, this will be followed by a thrust washer(s) and retaining ring or snap ring or a bearing and snap ring. The retaining/snap ring will often be the base for a thrust washer and another gear set.

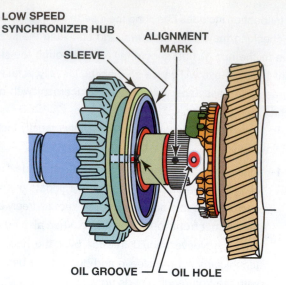

FIGURE 8–23 This synchronizer hub has an oil groove that must be aligned with the oil hole in the main shaft during assembly.

Pressing the shaft into a bearing normally completes the buildup of that end of the shaft.

STEP 5 After installing all the parts, check the assembly by shifting the synchronizer sleeves into neutral.

TRANSAXLE FINAL DRIVE SERVICE
Transaxle final drives (differentials) need to be partially or completely disassembled to replace the bearing cones, ring gear, or differential gears. The differential should be inspected and serviced whenever major transaxle service is performed.

SHIFT MECHANISM

TYPES Each mechanism set contains a fork for each synchronizer sleeve or gear to be shifted, and each fork is mounted on a rail or lever that moves it through its travel. Each shifter includes one or more spring loaded detent balls or cams and some form of interlock that allows only one shift fork to move at a time.

When visually inspecting the shift mechanisms, check the following:

- *Shift forks:* inspect for distortion, bends, cracks, broken or worn inserts, and step wear at both the sleeve and cam contact areas. ● **SEE FIGURE 8–24.**
- *Shift rails:* inspect for distortion, bends, burrs, scores, grooves, and elongated pinholes
- *Detent springs:* breakage

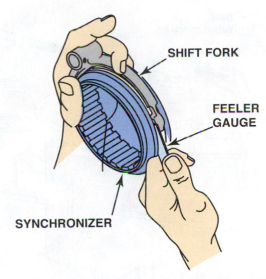

SHIFT FORK

FEELER GAUGE

SYNCHRONIZER

FIGURE 8–24 There should be a specified clearance, usually about 0.030 inch (0.8 mm), between the fork and the groove in the sleeve. Excess clearance indicates a worn fork or groove.

- *Detent cam:* (sometimes part of a rail): wear and scoring
- *Interlock plates:* burrs, wear, and scoring
- *Selector plates:* burrs, wear, and scoring
- *Reverse lockout mechanism/solenoid:* proper operation

Always have service information available as the transaxle/transmission is assembled, so each of these parts should be checked for complete movement and smooth operation. ● **SEE FIGURE 8–25.**

CASE AND COVERS

CLEANING AND INSPECTION

The case and all covers should be thoroughly cleaned and carefully checked for cracks, distortion or wear of bearing bores, stripped bolt threads, and worn release (throwout) bearing supports. Damaged cases are normally replaced. Some rebuilders machine the case and insert steel sleeves for worn bearing bores or throwout bearing supports to return them to the original diameter and provide stronger-than-new material.

SEAL INSTALLATION

Most cases include one or more seals, which are normally replaced during a rebuild. These seals include:

- Each shift shaft that passes through the case
- One or two output shaft seals
- Sometimes an input shaft seal

Old seals are normally removed by prying them out using a seal puller or prybar, or by driving them out from behind.

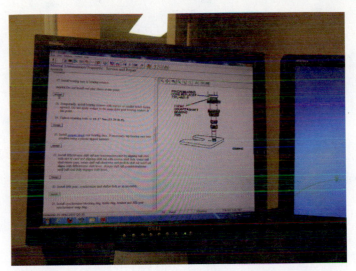

FIGURE 8–25 Having service information readily available is important so that each step can be checked as the unit is being reassembled.

 REAL WORLD FIX

The Case of the Worn Shift Fork

A 2007 BMW 325i (113,000 mi) had a problem of first-gear jump-out. The transmission was removed and rebuilt, and a new 1–2 guide sleeve and first gear was installed along with new transmission mounts and rubber shifter mounts. But, this did not fix the problem.

When the transmission was disassembled again, the shift fork was measured for wear. The shift fork measured at 0.145 to 0.170 inch, and the dimension of a new fork was 0.190 inch. Replacement of the fork fixed this transmission. The technician learned to check all possible parts involved that could cause the customer concern when the unit is apart.

☠ **WARNING**

Keep open flames away from transmission/transaxle cases. Most gear cases are cast from aluminum and, in a few cases, magnesium. Aluminum and magnesium have very similar properties except that magnesium burns. The metal will ignite at approximately 1,600°F (870°C) and burn with an intense white flame. Once combustion begins, it is extremely difficult to stop. Unpainted magnesium cases can be identified by a dull battleship-gray coating of magnesium oxide.

The Solder Trick

An alternative method of measuring the distance between the case and the bearing cup is to place two very thin strips of solder in place of the shim between the case and the bearing cup, install the shaft and bearing, install the case cover, and tighten the bolts to the correct torque. Disassemble the unit, and measure the thickness of the solder using a micrometer. This will be the shim size before adjusting for preload or end play.

REAL WORLD FIX

Find the Root Cause

The transmission in a 2008 Ford Explorer (150,000 mi) was rebuilt 5,000 miles ago. A damaged input shaft and all of the bearings were replaced using original equipment parts. The end play was adjusted as shown in the Ford service information. This transmission was repaired before for the same problem, a seized front bearing. It came back because of the same problem.

   It was determined that the damage was caused by a fluid loss. The leak was through three loose rubber plugs at the back of the top cover. Replacement of the damaged input shaft bearing and the three rubber sealing plugs fixed this problem.

New seals are driven into place using a seal driver that fits against the entire outer surface of the seal to prevent seal distortion.

END PLAY/PRELOAD CHECKS

During the reassembly of a transaxle/transmission that uses tapered roller bearings, the **preload** or **end play** of each shaft should be checked. A selective **shim** is located at a bearing at one end of each shaft, and the thickness of this shim controls the amount of preload or end play.

- Preload causes a slight drag as a shaft is rotated and it is usually measured using a torque wrench or spring scale.
- End play is a free, lengthwise movement of the shaft and is usually measured using a dial indicator or feeler gauge. ● **SEE FIGURE 8–26.**

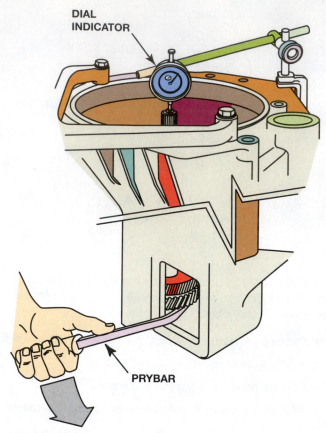

FIGURE 8–26 The dial indicator is set up to measure input shaft endplay as it is lifted and dropped using the prybar.

Gauging fixtures are available for some transaxles that allow for setting the clearance on all three of the shafts at one time. Without special fixtures, most shops will need to check the clearance on each shaft, one at a time. This must be done if a bearing, shaft, bearing retainer/case cover, or case has been replaced.

   To check and adjust bearing clearance/preload on a transaxle, perform the following steps:

STEP 1 Place the shaft to be checked with its bearings in the case. If new parts are used, adjustment is necessary. Use an adjusting shim that is too small, so there will be end play. A shim that is about 0.010 inch (0.25 mm) smaller than the one that was originally used, or the smallest one available, is normally used as a starter.

STEP 2 Install the bearing retainer or case cover, and tighten all bolts to the correct torque. Rotate the shaft several times as the bolts are tightened to seat the bearings.

STEP 3 Install a dial indicator with the indicating stylus at the end of and parallel to the shaft. Move the shaft up and down through its free travel several times while reading the end play or clearance on the dial indicator. ● **SEE FIGURE 8–27.**

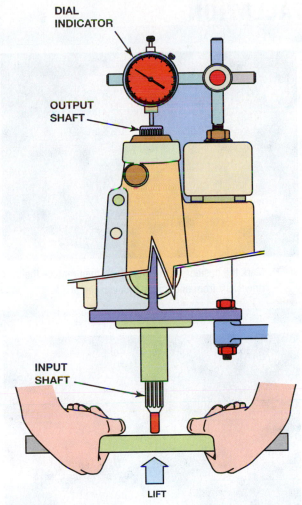

FIGURE 8–27 A dial indicator has been set up to measure the endplay that occurs as the cluster gear is lifted and dropped.

NOTE: Check end play at least three times or until consistent readings are obtained.

STEP 4 Compare the measured travel to the specifications.

STEP 5 If a shim change is required, remove the bearing retainer/case cover and remove the old shim. Measure the thickness of the shim. Add that size to the amount of change measured in the last step. Select and install a shim of the correct size, replace the bearing retainer/case cover, tighten the bolts, rotate the shaft to seat the bearings, and feel for end play. On preloaded shafts, there should not be any end play.

STEP 6 Using a torque wrench or spring scale and adapter, measure the torque required to keep the shaft rotating, not the breakaway or starting torque.

NOTE: An oversized socket can be used on splined shafts by placing cardboard or cloth

FIGURE 8–28 When using RTV to seal a transmission/transaxle case, be sure to surround each bolt hole to help prevent leakage.

over the shaft so a pressure is required to slide the socket in place.

Compare the preload reading to the specifications; if they are within the specifications, the shim is correct. Readings that are too high or too low indicate the wrong shim. In these cases, use the next larger or smaller shim to correct preload.

STEP 7 When the clearance/preload is correct, remove this shaft, and repeat this check on the next shaft.

CASE SEALANTS Most transaxles use **formed-in-place gaskets (FIPG)**. These are usually of the following two types:

- **Room-temperature vulcanizing (RTV)** liquid sealant. RTV is thick and very viscous as it comes out of the tube. Depending on temperature and humidity, it will set up to a rubber-like material in about 15 minutes.

- **Anaerobic sealants**. Anaerobic sealants are quite fluid and set up after the parts are assembled. Anaerobic sealants cure in the absence of air. RTV sealants are commonly used on covers that are less than perfectly flat, or on slightly flexible materials that do not necessarily make perfect joints. To make a good seal, an anaerobic sealant requires a wider, flatter, more perfect surface because it cures to a much thinner thickness than that of RTV. To make a good seal, both types of sealants require surfaces that are clean and oil-free when they are applied. ● **SEE FIGURE 8–28.**

FINAL CHECKS In neutral, both input and output shafts should turn freely of each other without drag. Shifts into each gear should be smooth, and the shafts should rotate easily and smoothly in each gear.

1 Start any transmission/transaxle removal procedure by disconnecting the negative battery cable.

2 Mark the position of the driveshaft, then remove the driveshaft from underneath the vehicle.

3 Use to tape or a rubber glove over the U-joint to keep the end caps from falling off and use a plug at the extension housing of the transmission to help keep transmission fluid from leaking.

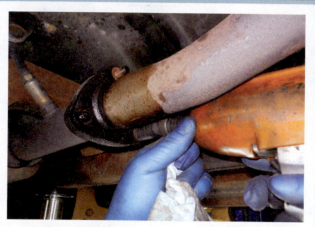

4 Removing the exhaust system was needed to be done to provide the clearance to remove the transmission.

5 Removing the bolts for the rear cross member by using an impact and extension to get to the fasteners inside the frame rail.

6 Removing the rear cross member but not before supporting the transmission with a transmission jack.

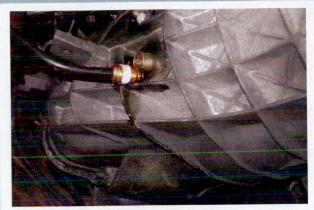

7 When the hydraulic clutch line was removed, hydraulic fluid (brake fluid) leaked out and into a catch pan.

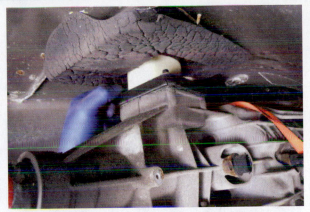

8 The transmission was lowered enough to disconnect the shifter from the transmission. This step helps save time by eliminating the need to remove the shifter and boot from inside the vehicle.

9 The bell housing bolts are removed using a long extension on the impact wrench.

10 The engine is being supported by a tall safety stand as the transmission is being removed.

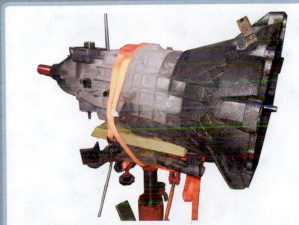

11 The transmission is lowered using the transmission jack and safety strap to help prevent it from falling off the jack.

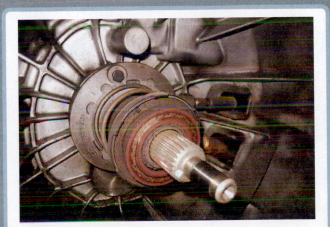

12 The original release bearing and clutch assembly is going to be replaced.

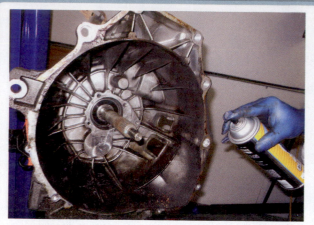

13 The bell housing area was cleaned after removing the release bearing.

14 The old pressure plate being removed from the flywheel.

15 After installing the new clutch assembly, the transmission was reinstalled and all of the fasteners tightened to factory specifications

16 The worn rear U-joint was replaced and then the driveshaft was installed.

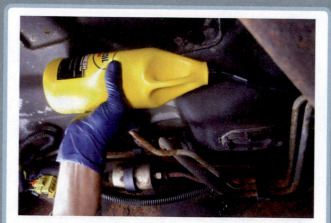

17 The specified gear lube was added to the manual transmission after it was fully installed.

18 The clutch fluid is being added, then the system bled and the truck was test driven to verify proper operation.

1 A NV-1500 five-speed manual transmission is used in two-wheel drive applications only.

2 The shifter assembly has been removed. Note the roll pin in the center of the shift lever socket.

3 Snap-ring pliers are being used to remove the snap ring retaining the input shaft bearing.

4 The upside down case is being separated showing the countershaft (top) and shift forks.

5 Before further disassembly can be accomplished, the shift lever socket roll pin must be driven out using a punch and a hammer.

6 The shift shaft and forks can now be removed.

CONTINUED ▶

7 The reverse idle gear is unbolted from the case and removed.

8 The output shaft assembly fifth gear (far left) and the synchronizer assemblies.

9 The bearing is being removed using a bearing splitter and a hydraulic press.

10 A speed gear (bottom) along with the double row needle bearing used between the shaft and the speed gear. The hub (center) is splined and rotates with the output shaft.

11 A synchronizer assembly being reassembled. It often takes several hands to hold the hub (center) and the sleeve (outer ring).

12 A hydraulic press is used to reassemble output shaft and bearing.

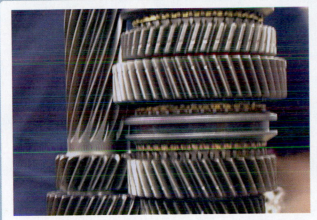

13 The assembled output shaft is held against the counter shaft to double check that all of the gears have been correctly assembled.

14 The assembled output shaft and counter shaft are being reinstalled in the transmission case.

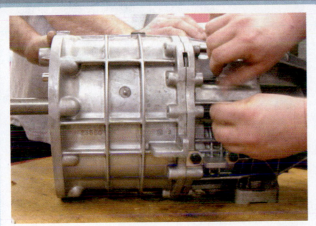

15 The case halves are bolted together.

16 The last step is to assembly the shift lever and check for proper operation in all gear positions.

1 After the transaxle has been removed from the vehicle and the fluid drained, place the transaxle on a work surface.

2 The bell housing case half containing the large output shaft front bearing (center) and the input shaft front bearing (smaller bearing on the left).

3 The differential assembly is simply lifted out of half of the case.

4 The input and output shafts are a press fit into the bearings and are also retained with a snap ring, which must be removed.

5 Using a special tool, the input and output shafts are pressed out of the housing using a hydraulic press.

6 The input shaft can be disassembled using a bearing splitter and a press, or two screwdrivers to pry the gears off the shaft.

7 This transaxle uses both brass and powdered metal synchronizer rings with a fiber (paper) inner cone surface.

8 Synchronizer ring gaps are being measured using a feeler (thickness) gauge. The factory specifications are usually 0.040 in. to 0.069 in.

9 The gear clutch teeth should be inspected for wear.

10 An assembled synchronizer assembly containing a sleeve, keys, springs, and detent.

11 The input shaft (left) and the output shaft (right) are checked for proper assembly before being installed into the case.

12 The differential bearing preload is determined by measuring for zero end play; then adding the thickness shim under the bearing cup.

CONTINUED ▶

13 The bearing cup is being installed using an installation tool and a hammer.

14 All of the shift forks and shift arms must be aligned properly before installing the components into the case.

15 All of the components, including the differential (upper right), the output shaft (center), and the input shaft (left), plus the shift linkage are installed and checked for proper positioning.

16 The case halves being reinstalled. The bearings (top) must be pressed back onto the input and output shafts using a press.

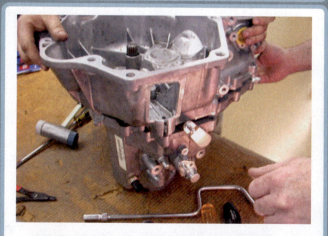

17 The bell housing case being reattached.

18 The completed assembly. Notice the bearing cover (top) has already been installed.

SUMMARY

1. Transmissions must have clean gear oil at the proper level and of the proper type.

2. Faulty shift linkage can cause problems.

3. The cause of improper transmission operation is determined using several diagnostic steps.

4. Internal transmission problems require that the transmission be removed from the vehicle. Transaxle removal is generally more difficult.

5. Transmission and transaxle disassembly and reassembly varies between different makes and models.

6. Presses and pullers are often required for complete disassembly.

7. A thorough cleanup is done so parts can be inspected.

8. Gears, bearings, synchronizer assemblies, shift forks, and transaxle differentials are the major wear components.

9. Synchronizer assemblies require careful assembly.

10. Shafts that use tapered roller bearings require end play adjustments as the unit is assembled.

REVIEW QUESTIONS

1. Where can the type and viscosity of transmission/transaxle lubricant be found?

2. How is the transmission fluid level determined?

3. What is a typical shifter adjustment procedure?

4. How should bearings be removed and installed on transmission/transaxle shafts?

5. What problems can a worn shift fork cause?

CHAPTER QUIZ

1. A transaxle lubricant level is being checked. Technician A says that the fluid level should be even with the bottom of the filler hole. Technician B says that it should be in the hatch-marked area of the dipstick. Which technician is correct?
   a. Technician A only
   b. Technician B only
   c. Both technicians A and B
   d. Neither technician A nor B

2. "Rust Dust" is an indication of what fault?
   a. Broken blocker rings
   b. Worn steel parts such as U-joints
   c. A slipping clutch
   d. Fluid leak

3. A transaxle shifts easily through all the gear ranges with the engine shut off, but with the engine running, the shifts into all forward gears are hard and there is a clash when shifting into reverse. Technician A says this problem could be caused by a worn shift fork. Technician B says there could be worn countershaft bearings. Which technician is correct?
   a. Technician A only
   b. Technician B only
   c. Both technicians A and B
   d. Neither technician A nor B

4. A typical transaxle repair kit includes _____.
   a. Seals
   b. Snap rings
   c. Gaskets
   d. All of the above

5. A transmission is noisy when driving in most gears. What is the most likely cause?
   a. A clutch that is not fully released
   b. Worn or defective bearing(s)

   c. Defective synchronizer blocker ring(s)
   d. Worn shift fork

6. All of the following should be observed carefully when checking bearings except:
   a. Bearings should be air-dried by spinning them with compressed air
   b. A rough bearing should be cleaned, dried, and rechecked
   c. A bearing is checked by rotating it feel and listen for roughness
   d. Bearing should be lightly oiled before checking

7. Before checking the fluid level in a manual transmission or transaxle, what should the technician do?
   a. Check service information for the specified procedure
   b. Loosen the fluid fill hole plug
   c. Check for the specified fluid type and viscosity
   d. All of the above

8. Blocker ring clearance can be checked using a _____.
   a. Dial bore gauge
   b. Feeler gauge
   c. Dial indicator
   d. Plastigauge

9. When installing a bearing over a shaft, where should the force be applied?
   a. On the outer (outside) race
   b. On the inner (inside) race
   c. On both the inner and outer races
   d. On the ball bearing themselves

10. Preload causes a slight drag as a shaft is rotated and it is usually measured using a _____.
    a. Feeler gauge
    b. Torque wrench
    c. Spring scale
    d. Either b or c

chapter 9

DRIVE SHAFTS AND CV JOINTS

LEARNING OBJECTIVES

After studying this chapter, the reader should be able to:

1. Describe driveshaft design and balance.
2. Describe the function and operation of U-joints.
3. Describe how CV joints work.
4. Discuss the two types of CV joints.

This chapter will help you prepare for Suspension and Steering (A4) ASE certification test content area "C" (Suspension and Steering Service).

KEY TERMS

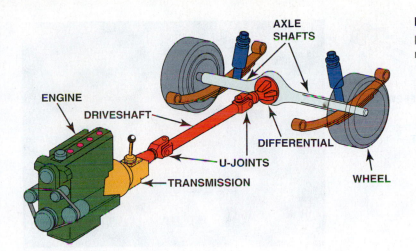

FIGURE 9–1 Typical rear-wheel-drive powertrain arrangement. The engine is mounted longitudinal (lengthwise).

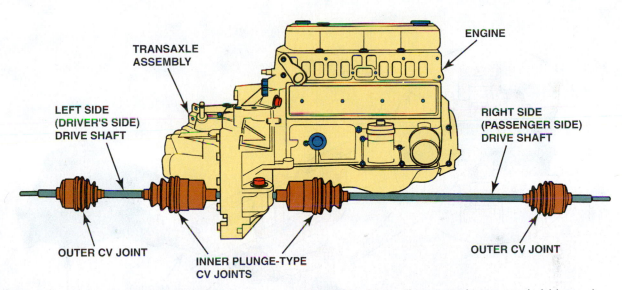

FIGURE 9–2 Typical front-wheel-drive powertrain arrangement. The engine is usually mounted transversely (sideways).

DRIVE SHAFTS

PURPOSE AND FUNCTION A drive shaft transmits engine torque from the transmission or transaxle (if front-wheel drive) to the rear axle assembly or drive wheels. ● SEE FIGURES 9–1 AND 9–2.

Driveshaft is the term used by the Society of Automotive Engineers (SAE) to describe the shaft between the transmission and the rear axle assembly on a rear-wheel-drive vehicle. General Motors and some other manufacturers use the term **propeller shaft** or *prop shaft* to describe this same part. The SAE term will be used throughout this textbook.

A typical driveshaft is a hollow steel tube. A splined end yoke is welded onto one end that slips over the splines of the output shaft of the transmission. ● SEE FIGURE 9–3. An end yoke is welded onto the other end of the driveshaft. Some driveshafts use a center support bearing.

DRIVESHAFT DESIGN Most driveshafts are constructed of hollow steel tubing. *The forces are transmitted through the surface of the driveshaft tubing.* The surface is therefore in tension, and cracks can develop on the outside surface of the driveshaft due to metal fatigue. Driveshaft tubing can bend and, if dented, can collapse. A dented driveshaft should be replaced and no attempt should be made to repair the dent. ● SEE FIGURE 9–4.

Most rear-wheel-drive cars and light trucks use a one-or two-piece driveshaft. A steel tube driveshaft has a maximum *length of about 65 inches (165 cm)*. Beyond this critical length, a **center support bearing**

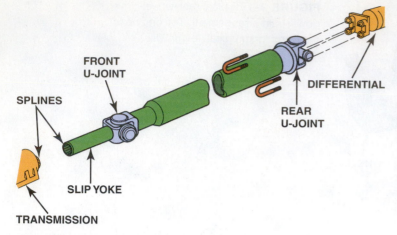

FIGURE 9–3 Typical driveshaft (also called a *propeller shaft*). The drivershaft transfers engine power from the transmission to the differential.

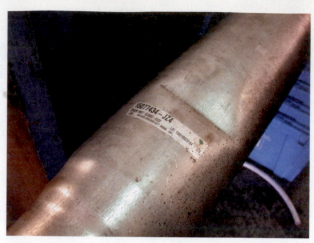

FIGURE 9–4 This driveshaft was found to be dented during a visual inspection and has to be replaced.

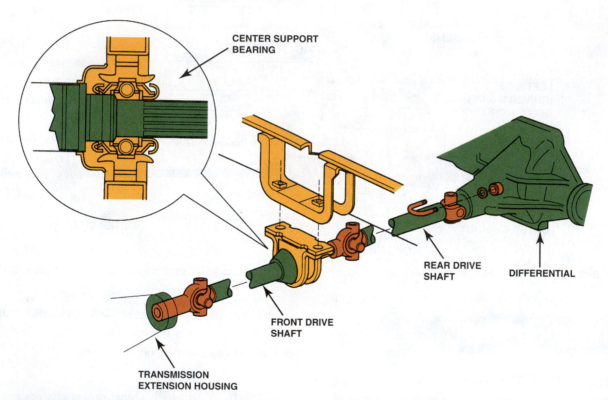

FIGURE 9–5 A center support bearing is used on many vehicles with long two-part driveshafts.

must be used, as shown in ● **FIGURE 9–5**. A center support bearing is also called a steady bearing or hanger bearing.

Some vehicle manufacturers use aluminum driveshafts; these can be as long as 90 inches (230 cm) with no problem. Many extended-cab pickup trucks and certain vans use aluminum driveshafts to eliminate the need (and expense) of a center support bearing. Composite-material driveshafts are also used

in some vehicles. These carbon-fiber-plastic driveshafts are very strong yet lightweight, and can be made in extended lengths without the need for a center support bearing.

To dampen driveshaft noise, it is common to line the inside of the hollow driveshaft with cardboard or rubber. This helps eliminate the tinny sound whenever shifting between drive and reverse in a vehicle equipped with an automatic transmission. ● **SEE FIGURE 9–6**.

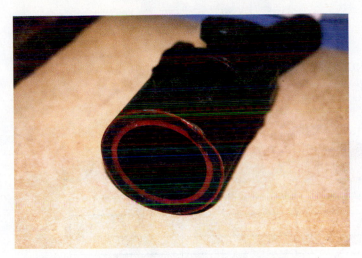

FIGURE 9–6 Some driveshafts use rubber between an inner and outer housing to absorb vibrations and shocks to the driveline.

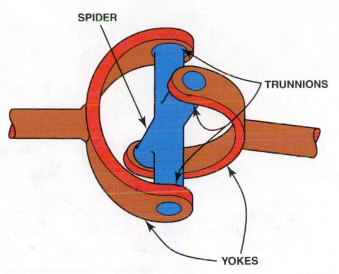

FIGURE 9–7 A simple universal joint (U-joint).

DRIVESHAFT BALANCE

All driveshafts are balanced. Generally, any driveshaft whose rotational speed is greater than 1000 RPM must be balanced. Driveshaft balance should be within 0.5% of the driveshaft weight. (This is one of the biggest reasons why aluminum or composite driveshafts can be longer because of their light weight.)

Driveshafts are often not available by make, model, and year of the vehicle. There are too many variations at the factory, such as transmission type, differential, or U-joint type. To get a replacement driveshaft, it is usually necessary to know the series of U-joints (type or style of U-joint) and the center-to-center distance between the U-joints.

U-JOINT DESIGN AND OPERATION

Universal joints (U-joints) are used at both ends of a driveshaft. U-joints allow the wheels and the rear axle to move up and down, remain flexible, and still transfer torque to the drive wheels. A simple universal joint can be made from two Y-shaped yokes connected by a crossmember called a cross or **spider**. The four arms of the cross are called **trunnions**. ● **SEE FIGURE 9–7** for a line drawing of a simple U-joint with all part names identified. A similar design is the common U-joint used with a socket wrench set.

Most U-joints are called cross-yoke joints or **Cardan joints**. *Cardan* is named for a sixteenth-century Italian mathematician who worked with objects that moved freely in any direction. Torque from the engine is transferred through the U-joint. The engine drives the U-joint at a constant speed, but the output speed of the U-joint changes because of the angle of the joint. The speed changes twice per revolution. *The greater the angle, the greater the change in speed (velocity).* ● **SEE FIGURE 9–8.**

If only one U-joint were used in a driveline, this change in speed of the driven side (output end) would generate vibrations in the driveline. To help reduce vibration, another U-joint is used at the other end of the driveshaft. If the angles of both joints are nearly equal, the acceleration and deceleration of one joint is offset by the alternate deceleration and acceleration of the second joint. *It is very important that both U-joints operate at about the same angle to prevent excessive driveline vibration.* ● **SEE FIGURE 9–9.**

ACCEPTABLE WORKING ANGLES Universal joints used in a typical driveshaft should have a *working angle* of 1/2 to 3 degrees. ● **SEE FIGURE 9–10.** The working angle is the angle between the driving end and the driven end of the joint.

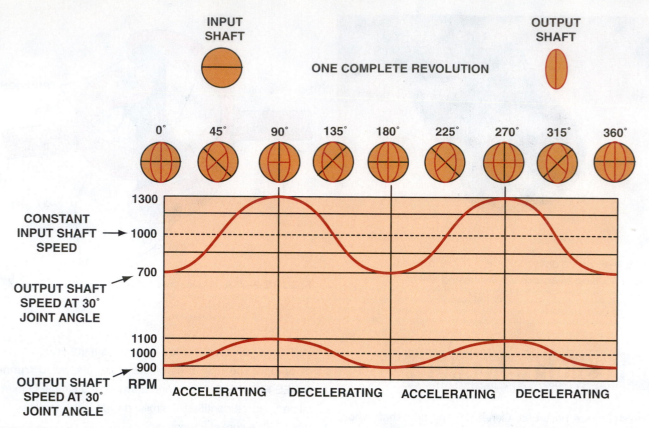

INPUT
SHAFT

OUTPUT
SHAFT

ONE COMPLETE REVOLUTION

0°   45°   90°   135°   180°   225°   270°   315°   360°

CONSTANT
INPUT SHAFT → 1000
SPEED

1300

700

OUTPUT SHAFT
SPEED AT 30°
JOINT ANGLE

1100
1000
900

OUTPUT SHAFT   RPM
SPEED AT 30°   ACCELERATING   DECELERATING   ACCELERATING   DECELERATING
JOINT ANGLE

FIGURE 9–8 How the speed difference on the output of a typical U-joint varies with the speed and the angle of the U-joint. At the bottom of the chart, the input speed is a constant 1000 RPM, while the output speed varies from 900 to 1100 RPM when the angle difference in the joint is only 10°. At the top of the chart, the input speed is a constant 1000 RPM, yet the output speed varies from 700 to 1200 RPM when the angle difference in the joint is changed to 30°.

If the driveshaft is perfectly straight (0 degree working angle), then the needle bearings inside the bearing cap are not revolving because there is no force (no difference in angles) to cause the rotation of the needle bearings. If the needle bearings do not rotate, they can exert a constant pressure in one place and damage the bearing journal. If a two-piece driveshaft is used, one U-joint (usually the front) runs at a small working angle of about 1/2 degree, just enough to keep the needle bearings rotating. The other two U-joints (from the center support bearing and rear U-joint at the differential) operate at typical working angles of a single-piece driveshaft.

If the U-joint working angles differ by more than a 1/2 degree between the front and the rear joint, a vibration is usually produced that is *torque sensitive.* As the vehicle is first accelerated from a stop, engine torque can create unequal driveshaft angles by causing the differential to rotate on its suspension support arms. This vibration is most noticeable when the vehicle is heavily loaded and being accelerated at lower speeds. The vibration usually diminishes at higher speeds due to decrease in the torque being transmitted. If the driveshaft angles are excessive (over 3 degrees), a vibration is usually produced that increases as the speed of the vehicle (and driveshaft) increases.

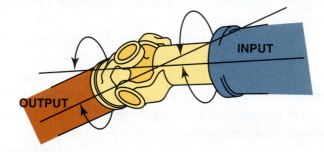

INPUT

OUTPUT

FIGURE 9–9 The joint angle is the difference between the angles of the joint.

FIGURE 9–10 The angle of this rear Cardan U-joint is noticeable.

FIGURE 9–11 A double-Cardan U-joint.

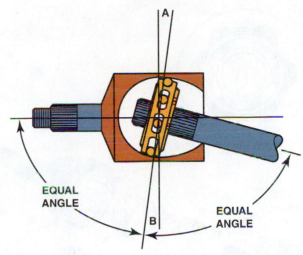

FIGURE 9–12 A constant velocity (CV) joint can operate at high angles without a change in velocity (speed) because the joint design results in equal angles between input and output.

CONSTANT VELOCITY JOINTS

PURPOSE AND FUNCTION Constant velocity joints, commonly called **CV joints**, are designed to rotate without changing speed. Regular U-joints are usually designed to work up to 12 degrees of angularity. If two Cardan-style U-joints are joined together, the angle at which this **double-Cardan joint** can function is about 18 to 20 degrees. ● **SEE FIGURE 9–11**.

Double-Cardan U-joints were first used on large rear-wheel-drive vehicles to help reduce drive line-induced vibrations, especially when the rear of the vehicle was fully loaded and driveshaft angles were at their greatest. As long as a U-joint (either single or double Cardan) operates in a straight line, the driven shaft will rotate at the same constant speed (velocity) as the driving shaft. As the angle increases, the driven shaft speed or velocity varies during each revolution. This produces pulsations and a noticeable vibration or surge.

NOTE: Many four-wheel-drive light trucks use standard Cardan-style U-joints in the front drive axles. If the front wheels are turned sharply and then accelerated, the entire truck often shakes due to the pulsations created by the speed variations through the U-joints. This vibration is normal and cannot be corrected. It is characteristic of this type of design and is usually not noticeable in normal driving.

RZEPPA JOINTS The first constant velocity joint was designed by Alfred H. Rzeppa (pronounced shep'pa) in the mid-1920s. The **Rzeppa joint** transfers torque through six round balls that are held in position midway between the two shafts. This design causes the angle between the shafts to be equally split regardless of the angle. ● **SEE FIGURE 9–12**. Because the angle is always split equally, torque is transferred equally without the change in speed (velocity) that occurs in

---

? FREQUENTLY ASKED QUESTION

What Is a 1350-Series U-Joint?

Most universal joints are available in sizes to best match the torque that they transmit. The larger the U-joint, the higher the amount of torque. Most U-joints are sized and rated by series numbers. See the accompanying chart for series numbers and sizes.

Series Number	Cap Diameter (inches)	Overall Length (inches)	Trunnion Diameter (inches)
1000	15/16	2 5/64	1/2
1100	15/16	2 13/64	1/2
1260/1270	1 1/16	2 31/32	19/32
1280	1 1/16	2 31/32	39/64
1310	1 1/16	2 31/32	21/32
1330	1 1/16	3 3/8	21/32
1350	1 3/16	3 3/8	49/64
1410	1 3/16	3 15/16	49/64
1480	1 3/8	3 7/8	57/64

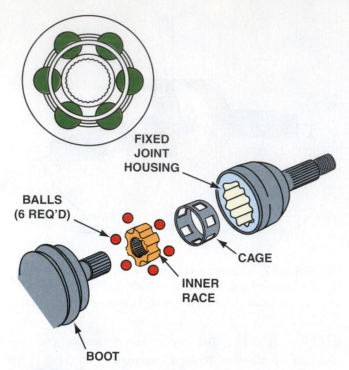

FIXED
JOINT
HOUSING

BALLS
(6 REQ'D)

CAGE

INNER
RACE

BOOT

FIGURE 9–13 A Rzeppa fixed joint. This type of CV joint is commonly used at the wheel side of the drive axle shaft. This joint can operate at high angles to compensate for suspension travel and steering angle changes.

Cardan-style U-joints. This style of joint results in a constant velocity between driving and driven shafts. It can also function at angles greater than simple U-joints can, up to 40 degrees.

NOTE: CV joints are also called LOBRÖ joints, the brand name of an original equipment manufacturer.

While commonly used today in all front-wheel-drive vehicles and many four-wheel-drive vehicles, its first use was on the front-wheel-drive 1929 Cord. Built in Auburn, Indiana, the Cord was the first front-wheel-drive car to use a CV-type drive axle joint.

OUTER CV JOINTS

The Rzeppa-type CV joint is most commonly used as an outer joint on most front-wheel-drive vehicles. ● SEE FIGURE 9–13. The outer joint must do the following:

1. Allow up to 40 degrees or more of movement to allow the front wheels to turn.

2. Allow the front wheels to move up and down through normal suspension travel in order to provide a smooth ride over rough surfaces.

3. Be able to transmit engine torque to drive the front wheels.

Outer CV joints are called **fixed joints**. The outer joints are also attached to the front wheels. They are more likely to suffer from road hazards that often can cut through the protective outer flexible boot. ● SEE FIGURE 9–14. Once this

FIGURE 9–14 The protective CV joint boot has been torn away on this vehicle and all of the grease has been thrown outward onto the brake and suspension parts. The driver of this vehicle noticed a "clicking" noise, especially when turning.

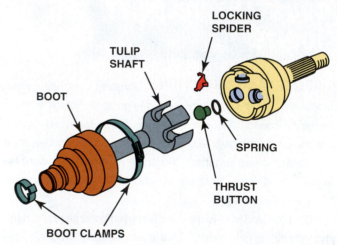

LOCKING
SPIDER

TULIP
SHAFT

BOOT

SPRING

THRUST
BUTTON

BOOT CLAMPS

FIGURE 9–15 A tripod fixed joint. This type of joint is found on some Japanese vehicles. If the joint wears out, it is to be replaced with an entire drive axle shaft assembly.

boot has been split open, the special high-quality grease is thrown out and contaminants such as dirt and water can enter. Some joints cannot be replaced individually if worn. ● SEE FIGURE 9–15.

NOTE: Research has shown that in as few as eight hours of driving time, a CV joint can be destroyed by dirt, moisture, and a lack of lubrication if the boot is torn. The technician should warn the owner as to the possible cost involved in replacing the CV joint itself whenever a torn CV boot is found.

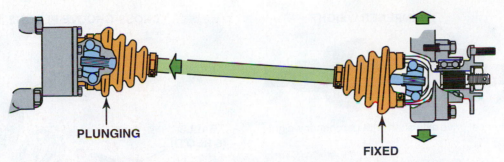

PLUNGING

FIXED

FIGURE 9–16 The fixed outer joint is required to move in all directions because the wheels must turn for steering as well as move up and down during suspension movement. The inner joint has to be able to not only move up and down but also plunge in and out as the suspension moves up and down.

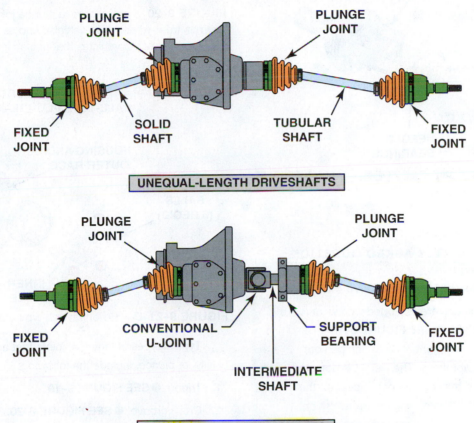

PLUNGE JOINT   PLUNGE JOINT

FIXED JOINT   SOLID SHAFT   TUBULAR SHAFT   FIXED JOINT

UNEQUAL-LENGTH DRIVESHAFTS

PLUNGE JOINT   PLUNGE JOINT

FIXED JOINT   CONVENTIONAL U-JOINT   SUPPORT BEARING   FIXED JOINT

INTERMEDIATE SHAFT

EQUAL-LENGTH DRIVESHAFTS

FIGURE 9–17 Unequal-length driveshafts result in unequal drive axle shaft angles to the front drive wheels. This unequal angle side to side often results in a steering of the vehicle during acceleration called torque steer. By using an intermediate shaft, both drive axles are the same angle and the torque steer effect is reduced.

INNER CV JOINTS Inner CV joints attach the output of the transaxle to the drive axle shaft. Inner CV joints are therefore inboard, or toward the center of the vehicle. ● SEE FIGURE 9–16.

Inner CV joints have to be able to perform two very important movements:

1. Allow the drive axle shaft to move up and down as the wheels travel over bumps.

2. Allow the drive axle shaft to change length as required during vehicle suspension travel movements (lengthening and shortening as the vehicle moves up and down; same as the slip yoke on a conventional RWD driveshaft). CV joints are also called **plunge joints**.

DRIVE AXLE SHAFTS Unequal-length **drive axle shafts** (also called **half shafts**) result in unequal drive axle shaft angles to the front drive wheels. ● SEE FIGURE 9–17. This unequal angle often results in a pull on the steering wheel during acceleration. This pulling to one side during acceleration due to

FIGURE 9–18 A typical drive axle shaft with dampener weight.

TRIPOD-TYPE PLUNGE JOINT

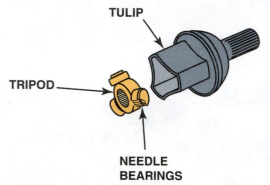

TULIP

TRIPOD

NEEDLE
BEARINGS

FIGURE 9–19 A tripod joint is also called a tripot, tripode, or tulip design.

? **FREQUENTLY ASKED QUESTION**

What Is That Weight for on the Drive Axle Shaft?

Some drive axle shafts are equipped with what looks like a balance weight. ● **SEE FIGURE 9–18**. It is actually a dampener weight used to dampen out certain drive line vibrations. The weight is not used on all vehicles and may or may not appear on the same vehicle depending on engine, transmission, and other options. The service technician should always try to replace a defective or worn drive axle shaft with the exact replacement. When replacing an entire drive axle shaft, the technician should always follow the manufacturer's instructions regarding either transferring or not transferring the weight to the new shaft.

unequal engine torque being applied to the front drive wheels is called torque steer. To help reduce the effect of torque steer, some vehicles are manufactured with an intermediate shaft that results in equal drive axle shaft angles. Both designs use fixed outer CV joints with plunge-type inner joints.

CROSS-GROOVE PLUNGE JOINT

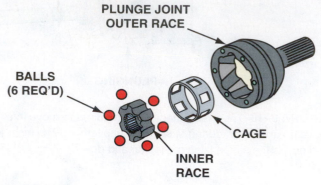

PLUNGE JOINT
OUTER RACE

BALLS
(6 REQ'D)

CAGE

INNER
RACE

FIGURE 9–20 A cross-groove plunge joint is used on many German front-wheel-drive vehicles and as both inner and outer joints on the rear of vehicles that use an independent-type rear suspension.

DOUBLE-OFFSET BALL-TYPE PLUNGE JOINT

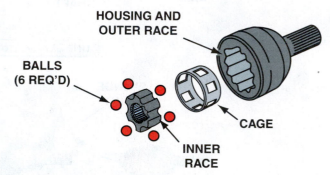

HOUSING AND
OUTER RACE

BALLS
(6 REQ'D)

CAGE

INNER
RACE

FIGURE 9–21 Double-offset ball-type plunge joint.

Typical types of inner CV joints that are designed to move axially, or *plunge,* include the following:

1. Tripod. ● **SEE FIGURE 9–19**.
2. Cross groove. ● **SEE FIGURE 9–20**.
3. Double offset. ● **SEE FIGURE 9–21**.

CV joints are also used in rear-wheel-drive vehicles and in many four-wheel-drive vehicles.

CV JOINT BOOT MATERIALS The pliable boot surrounding the CV joint, or **CV joint boot**, must be able to remain flexible under all weather conditions and still be strong enough to avoid being punctured by road debris. There are four basic types of boot materials used over CV joints:

1. *Natural rubber* (black) uses a bridge-type stainless steel clamp to retain.
2. *Silicone rubber* (gray) is a high-temperature-resistant material that is usually used only in places that need heat protection, such as the inner CV joint of a front-wheel-drive vehicle.

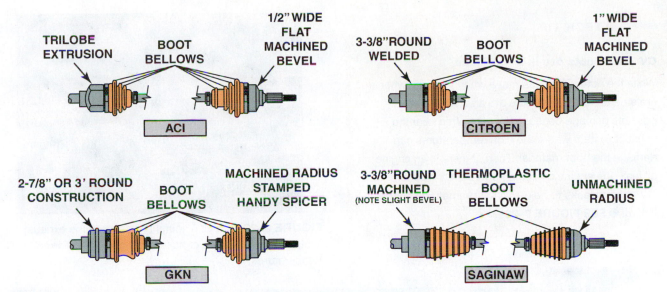

FIGURE 9–22 Getting the correct boot kit or parts from the parts store is more difficult on many Chrysler front-wheel-drive vehicles because Chrysler has used four different manufacturers for its axle shaft assemblies.

3. *Hard thermoplastic* (black) is a hard plastic material requiring heavy-duty clamps and a lot of torque to tighten (about 100 lb-ft!).

4. *Urethane* (usually blue) is a type of boot material usually found in an aftermarket part. ● **SEE FIGURE 9–22** for examples of various types of CV joint boots depending on the manufacturer of the CV joints and shafts.

NOTE: Some aftermarket companies offer a split-style replacement CV joint boot. Being split means that the boot can be replaced without having to remove the drive axle shaft. Vehicle manufacturers usually do *not* recommend this type of replacement boot because the joint cannot be disassembled and properly cleaned with the drive axle still in the vehicle. The split boots must also be kept perfectly clean (a hard job to do with all the grease in the joint) in order to properly seal the seam on the split boot.

It is important that boot seals be inspected regularly and replaced if damaged. The inboard (plunging joint) can often pump water into the joint around the seals or through small holes in the boot material itself because the joint moves in and out. Seal retainers are used to provide a leakproof connection between the boot seal and the housing or axle shaft.

CV JOINT GREASE   CV joints require special greases. Grease is an oil with thickening agents. Greases are named for the thickening agents used.

Most CV joint grease is molybdenum-disulfide-type grease, commonly referred to as *moly* grease. The exact composition of grease can vary depending on the CV joint manufacturer. *The grease supplied with a replacement CV joint or boot kit should be the only grease used*.

The exact mix of chemicals, viscosity (thickness), wear, and corrosion-resistant properties varies from one CV joint application to another. Some technicians mistakenly think that the *color* of the grease determines in which CV joint it is used. The color—such as black, blue, red, or tan—is used to identify the grease during manufacturing and packaging as well as to give the grease a consistent, even color (due to blending of various ingredients in the grease).

The exact grease to use depends on many factors, including the following:

1. The type (style) of CV joint. For example, outer (fixed) and inner (plunging) joints have different lubricating needs.

2. The location of the joint on the vehicle. For example, inner CV joints are usually exposed to the greatest amount of heat.

3. The type of boot. The grease has to be compatible with the boot material.

FIGURE 9–23 Many CV joints are close to the exhaust system where they are exposed to higher than normal temperatures.

SUMMARY

1. The driveshaft of a rear-wheel-drive vehicle transmits engine torque from the transmission to the differential.

2. Driveshaft length is usually limited to about 65 inches due to balancing considerations unless a two-piece or a composite-material shaft is used.

3. Universal joints (U-joints) allow the driveshaft to transmit engine torque while the suspension and the rear axle assembly are moving up and down during normal driving conditions.

4. Acceptable working angles for a Cardan-type U-joint fall within 1/2 to 3 degrees. Some angle is necessary to cause

the roller bearings to rotate; a working angle of greater than 3 degrees can lead to driveline vibrations.

5. Constant velocity (CV) joints are used on all front-wheel-drive vehicles and many four-wheel-drive vehicles to provide a smooth transmission of torque to the drive wheels regardless of angularity of the wheel or joint.

6. Outer or fixed CV joints commonly use a Rzeppa design, while inner CV joints are the plunging or tripod type.

REVIEW QUESTIONS

1. Explain why Cardan-type U-joints on a driveshaft must be within 1/2 degree working angles.

2. What makes a constant velocity joint able to transmit engine torque through an angle at a constant velocity?

3. What type of grease must be used in CV joints?

CHAPTER QUIZ

1. The name most often used to describe the universal joints on a conventional rear-wheel-drive vehicle driveshaft is _____.
   - a. Trunnion
   - b. Cardan
   - c. CV
   - d. Spider

2. A rear-wheel-drive vehicle shudders or vibrates when first accelerating from a stop. The vibration is less noticeable at higher speeds. The most likely cause is _____.
   - a. Driveshaft unbalance
   - b. Excessive U-joint working angles
   - c. Unequal U-joint working angles
   - d. Brinelling of the U-joint

3. All driveshafts are balanced.
   - a. True
   - b. False

4. The maximum difference between the front and rear working angle of a driveshaft is _____.
   - a. 1/4 degree
   - b. 1/2 degree
   - c. 1 degree
   - d. 3 degrees

5. Which series U-joint has the greatest torque capacity?
   - a. 1260
   - b. 1310
   - c. 1350
   - d. 1480

6. Two technicians are discussing torque steer on a front-wheel-drive vehicle. Technician A says that equal-length

drive axle shafts help reduce torque steer. Technician B says that equal drive axle shaft angles help reduce torque steer. Which technician is correct?

a. Technician A only   c. Both Technicians A and B
b. Technician B only   d. Neither Technician A nor B

7. The outer CV joints used on front-wheel-drive vehicles are _____.

a. Fixed type   b. Plunge type

8. The proper grease to use with a CV joint is _____.
   a. Black chassis grease
   b. Dark blue EP grease
   c. Red moly grease
   d. The grease that is supplied with the boot kit

9. Drive axle shafts are also called _____.
   a. Double-Cardan shafts   c. Driveshafts
   b. Half shafts   d. Propeller shafts

10. Two technicians are discussing a dented driveshaft. Technician A says that it should be repaired. Technician B says that it should be replaced. Which technician is correct?
    a. Technician A only
    b. Technician B only
    c. Both Technicians A and B
    d. Neither Technician A nor B

JOINT SERVICE

LEARNING OBJECTIVES

After studying this chapter, the reader should be able to:

1. Explain how to perform a U-joint inspection.
2. List the steps necessary to replace a U-joint.
3. Explain how to perform a measurement of the working angles of a U-joint.
4. Diagnose problems with CV joints and describe the service procedures for replacing CV joints.

This chapter will help you prepare for Suspension and Steering (A4) ASE certification test content area "C" (Related Suspension and Steering Service).

KEY TERMS

Inclinometer 179
Pin bushings 178
Pinch bolt 181
Spline bind 183

Synthetic retainers 177
Prevailing torque
   nut 182
U-joints 175

U-JOINT DIAGNOSIS

BACKGROUND The driveshaft of a typical rear-wheel-drive (RWD) vehicle rotates about three times faster than the wheels. This is due to the gear reduction that occurs in the differential. The differential not only provides gear reduction but also allows for a difference in the speed of the rear wheels that is necessary whenever turning a corner.

The driveshaft rotates at the same speed as the engine if the transmission ratio is 1 to 1 (1:1). The engine speed, in revolutions per minute (RPM), is transmitted through the transmission at the same speed. In lower gears, the engine speed is many times faster than the output of the transmission. Most transmissions today, both manual and automatic, have an overdrive gear. This means that at highway speeds, the driveshaft is rotating faster than the engine (the engine speed is decreased or over-driven to help reduce engine speed and improve fuel economy).

SYMPTOMS OF DEFECTIVE U-JOINTS

The driveshaft must travel up and down as the vehicle moves over bumps and dips in the road while rotating and transmitting engine power to the drive wheels. The driveshaft and universal joints should be carefully inspected whenever any of the following problems or symptoms occur:

1. Vibration or harshness at highway speed

2. A clicking sound whenever the vehicle is moving either forward or in reverse

3. A clunking sound whenever changing gears, such as moving from drive to reverse

NOTE: A click-click-click sound while moving in reverse is usually the first indication of a defective U-joint. This clicking occurs in reverse because the needle bearings are being forced to rotate in a direction opposite the usual.

DRIVESHAFT AND U-JOINT INSPECTION

The driveshaft should be inspected for the following:

1. Any dents or creases caused by incorrect hoisting of the vehicle or by road debris.

   CAUTION: A dented or creased driveshaft can collapse, especially when the vehicle is under load. This collapse of the driveshaft can cause severe damage to the vehicle and may cause an accident.

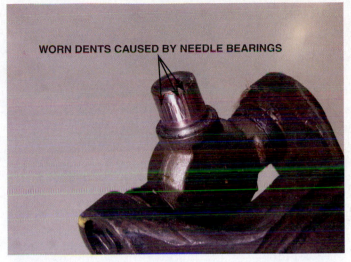

WORN DENTS CAUSED BY NEEDLE BEARINGS

FIGURE 10–1 Notice how the needle bearings have worn grooves, called Brinelling, into the bearing surface of the U-joint.

 REAL WORLD FIX

The Squeaking Pickup Truck

The owner of a pickup truck complained that a squeaking noise occurred while driving in reverse. The "eeee eeee eeee" sound increased in frequency as the truck increased in speed, yet the noise did not occur when driving forward.

Because there was no apparent looseness in the U-joints, the service technician at first thought that the problem was inside either the transmission or the rear end. When the driveshaft was removed to further investigate the problem, it became obvious where the noise was coming from. The U-joint needle bearing had worn the cross-shaft bearing surface of the U-joint. ● **SEE FIGURE 10–1**. The noise occurred only in reverse because the wear had occurred in the forward direction, and therefore only when the torque was applied in the opposite direction did the needle bearing become bound up and start to make noise. A replacement U-joint solved the squeaking noise in reverse.

2. Undercoating, grease, or dirt buildup on the driveshaft can cause vibrations.

3. Undercoating should be removed using a suitable solvent and a rag. Always dispose of used rags properly.

The **U-joints** should be inspected every time the vehicle chassis is lubricated, or four times a year. Original equipment

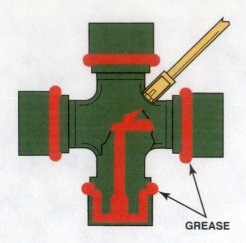

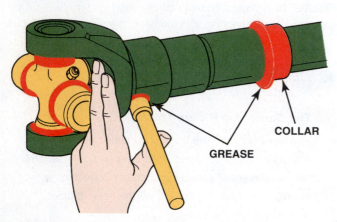

FIGURE 10–2 All U-joints and spline collars equipped with a grease fitting should be greased four times a year as part of a regular lubrication service. (*Courtesy of Dana Corporation*)

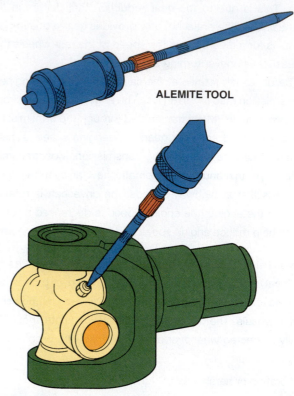

FIGURE 10–3 Many U-joints require a special grease gun tool to reach the grease fittings. (*Courtesy of Dana Corporation*)

(OE) U-joints are permanently lubricated and have no provision for greasing. If there is a grease fitting, the U-joint should be lubricated by applying grease with a grease gun. ● **SEE FIGURES 10–2 AND 10–3.**

In addition to periodic lubrication, the driveshaft should be grabbed and moved to see if there is any movement of the U-joints. If *any* movement is noticed when the driveshaft is moved, the U-joint is worn and must be replaced.

NOTE: U-joints are not serviceable items and cannot be repaired. If worn or defective, they must be replaced.

U-joints can be defective and still not show noticeable free movement. *A proper U-joint inspection can be performed only by removing the driveshaft from the vehicle.*

Before removing the driveshaft, always mark the position of all mating parts to ensure proper reassembly. White correction fluid, also known as "White Out" or "Liquid Paper," is an easy and fast-drying marking material. ● **SEE FIGURE 10–4.**

To remove the driveshaft from a rear-wheel-drive vehicle, remove the four fasteners at the rear U-joint at the differential. ● **SEE FIGURE 10–5.**

Push the driveshaft forward toward the transmission and then down and toward the rear of the vehicle. The driveshaft should slip out of the transmission spline and can be removed from underneath the vehicle.

NOTE: With the driveshaft removed, transmission lubricant can leak out of the rear extension housing. To prevent a mess, use an old spline the same size as the one being removed or place a plastic bag over the extension housing to hold any escaping lubricant. A rubber band can be used to hold the bag onto the extension housing.

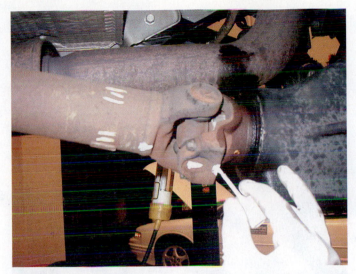

FIGURE 10–4 Always mark the original location of U-joints before disassembly.

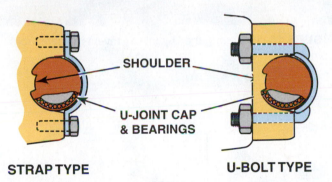

SHOULDER

U-JOINT CAP & BEARINGS

STRAP TYPE   U-BOLT TYPE

FIGURE 10–5 Two types of retaining methods that are commonly used at the rear U-joint at the differential.

To inspect U-joints, move each joint through its full travel, making sure it can move (articulate) freely and equally in all directions. ● SEE FIGURE 10–6.

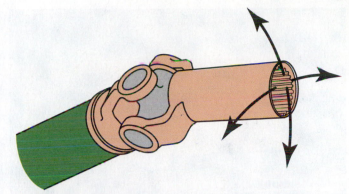

FIGURE 10–6 The best way to check any U-joint is to remove the driveshaft from the vehicle and move each joint in all directions. A good U-joint should be free to move without binding.

FIGURE 10–7 Typical U-joint that uses an outside snap ring. This style of joint bolts directly to the companion flange that is attached to the pinion gear in the differential.

U-JOINT REPLACEMENT

All movement in a U-joint should occur between the trunnions and the needle bearings in the end caps. The end caps are press-fit to the yokes, which are welded to the driveshaft. Three types of retainers are used to keep the bearing caps on the U-joints: the outside snap ring (● SEE FIGURE 10–7), the inside retaining ring, and injected synthetic (usually nylon). (● SEE FIGURE 10–8).

After removing the retainers, use a press or a vise to separate the U-joint from the yoke. ● SEE FIGURE 10–9.

U-joints that use **synthetic retainers** must be separated using a press and a special tool to press onto both sides of

TECH TIP

Use Tape to Be Safe

When removing a driveshaft, use tape to prevent the rear U-joint caps from falling off. If the caps fall off the U-joint, all of the needle bearings will fall out and scatter over the floor. ● SEE FIGURE 10–10.

the joint in order to shear the plastic retainer, as shown in ● FIGURE 10–11.

Replacement U-joints use spring clips instead of injected plastic. Remove the old U-joint from the yoke, as shown in ● FIGURE 10–12, and replace with a new U-joint.

FIGURE 10–8 A U-joint that is held together by nylon and usually requires that heat be applied to remove from the yoke.

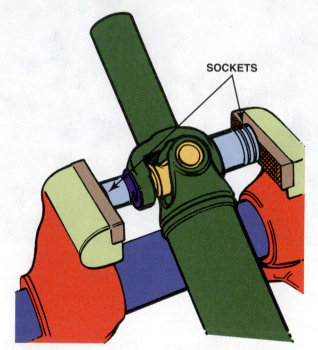

FIGURE 10–9 Use a vise and two sockets to replace a U-joint. One socket fits over the bearing cup and the other fits on the bearing to press-fit the cups from the crosspiece.

Replacement U-joints should be *forged* (never cast) and use up to 32 needle bearings (also called **pin bushings**) instead of just 24 needle bearings, as used in lower-quality U-joints. Replacement U-joints usually have a grease fitting so that the new replacement U-joint can be properly lubricated. ● **SEE FIGURE 10–13**.

After removing any dirt or burrs from the yoke, press in a new U-joint. Rotate the new joint after installation to make sure it moves freely, without binding or stiffness. If a U-joint is stiff, it can cause a vibration.

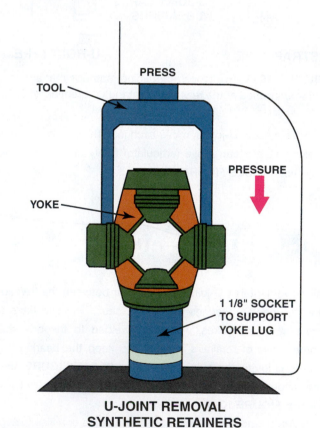

FIGURE 10–10 Taping the U-joint to prevent the caps from coming off.

U-JOINT REMOVAL SYNTHETIC RETAINERS

FIGURE 10–11 A special tool being used to press apart a U-joint that is retained by injected plastic. Heat from a propane torch may be necessary to soften the plastic to avoid exerting too much force on the U-joint.

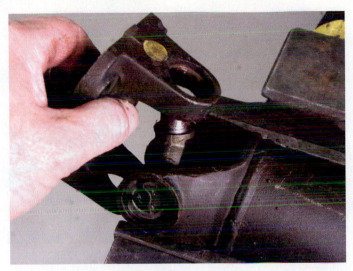

FIGURE 10–12 Removing the worn cross from the yoke.

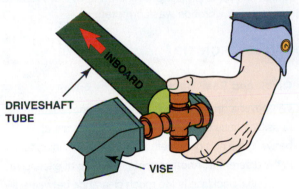

FIGURE 10–13 When installing a new U-joint, position the grease fitting on the inboard side (toward the driveshaft tube) and in alignment with the grease fitting of the U-joint at the other end.

NOTE: If a U-joint is slightly stiff after being installed, strike the U-joint using a brass punch and a light hammer. This often frees a stiff joint and is often called "relieving the joint." The shock aligns the needle bearings in the end caps.

U-JOINT WORKING ANGLES

Unequal or incorrect U-joint working angles can cause severe vibrations. Driveshaft and U-joint angles may change from the original factory setting due to one or more of the following:

1. Defective or collapsed engine or transmission mounts

2. Defective or sagging springs, especially the rear springs due to overloading or other causes

3. Accident damage or other changes to the chassis of the vehicle

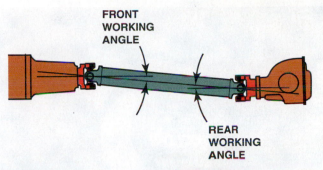

FIGURE 10–14 The working angle of most U-joints should be at least 1/2 degree (to permit the needle bearing to rotate in the U-joints) and should not exceed 3 degrees or a vibration can occur in the driveshaft, especially at higher speeds. The difference between the front and rear working angles should be within 1/2 degree of each other.

4. Vehicle modification that raises or lowers the ride height

Replace any engine or transmission mount that is cracked or collapsed. When a mount collapses, the engine drops from its original location. Now the driveshaft angles are changed and a vibration may be felt.

Rear springs often sag after many years of service or after being overloaded. This is especially true of pickup trucks. Many people carry as much as the cargo bed can hold, often exceeding the factory-recommended carry capacity or gross vehicle weight (GVW) of the vehicle.

To measure U-joint and driveshaft angles, the vehicle must be hoisted using an axle contact or drive-on-type lift so as to maintain the same driveshaft angles as the vehicle has while being driven.

The working angles of the two U-joints on a driveshaft should be within 1/2 degree of each other in order to cancel out speed changes. ● **SEE FIGURE 10–14.**

To measure the working angle of a U-joint, follow these steps:

STEP 1 Place an **inclinometer** (a tool used to measure angles) on the rear U-joint bearing cap. Level the bubble and read the angle. ● **SEE FIGURE 10–15**; the pictured reading is 19.5 degrees.

STEP 2 Rotate the driveshaft 90 degrees and read the angle of the rear yoke. For example, this reading is 17 degrees.

STEP 3 Subtract the smaller reading from the larger reading to obtain the working angle of the joint. In this example, it is 2.5 degrees (19.5 degrees – 17 degrees = 2.5 degrees).

Repeat the same procedure for the front U-joint. The front and rear working angles should be within 0.5 degrees. If the two working angles are not within 0.5 degrees, shims can be added to bring the two angles closer together. The angle of the rear joint is changed by installing a tapered shim between the leaf spring and the axle, as shown in ● **FIGURE 10–16.**

FIGURE 10–15 An inclinometer with a magnetic base is being used to measure the angle of the driveshaft at the rear U-joint.

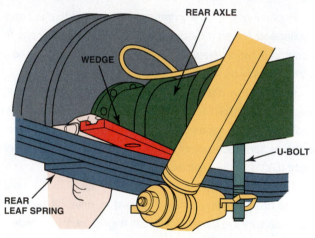

FIGURE 10–16 Placing a tapered metal wedge between the rear leaf spring and the rear axle pedestal to correct rear U-joint working angles.

CAUTION: Use caution whenever using wedges between the differential and the rear leaf spring to restore the correct U-joint working angle. Even though wedges are made to raise the front of the differential, the tilt often prevents rear-end lubricant from reaching the pinion bearing, resulting in pinion bearing noise and eventual failure.

The angle of the front joint is changed by adding or removing shims from the mount under the transmission. Sometimes the drive shaft working angles can change due to wear or failure of the engine or transmission mounts. ● SEE FIGURE 10–17.

CV JOINT DIAGNOSIS

When a CV joint wears or fails, the most common symptom is noise while driving. An outer fixed CV joint will most likely be heard when turning sharply and accelerating at the same time. This noise is usually a clicking sound. While inner joint

FIGURE 10–17 A transmission oil pan gasket leak allowed automatic transmission fluid (ATF) to saturate the rear transmission mount rubber, causing it to collapse. After replacing the defective mount, proper driveshaft angles were restored and the driveline vibration was corrected.

TECH TIP

Quick and Easy Backlash Test

Whenever a driveline clunk is being diagnosed, one possible cause is excessive backlash (clearance) between the ring gear teeth and differential pinion teeth in the differential. Another common cause of excessive differential backlash is too much clearance between differential carrier pinion teeth and side gear teeth. A quick test to check backlash involves three easy steps:

STEP 1 Hoist the vehicle on a frame contact lift, allowing the drive wheels to be rotated.

STEP 2 Have an assistant hold one drive wheel and the driveshaft to keep them from turning.

STEP 3 Move the other drive wheel, observing how far the tire can rotate. This is the amount of backlash in the differential; it should be less than 1 inch (25 mm) of movement measured *at the tire*.

If the tire can move more than 1 inch (25 mm), then the differential should be inspected for wear and parts should be replaced as necessary. If the tire moves *less* than 1 inch (25 mm), then the backlash between the ring gear and pinion is probably *not* the cause of the noise.

failure is less common, a defective inner CV joint often creates a loud clunk while accelerating from rest. To help verify a defective joint, drive the vehicle in reverse while turning and accelerating. This almost always will reveal a defective outer joint.

REPLACEMENT SHAFT ASSEMBLIES

Front-wheel-drive vehicles were widely used in Europe and Japan long before they became popular in North America. The standard repair procedure used in these countries is the replacement of the entire drive assembly if there is a CV joint failure. Replacement boot kits are rarely seen in Europe because it is felt that even a slight amount of dirt or water inside a CV joint is unacceptable. Vehicle owners simply wait until the joint wear causes severe noise, and then the entire assembly is replaced.

The entire drive axle shaft assembly can easily be replaced and the defective unit can be sent to a company for remanufacturing. Even though cost to the customer is higher, the parts and repair shop does not have to inventory every type, size, and style of boot kit and CV joint. Service procedures and practices therefore vary according to location and the availability of parts. For example, some service technicians use replacement drive axle assemblies from salvage yards with good success.

NOTE: Some drive axle shafts have a weight attached between the inner and outer CV joints. This is a dampener weight. It is not a balance weight, and it need not be transferred to the replacement drive axle shaft (half shaft) unless instructed to do so in the directions that accompany the replacement shaft assembly.

CV JOINT SERVICE

The hub nut must be removed whenever servicing a CV joint or shaft assembly on a front-wheel-drive vehicle. Since these nuts are usually torqued to almost 200 lb-ft (260 N-m), keep the vehicle on the ground until the hub nut is loosened and then follow these steps (● **SEE FIGURE 10–18**):

STEP 1 Remove the front wheel and hub nut.

> **NOTE: Most manufacturers warn against using an air impact wrench to remove the hub nut. The impacting force can damage the hub bearing.**

STEP 2 To allow the knuckle room to move outward enough to remove the drive axle shaft, some or all of the following will have to be disconnected:

   a. Lower ball joint or **pinch bolt** (● **SEE FIGURE 10–19**).
   b. Tie rod end (● **SEE FIGURE 10–20**).
   c. Stabilizer bar link.
   d. Front disc brake caliper.

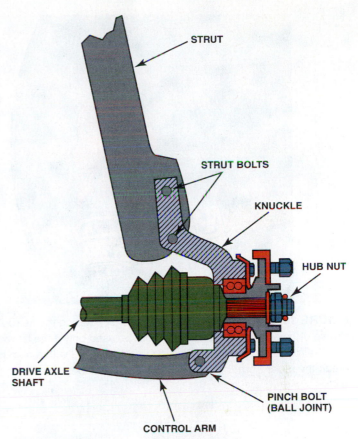

FIGURE 10–18 The hub nut must be removed before the hub bearing assembly or drive axle shaft can be removed from the vehicle.

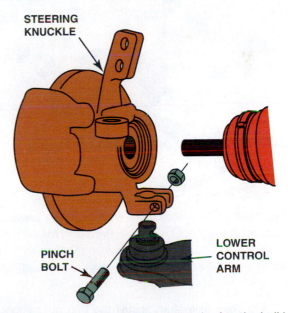

FIGURE 10–19 Many knuckles are attached to the ball joint on the lower control arm by a pinch bolt.

STEP 3 Remove the splined end of the axle from the hub bearing. Sometimes a special puller may be necessary, but in most cases the shaft can be tapped inward through the hub bearing with a light hammer and a brass punch can be used. To protect the threads of

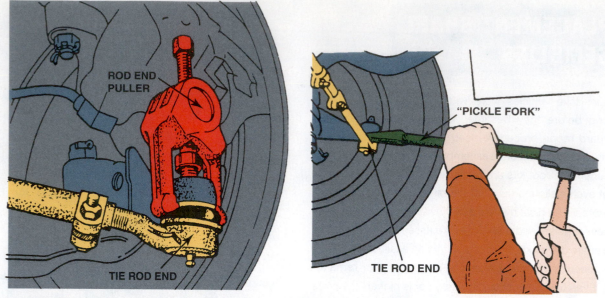

FIGURE 10–20 The preferred method for separating the tie rod end from the steering knuckle is to use a puller such as the one shown. A "pickle-fork"-type tool should be used only if the tie rod is going to be replaced. A pickle-fork-type tool can damage or tear the rubber grease boot. Striking the tie rod end with a hammer while holding another hammer behind the joint to shock and break the taper from the steering knuckle can also be used.

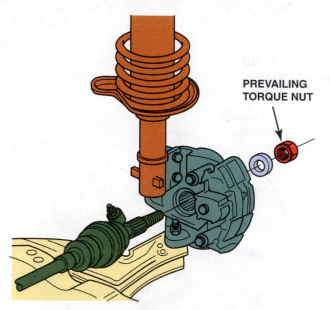

FIGURE 10–21 Many drive axles are retained by **prevailing torque nut** that must not be reused. Prevailing torque nuts are slightly deformed or contain a plastic insert that holds the nut tight (retains the torque) to the shaft without loosening.

FIGURE 10–22 A special General Motors tool is being used to separate the drive axle shaft from the wheel hub bearing.

the drive axle shaft, install the hub nut temporarily. ● **SEE FIGURES 10–21 AND 10–22.**

STEP 4 Use a prybar or special tool with a slide hammer, as shown in ● **FIGURE 10–23**, and remove the inner joint from the transaxle.

STEP 5 Disassemble, clean, and inspect all components. ● **SEE FIGURES 10–24 THROUGH 10–30.**

STEP 6 Replace the entire joint if there are *any* worn parts. Pack *all* the grease that is supplied into the assembly or joint. ● **SEE FIGURE 10–31.** Assemble the joint and position the boot in the same location as marked. Before clamping the last seal on the boot, be sure to release trapped air to prevent the boot from expanding when heated and collapsing when cold. This is sometimes called *burping the boot.* Clamp the boot according to the manufacturer's specifications.

STEP 7 Reinstall the drive axle shaft in the reverse order of removal, and torque the drive axle nut to factory specifications. ● **SEE FIGURE 10–32.**

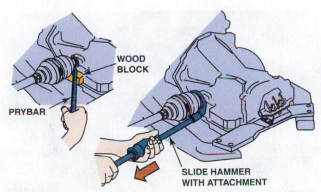

FIGURE 10–23 Most inner CV joints can be separated from the transaxle with a prybar.

FIGURE 10–24 When removing a drive axle shaft assembly, use care to avoid pulling the plunge joint apart.

FIGURE 10–25 If other service work requires that just one end of the drive axle shaft be disconnected from the vehicle, be sure that the free end is supported to prevent damage to the protective boots or allowing the joint to separate.

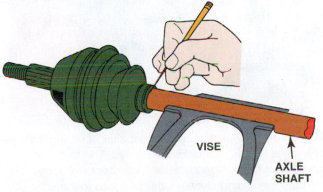

FIGURE 10–26 With a scribe, mark the location of the boots before removal. The replacement boots must be in the same location.

TECH TIP

Spline Bind Cure

Driveline "clunk" often occurs in rear-wheel-drive vehicles when shifting between drive and reverse or when accelerating from a stop. Often the cause of this noise is excessive clearance between the teeth of the ring and pinion in the differential. Another cause is called **spline bind**, where the changing rear pinion angle creates a binding in the spline when the rear springs change in height. For example, when a pickup truck stops, the weight transfers toward the front and unloads the rear springs. The front of the differential noses downward and forward as the rear springs unload. When the driver accelerates forward, the rear of the truck squats downward, causing the drive shaft to be pulled rearward when the front of the differential rotates upward. This upward movement on the spline often causes the spline to bind and make a loud clunk when the bind is finally released.

The method recommended by vehicle manufacturers to eliminate this noise is to follow these steps:

1. Remove the driveshaft.
2. Clean the splines on both the driveshaft yoke and the transmission output shaft.
3. Remove any burrs on the splines with a small metal file (remove all filings).
4. Apply a high-temperature grease to the spline teeth of the yoke. Apply grease to each spline, but do not fill the splines. Synthetic chassis grease is preferred because of its high temperature resistance.
5. Reinstall the driveshaft.

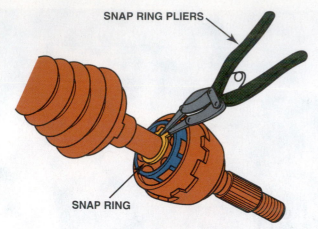

FIGURE 10–27 Most CV joints use a snap ring to retain the joint on the drive axle shaft.

SNAP RING PLIERS

SNAP RING

FIGURE 10–28 After releasing the snap ring, most CV joints can be tapped off the shaft using a brass or shot-filled plastic (dead-blow) hammer.

FIGURE 10–29 Typical outer CV joint after removing the boot and the joint from the drive axle shaft. This joint was removed from the vehicle because a torn boot was found. After disassembly and cleaning, this joint was found to be OK and was put back into service. Even though the grease looks terrible, there was enough grease in the joint to provide lubrication to prevent any wear from occurring.

FIGURE 10–30 The cage of this Rzeppa-type CV joint is being carefully inspected before being reassembled.

FIGURE 10–31 Be sure to use *all* of the grease supplied with the replacement joint or boot kit. Use only the grease supplied and do not use substitute grease.

 REAL WORLD FIX

The Vibrating Buick

The owner of a front-wheel-drive Buick complained that it vibrated during acceleration only. The vehicle would also pull toward one side during acceleration. An inspection discovered a worn (cracked) engine mount. After replacing the mount, the CV joint angles were restored and both the vibration and the pulling to one side during acceleration were solved. ● SEE **FIGURE 10–33**.

FIGURE 10–32 A punch being used to keep the rotor from rotating while torquing the axle shaft spindle nut.

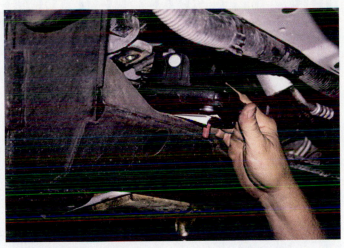

FIGURE 10–33 The engine had to be raised higher to get the new (non-collapsed) engine mount installed.

DRIVE AXLE SHAFT REPLACEMENT

1 Tools needed to replace a drive axle shaft on a General Motors vehicle include a drift, sockets, plus a prybar bearing/axle shaft special tool.

2 The drive axle shaft retaining nut can be loosened with the tire on the ground, or use a drift inserted into the rotor cooling fins before removing the nut.

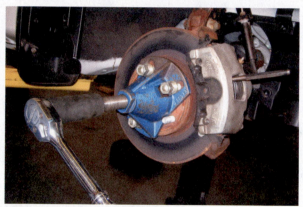

3 Using a special tool to push the drive axle splines from the bearing assembly.

4 Remove the disc brake caliper and support it out of the way. Then, remove the disc brake rotor.

5 To allow for the removal of the drive axle shaft, the strut is removed from the steering knuckle assembly.

6 A prybar is used to separate the inner drive axle shaft joint from the transaxle.

PRY BAR

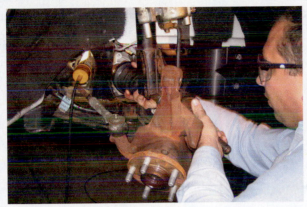

7 After the inner joint splines have been released from the transaxle, carefully remove the drive axle shaft assembly from the vehicle.

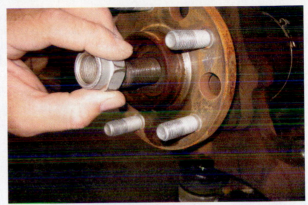

8 To install, reverse the disassembly procedure and be sure to install the washer under the retainer-nut, and always use a new prevailing torque nut.

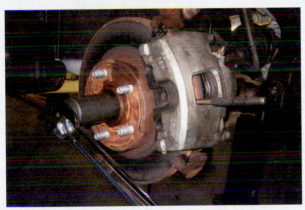

9 Reinstall the disc brake rotor and caliper and then torque the drive axle shaft retaining nut to factory specifications.

SUMMARY

1. A defective U-joint often makes a *clicking* sound when the vehicle is driven in reverse. Severely defective U-joints can cause driveline vibrations or a *clunk* sound when the transmission is shifted from reverse to drive or from drive to reverse.

2. Incorrect driveshaft working angles can result from collapsed engine or transmission mounts.

3. Driveline clunk noise can often be corrected by applying high-temperature chassis grease to the splines of the front yoke on the driveshaft.

4. CV joints require careful cleaning, inspection, and lubrication with specific CV joint grease.

REVIEW QUESTIONS

1. List two items that should be checked when inspecting a driveshaft.

2. List the steps necessary to measure driveshaft U-joint working angles.

3. Describe how to replace a Cardan-type U-joint.

4. Explain the proper steps to perform when replacing a CV joint.

CHAPTER QUIZ

1. Two technicians are discussing U-joints. Technician A says that a defective U-joint could cause a loud clunk when the transmission is shifted between drive and reverse. Technician B says a worn U-joint can cause a clicking sound only when driving the vehicle in reverse. Which technician is correct?
   a. Technician A only
   b. Technician B only
   c. Both Technicians A and B
   d. Neither Technician A nor B

2. Incorrect or unequal U-joint working angles are most likely to be caused by _____.
   a. A bent driveshaft
   b. A collapsed engine or transmission mount
   c. A dry output shaft spline
   d. Defective or damaged U-joints

3. A defective outer CV joint will usually make a _____.
   a. Rumbling noise
   b. Growling noise
   c. Clicking noise
   d. Clunking noise

4. The last step after installing a replacement CV boot is to _____.
   a. "Burp the boot"
   b. Lubricate the CV joint with chassis grease
   c. Mark the location of the boot on the drive axle shaft
   d. Separate the CV joint before installation

5. A Cardan-type U-joint may require what tool(s) to replace? _____
   a. A special tool
   b. A torch
   c. A press or a vise
   d. May require any of the above

6. What needs to be removed to replace a drive axle shaft from a front-wheel-drive vehicle?
   a. Tie rod end
   b. Lower control arm or ball joint
   c. Hub nut
   d. All of the above

7. The splines of the driveshaft yoke should be lubricated to prevent _____.
   a. A vibration
   b. Spline bind
   c. Rust
   d. Transmission fluid leaking from the extension housing

8. It is recommended by many experts that an air impact wrench *not* be used to remove or install the drive axle shaft nut because the impacting force can damage the hub bearing.
   a. True
   b. False

9. Front and rear driveshaft U-joint working angles should be within _____ degrees of each other.
   a. 0.5
   b. 1.0
   c. 3.0
   d. 4.0

10. A defective (collapsed) engine mount on a front-wheel-drive vehicle can cause a vibration.
    a. True
    b. False

chapter 11

WHEEL BEARINGS AND SERVICE

LEARNING OBJECTIVES

After studying this chapter, the reader will be able to:

1. Explain the diagnosis of defective wheel bearings.
2. Discuss rear drive axle classifications.
3. State the reasons for bearing failure.

This chapter will help you prepare for Suspension and Steering (A4) ASE certification test content area "C" (Related Suspension and Steering Service).

KEY TERMS

Antifriction bearings 191
Axial load 191
Ball bearings 191
Brinelling 206
Cage 192
Cone (inner ring) 192
Cup (outer ring) 192
Dynamic seals 194
Garter spring 194
GC-LB 194

Grease 193
Grease seal 198
Needle rollers 191
NLGI 194
Radial load 191
Retainer plate-type axle 201
Roller bearings 191
Spalling 204
Static seal 194
Tapered roller bearings 191

FIGURE 11–1 Rolling contact bearings include (left to right) ball, roller, needle, and tapered roller.

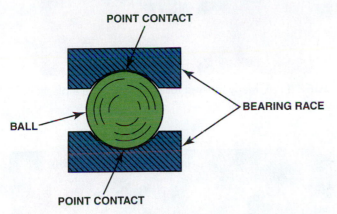

FIGURE 11–2 Ball bearing point contact.

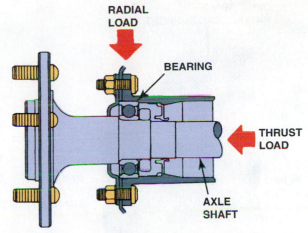

FIGURE 11–3 Radial load is the vehicle weight pressing on the wheels. The thrust load occurs as the chassis components exert a side force during cornering.

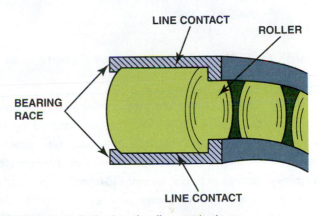

FIGURE 11–4 Roller bearing line contact.

ANTIFRICTION BEARINGS

PURPOSE AND FUNCTION   Bearings allow the wheels of a vehicle to rotate and still support the weight of the entire vehicle. **Antifriction bearings** use rolling parts inside the bearing to reduce friction. Four styles of rolling contact bearings include ball, roller, needle, and tapered roller bearings, as shown in ● **FIGURE 11–1**. All four styles convert sliding friction into rolling motion. All of the weight of a vehicle or load on the bearing is transferred through the rolling part. In a ball bearing, the entire load is concentrated into small spots where the ball contacts the *inner and outer race (rings)*. ● **SEE FIGURE 11–2**.

BALL BEARINGS   **Ball bearings** use hardened steel balls between the inner and outer race to reduce friction. While ball bearings cannot support the same weight as roller bearings, there is less friction in ball bearings and they generally operate at higher speeds. ● **SEE FIGURE 11–3**. Ball bearings can control thrust movement of an axle shaft because the balls ride in grooves on the inner and outer races. The groove walls resist lateral movement of the wheel on the spindle. The most frequent use of ball bearings is at the rear wheels of a rear-wheel-drive vehicle with a solid rear axle. These bearings are installed into the axle housing and are often press fitted to the axle shaft. Many front-wheel-drive vehicles use sealed double-row ball bearings as a complete sealed unit and are non-serviceable except as an assembly.

ROLLER BEARINGS   **Roller bearings** use rollers between the inner and outer race to reduce friction. A roller bearing having a greater (longer) contact area can support heavier loads than a ball bearing. ● **SEE FIGURE 11–4**.

A needle bearing is a type of roller bearing that uses smaller rollers called **needle rollers**. The clearance between the diameter of the straight roller is manufactured into the bearing to provide the proper *radial clearance* and is *not adjustable*.

TAPERED ROLLER BEARINGS   The most commonly used automotive wheel bearing is the **tapered roller bearing**. Not only is the bearing itself tapered, but the rollers are also tapered. By design, this type of bearing can withstand **radial loads** (up and down) as well as **axial loads** (thrust) in one direction. ● **SEE FIGURE 11–5**.

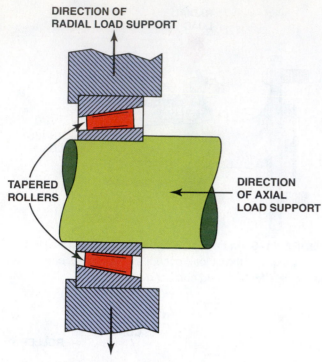

FIGURE 11–5 A tapered roller bearing will support a radial load and an axial load in only one direction.

FIGURE 11–6 Many tapered roller bearings use a plastic cage to retain the rollers.

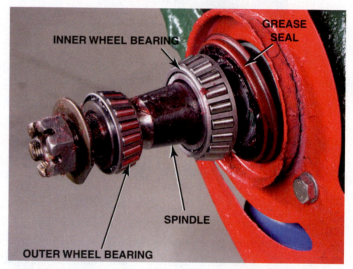

FIGURE 11–7 Non-drive-wheel hub with inner and outer tapered roller bearings. By angling the inner and outer in opposite directions, axial (thrust) loads are supported in both directions.

Many non-drive-wheel bearings use tapered roller bearings. The taper allows more weight to be handled by the friction-reducing bearings because the weight is directed over the entire length of each roller rather than concentrated on a small spot, as with ball bearings. The rollers are held in place by a **cage** between the inner race (also called the **inner ring or cone**) and the outer race (also called the **outer ring or cup**). Tapered roller bearings must be loose in the cage to allow for heat expansion. Tapered roller bearings should always be adjusted for a certain amount of free play to allow for heat expansion. On non-drive-axle vehicle wheels, the cup is tightly fitted to the wheel hub and the cone is loosely fitted to the wheel spindle. New bearings come packaged with the rollers, cage, and inner race assembled together with the outer race wrapped with moisture-resistant paper. ● **SEE FIGURE 11–6**.

INNER AND OUTER WHEEL BEARINGS Many rear-wheel-drive vehicles use an inner and an outer wheel bearing on the front wheels. The inner wheel bearing is always the larger bearing because it is designed to carry most of the vehicle weight and transmit the weight to the suspension through to the spindle. Between the inner wheel bearing and the spindle, there is a grease seal, which prevents grease from getting onto the braking surface and prevents dirt and moisture from entering the bearing. ● **SEE FIGURE 11–7**.

STANDARD BEARING SIZES Bearings use standard dimensions for inside diameter, width, and outside diameter.

The standardization of bearing sizes helps interchangeability. The dimensions that are standardized include bearing bore size (inside diameter), bearing series (light to heavy usage), and external dimensions. When replacing a wheel bearing, note the original bearing brand name and number. Replacement bearing catalogs usually have cross-over charts from one brand to another. The bearing number is usually the same because of the interchangeability and standardization within the wheel bearing industry.

SEALED FRONT-WHEEL-DRIVE BEARINGS Most front-wheel-drive vehicles use a sealed nonadjustable front wheel bearing. This type of bearing can include either two

BALL-BEARING ASSEMBLY

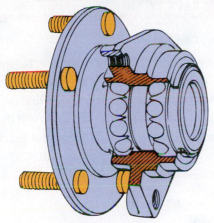

TAPERED ROLLER BEARING ASSEMBLY

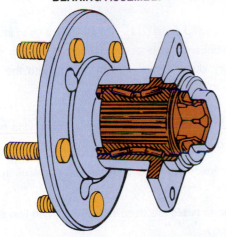

FIGURE 11–8 Sealed bearing and hub assemblies are used on the front and rear wheels of many vehicles.

preloaded tapered roller bearings or a double-row ball bearing. This type of sealed bearing is also used on the rear of many front-wheel-drive vehicles.

Double-row ball bearings are often used because of their reduced friction and greater seize resistance. ● **SEE FIGURES 11–8 AND 11–9.**

BEARING GREASES

DEFINITION OF GREASE Vehicle manufacturers specify the type and consistency of grease for each application. The technician should know what these specifications mean. **Grease** is oil with a thickening agent to allow it to be installed in places where a liquid lubricant would not stay. Greases are named for their thickening agent, such as aluminum, barium, calcium, lithium, or sodium.

GREASE ADDITIVES Commonly used additives in grease include the following:

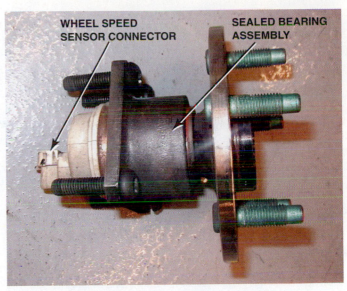

WHEEL SPEED SENSOR CONNECTOR   **SEALED BEARING ASSEMBLY**

FIGURE 11–9 Sealed bearing and hub assemblies are serviced as a complete unit as shown. This hub assembly includes the wheel speed sensor.

> **?** **FREQUENTLY ASKED QUESTION**
>
> **What Do Different Grease Colors Mean?**
>
> Nothing. According to grease manufacturers, grease is colored for identification, marketing, and for consistency of color reasons.
>
> - **Identification.** The color is often used to distinguish one type of grease from another within the same company. The blue grease from one company may be totally different from the blue grease produced or marketed by another company.
> - **Marketing.** According to grease manufacturers, customers tend to be attracted to a particular color of grease and associate that color with quality.
> - **Consistency of color.** All greases are produced in batches, and the color of the finished product often varies from one batch to another. By adding color to the grease, the color can be made consistent.
>
> Always use the grease recommended for the service being performed.

- Antioxidants
- Antiwear agents
- Rust inhibitors
- Extreme pressure (EP) additives such as sulfurized fatty oil or chlorine

Grease also contains a dye to not only provide product identification but also to give the grease a consistent color.

The grease contains a solid such as graphite or molybdenum disulfide (moly), which acts as an antiseize additive.

NLGI CLASSIFICATION The **National Lubricating Grease Institute (NLGI)** uses the penetration test as a guide to assign the grease a number. Low numbers are very fluid and higher numbers are more firm or hard. Number 2 grease is the most commonly used. See the chart for other numbers.

NATIONAL LUBRICATING GREASE INSTITUTE (NLGI) NUMBERS	
NLGI NUMBER	**RELATIVE CONSISTENCY**
000	Very fluid
00	Fluid
0	Semi-fluid
1	Very soft
2	Soft (typically used for wheel bearings)
3	Semi-firm
4	Firm
5	Very firm
6	Hard

Grease is also classified according to quality. Wheel bearing classifications include the following:

- GA—mild duty
- GB—moderate duty
- GC—severe duty, high temperature (frequent stop-and-go service)

GC indicates the highest quality. Chassis grease, such as is used to lubricate steering and suspension components, includes the following classifications:

- LA—mild duty (frequent relubrication)
- LB—high loads (infrequent relubrication)

LB indicates the highest quality. Most multipurpose greases are labeled with both wheel bearing and chassis grease classifications such as **GC-LB**.

More rolling bearings are destroyed by overlubrication than by underlubrication because the heat generated in the bearings cannot be transferred easily to the air through the excessive grease. The cavity between the inner and out bearings should never be filled beyond one-third to one-half of their grease capacity by volume.

SEALS

PURPOSE AND FUNCTION Seals are used in all vehicles to keep lubricant, such as grease, from leaking out and to prevent dirt, dust, or water from getting into the bearing or lubricant.

TYPES OF SEALS Two general applications of seals are static and dynamic.

- **Static seals** are used between two surfaces that do not move.
- **Dynamic seals** are used to seal between two surfaces that move.

Wheel bearing seals are dynamic-type seals that must seal between rotating axle hubs and the stationary spindles or axle housing. Most dynamic seals use a synthetic rubber lip seal encased in metal. The lip is often held in contact with the moving part with the aid of a **garter spring**, as seen in ●**FIGURE 11–10.** The sealing lip should be installed toward the grease or fluid being contained. ●**SEE FIGURE 11–11.**

BEARING DIAGNOSIS

SYMPTOMS OF A DEFECTIVE BEARING Wheel bearings control the positioning and reduce the rolling resistance of vehicle wheels. Whenever a bearing fails, the wheel may not be kept in position and noise is usually heard. Symptoms of defective wheel bearings include the following:

1. A hum, rumbling, or growling noise that increases with vehicle speed
2. Roughness felt in the steering wheel that changes with the vehicle speed or cornering

FIGURE 11–10 Typical lip seal with a garter spring.

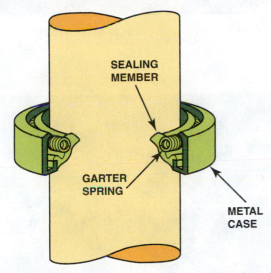

FIGURE 11–11 A garter spring helps hold the sharp lip edge of the seal tight against the shaft.

3. Looseness or excessive play in the steering wheel, especially while driving over rough road surfaces

4. A loud grinding noise in severe cases, indicating a defective front wheel bearing

5. Pulling during braking

DETERMINING BEARING NOISE FROM TIRE NOISE

A defective wheel bearing is often difficult to diagnose because the noise is similar to a noisy winter tire or a severely cupped tire. Customers often request that tires be replaced as a result of the noise when the real problem is a bad wheel bearing. To help determine if the noise is caused by a wheel bearing or a tire, try the following tests:

TEST #1 Drive the vehicle over a variety of road surfaces. If the noise changes with a change in road surface, then the noise is caused by a tire(s). If the noise remains the same, then the cause is a defective wheel bearing.

TEST #2 Try temporarily overinflating the tires. If the noise changes, then the tires are the cause. If the noise is the same, then defective wheel bearings are the cause.

TESTING A WHEEL BEARING

With the vehicle off the ground, rotate the wheel by hand, listening and feeling carefully for bearing roughness. Grasp the wheel at the top and bottom and wiggle it back and forth, checking for bearing looseness.

WHEEL BEARING SERVICE

The steps in a non-drive-wheel bearing inspection include the following:

1. Hoist the vehicle safely.

2. Remove the wheel.

3. Remove the brake caliper assembly and support it with a coat hanger or other suitable hook to avoid allowing the caliper to hang by the brake hose.

4. Remove the grease cap (dust cap). ●SEE FIGURE 11–12.

5. Remove the old cotter key and discard.

NOTE: The term *cotter*, as in cotter key or cotter pin, is derived from the Old English verb meaning "to close or fasten."

FIGURE 11–12 Removing the grease cap with grease cap pliers.

FIGURE 11–13 Using a seal puller to remove the grease seal.

FIGURE 11–14 Cleaning a wheel bearing with a parts brush and solvent.

6. Remove the spindle nut (castle nut).

7. Remove the washer and the outer wheel bearing.

8. Remove the bearing hub from the spindle. The inner bearing will remain in the hub and may be removed (simply lifted out) after the grease seal is pried out. ● **SEE FIGURE 11–13.**

9. Most vehicle and bearing manufacturers recommend cleaning the bearing thoroughly in solvent or acetone. ● **SEE FIGURE 11–14.** If there is no acetone, clean the solvent off the bearings with denatured alcohol or brake cleaner to make certain that the thin solvent layer is completely washed off and dry. *All solvent must be removed or allowed to dry from the bearing because the new grease will not stick to a layer of solvent.*

CAUTION: Never use compressed air to spin a bearing because the bearing can be damaged.

10. Carefully inspect the bearings and the races for the following:

   a. The outer race for lines, scratches, or pits.

   b. The cage should be round. If the round cage has straight sections, this is an indication of an overtightened adjustment or a dropped cage. ● **SEE CHART 11–1.**

   If either of the above is observed, then the bearing, including the outer race, must be replaced. Failure to

replace the outer race (which is included when purchasing a bearing) could lead to rapid failure of the new bearing. ● **SEE FIGURES 11–15 AND 11–16.**

11. Pack the cleaned or new bearing thoroughly with clean, new, approved wheel bearing grease. Always clean out all of the old grease before applying the recommended type of new grease. *Because of compatibility problems, it is not recommended that greases be mixed.* There are several different ways to pack wheel bearings including:

   ▪ **By hand.** Place some grease in the palm of the hand and then force the grease through the bearing until grease can be seen out the other side. ● **SEE FIGURE 11–17.**

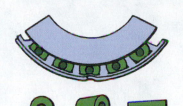

BENT CAGE

CAGE DAMAGE CAUSED BY IMPROPER HANDLING OR TOOL USE

GALLING

METAL SMEARS ON ROLLER ENDS CAUSED BY OVERHEATING, OVERLOADING, OR INADEQUATE LUBRICATION

STEP WEAR

NOTCHED WEAR PATTERN ON ROLLER ENDS CAUSED BY ABRASIVES IN THE LUBRICANT

ETCHING AND CORROSION

EATEN AWAY BEARING SURFACE WITH GRAY OR GRAY-BLACK COLOR CAUSED BY MOISTURE CONTAMINATION OF THE LUBRICANT

PITTING AND BRUISING

PITS, DEPRESSIONS, AND GROOVES IN THE BEARING SURFACES CAUSED BY PARTICULATE CONTAMINATION OF THE LUBRICANT

SPALLING

FLAKING AWAY OF THE BEARING SURFACE METAL CAUSED BY FATIGUE

MISALIGNMENT

SKEWED WEAR PATTERN CAUSED BY BENT SPINDLE OR IMPROPER BEARING INSTALLATION

HEAT DISCOLORATION

FAINT YELLOW TO DARK BLUE DISCOLORATION FROM OVERHEATING CAUSED BY OVERLOADING OR INADEQUATE LUBRICATION

BRINELLING

INDENTATIONS IN THE RACES CAUSED BY IMPACT LOADS OR VIBRATION WHEN THE BEARING IS NOT TURNING

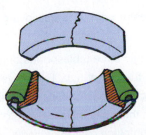

CRACKED RACE

CRACKING OF THE RACE CAUSED BY EXCESSIVE PRESS FIT, IMPROPER INSTALLATION, OR DAMAGED BEARING SEATS

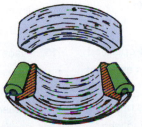

SMEARING

SMEARED METAL FROM SLIPPAGE CAUSED BY POOR FIT, POOR LUBRICATION, OVERLOADING, OVERHEATING, OR HANDLING DAMAGE

FRETTAGE

ETCHING OR CORROSION CAUSED BY SMALL RELATIVE MOVEMENTS BETWEEN PARTS WITH NO LUBRICATION

CHART 11–1

Wheel bearing inspection chart. Replace the bearing if it has any of the faults shown.

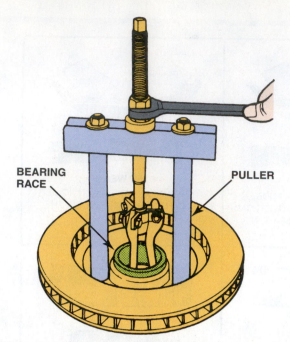

FIGURE 11–15 A wheel bearing race puller.

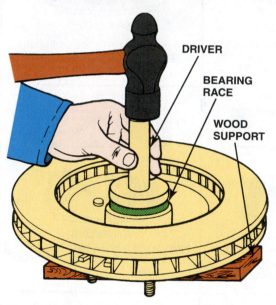

FIGURE 11–16 Installing a bearing race with a driver.

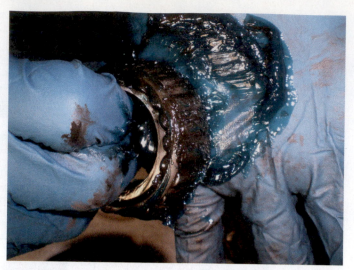

FIGURE 11–17 Notice the new blue grease has been forced through the bearing.

FIGURE 11–18 A commonly used hand-operated bearing packer.

- **By hand-operated bearing packer.** A hand-operated bearing packer is faster to use and produces excellent results. ● **SEE FIGURE 11–18.**
- **Grease gun-type bearing packer.** This type of bearing packer uses a grease gun to fill the bearing with grease. The grease gun can be hand-operated or powered by electric or air. ● **SEE FIGURE 11–19.**

12. Place a thin layer of grease on the outer race.

13. Apply a thin layer of grease to the spindle, being sure to cover the outer bearing seat, inner bearing seat, and shoulder at the grease seal seat.

14. Install a new **grease seal** (also called a *grease retainer*) flush with the hub using a seal driver.

15. Place approximately three tablespoons of grease into the grease cavity of the wheel hub. Excessive grease could cause the inner grease seal to fail, with the possibility of grease getting on the brakes. Place the rotor with the inner bearing and seal in place over the spindle until the grease seal rests on the grease seal shoulder.

16. Install the outer bearing and the bearing washer.

17. Install the spindle nut and, while rotating the tire assembly, tighten to about 12 to 30 lb-ft with a wrench to "seat" the bearing correctly in the race (cup) and on the spindle. ● **SEE FIGURE 11–20.**

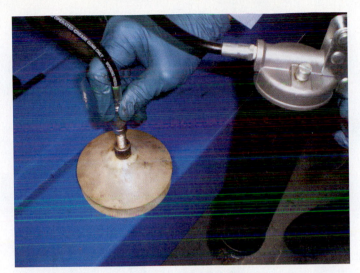

FIGURE 11–19 The wheel bearing is placed between two nylon cones and then a grease gun is used to inject grease into the center of the bearing.

18. While still rotating the tire assembly, loosen the nut approximately one-half turn and then *hand tighten only* (about 5 lb-in.).

NOTE: If the wheel bearing is properly adjusted, the wheel will still have about 0.001 to 0.005 inch (0.03 to 0.13 mm) end play. To check for proper clearance, grasp the wheel at the top and bottom and check for a slight looseness. This looseness is necessary to allow the tapered roller bearing to expand when hot and not bind or cause the wheel to lock up.

19. Install a new cotter key. (An old cotter key could break a part off where it was bent and lodge in the bearing, causing major damage.)

NOTE: Most vehicles use a cotter key that is 1/8 inch in diameter by 1 1/2 inch long.

20. If the cotter key does not line up with the hole in the spindle, loosen slightly (no more than 1/16 inch of a turn) until the hole lines up. Never tighten more than hand tight.

21. Bending the cotter key ends up and around the nut, not over the end of the spindle where the end of the cotter key could rub on the grease cap, causing noise. ● **SEE FIGURE 11–21.**

22. Install the grease cap (dust cap) with a rubber mallet or soft-faced hammer to help prevent denting or distorting the grease cap. Install the wheel cover or hub cap.

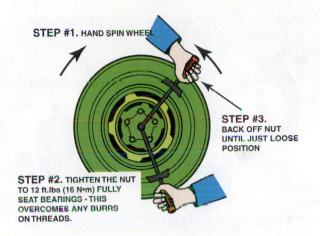

STEP #1. HAND SPIN WHEEL

STEP #3. BACK OFF NUT UNTIL JUST LOOSE POSITION

STEP #2. TIGHTEN THE NUT TO 12 ft.lbs (16 N•m) FULLY SEAT BEARINGS - THIS OVERCOMES ANY BURRS ON THREADS.

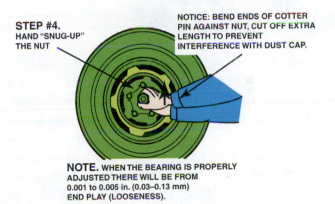

STEP #5. LOOSEN NUT UNTIL EITHER HOLE IN THE SPINDLE LINES UP WITH A SLOT IN THE NUT – THEN INSERT COTTER PIN.

STEP #4. HAND "SNUG-UP" THE NUT

NOTICE: BEND ENDS OF COTTER PIN AGAINST NUT, CUT OFF EXTRA LENGTH TO PREVENT INTERFERENCE WITH DUST CAP.

NOTE. WHEN THE BEARING IS PROPERLY ADJUSTED THERE WILL BE FROM 0.001 to 0.005 in. (0.03–0.13 mm) END PLAY (LOOSENESS).

FIGURE 11–20 The wheel bearing adjustment procedure as specified for rear-wheel-drive vehicles. Always check service information for the specified procedure to follow.

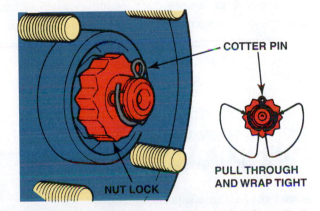

COTTER PIN

NUT LOCK

PULL THROUGH AND WRAP TIGHT

FIGURE 11–21 A properly secured wheel bearing adjust nut.

23. Clean grease off the disc brake rotors or drums after servicing the wheel bearings. Use a brake cleaner and a shop cloth. Even a slight amount of grease on the friction surfaces of the brakes can harm the friction lining and/or cause brake noise.

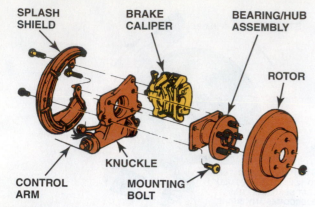

FIGURE 11–22 A rear wheel sealed bearing hub assembly.

Labels on figure: SPLASH SHIELD, BRAKE CALIPER, BEARING/HUB ASSEMBLY, ROTOR, KNUCKLE, CONTROL ARM, MOUNTING BOLT

SEALED BEARING REPLACEMENT

Diagnosing a defective front bearing on a front-wheel-drive vehicle is sometimes confusing. A defective wheel bearing is usually noisy while driving straight, and the noise increases with vehicle speed (wheel speed). A drive axle shaft U-joint (CV joint) can also be the cause of noise on a front-wheel-drive vehicle, but usually makes *more noise* while turning and accelerating. Most front-wheel-drive vehicles use a sealed bearing assembly that is bolted to the steering knuckle and supports the drive axle or the rear, as shown in ● FIGURE 11–22.

Many front-wheel-drive vehicles use a bearing that must be pressed off the steering knuckle. Special aftermarket tools are also available to remove many of the bearings without removing the knuckle from the vehicle. Check the service information for the exact procedures to follow for the vehicle being serviced. ● SEE FIGURES 11–23 AND 11–24.

REAR DRIVE AXLE CLASSIFICATIONS

There are three rear drive axle classifications:

- Full-floating
- Three-quarter-floating
- Semi-floating

These classifications indicate whether the axle shafts or the axle housing supports the wheel. The category of a rear drive axle is determined by how the wheel and wheel bearing mount to the axle or housing.

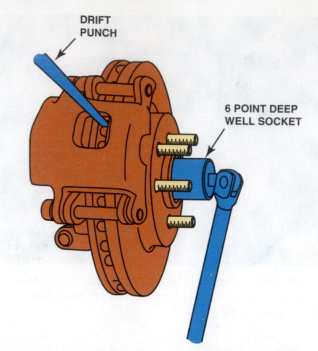

FIGURE 11–23 Removing the drive axle shaft hub nut. This nut is usually very tight and the drift (tapered) punch wedged into the cooling fins of the brake rotor keeps the hub from revolving when the nut is loosened. Never use an air impact wrench to loosen or tighten the drive axle shaft nut because the hammering action will damage the bearings.

Labels on figure: DRIFT PUNCH, 6 POINT DEEP WELL SOCKET

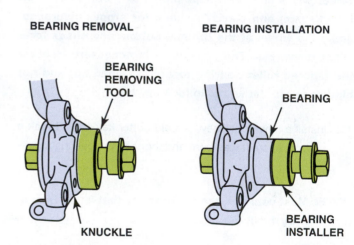

BEARING REMOVAL BEARING INSTALLATION

Labels on figure: BEARING REMOVING TOOL, KNUCKLE, BEARING, BEARING INSTALLER

FIGURE 11–24 A special puller makes the job of removing the hub bearing from the knuckle easy without damaging any component.

FULL-FLOATING AXLE On a full-floating axle, the bearings are mounted and retained in the hub of the brake drum or rotor. The hub and bearing mount onto the axle housing, and are held in place by a bearing retainer or adjustment nuts and safety locks. The flanged end of the drive axle is attached to the hub by bolts or nuts. The inner end of the axle splines into the differential side gears. The wheel mounts onto the hub, and lug bolts or nuts retain it. In this design, the axle shafts "float"

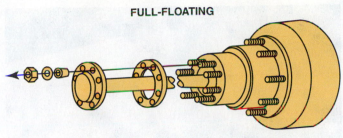

FIGURE 11–25 A typical full-floating rear axle assembly.

THREE-QUARTER-FLOATING

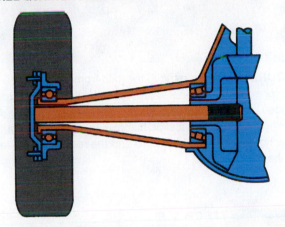

FIGURE 11–26 A three-quarter-floating rear axle.

SEMI-FLOATING

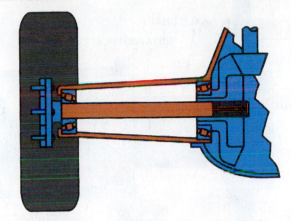

FIGURE 11–27 A semi-floating rear axle housing is the most commonly used in light rear-wheel-drive vehicles.

other end keeps the axle shaft in the housing. The brake drum or rotor fits onto the end of the axle, and lug bolts or nuts fasten the wheel to the drum or rotor and to the axle. These axles are called "semi-floating" because only the inboard ends of the axle shaft "float" in the housing. The outboard end of the shaft retains the wheel and transmits the weight of the wheel to the housing. Most solid-axle rear-wheel-drive cars and light trucks use a semi-floating type of axle. ● **SEE FIGURE 11–27.**

in the axle housing and drive the wheels without supporting their weight. Because the axle shafts do not retain the wheel, the axle shafts can usually be removed from the vehicle while it is standing on the wheels. Many three-quarter-ton pickups, all heavy-duty truck tractors, and trailers use full-floating axles. ● **SEE FIGURE 11–25.**

THREE-QUARTER-FLOATING AXLE

The bearings in a three-quarter-floating axle are mounted and retained in the brake drum or rotor hub, which mounts onto the axle housing. The outer extension of the hub fits onto the end of the axle, which is usually splined and tapered, and a nut and cotter pin secure the hub to the axle. The axle shaft splines to the side gears inside the differential. The wheels are mounted on the hub and retained by lug bolts or nuts. As in the full-floating axle, the axle housing and bearings in the hub support the weight in a three-quarter-floating axle. Because of the construction of a three-quarter-floating axle, the wheel must be removed before removing the axle shaft from the vehicle. ● **SEE FIGURE 11–26.**

SEMI-FLOATING AXLE

The wheel bearings in a semi-floating axle either press onto the axle shaft or are installed in the outer end of the axle housing. A retainer plate at the outer end of the axle shaft or a C-clip inside the differential at the

REAR AXLE BEARING AND SEAL REPLACEMENT

The rear bearings used on rear-wheel-drive vehicles are constructed and serviced differently from other types of wheel bearings. Rear axle bearings are either sealed or lubricated by the rear-end lubricant. The rear axle must be removed from the vehicle to replace the rear axle bearing. There are two basic types of axle retaining methods:

- **Retainer plate-type**
- **C-lock**

RETAINER PLATE-TYPE REAR AXLES

The retainer plate-type rear axle uses four fasteners that retain the axle in the axle housing. To remove the axle shaft and the rear axle bearing and seal, the retainer bolts or nuts must be removed.

NOTE: If the axle flange has an access hole, then a retainer plate-type axle is used.

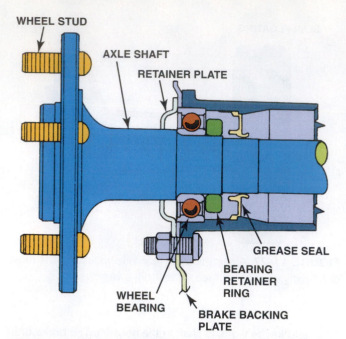

FIGURE 11–28 A retainer plate-type rear axle bearing. Access to the fasteners is through a hole in the axle flange.

FIGURE 11–29 A slide-hammer-type axle puller can be used to remove an axle.

The hole or holes in the wheel flange permit a socket wrench access to the fasteners. After the fasteners have been removed, the axle shaft must be removed from the rear axle housing. With the retainer plate-type rear axle, the bearing and the retaining ring are press fit onto the axle and the bearing cup (outer race) is also tightly fitted into the axle housing tube. ● SEE FIGURE 11–28. ● SEE FIGURE 11–29 for method to remove the axle shaft using a rear axle puller.

C-LOCK-TYPE AXLES
Vehicles that use C-locks (clips) use a straight roller bearing supporting a semi-floating axle shaft inside the axle housing. The straight rollers do not have

FIGURE 11–30 To remove the axle from this vehicle equipped with a retainer-plate rear axle, the brake drum was placed back onto the axle studs backward so that the drum itself can be used as a slide hammer to pull the axle out of the axle housing. A couple of pulls and the rear axle is pulled out of the axle housing.

🔧 TECH TIP

The Brake Drum Slide Hammer Trick

To remove the axle from a vehicle equipped with a retainer plate-type rear axle, simply use the brake drum as a slide hammer to remove the axle from the axle housing. ● SEE FIGURE 11–30. If the brake drum does not provide enough force, a slide hammer can also be used to remove the axle shaft.

an inner race. The rollers ride on the axle itself. If a bearing fails, both the axle and the bearing usually need to be replaced. The outer bearing race holding the rollers is pressed into the rear axle housing. The axle bearing is usually lubricated by the rear-end lubricant and a grease seal is located on the outside of the bearing.

NOTE: Some replacement bearings are available that are designed to ride on a fresh, unworn section of the old axle. These bearings allow the use of the original axle, saving the cost of a replacement axle.

The C-lock-type rear axle retaining method requires that the differential cover plate be removed. After removal of the cover, the differential pinion shaft has to be removed before the C-lock that retains the axle can be removed. ● SEE FIGURES 11–31 AND 11–32.

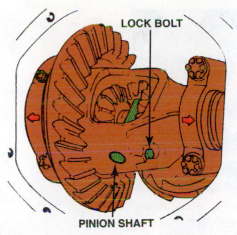

FIGURE 11–31 To remove the C-lock (clip), the lock bolt must be removed before the pinion shaft is taken out.

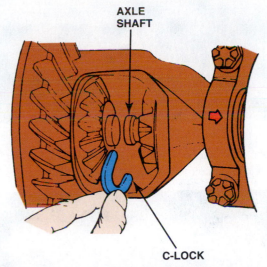

FIGURE 11–32 The axle must be pushed inward slightly to allow the C-lock to be removed. After the C-lock has been removed, the axle can be easily pulled out of the axle housing.

NOTE: When removing the differential cover, rear axle lubricant will flow from between the housing and the cover. Be sure to dispose of the old rear axle lubricant in the environmentally approved way, and refill with the proper type and viscosity (thickness) of rear-end lubricant. Check the vehicle specifications for the recommended grade.

Once the C-lock has been removed, the axle simply is pulled out of the axle tube. Axle bearings with inner races are pressed onto the axle shaft and must be pressed off using a hydraulic press. A bearing retaining collar should be chiseled or drilled into to expand the collar, allowing it to be removed. ● **SEE FIGURE 11–33.**

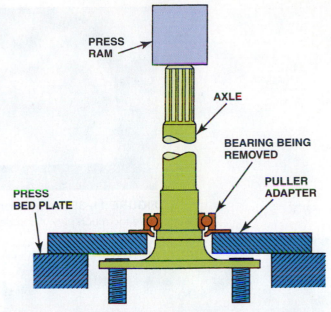

FIGURE 11–33 Using a hydraulic press to press an axle bearing from the axle. When pressing a new bearing back onto the axle, pressure should only be on the inner bearing race to prevent damaging the bearing.

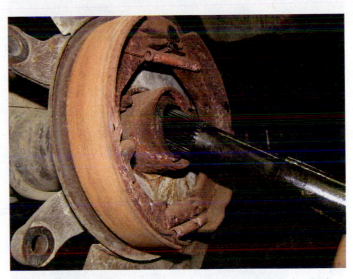

FIGURE 11–34 Removing an axle seal using the axle shaft as the tool. While this procedure is done in some shops, the preferred and specified procedure is to use a seal puller.

Always follow the manufacturer's recommended bearing removal and replacement procedures. Always replace the rear axle seal whenever replacing a rear axle bearing. ● **SEE FIGURE 11–34** for an example of seal removal.

All differentials use a vent so make sure it is clear. A clogged vent can cause excessive pressure to build up inside the differential and cause the rear axle seals to leak. If rear-end lubricant gets on the brake linings, the brakes will not have the proper friction and the linings themselves are ruined and must be replaced.

FIGURE 11–35 This is a normally worn bearing. If it does not have too much play, it can be reused. *(Courtesy SKF USA Inc.)*

(a)

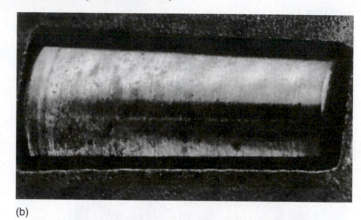

(b)

FIGURE 11–36 (a) When corrosion etches into the surface of a roller or race, the bearing should be discarded. (b) If light corrosion stains can be removed with an oil-soaked cloth, the bearing can be reused. *(Courtesy SKF USA Inc.)*

(a)

(b)

FIGURE 11–37 (a) When just the end of a roller is scored, it is because of excessive preload. Discard the bearing. (b) This is a more advanced case of pitting. Under load, it will rapidly lead to spalling. *(Courtesy SKF USA Inc.)*

BEARING FAILURE ANALYSIS

Whenever a bearing is replaced, the old bearing must be inspected and the cause of the failure eliminated. ● **SEE FIGURES 11–35 THROUGH 11–41** for examples of normal and abnormal bearing wear.

A wheel bearing may also fail for reasons that include the following:

METAL FATIGUE Long vehicle usage, even under normal driving conditions, causes metal to fatigue. Cracks often appear, and eventually these cracks expand downward into the metal from the surface. The metal between the cracks can break out into small chips, slabs, or scales of metal. This process of breaking up is called **spalling.** ● **SEE FIGURE 11–42.**

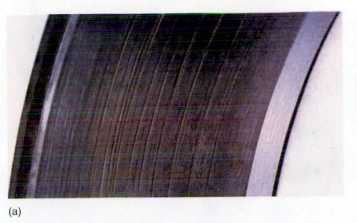

(a)

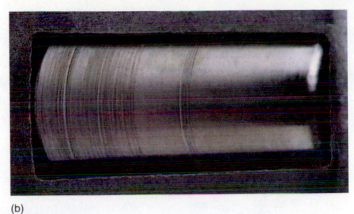

(b)

FIGURE 11–38 (a) Always check for faint grooves in the race. This bearing should not be reused. (b) Grooves like this are often matched by grooves in the race. Discard the bearing. *(Courtesy SKF USA Inc.)*

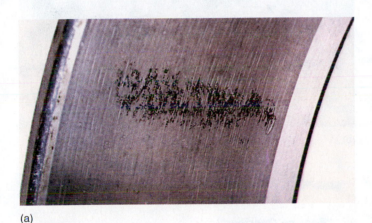

(a)

(b)

FIGURE 11–39 (a) Regular patterns of etching in the race are from corrosion. This bearing should be replaced. (b) Light pitting comes from contaminants being pressed into the race. Discard the bearing. *(Courtesy SKF USA Inc.)*

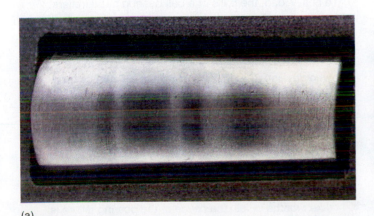

(a)

(b)

FIGURE 11–40 (a) This bearing is worn unevenly. Notice the stripes. It should not be reused. (b) Any damage that causes low spots in the metal renders the bearing useless. *(Courtesy SKF USA Inc.)*

(a)

(b)

FIGURE 11–41 (a) In this more advanced case of pitting, you can see how the race has been damaged. (b) Discoloration is a result of overheating. Even a lightly burned bearing should be replaced. *(Courtesy SKF USA Inc.)*

(a)

(b)

FIGURE 11–42 (a) Pitting eventually leads to spalling, a condition where the metal falls away in large chunks. (b) In this spalled roller, the metal has actually begun to flake away from the surface. *(Courtesy SKF USA Inc.)*

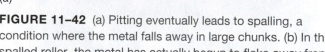
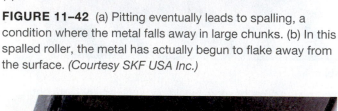

FIGURE 11–43 These dents resulted from the rollers "hammering" against the race, such as what occurs when the heavily loaded vehicle hits a bump or is shock loaded. This condition is called brinelling. *(Courtesy SKF USA Inc.)*

ELECTRICAL ARCING Bearings can be damaged by poor ground wires or improper welding on the vehicle.

SHOCK LOADING Dents can be formed in the race of a bearing, which eventually leads to bearing failure. ● **SEE FIGURE 11–43**.

🔧 **TECH TIP**

"Bearing Overload"

It is not uncommon for vehicles to be overloaded. This is particularly common with pickup trucks and vans. Whenever there is a heavy load, the axle bearings must support the entire weight of the vehicle, including its cargo. If a bump is hit while driving with a heavy load, the balls of a ball bearing or the rollers of a roller bearing can make an indent in the race of the bearing. This dent or imprint is called **brinelling**, named after Johann A. Brinell, a Swedish engineer who developed a process of testing for surface hardness by pressing a hard ball with a standard force into a sample material to be tested.

Once this imprint is made, the bearing will make noise whenever the roller or ball rolls over the indent. Continued use causes wear to occur on all of the balls or rollers and eventual failure. While this may take months to fail, the *cause* of the bearing failure is often overloading of the vehicle. Avoid shock loads and overloading for safety and for longer vehicle life.

1 After safely hoisting the vehicle, remove the rear wheels and brake drums.

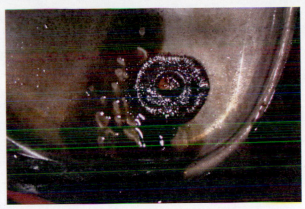

2 Remove the rear differential cover and inspect the magnet for metal particles that would indicate serious wear or damage.

3 Remove the retaining bolt and allow the pinion shaft to be removed.

4 Push the axle inward toward the center of the vehicle to free the axle clip.

5 After removing the clip, the axle can then be removed. Note that the backing plate is wet, indicating that the axle seal has been leaking.

6 A seal removal tool being used to remove the axle seal.

CONTINUED ▶

7 If a retainer-type axle is being serviced, the bearing and seal need to be pressed off of the axle.

8 After installing a new bearing and seal, insert the axle and install the clip, then the pinion shaft.

9 Clean the differential housing before installing the cover gasket and cover. Refill the differential with the specified fluid.

SUMMARY

1. Wheel bearings support the entire weight of a vehicle and are used to reduce rolling friction. Ball and straight roller-type bearings are nonadjustable while tapered roller-type bearings must be adjusted for proper clearance.

2. Most front-wheel-drive vehicles use sealed bearings, either two preloaded tapered roller bearings or double-row ball bearings.

3. Most wheel bearings are standardized sizes.

4. A defective bearing can be caused by metal fatigue that leads to spalling, shock loads that cause brinelling, or damage from electrical arcing due to poor body ground wires or improper electrical welding on the vehicle.

5. Bearing grease is an oil with a thickener. The higher the NLGI number of the grease, the thicker or harder the grease consistency.

6. Tapered wheel bearings must be adjusted by hand tightening the spindle nut after properly seating the bearings. A new cotter key must always be used.

7. A defective wheel bearing is usually noisy while driving straight, and the noise increases with vehicle speed (wheel speed). A drive axle shaft U-joint (CV joint) can also be the cause of noise on a front-wheel-drive vehicle, but usually makes more noise while turning and accelerating.

8. All bearings must be serviced, replaced, and/or adjusted using the vehicle manufacturer's recommended procedures as stated in the service manual.

REVIEW QUESTIONS

1. List three common types of automotive antifriction bearings.

2. Explain the adjustment procedure for a typical tapered roller wheel bearing.

3. List four symptoms of a defective wheel bearing.

4. Describe how the rear axle is removed from a C-lock-type axle.

CHAPTER QUIZ

1. Which type of automotive bearing can withstand radial and thrust loads, yet must be adjusted for proper clearance?
   a. Roller bearing
   b. Tapered roller bearing
   c. Ball bearings
   d. Needle roller bearing

2. Most sealed bearings used on the front wheels of front-wheel-drive vehicles are usually which type?
   a. Roller bearing
   b. Single tapered roller bearing
   c. Double-row ball bearing
   d. Needle roller bearing

3. On a bearing that has been shock loaded, the race (cup) of the bearing can be dented. This type of bearing failure is called _____.
   a. Spalling
   b. Arcing
   c. Brinelling
   d. Fluting

4. The bearing grease most often specified is rated NLGI _____.
   a. #00
   b. #0
   c. #1
   d. #2

5. A non-drive-wheel bearing adjustment procedure includes a final spindle nut tightening torque of _____.
   a. Finger tight
   b. 5 lb-in.
   c. 12 to 30 lb-ft
   d. 12 to 15 lb-ft plus 1/16 inch turn

6. After a non-drive-wheel bearing has been properly adjusted, the wheel should have how much end play?
   a. Zero
   b. 0.001 to 0.005 inch
   c. 0.10 to 0.30 inch
   d. 1/16 to 3/32 inch

7. The differential cover must be removed before removing the rear axle on which type of axle?
   a. Retainer plate
   b. C-lock
   c. Press fit
   d. Welded tube

8. What part(s) should be replaced when servicing a wheel bearing on a non-drive wheel?
   a. The bearing cup
   b. The grease seal
   c. The cotter key
   d. Both the grease seal and the cotter key

9. Technician A says that a defective wheel or axle bearing often makes a growling or rumbling noise. Technician B says that a defective wheel or axle bearing often makes a noise similar to a tire with an aggressive mud or snow design. Which technician is correct?
   a. Technician A only
   b. Technician B only
   c. Both Technicians A and B
   d. Neither Technician A nor B

10. Two technicians are discussing differentials. Technician A says all differentials are vented. Technician B says that a clogged vent can cause the rear axle seal to leak. Which technician is correct?
   a. Technician A only
   b. Technician B only
   c. Both Technicians A and B
   d. Neither Technician A nor B

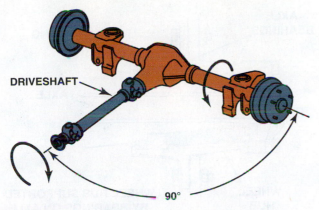

FIGURE 12–1 The differential assembly changes the direction of engine torque and increases the torque to the drive wheels.

DRIVE AXLE TERMINOLOGY

All rear-wheel-drive (RWD) vehicles use a drive axle assembly to transfer power from the driveshaft to the drive wheels. Because it is powered, it is sometimes called a **live axle**. Front-wheel-drive (FWD) cars use a **dead axle** or non-powered rear axle. The major parts of a drive axle include:

- The ring and pinion gears
- Differential
- Axle shafts

Many 4WD and AWD vehicles use a similar axle at the front, the major difference being steerable drive wheels.

DRIVE AXLE ASSEMBLY

PURPOSE AND FUNCTION   The purpose and function of a drive axle assembly include the following:

1. *Changing the direction of engine torque*—This is achieved using a ring and pinion gears. ● **SEE FIGURE 12–1.**

2. *Allowing the drive wheels to rotate at different speeds*—This is achieved using a differential assembly. ● **SEE FIGURE 12–2.**

3. *Support the weight of the vehicle*—This is achieved by using a robust drive axle assembly that is capable of supporting the suspension and the carrying the load of the vehicle itself plus the carrying capability of the vehicle.

4. *Drive the wheels through axles*—The drive axles are splined to the side gears and attached to the drive wheels at the outer end.

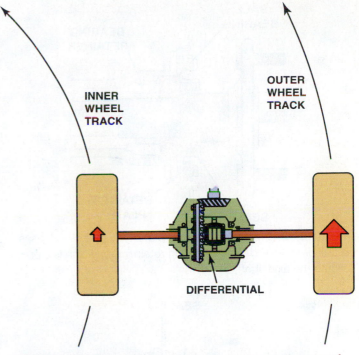

FIGURE 12–2 The difference between the travel distance of the drive wheels is controlled by the differential.

AXLE DESIGNS

AXLE SHAFTS   On most passenger vehicles and pickups, the axle shafts transfer the torque from the differential side gears to the drive wheels and support the weight of the vehicle. To give them the necessary strength to transfer the torque, axles are made of forged steel. The inner ends are splined to match the splines of the differential side gears.

SEMI-FLOATING AXLES   Axle shafts can be classified by the way the axle is loaded and how the axle is retained in the housing. Currently, all rear-wheel-drive passenger vehicles use **semi-floating axles**.

- The inner end floats because it is supported by a gear, not a bearing.
- The outer end uses a bearing in the end of the housing. This bearing transfers the load of the vehicle to the axle, which, in turn, transfers it to the wheel.
- If the axle were to break outboard of the bearing, the wheel would fall off and the vehicle would drop.

There are two types of semi-floating axles:

1. **Retainer-plate type**—A retainer-plate-type axle usually uses a ball bearing. With a ball bearing axle, the side

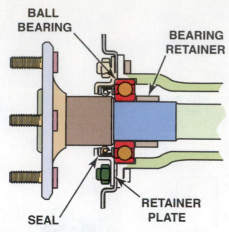

FIGURE 12–3 A typical retainer-plate-type axle, which uses a ball bearing and uses a bearing retainer ring which is a press fit into the axle shaft.

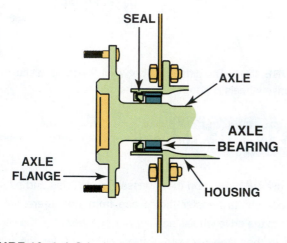

FIGURE 12–4 A C-lock type axle uses a straight roller bearing which is lubricated by the drive axle lube.

thrust is transferred from the axle to the axle tube through the bearing and the retainer plate. ●SEE FIGURE 12–3.

2. **C-Lock—**A C-lock axle uses a straight roller bearing and uses the axle shaft itself as the inner race. The C-locks keep the axle shafts from moving outward and the differential pinion shafts prevents axle movement inward. ●SEE FIGURE 12–4.

FULL-FLOATING AXLES
All heavy trucks use a full-floating axle design. The wheel hub has a pair of large tapered roller bearings that transfer all of the vehicle loads except torque from the axle housing to the wheel. The axle shaft slides into mesh with the axle gear and is bolted to the hub. Even if the axle shaft is removed, the vehicle will still roll down the road. ●SEE FIGURE 12–5.

THREE-QUARTER AXLES
A few older vehicles used three-quarter-floating axles. This design uses a single roller or ball bearing between the hub and axle housing. Vertical loads

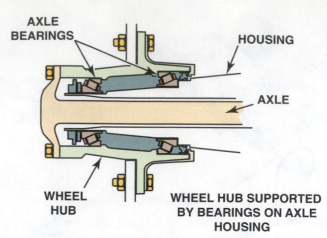

FIGURE 12–5 In a full-floating axle the axle itself slides through the center of the wheel hub assembly and does not support the weight of the vehicle.

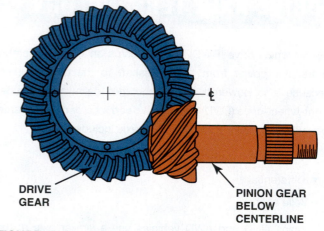

FIGURE 12–6 A hypoid gear set uses a drive pinion that meshes with the ring gear below the center line of the ring gear.

pass from the hub through this bearing to the housing, but cornering loads, which try to pull the axle out of the housing, act on the axle. If the axle breaks, it can slide out of the housing.

RING AND PINION GEARS

FINAL GEAR RATIO The **ring** and **pinion gears** are the **final drive** reduction gears.

- The final drive gear ratio and tire size are selected to provide the best engine RPM for cruise speed. Sometimes the ratio must be selected so that it will provide sufficient torque for low-speed operation.
- The ring and pinion gear set must also turn the power flow from the driveshaft 90° to align with the axles.

HYPOID GEAR SET The ring and pinion gear set is a hypoid type. These are similar to spiral bevel gears except for the location of the pinion gear. ●SEE FIGURE 12–6.

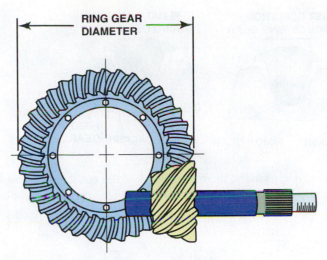

FIGURE 12–7 A 9 inch axle has a ring gear with a rough diameter of 9 inches.

FREQUENTLY ASKED QUESTION

What Does the 9-Inch Refer to When Describing a Drive Axle?

A 9 inch drive axle actually is referring to the rough diameter of the ring gear. A 9-inch gear set is bigger and stronger than an 8-inch gear set. ● SEE FIGURE 12–7.

A **hypoid gear set** has the pinion gear below the center line. This accomplishes two purposes:

1. Allows a lower the driveshaft so that the tunnel or hump in the floor of the vehicle can be smaller.

2. Allows a larger and stronger drive pinion gear in which the pinion gear teeth slide across the teeth of the ring gear. This also makes a hypoid gear set quieter. The sliding, wiping action of the gear teeth requires a special GL-4 or GL-5 lubricant.

HYPOID GEAR SET MANUFACTURING

As a gear set is made, after the gears have been cut, hardened, and ground to shape, the ring and pinion are run against each other in a machine with abrasive compound on their teeth. This laps or wears them to match each other perfectly. At this point, they become a matched set, and damage to one will require replacement of both with another matched set. There is normally a mark etched on the head of the pinion gear and on the side of the ring gear to identify a particular set. There is often a stamping that indicates the gear ratio or part number,

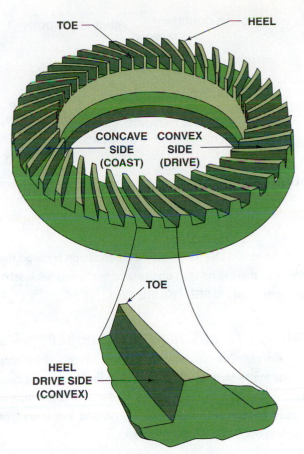

FIGURE 12–8 The drive side is the convex side of the ring gear except for some front axles used in four-wheel vehicles, and they often use the concave side on the drive side.

and sometimes there will also be a marking that indicates the pinion gear depth.

HYPOID GEAR TOOTH TERMINOLOGY

When a hypoid ring and pinion gear set is adjusted, reference is often made to particular parts of the gears and their teeth. The outer ends of the ring gear teeth are called the **heel** and the inner ends the **toe**. ● SEE FIGURE 12–8.

The **pitch line** is the design center of contact between the two gears and is about halfway up the tooth. The **face** of the tooth is above the pitch line, and the **flank** is below it.

The **drive side** of the ring gear teeth is the vertical, *convex* side of the tooth. This is the side of the tooth that contacts the pinion gear while the engine is driving the vehicle forward.

There should be a clearance at the coast side of the tooth which is called **backlash**. The **coast side** of ring gear teeth is the slanted, *concave* side of the tooth. This surface receives pressure while the vehicle is coasting and the vehicle is driving the engine. While coasting, the backlash will be at the drive

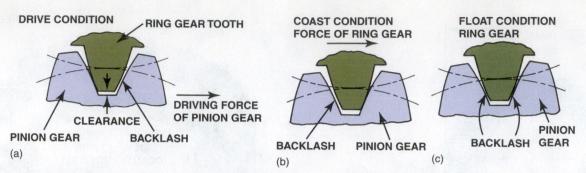

FIGURE 12–9 (a) During a drive condition, the pinion gear is driving the ring gear and there is backlash at the coast side of the ring gear tooth. (b) During a coast condition, this action is reversed. (c) During a float condition, lash is split between both sides of the tooth.

side of the tooth. The third tooth-load condition is called **float**. During float there is no load on the gear teeth, and backlash will be on both sides. ● **SEE FIGURE 12–9.**

HUNTING AND NON-HUNTING GEAR SET

The final drive gear ratio determines how many times a drive pinion tooth will make contact with a particular ring gear tooth during one revolution. This affects final drive gear set manufacture and service. Final drive gear sets may be divided into three types, depending on the final drive gear ratio.

1. **Hunting gear sets** are gear sets with final drive ratios expressible in a fraction that cannot be reduced to any lower terms. An example of a hunting gear set is one that has 41 teeth on the ring gear and 11 teeth on the drive pinion. This combination creates a 3.73:1 axle ratio. This type of gear set requires no timing marks or alignment during assembly. As the pinion gear drives the ring gear, each pinion tooth will hunt for, or seek, contact with every ring gear tooth.

2. **Non-hunting gear sets** are gear sets with final drive ratios expressible as a whole number. An example of a non-hunting gear set is a differential that uses 39 teeth on the ring gear and 13 teeth on the pinion gear which gives a 3.00:1 gear ratio. Non-hunting gear sets require *timing marks*. As the pinion gear drives the ring gear, each pinion tooth contacts only a few ring gear teeth during each revolution.

3. **Partially non-hunting gear sets** are gear sets with final drive ratios expressible as a reducible fraction not equaling a whole number. An example of a partial non-hunting gear set is an axle ratio of 3.50:1. Partially non-hunting gear sets also require timing marks. During final drive operation, each pinion tooth contacts only some of the ring pinion teeth. For the pinion teeth to make contact with the highest number of ring gear teeth, the pinion gear must drive the ring gear more than one revolution. On non-hunting and

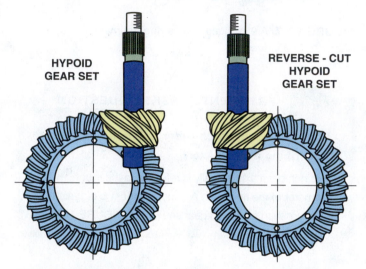

FIGURE 12–10 A reverse-cut gear set is a mirror image of the normal hypoid gear set.

partially non-hunting gears, manufacturers lap (provide a surface finish) the contacting gear teeth to decrease wear. For this reason, these gear sets are marked to ensure proper alignment during assembly procedures. To preserve the wear patterns, the gear sets should be reassembled using the same alignment. This prolongs the life of the gear set and decreases operational noise.

REVERSE-CUT RING AND PINION GEARS

Reverse-cut ring and pinion gears were primarily designed for front-wheel drive applications to take advantage of their increased strength. The gears have the teeth spirally cut in the opposite direction of standard gears. ● **SEE FIGURE 12–10.**

Some 4WD vehicles use a standard rear-drive axle that has been turned around for the front, but this arrangement drives on the coast side of the gear tooth which results in a gear that is 15% to 30% weaker. Reverse-cut gears are stronger when used in the front axle and move the drive pinion above the centerline of the ring gear. When the drive pinion is above

FIGURE 12–11 Two front drive axles. The left one has a standard-cut ring and pinion, whereas the one at the right has high-pinion, reverse-cut ring and pinion gears.

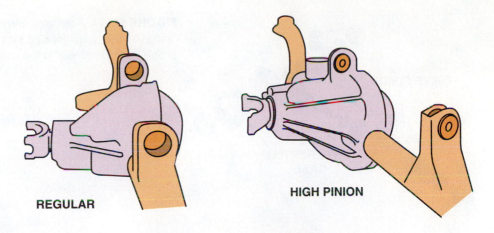

REGULAR

HIGH PINION

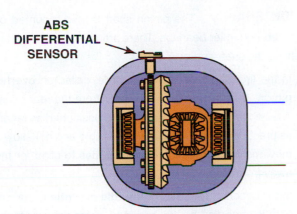

ABS DIFFERENTIAL SENSOR

FIGURE 12–12 Some vehicles with ABS will have a single rear wheel speed sensor at the ring gear or a speed sensor at each axle shaft. Some will use a similar sensor at the drive pinion shaft.

the centerline of the ring gear (high-mounted), the angle of the driveshaft will be decreased and this is especially useful when the vehicle has been lifted for additional ground clearance. The housing is especially designed with different oiling passages to properly lubricate the gears. ● **SEE FIGURE 12–11.**

ABS RELUCTOR WHEEL   On rear-wheel-drive vehicles with antilock braking system (ABS), the rear wheel speed sensor(s) is attached to the rear axle assembly. Some older vehicles that are equipped with a three-channel ABS will use one speed sensor mounted to the driveshaft flange, drive pinion shaft, or ring gear, whereas others use a pair of sensors near the end of the axle at each wheel hub. Because they include a magnetic core, sensors that are in the axle housing can be affected by metal particles worn from the gears or bearings. Sensors at the axle shafts can be affected by worn axle bearings. ● **SEE FIGURE 12–12.**

GEAR AND PINION MOUNTING   The ring and pinion gears must be mounted securely because of the large torque load involved. Gear separation forces try to move the gears

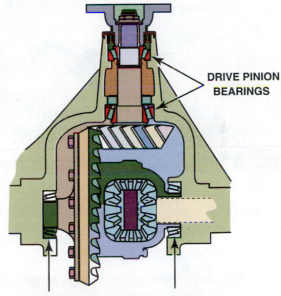

DRIVE PINION BEARINGS

DIFFERENTIAL CARRIER BEARINGS

FIGURE 12–13 A pair of tapered roller bearings called carrier bearings is used to locate the drive pinion gear and the differential case and ring gear. Another pair of bearings locates the drive pinion gear.

away from each other. The ring gear is bolted or riveted to the differential case. Rivets provide a secure and permanent mounting, but they make it harder to remove the ring gear. The differential case is mounted on a pair of tapered roller bearings, which are commonly called **carrier bearings** or **side bearings.** ● **SEE FIGURE 12–13.**

DIFFERENTIAL CARRIERS

PURPOSE AND FUNCTION   The **differential** is responsible for allowing the drive wheels to rotate at different speeds when turning or when the vehicle is traveling over uneven road surface. The *differential carrier* is the heavy cast iron portion of the rear axle assembly that provides

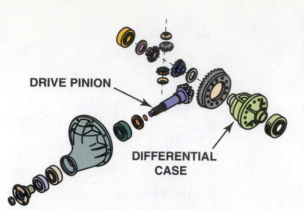

FIGURE 12–14 A removal carrier such as this Ford 9 inch unit. This older design uses an axle housing that is often called a "banjo" because of the shape, which is similar to the musical instrument.

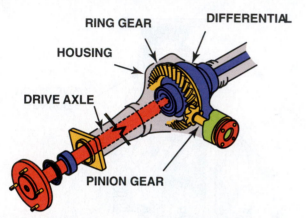

FIGURE 12–15 An integral carrier axle assembly is the most commonly used design of drive axle.

mounting points for the drive pinion shaft bearings and the carrier bearings. Many carriers have special reinforcing webs to contain the gear separation forces of the ring and pinion gear set.

TYPES OF CARRIERS

Removable carriers—Most early trucks and passenger vehicle drive axles had removable carriers, which could be unbolted and removed from the housing for service. They are also known as

- Third member
- Drop-out
- Pumpkin ● SEE FIGURE 12–14.

Integral carriers—Most rear-wheel-drive passenger vehicles and light trucks use integral carriers, and the axle tubes are welded to extensions of the carrier. An integral carrier is stronger in the areas around the carrier bearings. An integral carrier axle assembly, sometimes called a *Salisbury* or *Spicer axle*, has a removable rear cover for access to the differential and other internal parts. ● SEE FIGURE 12–15.

PINION SHAFTS The pinion shaft is also mounted on a pair of tapered roller bearings. There are two common styles of mounting the shaft and gear.

1. In the first and most common style, called an **overhung pinion**, the pinion gear hangs over from the rear bearing. The two tapered roller bearings are positioned as far apart as practical to hold the pinion shaft rigid and not allow any movement of the pinion gear as it tries to climb or move away from the ring gear.

2. In the second style, called **straddle mounting**, the pinion gear is straddled by two bearings where the rear tapered roller bearing is located in front of the gear and a pilot bearing behind the gear. The pilot bearing is usually a smaller roller bearing. Straddle mounting is the strongest, in that the pilot bearing prevents any flexing of the pinion shaft. It also eliminates any gear-to-bearing leverage effects and allows the two tapered roller bearings to be placed fairly close to each other.

DIFFERENTIALS

PURPOSE AND FUNCTION A differential, inside the drive axle housing splits torque equally to the drive wheels. The differential allows engine torque to be applied to both drive axles, which rotate at varying speeds during cornering and while traveling over bumps and dips in the road.

A differential is a mechanical addition and subtraction assembly. A differential is sometimes referred to as *torque equalizer* because it splits the engine torque equally to the drive wheels. When the vehicle is turning a corner, the torque forces cause the side gear and pinion gears to subtract torque from one side and add torque to the opposite side. ● SEE FIGURE 12–16.

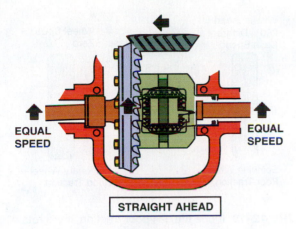

EQUAL SPEED — EQUAL SPEED

STRAIGHT AHEAD

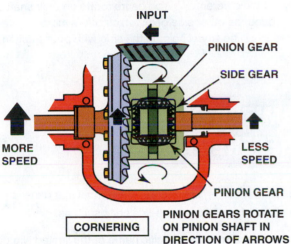

INPUT

PINION GEAR

SIDE GEAR

MORE SPEED — LESS SPEED

PINION GEAR

CORNERING

PINION GEARS ROTATE ON PINION SHAFT IN DIRECTION OF ARROWS

FIGURE 12–16 When the vehicle turns a corner, the inner wheel slows and the outer wheel increases in speed to compensate. This difference in rotational speed causes the pinion gears to "walk" around the slower side gear.

PARTS AND OPERATION

A drive axle assembly must include a differential to allow the drive wheels to rotate at different speeds on corners. The differential used in most drive axles includes:

- Two or more differential pinion gears mounted on a differential pinion shaft(s)
- Two side or axle gears which are splined to the axle shafts

The differential pinion shaft runs through the case and has the two differential pinion gears (sometimes called spider gears) floating on it. These gears are not secured to the shaft. They are located between the differential case and the two **side gears**, which are also called *axle gears*. ● **SEE FIGURE 12–17.**

The axle gears also float in the case, but they have internal splines so they can drive the axle shafts. All four of these gears are spur bevel gears. The spur bevel gears can usually be operated by lifting both drive wheels and rotating one wheel by hand. When one wheel is turned, note that the other wheel is rotating in the opposite direction because the pinion gears

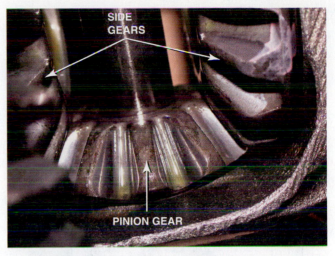

SIDE GEARS

PINION GEAR

FIGURE 12–17 A close-up view of the side gears and spider (pinion) gear. Note the ridges on the gear teeth. These ridges are manufactured into the gear teeth to help retain lubricant so that no metal-to-metal contact occurs.

? FREQUENTLY ASKED QUESTION

Why Does One Wheel Spin When the Other Wheel Is on Dry Pavement?

A standard, called an *open differential* splits torque equally to the drive wheels. If one tire is on a slippery surface and only 50 pounds-feet of torque can be applied to the road, the other side will also have the same 50 pounds-feet. Even if the tire on the other side from the one on a slippery surface is on dry pavement, the force being sent to the drive wheel (50 pounds) is not enough to propel the vehicle. ● **SEE FIGURE 12–18.**

are acting like idlers between the two side gears. The load of the side gears determines what the differential pinion gears do.

- If both side gears are loaded the same and offer the same resistance, the differential pinion gears remain motionless on their shaft and the entire differential assembly rotates as one unit with no internal gear movement.
- When a vehicle goes around a corner, the side gears are equally loaded, but the one connected to the outer wheel will rotate faster. At this time, the differential pinion gears will rotate on their shafts to compensate for this change in speed. The outer wheel will speed up relative to the vehicle and differential, and the inner wheel will slow down the same amount. For example, if the outer wheel speeds up 20% from 100 RPM to 120 RPM, the inner wheel will slow down by the same percentage.

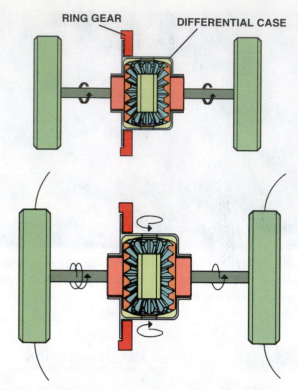

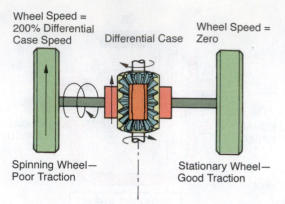

FIGURE 12–19 If one tire has poor traction, it will rotate easily, so the differential pinion gears rotate on their shaft and walk around the other side gear, which offers more resistance. The result will be wheel spin on the side with poor traction.

FIGURE 12–18 If one tire has poor traction, it will rotate easily, so the differential pinion gears rotate on their shaft and "walk" around the other side gear, which offers more resistance. The result will be wheel spin on the side with poor traction.

TYPES OF DIFFERENTIALS
Pickups and rear-wheel-drive vehicles encounter more single-wheel traction problems than front-wheel-drive vehicles basically because the weight is over the drive wheels on a front-wheel-drive vehicle. Therefore, rear-wheel-drive vehicles encounter more driving conditions in which the open differential action is not suitable. One tire cannot receive more torque than either tire can transmit to the ground. ● **SEE FIGURE 12–19.**

The three major types of differentials are as follows:

1. **Open differential** This type of differential is used in most passenger vehicles.

2. **Limited Slip differential (LSD)** This type of differential can send more torque to the wheel with traction than the wheel with poor traction.

3. **Locked differential** This type of differential connects both axle shafts together to eliminate differential action, but rarely used in original equipment (OE) applications except for vehicles that are designed for off-road travel, and then only at low speeds.

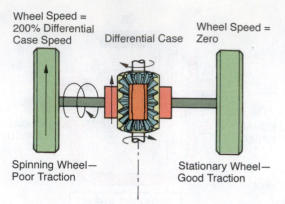

LIMITED SLIP DIFFERENTIALS

TERMINOLOGY Limited slip differential is a generic name for a group of specific vehicle-line units such as:

- **Positraction** is the specific name of the limited slip differential used in Chevrolet vehicles

- Trac-Lok® for a Ford

- Sure-Grip or Anti-Spin for a Chrysler/Jeep

DIFFERENTIAL TORQUE BIAS RATIO An open differential has a **torque bias ratio (TBR)** of 1:1. A 1:1 TBR indicates that the torque applied to each wheel is the same. This means that the available torque that can be sent to the two wheels is twice that of the tire with the least traction. Any more torque than this will cause the tire with poor traction to spin. If the poor-traction tire spins at 50 pound-feet of torque, only 50 pound-feet of torque can be sent to the good-traction tire.

Limited slip differentials can deliver as much as five times the torque to the tire with good traction which would be a TBR of 5:1. If the differential has a TBR of 2.5:1 and 50 pounds-feet of torque can be sent to the poor traction tire, then 50 × 2.5 or 125 pounds-feet of torque can be sent to the good traction tire. A total of 175 pounds-feet of torque can be sent to both tires.

NOTE: Limited slip differentials are *torque biasing devices* (TBD) that have been traditionally used to

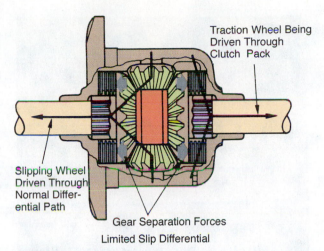

Traction Wheel Being Driven Through Clutch Pack

Slipping Wheel Driven Through Normal Differential Path

Gear Separation Forces

Limited Slip Differential

FIGURE 12–20 Limited slip differentials transfer most of the torque through the pinion shaft and gears like a conventional differential. Some torque is also transferred through the clutch pack going from the case through the clutch to the side gear (right).

improve traction for both off-road and on-road driving. These devices are also used with the recent all-wheel-drive (AWD) vehicle where on-road handling in both good and bad traction conditions is a major priority. Electronic wheel speed, steering, and yaw sensors determine what the vehicle is doing relative to what the driver is requesting it to do, and the TBD is electronically actuated to send more torque to the tire most able to improve the situation.

TYPES OF LIMITED SLIP DIFFERENTIALS There are several different styles of limited slip differentials used in production vehicles including the following:

1. Preloaded clutches
2. Self-applying clutches
3. Viscous couplings
4. Eaton locker differential
5. Hydraulic applied clutches
6. Cone type

PRELOADED CLUTCH DIFFERENTIAL Differentials with a preloaded clutch(es) provide two different differential power paths. ● SEE FIGURE 12–20.

One path is through the differential gears as in other differentials, and the other path is directly through the clutch pack(s). Most of these units use two clutch packs, one on each side, but a few designs use a single clutch pack. The operation is essentially the same. Flat, hardened-steel plates with various-shaped oiling grooves are used for the clutch plates. Half of them are splined to the axle gear and the other half are splined to the differential case.

To provide the preload force to apply the clutch, spring pressure forces the axle gear against the clutch pack. The

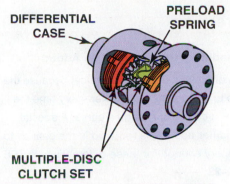

DIFFERENTIAL CASE   PRELOAD SPRING

MULTIPLE-DISC CLUTCH SET

FIGURE 12–21 A limited slip differential showing the preload spring and how the steel plates of the clutch pack are held to the differential case.

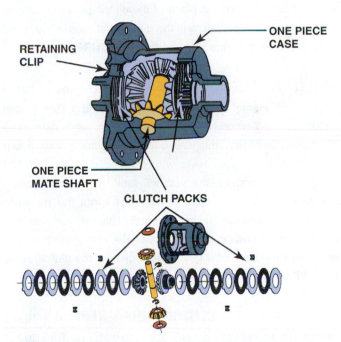

RETAINING CLIP

ONE PIECE CASE

ONE PIECE MATE SHAFT

CLUTCH PACKS

FIGURE 12–22 This type of limited slip differential uses the preload force from a spring and the torque generated by the side gears as the two axles rotate at different rates to apply the clutches and limit the amount of difference in the speed of two axles.

spring can be a single coil spring, a group of coil springs, an S-shaped spring, or one or more Belleville springs. ● SEE FIGURE 12–21.

This style of differential has a tendency to lock up under high-torque conditions such as during hard acceleration. This is due to the gear separation force between the differential pinions and the side gears. The applied torque will try to move the side gears away from the differential pinion gears. The separation force, also called *torque loading*, will increase the applied force at the clutch packs. ● SEE FIGURE 12–22.

TECH TIP

Friction Modified Additive May Be Added

Lubrication of the clutch plates is critical because the plates have to slip across each other every time the vehicle turns a corner or rounds a curve. A special **friction modifier** additive is required in the gear oil to make it slippery enough for these differentials. ● **SEE FIGURE 12–23.**

CONE CLUTCH DESIGN   Some limited slip differentials use a pair of cone clutches in place of the clutch plates. A cone is splined to each axle shaft, and the differential case is machined to form the mating cone surface. ● **SEE FIGURE 12–24.**

EATON LOCKER DIFFERENTIAL The Eaton "locker" differential used in some pickups and light trucks includes a governor, latching mechanism, and differential cam gear. Normally, this unit will operate as a limited slip differential, but if a wheel-to-wheel speed difference of 100 RPM or more occurs, the unit will lock up. Lockup occurs because the spinning cam in the case turns the governor weights fast enough to fly outward. This, in turn, causes the latching operation, which causes the cam gear to rotate relative to the cam side gear, and locks up the clutch pack. ● **SEE FIGURE 12–25.**

SELF-APPLYING CLUTCH DIFFERENTIAL Some limited slip differentials use self-applying clutches. They do not maintain a constant preload on the clutch packs, so differential action during normal driving is free of clutch drag. These differentials used a four-pinion differential with two separate differential pinion shafts. The two shafts called *mate shafts* are fitted into the case in an opposing manner, with ramplike attachments to the case.

While going down the road, the two shafts stay centered by pushing toward each other with equal force because of the equal driving loads and differential gear separation forces. If one wheel loses traction, the driving load on one of the pinion shafts drops off. The load on the other pinion shaft causes it to lag behind the differential case and move sideways because of the case ramps. This force from the differential pinion gears through the axle gear applies the clutch on the side with good traction. The result is that this differential applies the clutch needed to drive the other wheel from the one with poor traction. ● **SEE FIGURE 12–27.**

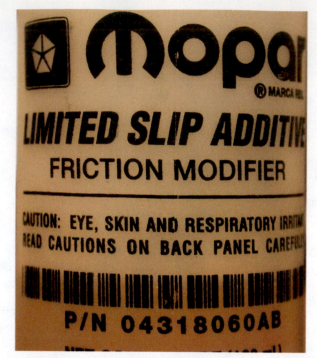

FIGURE 12–23 A friction additive is needed to be added to the gear lube if using a preloaded clutch-type differential.

 REAL WORLD FIX

I Used to Have a Limited Slip Differential

An owner of a Chevrolet S-10 pickup truck equipped with a V-6 and five-speed manual transmission complained that he used to be able to spin both rear tires on dry pavement, but lately only one tire spins. The service technician assigned to the repair order was very familiar with what might have occurred. Many General Motors pickup trucks are equipped with an Eaton locking differential that uses a torque limiting disc. The teeth of this disc are designed to shear to prevent the possibility of breaking an axle. The service procedure to correct the customer's concern is to replace the left-hand clutch plates. Usually, the shearing of the torque-linking teeth is associated with a loud bang in the rear axle. The differential will continue to operate normally as a standard (open) differential. ● **SEE FIGURE 12–26** on page 222.

VISCOUS COUPLING DIFFERENTIAL   Viscous coupling differentials use a stack of intermeshed clutch plates that run in a bath of silicone fluid and are not spring loaded. The thickness of the fluid causes a drag that tries to keep the two sets of plates at the same speed. Slippage between the plates heats the fluid

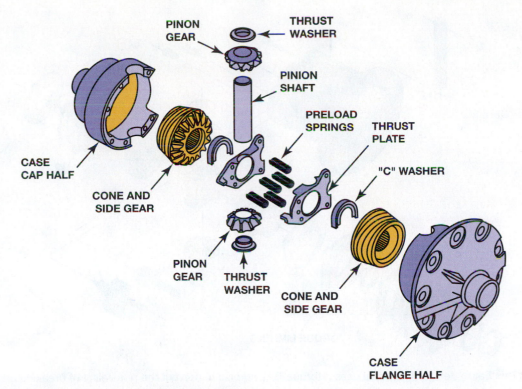

FIGURE 12–24 Exploded view of a limited slip differential using cone-type clutches.

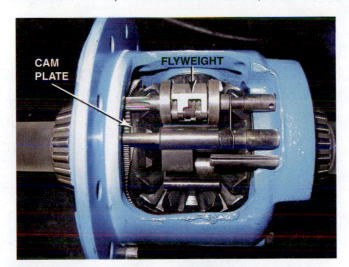

FIGURE 12–25 A locker-type differential operates as a limited slip differential until there is a wheel-to-wheel speed difference of 100 RPM or more. At that point, the governor weights move outward and cause the mechanism to lock the clutch pack.

causing it to expand. A unique feature of silicone fluid is that the drag increases as the slip speed of the plates increases. Single-wheel spinning tends to lock up the differential. The plates and silicone fluid must be isolated within a chamber inside the differential case and must be kept separate from the gear oil in the axle. ● SEE FIGURE 12–28.

HYDRAULIC APPLIED CLUTCH DIFFERENTIAL

Normally, a limited slip differential cannot be used on the front axle.

If both front wheels turn at the same speed, the vehicle cannot turn and it will travel straight ahead. One type is the Hydra-Lok differential from Dana-Spicer. Jeep uses the name *Vari-Lock* for this differential. This design of differential uses a set of clutch plates between one axle gear and the differential case, and these clutch plates have a clearance for free running. There is also a gerotor oil pump built into the differential case. The fluid pressure developed is dependent on the speed difference between the axle gear and the case. The fluid pressure applies to the clutch plates, so torque will be transferred to both the drive axles. The Hydra-Lok differential can be tuned to operate in both front and rear drive axles. ● SEE FIGURE 12–29.

TORSEN® DIFFERENTIAL

The **Torsen®** differential is a pure mechanical worm gear differential. The name is derived from *torque sensing*. Two helical gears, called "side gears," are connected to the axle shafts. Three pairs of worm gears are mounted in the differential case, and these are called "element gears." Each element gear has the worm gear in the center and a spur gear at each end. The spur gears mesh with the spur gears of the mating element gear. If one of the element gears rotates in the case, its mate must rotate in the opposite direction. Note that all three pairs of element gears must rotate at the same time. Gleason, the company that developed Torsen® differentials, calls the element and side gears *Invex gearing*. ● SEE FIGURE 12–30.

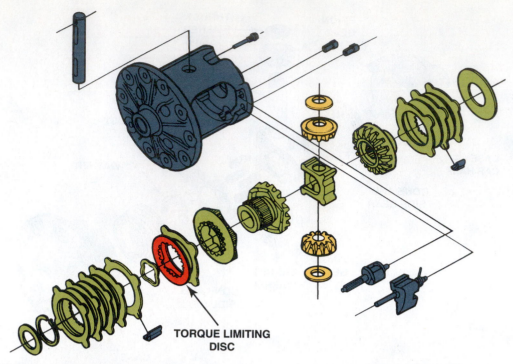

TORQUE LIMITING DISC

FIGURE 12–26 This Eaton design differential uses a torque-limiting disc to prevent the possibility of breaking an axle in the event of a high-torque demand. When the disc tangs shear, the differential will continue to function but as an open rather than as a limited slip differential.

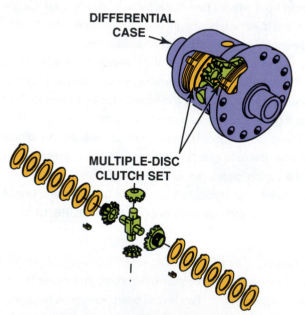

DIFFERENTIAL CASE

MULTIPLE-DISC CLUTCH SET

FIGURE 12–27 This limited slip differential uses the action of the pinion mate shafts and ramps in the differential case to apply pressure on the clutch pack and send torque to the wheel with traction.

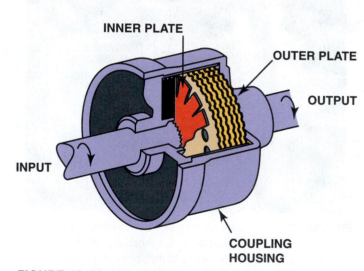

INNER PLATE

OUTER PLATE

OUTPUT

INPUT

COUPLING HOUSING

FIGURE 12–28 In a viscous coupling, silicone fluid is placed between the plates in a seal assembly. When the two axles are moving at different speeds, the fluid becomes hot and expands, which forces the clutch plates to rotate together.

ELECTRIC LOCKING DIFFERENTIALS

A locking differential eliminates any differential action by coupling two of the differential parts together. When the axle shaft or side gear is connected to the differential case, the differential becomes locked.

Electric locking differentials use an electric motor or magnetic clutch assembly to move the locking mechanism. Current flow to the motor can be electronically controlled by the powertrain control module (PCM). Locking differentials are used in both rear and front axles.

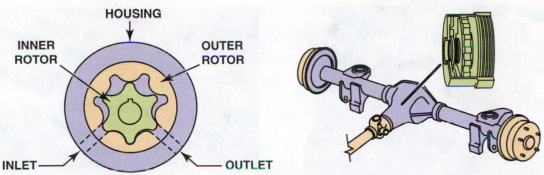

FIGURE 12-29 (a) In a hydraulically operated locking differential, if one wheel turns faster than the other drive wheel, the elements of the fluid pump create fluid pressure which then applies the clutch pack. (b) The pump assembly is similar to a type of fluid pump used in many engines or automatic transmissions.

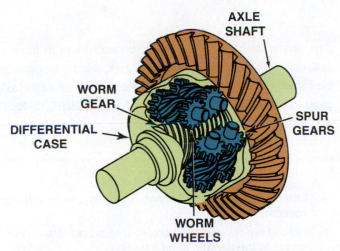

FIGURE 12-30 A torque sensing differential is used in the front drive axle in front-wheel drive vehicles as well as in the rear in rear wheel drive or all-wheel drive vehicles.

ELECTRONIC TORQUE MANAGEMENT
Some vehicles are using a variable torque rear drive axle. These are basically front-wheel-drive vehicles that have a rear drive axle with no differential with the ring gear mounted on a spool to drive two clutches.

The pair of electronically controlled wet clutch packs is used to send power to the rear axle shafts. The clutches can be engaged at times of poor traction for AWD or they can be engaged to provide high-speed vehicle stability. The latter is called *automatic yaw control (AYC)* and it drives one or both rear wheels as needed to keep the vehicle under control. Clutch control comes from an electronic control module (ECM), which receives signals from front and rear wheel speed sensors and engine speed and load sensors.

The Honda Super Handling All Wheel Drive system, SH-AWD, uses a similar rear drive axle that includes an

TECH TIP

Check Tire Size

A common problem encountered with limited slip differentials is a stick/slip condition in which the plates stick together, break apart, and stick together instead of sliding smoothly over each other. This problem shows up as a series of clunks or chuckle sounds as a vehicle rounds a corner. It is very important to keep the drive tires the same diameter with these differentials. Having tires of different diameters will cause the clutch stacks to slip continuously, which, in turn, will cause early failure.

? FREQUENTLY ASKED QUESTION

How Does Electronic Traction Control Work?

Many recent vehicles use **electronic traction control (ETC)** to prevent single-wheel spin. ETC uses the wheel speed sensors, control module, and hydraulic modulator of the antilock brake system (ABS) to sense wheel spin and, if spin occurs, to apply the brake on that wheel. This will transfer torque to the other drive wheel.

electronically controlled gear assembly to increase wheel speed. When necessary, AYC drives one or both rear wheels as needed to keep the vehicle under control during cornering maneuvers. ● **SEE FIGURE 12–31.**

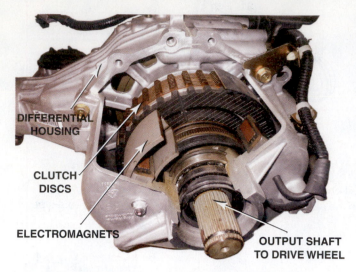

FIGURE 12–31 A cutaway of a Honda SH-AWD differential showing magnetic clutch assembly.

FIGURE 12–32 An independent rear suspension is used to reduce the amount of weight that the suspension has to carry to improve ride and handling. The differential is attached to the frame of the vehicle and does not move when the rear wheels travel over bumps in the road.

INDEPENDENT REAR SUSPENSION DRIVE AXLES

Vehicles with **independent rear suspension (IRS)** have wheels that are supported by the suspension system and the drive shafts, also called *half shafts*, connect them to the axle assembly. The axle housing is very short, slightly bigger than the carrier, and short output shafts are used to connect the axle gears to the U-joint half shaft flanges. ● **SEE FIGURE 12–32.**

SUMMARY

1. A drive axle combines the hypoid final drive gears with the differential and two axle shafts.

2. Hypoid ring and pinion gears must be adjusted correctly for long life and quiet operation.

3. The pinion gear and shaft are supported by two pinion bearings, and the ring gear and differential case are supported by two carrier bearings.

4. Differentials allow two wheels to be driven at different speeds.

5. Limited slip differentials increase torque bias to send more torque to the tire with good traction.

6. Several bearing types are used at the axle wheel ends. Axle shafts can be retained by the axle retainer, a C-lock in the differential, or a full-floating axle is bolted to the hub.

REVIEW QUESTIONS

1. Why is a hypoid gear set used in drive axle assemblies?

2. What is the difference between a hunting and non-hunting gear set?

3. What is the difference between an integral and removal carrier?

4. What are the six types of limited slip differentials?

5. Why is a friction modifier additive required for use in some rear drive axles?

CHAPTER QUIZ

1. In a rear axle, the drive pinion gear works with _____.
   a. A ring gear to change the direction of the power flow
   b. Side gears to provide differential action
   c. A ring gear to provide a gear reduction
   d. All of the above

2. Hypoid ring and pinion gears are used in passenger vehicle drive axles. Technician A says that the concave side of the ring gear tooth is called the drive side. Technician B says that the heel is the smaller, inner end of the ring gear tooth. Which technician is correct?
   a. Technician A only
   b. Technician B only
   c. Both technicians A and B
   d. Neither technician A nor B

3. An overhung pinion uses _____.
   a. One pinion bearing
   b. Two tapered roller pinion bearings
   c. Three roller pinion bearings
   d. Four ball-type pinion bearings

4. Which of the following is not true about a hypoid gear set?
   a. The pinion gear is mounted below the ring gear centerline.
   b. A special type of gear oil is required.
   c. This is an efficient gear set with very little friction.
   d. Special procedures are required to adjust it.

5. Which axle design is used for heavy duty vehicles?
   a. Full floating
   b. C-lock axle
   c. Retainer plate axle
   d. Semi-floating

6. A ring and pinion with a 3.76:1 ratio is classified as _____.
   a. Hunting
   b. Non-hunting
   c. Partial non-hunting.
   d. None of the above

7. What is the dimension that is used to identify a 9 inch axle?
   a. The distance between side bearings
   b. The diameter of the inspection cover
   c. The diameter of the ring gear
   d. The diameter of the axle tubes

8. The differential case _____.
   a. Provides a mounting point for the ring gear
   b. Encloses the differential gears
   c. Is supported by the carrier bearings
   d. All of these

9. A removal carrier is also called a _____.
   a. A third member
   b. A drop out
   c. Pumpkin
   d. Any of the above

10. Most limited slip differentials transfer torque through _____.
    a. The differential gears
    b. One or two clutch stacks
    c. Both a and b
    d. Neither a nor b

chapter 13

DRIVE AXLE AND DIFFERENTIAL DIAGNOSIS AND SERVICE

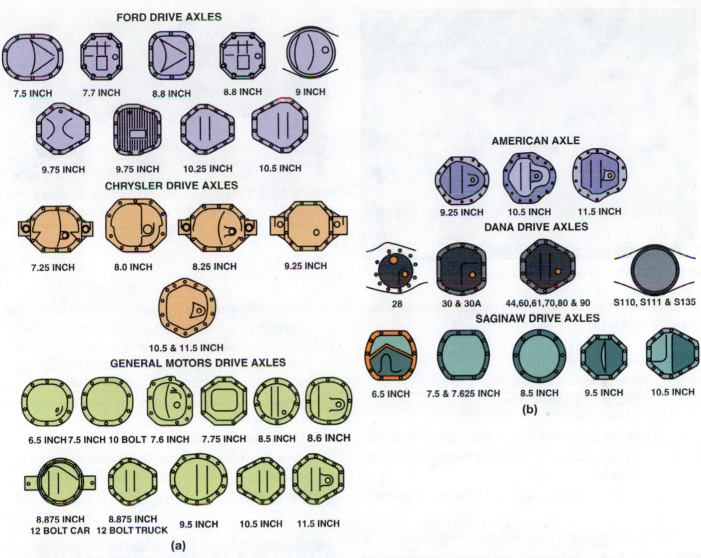

FIGURE 13–1 The drive axle can often be identified using the shape and counting the bolts on the inspection cover. This is most helpful if trying to locate a heavy duty drive axle at a wrecking (recycling) yard. (a) Drive axles sorted by the Detroit three vehicle manufacturers. (b) Axles sorted by axle manufacturers such as American Axle and Manufacturing (AAM), who supply axles to many vehicle manufacturers.

DRIVE AXLE SERVICE

STEPS INVOLVED When diagnosing drive axle concerns, perform the following steps:

STEP 1 The first step is to verify the customer complaint. This step usually includes test driving the vehicle to see if the complaint can be duplicated. If the problem cannot be duplicated, then the repair or service cannot be verified.

STEP 2 Identify the vehicle and the drive axle including the gear ratio so that the proper procedures and specifications will be used. The proper identification can include the following:

- Visual identification (number of bolts used on the cover and the cover design.) ● **SEE FIGURE 13–1**.

- *Regular production option* (RPO) code identification or *service parts identification*. This is found on a sticker located in the trunk or glove box in many vehicles. ● **SEE FIGURE 13–2**.

- Service information and axle identification label on axle assembly.

STEP 3 Check vehicle history and technical service bulletins (TSBs) for the vehicle or axle being serviced.

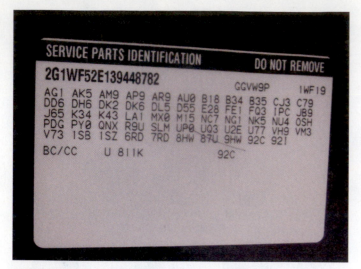

FIGURE 13–2 The service parts identification sticker includes the codes for major components parts and includes the drive axle ratio and other information needed by the parts department to get the correct parts.

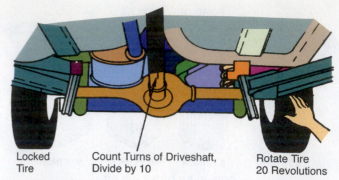

Locked Tire   Count Turns of Driveshaft, Divide by 10   Rotate Tire 20 Revolutions

FIGURE 13–3 The quickest way to check the drive axle ratio is to rotate one wheel with the other wheel locked and count the number of times the driveshaft rotates. If the driveshaft rotates 37 1/3 turns while the free tire rotates 20 turns, the ratio is 3.73:1.

STEP 4 Safely hoist the vehicle and remove the wheels. Visually check for the following:
- Proper gear lubricant level
- Leaks
- Obvious problems such a broken or damaged suspension parts that could affect the operation of the drive axle
- The driveshaft and U-joints for damage or excessive wear

STEP 5 Disassembly and inspect all internal components.

STEP 6 Test for proper backlash and correct operation of the limited slip unit, if equipped.

STEP 7 Replace all components that do not meet factory specifications.

STEP 8 Test drive the vehicle to verify that the repairs did correct the customer concern.

DETERMINING THE AXLE RATIO Sometimes the axle ratio has to be determined, especially if using a wrecking (recycling) yard unit. The axle ratio can often be identified from the tag attached to the axle housing or by the coding on some axles, but not all. The axle ratio can be determined by two other methods.

- **Gear Tooth Count:** The most accurate method of determining gear ratios, if the ring and pinion gears are exposed, is to read the tooth number markings on the ring gear or count the number of teeth on the two gears. Now divide the tooth count of the ring gear by that of the pinion gear, and the result is the ratio.

- **Counting Revolutions:** The axle ratio can be determined by counting the number of revolutions of the driveshaft that are required to turn the wheels one revolution. The best way of doing this is to lock one of the tires using the parking brake or a block. Now, turn the driveshaft until the free tire turns 20 revolutions, and divide the driveshaft revolutions by 10. For example, if there are 23 1/3 turns of the driveshaft to 20 turns of the free tire, the gear ratio is 2.33:1. With one wheel locked, the differential will cause the other wheel to turn twice as fast. ● SEE FIGURE 13–3.

DRIVE AXLE LUBRICATION

GEAR OIL MOVEMENT A drive axle is normally filled with gear oil to a point just below the filler hole. The action of the ring gear running in the bath of oil distributes the lubricant through the housing. Many carriers provide a trough to ensure adequate oiling of the front pinion shaft bearing. The gear oil is kept in the housing by one or more grease seals in each end of the axle housing and at the drive pinion shaft. ● SEE FIGURE 13–4.

VISCOSITY OF GEAR OIL The term viscosity means the "resistance to flow" and assigned a number by SAE (Society of Automotive Engineers). The higher the number, the less viscous the oil and is therefore thicker. The first number followed by the letter W is the viscosity rating when the oil is cold. The letter "W" stands for *winter*.

- The second number indicates the viscosity when tested at 212°F (100°C).

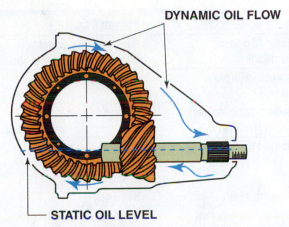

DYNAMIC OIL FLOW

STATIC OIL LEVEL

FIGURE 13–4 In most axles the gear oil level is at the bottom of the filler opening. When the axle operates, the ring gear will produce a dynamic oil flow to lubricate all the parts.

LUBE LEVEL/FILL PLUG

FIGURE 13–5 The fill/level plug is often located on the inspection cover but can also be located on the side.

The gear oil used in drive axles can include the following viscosities:

- SAE 75W-90
- SAE 80W-90
- SAE 85W-90
- SAE 85W-140
- SAE 90

NOTE: Some vehicle manufacturers specify the use of synthetic gear oil of the specified viscosity. Always check service information for the exact gear lubricant to use.

API GEAR OIL GRADE Because all differentials use hypoid gear sets, a special lubricant is necessary because the gears both roll and slide between their meshed teeth. Gear oils

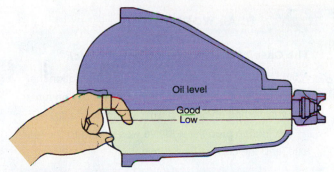

Oil level
Good
Low

FIGURE 13–6 The lubricant (oil) level is usually even with the bottom of the fill opening. If necessary, a finger can be used as a dipstick to determine the level.

labeled *gear lubricant* (GL) are specified by the American Petroleum Institute (API). Drive axles should use hypoid quality GL-5 (meets military Mil-L2150B requirements) gear lubricant of the specified viscosity. If the axle has a limited slip differential, the gear lubricant must meet the requirements for that differential type. A label is normally located near the filler opening on those axles to indicate the fluid required.

CHECKING DRIVE AXLE GEAR OIL LEVEL To check the gear oil level, perform the following steps.

STEP 1 Raise and securely support the vehicle on a hoist or safety stands to gain access to the axle. The vehicle should be raised so that the drive axle is in its normal position relative to level.

STEP 2 Locate the gear oil level plug, which can be in the side of the case or on the cover. Clean the area around it, and remove the plug. Be prepared for fluid to run out of the opening. ● **SEE FIGURE 13–5.**

STEP 3 In most axles the gear oil level should be even with the bottom of the opening. If the gear oil level cannot be seen, carefully insert a finger into the opening and bend it downward, using it as a level indicator. ● **SEE FIGURE 13–6.**

- The fluid level on some Ford axles should be a specified distance below the opening and requires a special dipstick, which can be shop-made. A high fluid level can flood the axle seals and can cause gear oil to leak into the brake drums or rotors. If the fluid level is too low, gear and bearing wear and overheating will occur.

- Gear oil normally has a mildly unpleasant rotten egg smell because of the additive's sulfur compounds. Its color should be the same as that of new oil. Metal particles in the oil indicate internal problems.

The Case of the Chattering Dodge Truck

A 5.9 L Dodge extended cab 4 × 4 had a vibration that felt like a clutch chatter that happened mostly on turns. The vehicle had an antispin (limited slip) rear axle.

A friction modifier additive was added to the rear axle, and the chatter was eliminated.

The "Steering Problem" That Was a Drive Axle Problem

A Honda CRV (All-wheel-drive) (130,000 mi) had an objectionable noise while turning. The vehicle owner complained that the problem must be in the power steering system because it only occurred when turning. An inspection of the power steering showed no problem. On a road test, the noise seemed to be coming from the rear so the rear driveshaft was removed, and the noise was gone.

The fluid was drained from the rear drive axle and replaced using the recommended oil, and this almost cured the noise problem. A second gear oil change was done, and this fixed this noise problem.

NOTE: Some similar faults have been corrected by replacing the transfer case lubricant.

DRIVE AXLE DIAGNOSIS

ROAD TEST Most drive axle problems are related to noise, vibration, leaks, and failure to transmit power.

The road test should include the following driving conditions:

- **Drive:** Light-to-moderate throttle acceleration
- **Cruise:** Enough throttle to maintain a constant speed
- **Float:** Just enough throttle to keep engine load off the drivetrain as the vehicle slows
- **Coast:** Closed throttle deceleration
- **Coast while in neutral:** Isolates transmission noises

NOISE DIAGNOSIS Drive axle noise problems normally fall into one of these categories:

- **Gear noise:** Howling or whining and is often torque sensitive but can be continuous.

WHEN NOISE OCCURS	POSSIBLE CAUSE
Under all driving conditions	Road and tires; wheel bearings; incorrect driveline angles
Changes with road surface	Tires
Noise becomes louder during cornering	Differential gears; axle bearings
Howling sound	Ring and pinion gears (incorrect adjustment, worn, or runout issues)
Growling sound	Bearing(s)
Whine noise concern	Check ring gear pattern for incorrect backlash or pinion depth
Clunk on speed change or going from forward to reverse or reverse to forward	Worn U-Joints, differential or driveshaft splines
Continuous low pitched whir	Worn U-joints
Low pitch rumble over 20 MPH (32 km/h)	Worn carrier bearings
Chatter during cornering	Incorrect gear oil or worn limited slip clutches

CHART 13–1

A summary chart showing the probable causes of various drive axle-related noise concerns.

- **Bearing noise:** Can be a high-pitched, whistlelike sound but is usually a rough growl or rumble. Bearings will often make a "wow-wow" type of sound at the speed frequency of the spinning shaft.

- **Clunk:** Heavy metallic slapping noise during reversal of power flow or engagement of power from neutral. This fault is caused by excessive slack or excessive clearances in the drivetrain and can be felt in the drive axle.

- **Chuckle:** A rattling noise, similar to a playing card against spinning bicycle spokes, during deceleration below 40 MPH (64 km/h). This fault is often caused by excessive clearance in the differential.

- **Chatter on corners:** A vibration or noise as the vehicle turns a corner, especially after prolonged straight driving. This noise is often called *chatter,* commonly caused by a stick/slip condition at the clutch plates of a limited slip differential. After changing the lubricant in a limited slip differential to cure a chatter problem, drive the vehicle through 10 to 12 figure-8 turns. This procedure will force the new lubricant between the clutch plates.

● **SEE CHART 13–1** for summary of noise-related faults and their possible causes.

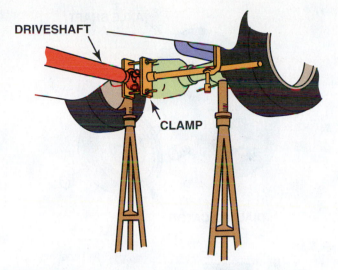

DRIVESHAFT

CLAMP

FIGURE 13–7 A drive axle can be checked for excessive play in the differential by blocking one drive wheel and the driveshaft

FIGURE 13–8 One way to lock one wheel is to lower the vehicle so one tire is resting on a barrel or something similar that will keep the wheel from moving.

LOCK LEFT REAR WHEEL

CHALK MARK

12"

FIGURE 13–9 The mark should be 1 inch or shorter. If the mark is less than 1 inch and there is a clunk in the driveline, the problem is NOT in the drive axle assembly.

TECH TIP

Noises Can Travel

While diagnosing noise problems, remember that they can come from the exhaust system (both normal air-transmitted noises and noises from metal-to-metal contact between the exhaust system and the vehicle body or frame), tires, and wind. Drivetrain noises can usually be heard while the vehicle is operated and being supported on a hoist or safety stands. Vehicle loads can be simulated by applying the brake for short periods of time.

STEP 3 Block the left wheel so that it cannot turn. ● **SEE FIGURE 13–8.**

STEP 4 Turn the right wheel slowly in one direction until it stops, loading the entire lash (clearance) to one side. Using chalk or marking crayon, place a mark on the side of the tire 12 inches (30 cm) from the center of the wheel.

STEP 5 Hold the chalk steady and rotate the tire in the opposite direction until it stops.

STEP 6 Measure the length of the chalk mark; this is the amount of drive axle backlash. More than 1 inch (25 mm) of lash is excessive and indicates that something in the axle is worn. ● **SEE FIGURE 13–9.**

IN-THE-SHOP INSPECTIONS

DRIVE AXLE BACKLASH A drivetrain clunk during a power change can be caused by too much internal **backlash**. To quickly determine if the drive axle is the cause of the noise due to backlash, perform the following steps:

STEP 1 Raise and securely support the vehicle on a hoist or jack stands and the wheels are free to turn.

STEP 2 Lock the driveshaft and drive pinion companion flange by clamping a bar to the companion flange and the body or rear suspension. ● **SEE FIGURE 13–7.**

AXLE SHAFT ENDPLAY To check axle shaft endplay, grip each wheel and attempt to move it in and out. If axle shaft endplay seems excessive, place index marks on the tire and the brake drum and remove them. Mount a dial indicator on the brake backing plate and position the stylus on the axle flange. Move the axle shaft in and out while looking at the endplay on the dial indicator. Check the results with the vehicle manufacturer specifications. Excessive endplay can mean a worn axle groove for the C-lock or a worn axle bearing. ● **SEE FIGURE 13–10.**

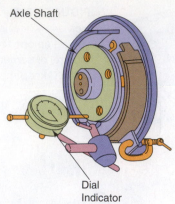

Axle Shaft

Dial
Indicator

FIGURE 13–10 Axle shaft endplay can be checked by mounting a dial indicator on the brake assembly or axle housing with the indicator stylus on the axle. The indicator will measure the endplay as the axle is moved in and out.

 REAL WORLD FIX

Pinion Bearing Fault

An all-wheel-drive (AWD) Buick Rendezvous (61,000 mi) came into the shop with loud drivetrain howl and vibration that varied with speed and load. Raising the vehicle on a hoist allowed the technician to narrow the problem down to the rear drive axle. The rear drive axle gear oil was clean and at the proper level.

A close inspection of the drive axle revealed rough pinion shaft bearings, possibly from the adjustment being too tight or poor lubrication. The technician was unable to get replacement bearings or a rebuilt assembly so a new axle was installed which fixed the problem.

AXLE FLANGE RUNOUT   To check wheel mounting flange runout, perform the following steps:

STEP 1   Raise and securely support the vehicle on a hoist or safety stands and remove the tire/wheel assembly and drum/disc.

STEP 2   Install a dial indicator and while pushing the axle inward to remove any end-play, measure lateral (side-to-side) and radial (out-of-round) ends of the axle flange. Lateral runout of 0.005 inch (0.1 mm) or less is acceptable.

- Radial runout of 0.030 inch (0.76 mm) or less is acceptable.
- If the runout is more than the specifications, the axle should be replaced. ● **SEE FIGURE 13–11**.

LEAK DETECTION   Most gear oil leaks will be found at the following locations:

AXLE SHAFT

DIAL INDICATOR

(a)

AXLE HUB

(b)

FIGURE 13–11   (a) This dial indicator is set up to measure axle flange lateral runout, which can cause the wheel to wobble. (b) This dial indicator is set up to measure radial runout of the drum and wheel pilot, which can cause the wheel to run off-center.

- Axle shaft seals
- Drive pinion seals
- Rear cover
- Carrier-to-housing gasket (on removable carrier type).

Occasionally, a leak is found in a porous casting or a faulty weld in the housing. A porous casting can be repaired using epoxy. A leaky weld, however, is a sign of a potentially dangerous stress crack or fracture, and the housing should be replaced. ● **SEE FIGURE 13–12**.

LIMITED SLIP DIFFERENTIAL CHECK   To confirm that a limited slip differential is able to drive both drive wheels requires a special adapter and a torque wrench. ● **SEE FIGURE 13–13**.

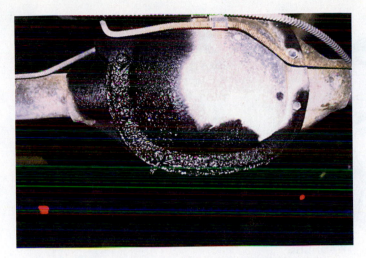

FIGURE 13–12 Many leaks are caused by defective gaskets but some axle oil leaks can be caused by a porous casting or cracked welds. A casting problem can be repaired using epoxy sealant, whereas a cracked weld requires housing replacement.

To do so, perform the following steps:

STEP 1 Attach an adapter to one of the rear hubs. Some adapters require removal of the wheel and tire.

STEP 2 Raise the wheel with the adapter off the floor and leave the other wheel on the floor and place the transmission in neutral.

STEP 3 Attach a torque wrench to the adapter and read the amount of torque required as the wheel is rotated. Compare the reading to factory specifications. If no torque specifications are available, some technicians will use a rule-of-thumb of 35 to 40 lb-ft (48 to 54 N-m) minimum. Readings lower than this indicates a badly worn clutch pack in the differential.

ON-VEHICLE SERVICE OPERATIONS

ITEMS THAT CAN BE SERVICED   On-vehicle operations include the following:

- Wheel stud replacement
- Axle seal replacement
- Axle shaft
- Axle bearing
- Drive pinion seal replacement

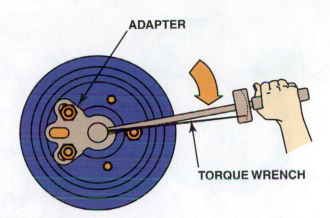

FIGURE 13–13 A special tool has been attached to two wheel studs, allowing a torque wrench to be used to measure the torque required to turn this wheel. The opposite wheel is on the ground with the transmission in neutral. A low reading indicates limited slip differential wear.

🔧 **TECH TIP**

Look for the Hole in the Retainer Plate

Most axle flanges include a hole so that a socket and extension bar can be used to remove and replace the retainer bolts. If the axle does not have a hole in the retainer plate, then the axle uses a C-lock-type retaining method.

WHEEL STUD REPLACEMENT   Wheel studs are held in the axle flange by an interference fit between a serrated portion of the stud and the hole in the flange. Wheel studs should be carefully inspected and replaced if the threads are stripped or damaged. Damaged wheel studs can be replaced without removing the axle. ● **SEE FIGURE 13–14**.

AXLE REMOVAL   Passenger car and light pickup axles are semi-floating and are retained in the housing by either a C-lock at the inner end of the axle or by the axle bearing retainer at the outer end. Axle service includes removing the axle for bearing or seal replacement and bent or broken axle replacement. ● **SEE FIGURES 13–15 AND 13–16**.

C-LOCK AXLE SEAL REPLACEMENT   The axle seal is located next to the bearing and seals against a smooth area of the axle shaft.

Both the bearing and the seal are removed from the housing using a slide hammer and special adapter. ● **SEE FIGURE 13–17**.

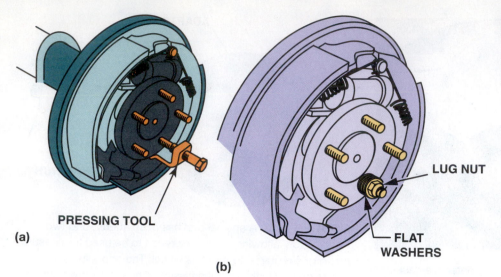

FIGURE 13–14 (a) A tight stud should be removed using a pressing tool so as not to bend the axle flange. (b) A new wheel stud is installed by tightening the lug nut against a stack of flat washers.

C-Lock Retained Axle

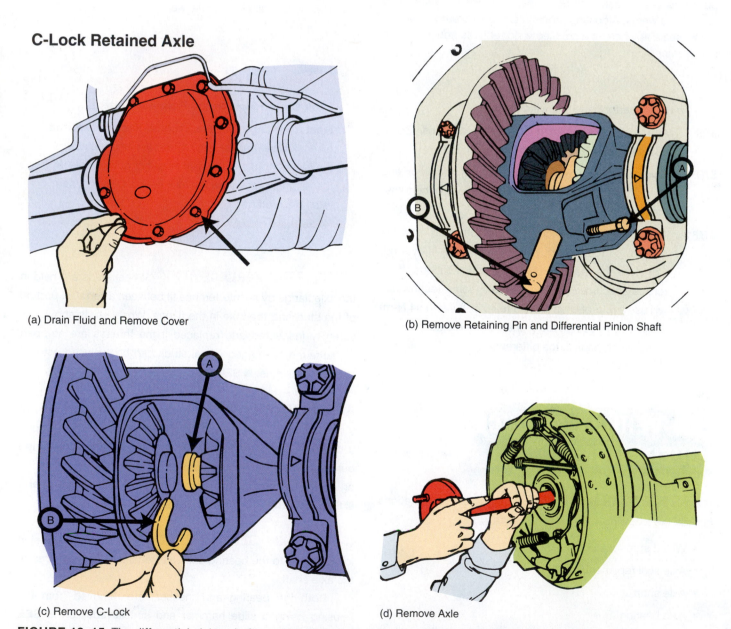

(a) Drain Fluid and Remove Cover

(b) Remove Retaining Pin and Differential Pinion Shaft

(c) Remove C-Lock

(d) Remove Axle

FIGURE 13–15 The differential pinion shaft must be removed to allow the C-lock and axle to be removed.

BEARING RETAINED AXLE

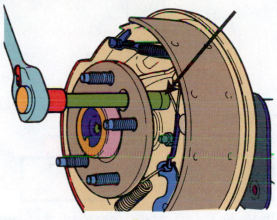

(a) Remove Retainer Nuts/Bots

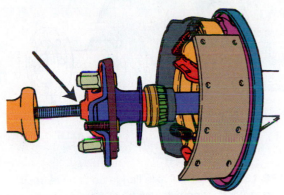

(b) Attach Slide Hammer and Remove Axle

FIGURE 13–16 The retainer nuts/bolts are removed before sliding the bearing-retained axle from the housing.

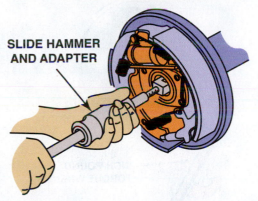

SLIDE HAMMER AND ADAPTER

FIGURE 13–17 The bearing and seal are removed from the housing with a slide hammer and adapter.

Pull the seal first and then, if needed, remove the bearing. After they are removed, the recesses where they fit should be checked for scratches or gouges that might let gear oil past the seal. Another special tool is required to install the bearing. It should be slightly smaller than the diameter of the bearing and have a face that meets the face of the bearing to prevent damaging the bearing during installation. The new bearing is driven straight into the housing to the end of its recess. The same installation procedure and tool is used to install the new seal.

RETAINER AXLE BEARING AND SEAL REMOVAL AND REPLACEMENT

The retainer bearing type axle bearing is press fit on the axle and requires a hydraulic press and special adapters to remove and install. Extreme caution should be observed when performing this procedure to avoid serious injuries from possible bearing explosion during the pressing procedure. Most axle bearing removal tools enclose the bearing completely to contain the bearing if it explodes.

CAUTION: When pressing a bearing off an axle, place a brake drum over the bearing as a shatter shield.

? FREQUENTLY ASKED QUESTION

How Is the Axle Removed from a Full-Floating-Type Axle?

The full-floating axle is used in medium and heavy-duty trucks and in many larger pickups and vans. Axles are removed to replace the shaft, gain access to the wheel bearings, and allow removal of the hub and brake drum and the carrier.

1. Remove the bolts that attach the axle shaft flange to the hub and mark the location of the axle and hub.
2. Using a soft hammer, strike the axle flange to break the gasket loose.
3. Slide the axle out of the housing. ● **SEE FIGURE 13–18**.

To remove and replace a bearing pressed on an axle shaft, perform the following steps:

STEP 1 Position the axle so that the lock ring rests on the edge of the anvil portion of a vise or a sturdy bench-top. Using a hammer and cold chisel, make a series of six or eight cuts into the ring. Strike each location once or twice using fairly strong blows to expand the ring slightly so that it will relax its grip on the axle. ● **SEE FIGURE 13–19**.

STEP 2 Select the correct size adapter for the bearing, and install the adapter and fixture on the axle.

STEP 3 Place the fixture in the bed of a press and press the axle out of the bearing and lock ring.

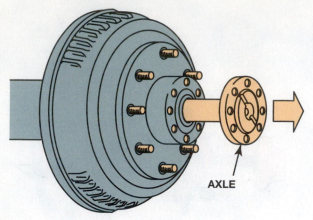

FIGURE 13–18 After the axle flange bolts have been removed, a full-floating axle can be slid out of the housing. This permits access to the axle, wheel bearings, and brakes.

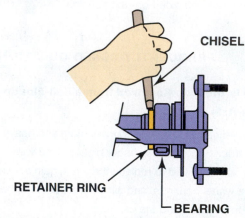

FIGURE 13–19 The axle bearing retainer ring should be cut or stretched using a drill and a chisel to make six to eight blows before trying to press the bearing off the axle.

CAUTION: Be ready to catch the axle as it moves through the bearing as it will fall freely after moving about an inch (25 mm).

To press a bearing onto an axle, perform the following steps:

STEP 1 Clean the bearing retainer and the end of the axle, and place the bearing retainer onto the axle.

STEP 2 Place the bearing on the axle and press the axle into the bearing to the correct position. Be sure to press only on the inner race of the axle bearing. ● SEE FIGURE 13–20.

STEP 3 Place the lock ring on the axle and press the axle into the ring until the ring contacts the bearing.

PINION SHAFT SEAL REPLACEMENT

PROCEDURE A leaking pinion shaft seal can be replaced in-vehicle without removing the pinion shaft from the carrier or drive axle/carrier from the vehicle. The driveshaft flange

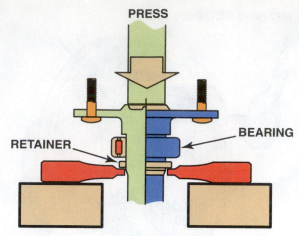

FIGURE 13–20 The axle is being pressed into the bearing and retainer plate.

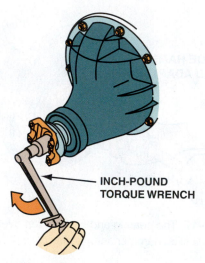

FIGURE 13–21 A leaky drive pinion seal is repaired by first measuring the axle preload. After removing the wheels and eliminating any brake drag, use an inch-pound torque wrench to measure the pinion bearing preload. It should be between 17 and 22 inch-pounds or slightly lower in most applications.

is removed and then the seal is removed and replaced. An important requirement while performing this operation is to not disturb the drive **pinion bearing preload** adjustment.

NOTE: Measuring the drive axle preload in step 2 provides the information for tightening the pinion nut in step 7.

To remove and replace a drive pinion seal, perform the following steps:

STEP 1 Disconnect the driveshaft from the companion flange, and support the driveshaft so it does not hang from the front U-joint.

STEP 2 Measure the torque required to rotate the pinion shaft (pinion and carrier bearing preload) using an inch-pound torque wrench, and record this measurement. ● SEE FIGURE 13–21.

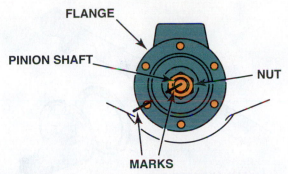

FLANGE

PINION SHAFT

NUT

MARKS

FIGURE 13–22 Mark the pinion flange, pinion nut, and the pinion shaft before removing the pinion nut.

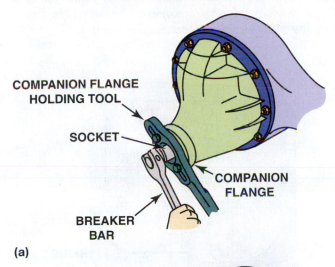

COMPANION FLANGE HOLDING TOOL

SOCKET

BREAKER BAR

COMPANION FLANGE

(a)

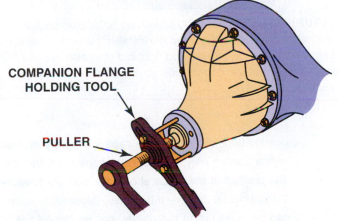

COMPANION FLANGE HOLDING TOOL

PULLER

(b)

FIGURE 13–23 (a) A companion flange holding tool is used to keep the companion flange from rotating as the pinion nut is loosened. (b) After the pinion nut has been removed, a puller is used to remove the companion flange.

STEP 3 Place index marks on the end of the pinion shaft, pinion nut, and the companion flange so that the flange can be installed back on the same spline. ● **SEE FIGURE 13–22.**

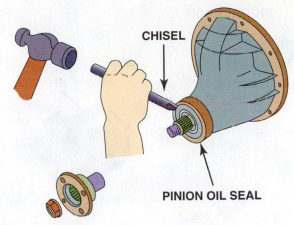

CHISEL

PINION OIL SEAL

FIGURE 13–24 Use a chisel to separate the seal from the axle housing, then use a seal remover to pry the seal off.

STEP 4 Remove the drive pinion nut, washer, and companion flange. ● **SEE FIGURE 13–23.**

STEP 5 Remove the pinion seal. ● **SEE FIGURE 13–24.**

STEP 6 Check the bearing pocket for damage. Then, apply a thin film of gear oil to the lip of the seal and the sealing surface of the flange. ● **SEE FIGURE 13–25.**

STEP 7 Replace the companion flange and install a new pinion nut with a washer and tighten the nut until the parts align as per the marks that were made in step 3. Check that the bearing preload is slightly greater than that recorded in step 2. The pinion nut should be very tight.

STEP 8 Replace the driveshaft.

DIFFERENTIAL CARRIER SERVICE

TYPICAL STEPS INVOLVED Differential carrier service usually includes the following steps:

- An inspection of the gears and bearings before teardown
- A check for ring gear runout
- Removal and replacement of the differential and ring gear
- Removal and replacement of the pinion gear
- Inspection and repair of the differential
- Assembly adjustments for pinion depth, pinion bearing preload, backlash, and carrier bearing preload.

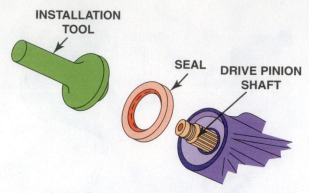

FIGURE 13–25 Use a seal driver (installation tool) to seat the new seal in the axle housing.

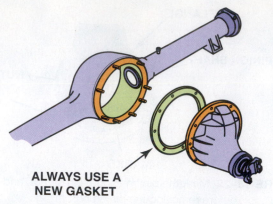

FIGURE 13–26 The carrier (third member) is removed from the drive axle housing by removing the retaining nuts, and then the heavy assembly is carefully removed.

REMOVABLE CARRIER REMOVAL

On removable carrier axles, the carrier is removed from the axle housing to service or repair the differential, ring and pinion gears, or any of the bearings.

To remove a carrier, perform the following steps:

STEP 1 Raise and securely support the vehicle on a hoist or safety stands.

STEP 2 Remove the axles and the driveshaft.

STEP 3 Place a drain pan under the axle assembly, and remove the nuts or bolts that are securing the carrier to the housing. Also remove the copper washers used to seal the studs. ● **SEE FIGURE 13–26.**

INTEGRAL CARRIER REMOVAL

To remove an integral carrier, perform the following steps:

STEP 1 Raise and securely support the vehicle on a hoist or safety stands and remove both axles.

STEP 2 Using a punch and hammer or permanent marker, place index marks on each of the bearing caps. ● **SEE FIGURE 13–27.**

STEP 3A On units with threaded adjusters, remove the adjustment locks, the carrier bearing cap mounting bolts, and the bearing caps. On threaded adjusters, remove the adjuster and lift the differential with bearing cups out of the carrier. Mark or tag the bearing cups. On shim-adjusted carriers, remove the bearing cap mounting bolts and the bearing caps.

STEP 3B On shim-adjusted carriers, remove the bearing cap mounting bolts and the bearing caps. Mark or tag the

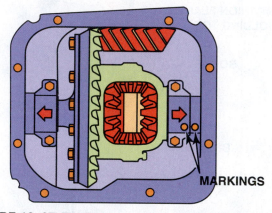

FIGURE 13–27 The bearing caps have to be stamped or marked to make sure that they are installed back in the exact same location. Not only left and right but they also need to be installed with the correct side up, the same as they were installed originally.

bearing cups. Some bearing caps are factory marked with an arrow only, so mark the caps right and left. The preload at the shims should be too tight to allow easy removal of the differential. Most differentials can be pried out of the carrier, but be careful not to damage the gasket surface on the carrier. ● **SEE FIGURE 13–28.**

NOTE: Some differentials can be removed by placing a box wrench on one of the ring gear bolts and turning the pinion gear so that the wrench pushes against the carrier and lifts up the differential.

Some manufacturers recommend the use of a spreader tool to stretch the carrier. Stretching the carrier will take the

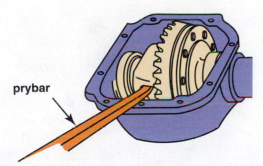

prybar

FIGURE 13–28 Use a prybar to gently pry the carrier from the housing.

pressure off the shims and bearings. When using a spreader tool, do not spread the carrier more than the manufacturer's limits, or 0.015 inch (0.4 mm).

STEP 4 As the carrier is removed from the housing, tag or mark the shims and bearing cup from each side.

STEP 5 The drive pinion gear is held in place by the companion flange, and the self-locking nut that secures it. It will require a lot of torque to loosen, often 150 to 300 lb-ft (203 to 407 N-m). Follow the steps mentioned for pinion seal replacement for removal.

INSPECTION AND CLEANING Inspection begins with a complete cleanup. After cleaning, visually inspect the ring gear and differential gears for obvious damage. The surface of the teeth should be smooth and have a polished sheen. Common ring gear wear appears as a rough, scored tooth surface or chipped or nicked teeth.

DIFFERENTIAL ASSEMBLY SERVICE

INSPECTION After cleaning, visually inspect the ring gear and differential gears for obvious damage. The surface of the teeth should be smooth and have a polished sheen. Common ring gear wear appears as a rough, scored tooth surface or chipped or nicked teeth.

RING GEAR RUNOUT **Ring gear runout** is checked if there is evidence of damage to the ring gear. Runout is usually caused by a faulty or bent differential case or an improper mounting of the ring gear onto the case. Because gear runout will cause backlash to change, it is sometimes referred to as **backlash variation**.

To check ring gear runout, perform the following steps:

- Mount a dial indicator with the stylus on the back of the ring gear at 90° to the gear surface The runout of a differential case can be checked using a similar procedure. ● **SEE FIGURE 13–29.**

- Rotate the ring gear and observe the indicator needle movement. This is the total indicated runout (TIR).

RING GEAR REPLACEMENT Ring gear replacement on most differentials is a matter of removing the bolts and then the gear.

NOTE: Due to the precise fit between the ring gear and the carrier, it is often difficult to remove the ring gear with binding. Take care when removing the ring gear to avoid damaging the carrier of the ring gear.

When installing the ring gear, heating the gear is required to seat it properly onto the case. The ring gear mounting bolts must be tightened to the correct torque and in an alternating pattern, back and forth across the gear. Replacement ring gears have threaded holes and are furnished with new bolts.

FIGURE 13–29 Ring gear runout should be less than 0.002 inch (0.05 mm) as measured by a dial indicator.

 TECH TIP

Loosen Ring Gear Bolts First

An experienced technician will loosen the ring gear mounting bolts before removing the differential from the differential case. These bolts are normally very tight, and the differential is hard to hold when it is out of the carrier. While still in the carrier, the differential case can be held stationary by placing a block of wood between the ring and pinion gears or by placing a box wrench on one of the ring gear bolts and against the side of the carrier.

NOTE: Sometimes the ring gear is installed using rivets. These are normally removed by drilling through the rivet head, cutting the remainder of the head off with a chisel, and driving the rest of the rivet out using a punch.

PINION GEAR REMOVAL
To remove a drive pinion from the housing, perform the following steps:

STEP 1 Place index marks on the end of the pinion shaft, pinion nut, and the companion flange so that the flange can be installed back on the same spline.

STEP 2 Attach a holding tool to the flange and use a socket and the longest handle available to loosen the nut.

CAUTION: Most vehicle manufactures warn to not use an impact wrench for removing or installing a pinion

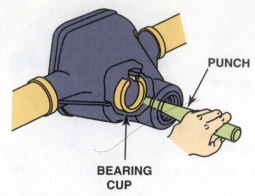

FIGURE 13–30 A damaged bearing cup can be driven out of the housing using a long punch.

shaft nut. The hammering forces can easily cause the pinion shaft bearing rollers to dent the races. Use only hand tools to avoid shock loading the pinion bearings.

STEP 3 Slide the companion flange off the drive pinion shaft. If necessary, use a puller to remove the flange.

STEP 4 Use a soft hammer or brass punch to tap the pinion shaft into the carrier. Be ready to catch the pinion gear as it slides out.

PINION BEARINGS
After disassembly, the parts should be cleaned in a solvent and inspected to ensure their usability.

If new pinion bearings are required, then the old bearing cups must also be replaced. Worn drive pinion bearing cups are normally removed from the carrier using a punch and hammer. ● SEE FIGURE 13–30.

New pinion bearing cups are installed by driving them into place using a bearing cup driver and hammer.

CAUTION: Never hammer directly on the new cup.

SIDE BEARINGS
Normally during disassembly, the carrier bearings are left on the differential case unless they or the shim located behind them need to be replaced. A puller is normally required to remove the side bearings. Some manufacturers recommend the use of a special puller while others use a sturdy two-jaw bearing puller and a step-plate adapter. ● SEE FIGURE 13–31.

The new bearing is installed using a special bearing installer. Many shops will use a section of an iron pipe of the correct diameter that fits the inner bearing race.

DIFFERENTIAL CASE CLEARANCE CHECKS
Differential case clearance is usually checked by using a dial indicator with the stylus on a side gear tooth. Hold the other side gear stationary as the first gear is moved back and forth against

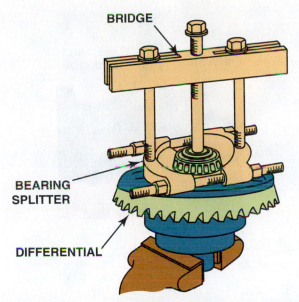

FIGURE 13–31 A puller and bearing splitter are set up to remove the differential side bearing.

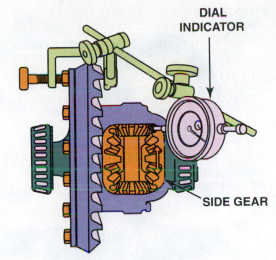

FIGURE 13–32 Differential case wear can be checked by measuring the side gear backlash using a dial indicator.

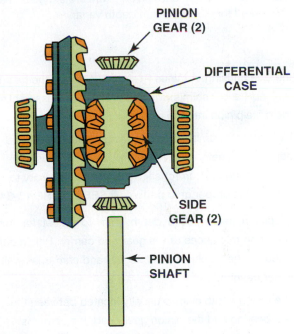

FIGURE 13–33 With the pinion shaft removed, the pinion gears can be rolled to the case windows and removed; then the side gears can be lifted out of the case.

the lash. The amount of lash is shown by the dial indicator needle movement. One manufacturer gives a specification of 0 to 0.009 inch (0 to 23 mm). ● SEE FIGURE 13–32.

- Too much clearance can be reduced in some differentials by using thicker thrust washers behind the differential pinion and side gears.
- Other differentials do not use thrust washers, so the only way to reduce the clearance is to replace the worn differential parts.

NOTE: Excessive clearance in the differential gear set can cause a clunk as the lash is taken up when either the manual transmission clutch or automatic transmission is engaged. This is especially noticeable when changing direction, low to reverse, or reverse to low.

DISASSEMBLING THE DIFFERENTIAL CASE ASSEMBLY

To disassemble the differential case assembly, perform the following steps.

STEP 1 Remove the pinion shaft lock pin.

STEP 2 Slide the pinion shaft out of the case and check it for step wear.

STEP 3 Roll the pinion gears to the case window(s) and remove the pinion gears and thrust washers and the axle side gears and their thrust washers. ● SEE FIGURE 13–33.

STEP 4 Inspect the gears, thrust washers, and case surfaces for scoring and wear. Reverse this procedure to reassemble the differential.

DRIVE PINION SHAFT

DRIVE PINION DEPTH The drive pinion gear and ring gear are manufactured as a matched set and must be installed as a set. Due to variances in the production of these gears, it is often necessary to vary the thickness of a shim needed to create the proper ring gear-to-drive pinion pattern:

- A plus (+) sign means the gear is too long and removing a shim(s) is required when assembling the drive pinion into

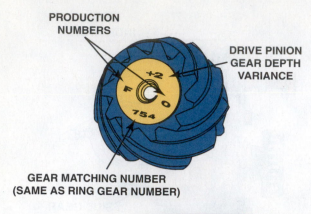

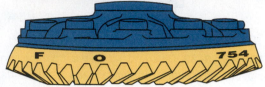

FIGURE 13–34 The ring and pinion gears are a matched set and are marked for correct pinion depth variance.

(a)

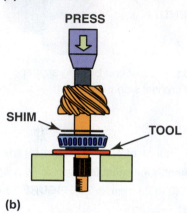

(b)

FIGURE 13–35 (a) A bearing splitter and a hydraulic press is needed to remove the pinion shaft bearing and get access to the shim. (b) The setup for pressing the bearing onto the pinion shaft with the shim in place.

the axle housing. A minus (-) sign means that the gear is too short and a shim(s) will be needed when assembling the drive pinion into the axle housing.

- Pinion depth can be checked using a gauging set and depth micrometer. This is a common method used to determine the correct shim thickness necessary to provide the proper gear pattern. ● SEE FIGURE 13–34.

All pinion gears use a depth shim to adjust for minor manufacturing tolerances of the gear and carrier. Pinion depth is affected by the machining of the gear and carrier, as well as by the rear bearing.

- The pinion depth shim is usually located between the rear bearing and the pinion gear head. If a carrier is assembled with the wrong pinion depth shim, it will need to be disassembled so that the shim can be changed.

Some adjustments require that while inserting a shim, press the bearing in place, and then check to see if the inserted a shim is the correct size. If a change in the shim is needed, the pinion bearing will have to be pressed off. ● SEE FIGURE 13–35.

PINION DEPTH SHIM SELECTION
There are four different methods used to determine the correct size for a pinion depth shim, including the following:

1. + or – markings on the pinion gear
2. Gauge block and fixtures
3. Contact patterns

At one time, many passenger vehicle drive pinion gears were marked with a + or – and a number that indicated the position of that gear relative to a perfect gear. The + or – indicated the direction, and the number (up to about 0.005 inch) indicated the distance. This number was etched or painted on the head or stem of the gear. When a ring and pinion gear set is replaced, the technician checks the markings on both the old and new pinion gears and changes the shim to compensate for any difference. ● SEE CHART 13–2.

OLD SHIM MARKING	NEW SHIM MARKING −4	NEW SHIM MARKING −3	NEW SHIM MARKING −2	NEW SHIM MARKING −1	NEW SHIM MARKING 0	NEW SHIM MARKING +1	NEW SHIM MARKING +2	NEW SHIM MARKING +3	NEW SHIM MARKING +4
+4	+0.008	+0.007	+0.006	+0.005	+0.004	+0.003	+0.002	+0.001	0.000
+3	+0.007	+0.006	+0.005	+0.004	+0.003	+0.002	+0.001	0.000	−0.001
+2	+0.006	+0.005	+0.004	+0.003	+0.002	+0.001	0.000	−0.001	−0.002
+1	+0.005	+0.004	+0.003	+0.002	+0.001	0.000	−0.001	−0.002	−0.003
0	+0.004	+0.003	+0.002	+0.001	0.000	−0.001	−0.002	−0.003	−0.004
−1	+0.003	+0.002	+0.001	0.000	−0.001	−0.002	−0.003	−0.004	−0.005
−2	+0.002	+0.001	0.000	−0.001	−0.002	−0.003	−0.004	−0.005	−0.006
−3	+0.001	0.000	−0.001	−0.002	−0.003	−0.004	−0.005	−0.006	−0.007
−4	0.000	−0.001	−0.002	−0.003	−0.004	−0.005	−0.006	−0.007	−0.008

CHART 13–2

A chart can be used to determine the size of the depth shim needed. These markings are no longer used by all manufacturers.

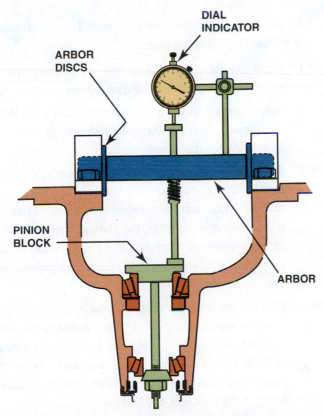

FIGURE 13–36 Special tool kit used for determining the correct pinion shaft shim thickness.

Most vehicle manufacturers use a set of pinion depth gauge blocks to select the correct depth shim. These gauges are installed in the carrier, usually using the rear drive pinion bearing. Universal pinion depth measuring tools are available that can be used to determine the pinion depth. ● SEE FIGURE 13–36.

PINION BEARINGS The pinion shaft usually has two tapered roller bearings where the small diameter of each bearing faces each other. This arrangement allows the two bearings to absorb thrust load in both directions. When tapered roller bearings are used in a differential, it is very important that they have the proper preload. If a tapered roller bearing is too loose (too little preload), then the bearing cannot properly support and position the pinion shaft. If the preload is too great, excessive heat will quickly destroy the bearing as it expands with heat during normal operation of the rear axle assembly.

DRIVE PINION BEARING PRELOAD ADJUSTMENT

After installation of the pinion depth shim, pinion seal, and rear bearing, the bearing spacer is placed on the pinion shaft and the pinion gear is installed in the carrier. The **bearing spacer** will be either a collapsible **crush sleeve** or a fixed-length solid spacer. ● SEE FIGURE 13–37.

This spacer keeps the two tapered roller bearings apart as the companion flange nut is tightened. The spacer allows the bearings to be squeezed against their races just tight enough to obtain the proper preload. The length of a fixed spacer is adjusted by adding or removing thin selective-size shims. A crush sleeve starts out too long and is collapsed to the proper length as the drive pinion nut is tightened. Collapsing a crush sleeve takes a substantial amount of force.

To adjust drive pinion bearing preload using a collapsible spacer, perform the following steps:

STEP 1 Lubricate the bearings and slide the pinion gear with the rear bearing, depth shim, and new collapsible spacer into the carrier through the front bearing and seal.

STEP 2 Lubricate the splines and seal area, and install the companion flange, being sure to align the index marks.

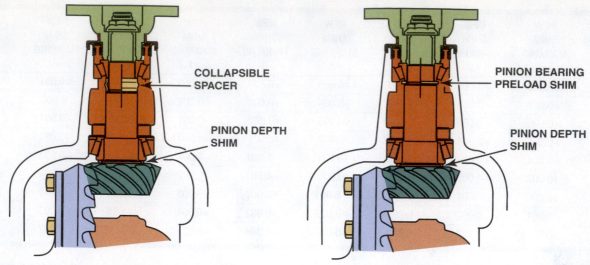

FIGURE 13–37 The pinion on the left uses a collapsible spacer, and the pinion on the right uses shims to provide the necessary preload to the pinion shaft bearings.

FIGURE 13–38 Using an inch-pound torque wrench to check the rotating torque of the drive pinion. This procedure is very important if the axle uses a collapsible spacer. The drive pinion nut should be gradually tightened and the rotating torque checked to prevent over-tightening the nut. If the rotating torque is higher than specifications, the collapsible spacer will require replacement and the installation procedure must be repeated.

STEP 3   Oil the inner face of the new nut and special washer, and then install them on the pinion shaft.

STEP 4   Attach a holding tool to the flange and begin tightening the nut.

STEP 5   Continue tightening the nut with a foot-pound torque wrench as two things are checked:

1. The minimum torque to obtain the preload and the amount of preload using an inch-pound torque wrench.

2. Stop tightening when the preload is within specifications. ● **SEE FIGURE 13–38.**

To adjust drive pinion bearing preload using a solid spacer, perform the following steps:

STEP 1   Install the solid spacer onto the pinion shaft with a starting shim that should be thicker than needed.

STEP 2   Follow steps 1 through 4 of the procedure used with a collapsible spacer. Torque-tighten the nut to about 50 ft-lb (68 N-m) of torque.

STEP 3   If there is no free play, measure the bearing preload as described in step 5 of the collapsible spacer procedure. If the preload is within specifications, go to step 8. If the preload is too high, the starting shim will have to be replaced with a thicker one. If the preload is too low, a thinner shim is needed. If there is no preload, as expected, move on to step 4.

STEP 4   Mount a dial indicator on the carrier and position the indicator stylus on the end of and parallel to the pinion shaft. For example, if there is a starting shim size of 0.030 inch, 0.010 inch of free play, and a factor of 0.003, the procedure would be 0.030 – 0.010 – 0.003 = 0.017 , for a shim size of 0.017 inch.

STEP 5   Move the pinion shaft through its free play and read the dial indicator needle movement to determine the free play.

STEP 6   Determine the shim change by subtracting a factor specified by the manufacturer and the free play from the size of the starting shim.

STEP 7   Remove the pinion gear and replace the starting shim with the size just determined. Repeat steps 1 through 3.

STEP 8   Tighten the pinion nut to the correct torque and check pinion bearing preload as described in step 3.

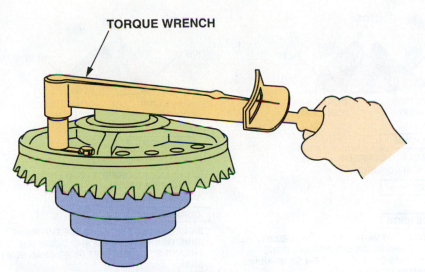

FIGURE 13-39 Torque the retaining bolts to factory specification and in the order specified in service information.

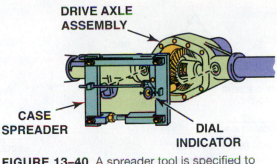

FIGURE 13-40 A spreader tool is specified to be used by some vehicle manufacturers when the differential case assembly is being installed in the housing. Always follow the vehicle manufacturer's recommended procedures.

CARRIER ASSEMBLY AND SETUP

INSTALLING THE RING GEAR

When installing the ring gear to the differential case, perform the following steps to insure that the gear is firmly seated:

- Use an Arkansas stone or a fine file to remove any burrs on the mating surface between the ring gear and the case.
- Sometimes heat from a torch is needed to expand the ring gear slightly so it fits over the case.
- Use guide pins to help align the ring gear fastener holes while installing the ring gear.
- Use new retaining bolts and torque them to factory specifications. ● SEE FIGURE 13-39.

INSTALLING THE CASE INTO THE HOUSING

Install the assembled differential case into the drive axle housing.

- Use the same shims that were removed when the case was removed from the housing as a starting point toward achieving the correct backlash and side bearing preload.
- Be sure to align the index marks on the gear teeth of non-hunting and partial non-hunting gear sets.
- Verify the bearing caps are installed in the same location as when they were removed. Some vehicle manufacturers specify the use of a spreader tool. ● SEE FIGURE 13-40.

GEAR MARKING COMPOUND

A tooth **contact pattern** test is an excellent method for checking proper drive pinion depth as well as proper backlash between the drive pinion and

the ring gear. **Gear marking compound** is available from some gear or vehicle manufacturers (GM gear marking compound, for example is part number 1052351).

Any faults in these areas will be reflected in the pattern. The pattern test involves the following steps:

STEP 1 Clean the gear teeth of the ring gear and the drive pinion.

STEP 2 Using a small brush, apply a light coating of iron oxide compound.

STEP 3 Use a small prybar to apply a load to the ring gear to achieve a more accurate contact pattern.

STEP 4 Rotate the drive pinion until the ring gear turns one revolution (about three revolutions of the drive pinion gear).

STEP 5 Repeat rotating the drive pinion in the opposite direction. This will create a contact pattern on both the drive side and the coast side of the ring gear.

NOTE: The drive side is the convex surface of the ring gear teeth. The coast side is the concave side of the ring gear. This is true except for many differentials used on the front of four-wheel-drive vehicles. In this case, the drive side in the front differential is the concave surface and the coast side is the convex surface of the ring gear teeth. Always check the service information for the vehicle being serviced for the correct interpretation of the pattern results. ● SEE FIGURE 13-41.

BACKLASH

Backlash and carrier side bearing preload adjustments are made as the ring gear and differential are installed into the carrier. Backlash is the operating clearance between the ring and pinion gears. It is adjusted by moving the ring gear toward the pinion gear (toward the right side) to

DRIVE SIDE (CONVEX) COAST SIDE (CONCAVE)

CONDITION

PINION DEPTH CORRECT.

BACKLASH INCORRECT - TOO MUCH CLEARANCE BETWEEN THE PINION AND RING GEARS.

CORRECTION

INCREASE THE THICKNESS OF THE LEFT (RING GEAR SIDE) SHIM AND DECREASE THE THICKNESS OF THE RIGHT SHIM AN EQUAL AMOUNT.

SERVICE HINTS

HOW TO CHECK PATTERNS:

BRUSH GEAR MARKING COMPOUND ON THE RING GEAR TEETH.

APPLY BRAKES SO THAT 50 LB. FT. IS NEEDED TO ROTATE THE PINION.

ROTATE THE PINION SIX TIMES CLOCKWISE AND SIX TIMES COUNTERCLOCKWISE.

OBSERVE THE TOOTH CONTACT PATTERN AND MAKE ANY NECESSARY CORRECTIONS.

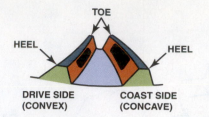

DRIVE SIDE (CONVEX) COAST SIDE (CONCAVE)

CONDITION

PINION DEPTH CORRECT.
BACKLASH CORRECT.

CORRECTION

NONE.

SERVICE HINTS

PATTERNS THAT VARY MAY BE CAUSED BY LOOSE BEARINGS ON THE PINION OR THE DIFFERENTIAL CASE. CHECK THESE BEARING PRELOAD SETTINGS:

TOTAL ASSEMBLY

DIFFERENTIAL CASE

PINION

IF THESE SETTINGS ARE GOOD, LOOK FOR DAMAGED OR INCORRECTLY ASSEMBLED PARTS.

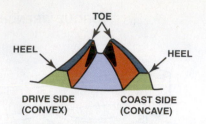

DRIVE SIDE (CONVEX) COAST SIDE (CONCAVE)

CONDITION

PINION DEPTH CORRECT.

BACKLASH INCORRECT - TOO LITTLE CLEARANCE BETWEEN THE PINION AND RING GEARS.

CORRECTION

INCREASE THE THICKNESS OF THE RIGHT (RING GEAR SIDE) SHIM AND DECREASE THE THICKNESS OF THE LEFT (RING GEAR SIDE) SHIM.

SERVICE HINTS

SIDE BEARING GEAR LOCATIONS:

BETWEEN THE SIDE BEARING CONES AND THE DIFFERENTIAL CASE.

BETWEEN THE SIDE BEARING CUPS AND THE REAR AXLE HOUSING.

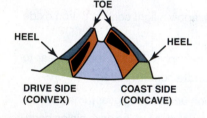

DRIVE SIDE (CONVEX) COAST SIDE (CONCAVE)

CONDITION

PINION DEPTH INCORRECT - PINION GEAR IS TOO FAR AWAY FROM THE RING GEAR.

BACKLASH CORRECT

CORRECTION

INCREASE THE PINION SHIM THICKNESS.

SERVICE HINTS

HOW TO CHECK PATTERNS:

BRUSH GEAR MARKING COMPOUND ON THE RING GEAR TEETH.

APPLY BRAKES SO THAT 50 LB. FT. IS NEEDED TO ROTATE THE PINION.

ROTATE THE PINION SIX TIMES CLOCKWISE AND SIX TIMES COUNTERCLOCKWISE.

OBSERVE THE TOOTH CONTACT PATTERN AND MAKE ANY NECESSARY CORRECTIONS.

FIGURE 13–41 Tooth contact pattern.

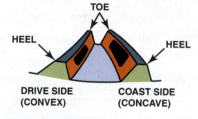

DRIVE SIDE (CONVEX) COAST SIDE (CONCAVE)

CONDITION

PINION DEPTH CORRECT.
BACKLASH CORRECT.

CORRECTION

NONE.

SERVICE HINTS

PATTERNS THAT VARY MAY BE CAUSED BY LOOSE BEARINGS ON THE PINION OR THE DIFFERENTIAL CASE. CHECK THESE BEARING PRELOAD SETTINGS:

TOTAL ASSEMBLY

DIFFERENTIAL CASE

PINION

IF THESE SETTINGS ARE GOOD, LOOK FOR DAMAGED OR INCORRECTLY ASSEMBLED PARTS.

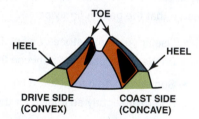

DRIVE SIDE (CONVEX) COAST SIDE (CONCAVE)

CONDITION

PINION DEPTH INCORRECT - PINION GEAR IS TOO CLOSE TO RING GEAR.

BACKLASH CORRECT.

CORRECTION

DECREASE THE PINION SHIM THICKNESS.

SERVICE HINTS

PINION DEPTH SHIM LOCATIONS:

BETWEEN THE INNER PINION BEARING CONE AND THE HEAD OF THE PINION GEAR.

BETWEEN THE INNER PINION BEARING CUP AND THE REAR AXLE HOUSING.

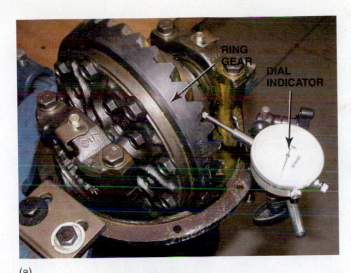

(a)

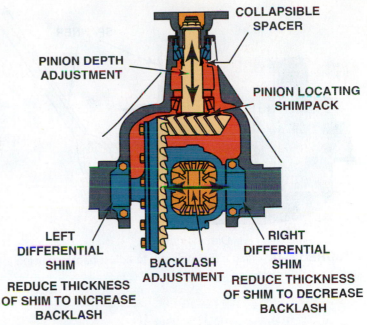

FIGURE 13–43 Backlash is adjusted by moving the position of the ring gear.

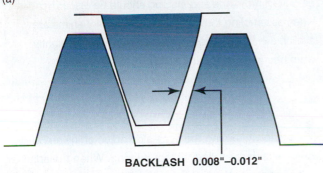

(b)

BACKLASH 0.008"–0.012"

FIGURE 13–42 (a) Backlash is determined by mounting a dial indicator to the differential housing and placing the button of the gauge against a tooth of the ring gear. Moving the ring gear back and forth will indicate on the dial indicator the amount of backlash. (b) Backlash is the clearance between the drive pinion and the ring gear teeth.

reduce backlash, or away from the pinion (toward the left side) to increase backlash. ● SEE FIGURE 13–42.

Incorrect backlash will cause the contact pattern on both sides of the gear tooth to be too close to the heel or too close to the toe. ● SEE FIGURE 13–43.

THREADED ADJUSTER PRELOAD/BACKLASH Carrier bearing preload places enough pressure on the carrier bearings to hold the ring gear in proper mesh with the pinion gear without putting unnecessary load and drag on the bearings. Preload is increased by moving one or both of the carrier bearing cups toward each other, and it is reduced by moving them away from each other. These adjustments are made using the threaded adjusters or by changing the shims.

To adjust backlash and carrier bearing preload using threaded adjusters, perform the following steps:

STEP 1 Clean the adjuster threads in the carrier and bearing caps. After carrier bearing preload has been adjusted, the overall preload of the carrier should increase by a noticeable amount, about 5 to 10 inch-pounds, from the pinion bearing preload.

This is often called *case bearing preload* or *carrier bearing preload*. Be sure to align the index marks on the gear teeth of non-hunting and partial non-hunting gear sets.

STEP 2 Place the threaded adjusters in position and thread them next to the bearing cups.

STEP 3 Turn the adjusters to move the ring gear completely into mesh with the pinion gear so that there is no backlash and no clearance at the bearings.

STEP 4 Install the bearing caps, making sure to align the index marks. Align the bearing caps by threading the bolts into their holes while holding the caps upward, and then drop the caps into position.
- Rotate the differential to seat the bearings as the adjustments are made.
- When the caps drop into place, they should sit right next to the carrier.

STEP 5 Tighten the bearing cap bolts so they are snug, about 10 to 20 ft-lb (13 to 27 N-m). Rotate the differential to seat the bearings.

STEP 6 Turn the adjusters to push the differential case to the left so there is a slight backlash and then back to the right until the backlash just disappears. This is zero backlash with no load between the gears.

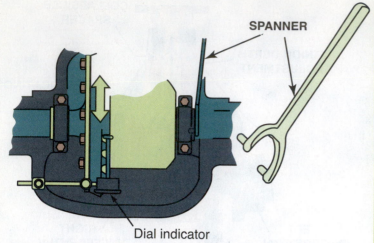

FIGURE 13–44 Using a dial indicator to adjust backlash using threaded adjusters.

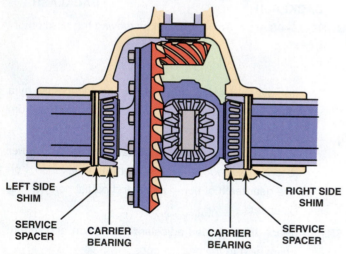

FIGURE 13–45 Cast iron production shim (OEM use), service spacer, and shim used to adjust backlash and carrier bearing preload.

STEP 7 Mount a dial indicator on the carrier. Position it so that the indicator stylus is on the heel of a ring gear tooth and parallel to the ring gear in one plane while being as close as possible to tangent with the ring gear in the other plane.

STEP 8 Hold the pinion gear stationary while the ring gear is moved back and forth. There should be no backlash or indicator needle motion.

STEP 9 Keep the left-side adjuster stationary as the right-side adjuster is threaded inward. Recheck backlash, and stop adjusting when the backlash is within specifications.

STEP 10 Confirm the preload adjustment by:
- Marking the right-side adjuster position and backing the adjuster off about one-half turn.

? FREQUENTLY ASKED QUESTION

Why Should Service Shims Be Used Instead of the Factory Shims?

During manufacture of a carrier, the bearings and gears are adjusted using a single, cast iron production shim at each carrier bearing. The sizes of these two shims are carefully selected to provide the proper backlash and carrier bearing preload. The production shims are normally replaced with a fixed-size **service spacer** and a selective-size shim when the carrier is adjusted. The service shims are made from steel and they can be driven into place. The factory cast iron shims cannot be driven into place and instead should be discarded when assembling the axle. The replacement shims are available in thicknesses needed to readjust the slightly worn bearings and gears. ● SEE FIGURE 13–45.

- Slowly turning the right-side adjuster inward and watch the rollers of that bearing. When the adjuster contacts the bearing cone, the rollers should begin to rotate.
- Turning the adjuster inward at least one full adjuster lock hole but not more than two. Stop at the point where the adjuster lock will line up.

OR:

- Back off the left adjuster one notch.
- Set up a dial indicator with stylus touching the side of the left bearing race.
- Turn the right bearing adjuster inward until the dial indicator shows movement of the race.
- Remove the dial indicator and turn the left adjuster back inward one notch.
- Turn the right adjuster inward one to two notches further.

OR:

- Set up a dial indicator between the carrier bearing caps to measure case spread. As the adjuster is turned inward to preload the bearings, the case will spread apart and the amount of spread can be read on the dial indicator. Some manufacturers provide a case spread specification.

STEP 11 Tighten the bearing cap bolts to the correct torque and rotate the differential to seat the bearings. ● SEE FIGURE 13–44.

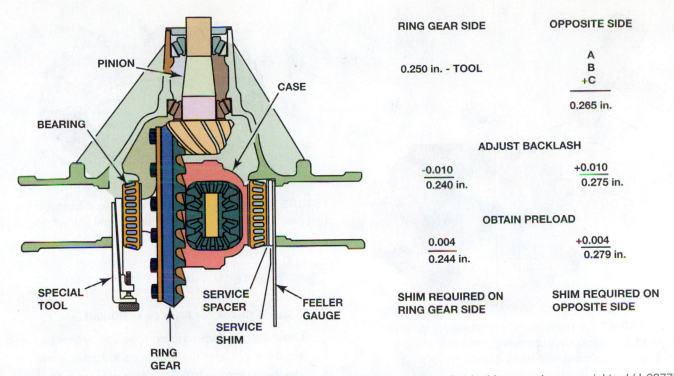

RING GEAR SIDE	OPPOSITE SIDE
0.250 in. - TOOL	A B +C ――― 0.265 in.

ADJUST BACKLASH

-0.010	+0.010
――――	――――
0.240 in.	0.275 in.

OBTAIN PRELOAD

0.004	+0.004
――――	――――
0.244 in.	0.279 in.

SHIM REQUIRED ON RING GEAR SIDE	SHIM REQUIRED ON OPPOSITE SIDE

FIGURE 13–46 Procedure used to measure and determine the correct shims. Note that in this example, a special tool (J-22779) is used to measure the gap on the left side, while a service spacer, shim, and feeler gauge are used on the right side.

STEP 12 Recheck backlash at four or more points around the ring gear, making sure that the backlash is within specifications and that there is not too much variation. Readjust the adjusters if backlash is incorrect. At this time, turn one adjuster out one notch and then the other one in one notch to maintain the bearing preload.

STEP 13 Install the adjuster locks, and then tighten the bolts to the correct torque.

PRELOAD/BACKLASH USING SHIMS

To adjust backlash and carrier bearing preload using shims, perform the following steps:

STEP 1 Set the carrier with the bearing cups into the differential housing.

STEP 2 Use a group of shims, spacers, and feeler gauge pairs on each side, between the bearing cups and the carrier, so that there will be zero backlash and preload at the ring and pinion gears as well as removing any clearance at the bearings.

- Insert two feeler gauges, one at each side of the shim, below the bearing cup boss so that the shims will not cock and cause a false reading.
- The feeler gauges should have a slight but definite drag. Be sure to rotate the differential during the final readings to ensure that the bearings are seated.

STEP 3 Add the spacer, shims, and feeler gauges used on each side, and record these as shim sizes. ● SEE **FIGURE 13–46**.

STEP 4 Adjust the shim sizes to obtain the correct backlash by subtracting the specified amount from the left side and adding that amount to the right side.

STEP 5 Adjust the shim packs to obtain the correct preload by adding the specified amount to each shim pack. This will be about 0.004 to 0.006 inch (0.1 to 0.15 mm) on each side.

STEP 6 Install the selected shim. It will be necessary to use a soft hammer or a special tool to tap the second shim into place. ● SEE **FIGURE 13–47**.

STEP 7 Install the bearing caps, and tighten the bolts to the correct torque.

STEP 8 Rotate the differential several turns to make sure that there is no binding and to seat the bearings. Measure the backlash as described in step 7 of the procedure for threaded adjusters. Measure the backlash at four or more locations around the ring gear to ensure that any variation is within the limits and that the backlash is within specifications. If there is too much or too little backlash, reduce the shim pack on one side and increase the shim pack on the other side by the same amount.

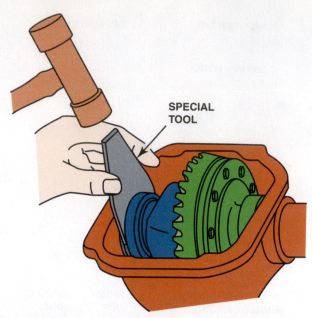

SPECIAL TOOL

FIGURE 13–47 On many axles, it is necessary to use a special tool to install steel spacers (shims) to achieve the specified backlash and side bearing preload.

🔧 **TECH TIP**

Quick and Easy Shim Trick

An alternative method of adjusting backlash and carrier bearing preload is to start with too small a shim at the left side and add enough shims to obtain zero bearing clearance and preload. Now, measure the backlash and adjust the shim packs to correct backlash. Next, increase the size of both shim packs to adjust the bearing preload.

NOTE: When changing shims to correct lash, moving 0.002 inch of shim will change the lash by about 0.001 inch.

LIMITED SLIP DIFFERENTIAL SERVICE

TYPICAL CHECKS In most cases, this operation involves disassembly and reassembly of the differential with replacement of worn parts. It can also include adjusting the clearance or preload of the clutch packs and bench check for rotating torque. Cone clutch limited slip differentials use a split case, which makes disassembly easy because the plate clutch units can be serviced through the case window.

NOTE: If the clutch plates are to be reused, they should be replaced in their original positions. Restacking the

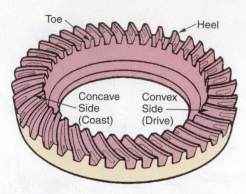

Toe — Heel

Concave Side (Coast) Convex Side (Drive)

FIGURE 13–48 A pattern that changes as it goes around the ring gear is caused by ring gear runout (one pattern change) or pinion gear runout (several pattern changes).

🔧 **TECH TIP**

A Quick Check for Ring Gear Runout

Check for a pattern variation. One steady change in pattern indicates ring gear runout. Two or more changes in pattern indicate pinion gear runout.
● **SEE FIGURE 13–48.**

plates in different positions will result in increased wear and diminished performance.

TYPICAL ASSEMBLY PROCEDURE To disassemble a plate clutch limited slip differential, perform the following steps:

STEP 1 Carefully remove the S-shaped preload spring by tapping it through the window.

STEP 2 Roll the differential pinions around the case windows, and remove them.

STEP 3 Remove the side gear and clutch packs as a group, and tag or mark them so that they can be reassembled on the same side of the differential.

STEP 4 Clean the parts by wiping the friction surfaces with a cloth and do *not* use any solvent. The differential case and pinion gears can be washed in a solvent.

STEP 5 The clutch plates or cones should be checked for scores, grooves, or galling. Reassembly of most limited slip differentials is the reverse of the disassembly procedure. Be sure to lubricate all of the friction surfaces with the recommended gear oil. Some differentials use a shim to set the clutch pack for the correct preload or clearance, which adds a step in the reassembly procedure for determining the pack height and shim size.

The clutch pack surfaces must be thoroughly lubricated with the proper lubricant during assembly. One manufacturer recommends soaking them in the lubricant for 20 minutes.

1 The rear axle fluid is drained by removing all of the inspection cover bolts except for the top one and then the cover is pried loose and the fluid drained into a suitable container.

2 The retaining pin is removed which will then allow the pinion shaft to be removed.

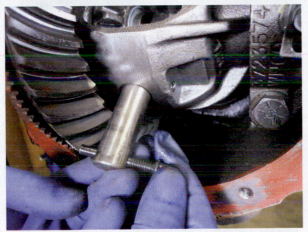

3 The pinion shaft is removed.

4 The axle is pushed inward and the C-lock removed.

5 The axle can then be removed.

6 The C-lock on the other axle is then removed and the second axle pulled out of the drive axle housing.

CONTINUED ▶

DRIVE AXLE SERVICE (CONTINUED)

7 After marking the bearing caps, the retaining bolts are removed, and then the differential case is removed from the drive axle housing.

8 The axle bearing and seals are removed and will be replaced as part of the overhaul of this drive axle assembly.

9 A long holding tool to keep the pinion flange from rotating as the pinion nut is removed.

10 After the pinion shaft has been removed, the pinion bearing is then removed from the front of the housing.

11 A hydraulic press is used to press the pinion bearing off the pinion shaft.

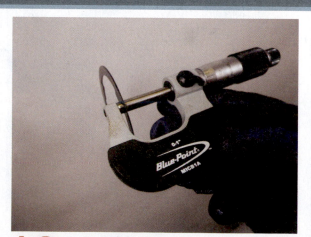

12 The pinion depth shim is measured and recorded for future reference.

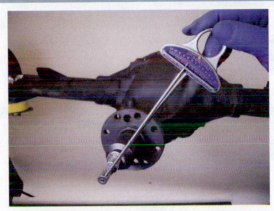

13 A special gauging tool is used to determine the proper pinion depth.

14 The pinion nut is tightened and the rotating toque checked using an inch-pound torque wrench.

15 The differential case is installed into the drive axle housing.

16 The pattern is checked and the backlash adjusted to factory specifications using threaded adjusters on this Jeep axle.

17 New bearings are installed.

18 The drive axle cover is installed using the specified RTV to seal the cover, and then it is filled with the specified gear oil.

1. Drive axles must have clean gear oil at the proper level and of the proper type.
2. The cause of improper drive axle operation is determined using several diagnostic steps.
3. Some drive axle problems can be repaired on-vehicle.
4. Major internal drive axle problems usually require that the assembly be removed from the vehicle.
5. Drive axle disassembly and reassembly procedures vary between makes and models.
6. Presses and pullers are often required for complete disassembly.
7. Parts must be cleaned before being inspected.
8. Gears and bearings, are the major wear components.
9. Four ring and pinion adjustments are required: pinion depth, pinion bearing preload, carrier bearing preload, and backlash.
10. Ring and pinion adjustment can be confirmed with a tooth contact pattern check.

REVIEW QUESTIONS

1. How can a drive axle be identified?
2. How can the gear ratio be determined?
3. How is a leak through the porous axle housing repaired?
4. What tool is needed to check pinion gear rotating torque?

CHAPTER QUIZ

1. A drive axle assembly can be identified by_____.
   a. The shape and the number of bolts for the cover
   b. RPO code
   c. Checking service information
   d. All of the above

2. Drive axles usually use gear oil labeled as _____ by the API.
   a. GL-5
   b. GL-4
   c. GL-3
   d. Any of the above

3. A worn or defective axle bearing will likely make what type of noise?
   a. Chuckle
   b. Growl
   c. Clunk
   d. Chatter

4. A low pitch rumble over 20 MPH (32 km/h) is likely caused by a worn or defective_____.
   a. Incorrect backlash or pinion depth
   b. Incorrect gear oil or worn limited slip clutches
   c. Worn carrier bearings
   d. Worn U-joints

5. To remove and replace a drive pinion seal, what should be marked before removing the pinion nut?
   a. Pinion flange
   b. Pinion nut
   c. Pinion shaft
   d. All of the above

6. The total indicated runout (TIR) of a ring gear should be_____.
   a. 0.002 inch (0.05 mm)
   b. 0.020 inch (0.5 mm)
   c. 0.200 inch (5.0 mm)
   d. 0.040 inch (1.0 mm)

7. Differential case clearance is usually checked by using a _____.
   a. Feeler gauge
   b. An inch-pound torque wrench
   c. Dial indicator
   d. Micrometer

8. Pinion depth is usually adjusted by _____.
   a. Changing the thickness of a shim under the pinion bearing
   b. Adjusting the position of the ring gear
   c. Tightening the side bearing cap bolts
   d. Adding or deleting side bearing shims

9. Backlash and carrier side bearing preload adjustments are made by_____.
   a. Adding a shim behind the pinion shaft bearing
   b. Threaded adjusters or by changing the shims
   c. Tightening or loosening the ring gear retainer bolts
   d. Using a case spreader

10. Backlash is normally_____.
    a. Less than 0.008 inch (0.2 mm)
    b. 0.008 to 0.012 inch (0.2 to 0.3 mm)
    c. 0.012 to 0.020 inch (0.3 to 0.5 mm)
    d. 0.100 to 0.120 inch (2.5 to 3.0 mm)

chapter 14

DRIVETRAIN ELECTRICITY AND ELECTRONICS

LEARNING OBJECTIVES

After studying this chapter, the reader should be able to:

1. Prepare for the Manual Drivelines and Axles (A2) ASE certification test content area "C" (Transmission/Transaxle Diagnosis and Repair).
2. Explain the characteristics of electricity.
3. Differentiate between conductors, insulators, and semiconductors.
4. Explain the units of electrical measurement.
5. List the parts of a complete circuit.
6. Discuss the types of electrical circuit faults.
7. Explain how to detect and measure electrical voltage, current, and resistance.
8. Discuss the purpose of terminals, connectors, relays, and switches.
9. Explain the operation of speed sensors and throttle position (TP) sensors.
10. State the need for networks and discuss network classifications.

KEY TERMS

Ammeter 267
Ampere 258
Conductors 257
Connector 269
Conventional theory 258
Crimp-and-seal connectors 271
Digital multimeter (DMM) 265
Digital volt-ohm-meter (DVOM) 265
Electricity 256
Electron theory 258
Hall Effect 275
High resistance 263

Insulators 257
Node 276
Ohmmeter 266
Ohms 259
Open circuit 261
Potentiometer 275
Relay 272
Schematic 260
Short-to-ground 261
Short-to-voltage 261
Semiconductor 258
Terminal 269
Volts 259
Voltmeter 265

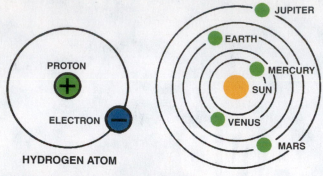

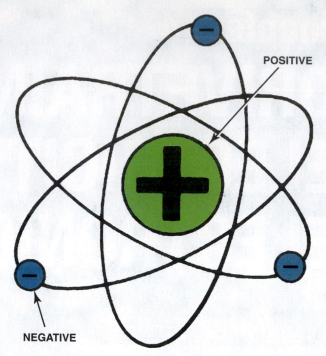

FIGURE 14–1 In an atom (left), electrons orbit protons in the nucleus just as planets orbit the sun in our solar system (right).

INTRODUCTION

The electrical system is one of the most important systems in a vehicle today. Every year more and more vehicle components and systems use electricity.

Electricity may be difficult for some people to learn for the following reasons.

- It cannot be seen.
- Only the results of electricity can be seen.
- It has to be detected and measured.

ELECTRICITY

BACKGROUND   Our universe is composed of matter, which is anything that has mass and occupies space. All matter is made from slightly over 100 individual components called elements. The smallest particle that an element can be broken into and still retain the properties of that element is known as an atom. ● **SEE FIGURE 14–1**.

DEFINITION   **Electricity** is the movement of electrons from one atom to another. The dense center of each atom is called the nucleus. The nucleus contains

- Protons, which have a positive charge
- Neutrons, which are electrically neutral (have no charge)
- Electrons, which have a negative charge, orbit the nucleus. Each atom contains an equal number of electrons and protons.

NOTE: As an example of the relative sizes of the parts of an atom, consider that if an atom were magnified so that the nucleus were the size of the period at the end of this sentence, the whole atom would be bigger than a house.

FIGURE 14–2 The nucleus of an atom has a positive (+) charge and the surrounding electrons have a negative (–) charge.

POSITIVE AND NEGATIVE CHARGES   The parts of an atom have different charges. The orbiting electrons are negatively charged, while the protons are positively charged. Positive charges are indicated by the "plus" sign (+), and negative charges by the "minus" sign (–). ● **SEE FIGURE 14–2**.

These same + and – signs are used to identify parts of an electrical circuit. Neutrons have no charge at all. They are neutral. In a normal or balanced atom, the number of negative particles equals the number of positive particles. That is, there are as many electrons as there are protons. ● **SEE FIGURE 14–3**.

MAGNETS AND ELECTRICAL CHARGE   An ordinary magnet has two ends, or poles. One end is called the south pole, and the other is called the north pole. If two magnets are brought close to each other with like poles together (south to south or north to north), the magnets will push each other apart, because like poles repel each other. If the opposite poles of the magnets are brought close to each other, south to north, the magnets will snap together, because unlike poles attract each other. The positive and negative charges within an atom are like the north and south poles of a magnet. Charges that are alike will repel each other, similar to the poles of a magnet. ● **SEE FIGURE 14–4**.

That is why the negative electrons continue to orbit around the positive protons. They are attracted and held by the opposite charge of the protons. The electrons keep moving in orbit because they repel each other.

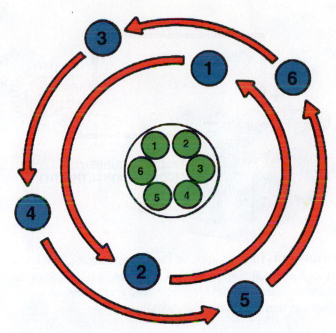

FIGURE 14–3 This figure shows a balanced atom. The number of electrons is the same as the number of protons in the nucleus.

FIGURE 14–4 Unlike charges attract and like charges repel.

ELECTRON ORBITS

Electrons orbit around the nucleus in rings and the outermost ring is called the "valence ring." Whether a material is a conductor or an insulator strictly depends on how many electrons are in the outer ring.

CONDUCTORS

Conductors are materials with fewer than four electrons in their atom's outer orbit. ● SEE FIGURE 14–5.

Copper is an excellent conductor because it has only one electron in its outer orbit. This orbit is far enough away from the nucleus of the copper atom that the pull or force holding the outermost electron in orbit is relatively weak. ● SEE FIGURE 14–6.

Copper is the conductor most used in vehicles because the price of copper is reasonable compared to the relative cost of other conductors with similar properties. Examples of commonly used conductors include:

- Silver
- Copper
- Gold
- Aluminum
- Steel
- Cast iron

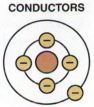

FIGURE 14–5 A conductor is any element that has one to three electrons in its outer orbit.

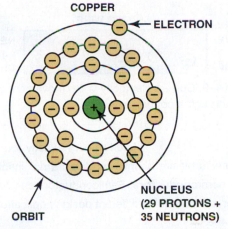

FIGURE 14–6 Copper is an excellent conductor of electricity because it has just one electron in its outer orbit, making it easy to be knocked out of its orbit and flow to other nearby atoms. This causes electron flow, which is the definition of electricity.

COPPER

ELECTRON

NUCLEUS
(29 PROTONS +
35 NEUTRONS)

ORBIT

FIGURE 14–7 Insulators are elements with five to eight electrons in the outer orbit.

INSULATORS

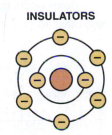

INSULATORS

Some materials hold their electrons very tightly; therefore, electrons do not move through them very well. These materials are called insulators. Insulators are materials with more than four electrons in their atom's outer orbit. Because they have more than four electrons in their outer orbit, it becomes easier for these materials to acquire (gain) electrons than to release electrons. ● SEE FIGURE 14–7.

Examples of insulators include:

- Rubber
- Plastic
- Nylon
- Porcelain
- Ceramic
- Fiberglass

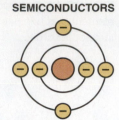

FIGURE 14–8 Semiconductor elements contain exactly four electrons in the outer orbit.

SEMICONDUCTORS

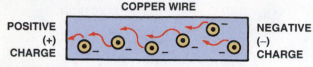

POSITIVE (+) CHARGE   COPPER WIRE   NEGATIVE (–) CHARGE

FIGURE 14–9 Current electricity is the movement of electrons through a conductor.

SEMICONDUCTORS

Materials with exactly four electrons in their outer orbit are neither conductors nor insulators, but are called **semiconductors**. Semiconductors can be either an insulator or a conductor in different design applications. ● SEE **FIGURE 14–8**.

Examples of semiconductors include:

- Silicon
- Germanium
- Carbon

Semiconductors are used mostly in transistors, computers, and other electronic devices.

HOW ELECTRONS MOVE THROUGH A CONDUCTOR

CURRENT FLOW

The following events occur if a source of power, such as a battery, is connected to the ends of a conductor—a positive charge (lack of electrons) is placed on one end of the conductor and a negative charge (excess of electrons) is placed on the opposite end of the conductor. For current to flow, there must be an imbalance of excess electrons at one end of the circuit and a deficiency of electrons at the opposite end. ● SEE **FIGURE 14–9**.

CONVENTIONAL THEORY VERSUS ELECTRON THEORY

- **Conventional theory**: It was once thought that electricity had only one charge and moved from positive to negative. This theory of the flow of electricity through a conductor is called the conventional theory of current flow. Most automotive applications use the conventional theory. ● SEE **FIGURE 14–10**.

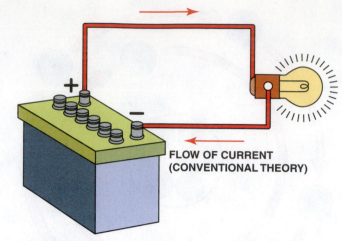

FLOW OF CURRENT (CONVENTIONAL THEORY)

FIGURE 14–10 Conventional theory states that current flows through a circuit from positive (+) to negative (–). Automotive electricity uses the conventional theory in all electrical diagrams and schematics.

POSITIVE (+) CHARGE   COPPER WIRE   6.28 BILLION BILLION ELECTRONS PER SECOND   NEGATIVE (–) CHARGE

(1 AMPERE)

FIGURE 14–11 One ampere is the movement of 1 coulomb (6.28 billion billion electrons) past a point in 1 second.

- **Electron theory**: The discovery of the electron and its negative charge led to the electron theory, which states that there is electron flow from negative to positive.

UNITS OF ELECTRICITY

Electricity is measured using meters or other test equipment. The three fundamentals of electricity-related units include the ampere, volt, and ohm.

AMPERE

The **ampere** is the unit used throughout the world to measure current flow. When 6.28 billion billion electrons (the name for this large number of electrons is a coulomb) move past a certain point in 1 second, this represents 1 ampere of current. ● SEE **FIGURE 14–11**.

The ampere is the electrical unit for the amount of electron flow, just as "gallons per minute" is the unit that can be used to measure the quantity of water flow. It is named for the French electrician Andrè Marie Ampére (1775–1836). The conventional abbreviations and measurement for amperes are as follows:

1. The ampere is the unit of measurement for the amount of current flow.

2. A and amps are acceptable abbreviations for amperes.

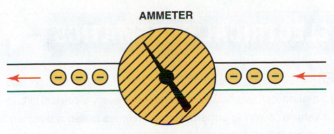

AMMETER

FIGURE 14–12 An ammeter is installed in the path of the electrons similar to a water meter used to measure the flow of water in gallons per minute. The ammeter displays current flow in amperes.

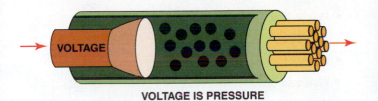

VOLTAGE IS PRESSURE

FIGURE 14–13 Voltage is the electrical pressure that causes the electrons to flow through a conductor.

FIGURE 14–14 This digital multimeter set to read DC volts is being used to test the voltage of a vehicle battery. Most multimeters can also measure resistance (ohms) and current flow (amperes).

3. The capital letter I, for intensity, is used in mathematical calculations to represent amperes.

4. Amperes do the actual work in the circuit. It is the movement of the electrons through a light bulb or motor that actually makes the electrical device work. Without amperage through a device, it will not work at all.

5. Amperes are measured by an ammeter (not ampmeter). ● **SEE FIGURE 14–12**.

VOLTS The **volt** is the unit of measurement for electrical pressure. It is named for an Italian physicist, Alessandro Volta (1745–1827). The comparable unit using water pressure as an example would be pounds per square inch (PSI). It is possible to have very high pressures (volts) and low water flow (amperes). It is also possible to have high water flow (amperes) and low pressures (volts). Voltage is also called electrical potential, because if there is voltage present in a conductor, there is a potential (possibility) for current flow. ● **SEE FIGURE 14–13**.

The conventional abbreviations and measurement for voltage are as follows:

1. The volt is the unit of measurement for the amount of electrical pressure.

2. Electromotive force, abbreviated EMF, is another way of indicating voltage.

3. V is the generally accepted abbreviation for volts.

4. The symbol used in calculations is E, for electromotive force.

5. Volts are measured by a voltmeter. ● **SEE FIGURE 14–14**.

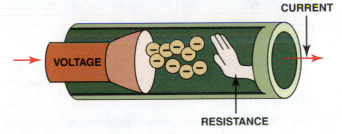

CURRENT

VOLTAGE

RESISTANCE

FIGURE 14–15 Resistance to the flow of electrons through a conductor is measured in ohms.

OHMS Resistance to the flow of current through a conductor is measured in units called **ohms**, named after the German physicist George Simon Ohm (1787–1854). The resistance to the flow of free electrons through a conductor results from the countless collisions the electrons cause within the atoms of the conductor. ● **SEE FIGURE 14–15**.

Resistance can be:

▪ Desirable when it is part of how a circuit works, such as the resistance of a filament in a light bulb.

▪ Undesirable, such as corrosion in a connection restricting the amount of current flow in a circuit.

The conventional abbreviations and measurement for resistance are as follows:

1. The ohm is the unit of measurement for electrical resistance.

2. The symbol for ohms is Ω (Greek capital letter omega), the last letter of the Greek alphabet.

3. The symbol used in calculations is R, for resistance.

4. Ohms are measured by an ohmmeter.

5. Resistance to electron flow depends on the material used.

ELECTRICAL CIRCUITS

DEFINITION   A circuit is a complete path that electrons travel from a power source (such as a battery) through a load such as a light bulb and back to the power source. It is called a circuit because the current must start and finish at the same place (power source). For any electrical circuit to work at all, it must be continuous from the battery (power), through all the wires and components, and back to the battery (ground). A circuit that is continuous throughout is said to have continuity.

PARTS OF A COMPLETE CIRCUIT   Every complete circuit contains the following parts

1. A power source, such as a vehicle's battery.

2. Protection from harmful overloads (excessive current flow). (Fuses, circuit breakers, and fusible links are examples of electrical circuit protection devices.)

3. The power path for the current to flow through, from the power source to the resistance. (This path from a power source to the load—a light bulb in this example—is usually an insulated copper wire.)

4. The electrical load or resistance, which converts electrical energy into heat, light, or motion.

5. A return path (ground) for the electrical current from the load back to the power source so that there is a complete circuit. (This return, or ground, path is usually the metal body, frame, ground wires, and engine block of the vehicle.) ●**SEE FIGURE 14–16**.

6. Switches and controls that turn the circuit on and off. ●**SEE FIGURE 14–17**.

ELECTRICAL SCHEMATICS

TERMINOLOGY   Automotive manufacturer's service information includes wiring schematics of every electrical circuit in a vehicle. A wiring **schematic**, sometimes called a *diagram,* shows electrical components and wiring using symbols and lines to represent components and wires. A typical wiring schematic may include all of the circuits combined, or they may be broken down to show individual circuits. All circuit schematics or diagrams include:

- Power-side wiring of the circuit
- All splices
- Connectors
- Wire size
- Wire color
- Trace color (if any)
- Circuit number
- Electrical components
- Ground return paths
- Fuses and switches

CIRCUIT INFORMATION   Many wiring schematics include numbers and letters near components and wires that may confuse readers of the schematic. Most letters used near or on a wire identify the color or colors of the wire.

- The first color or color abbreviation is the color of the wire insulation.
- The second color (if mentioned) is the color of the stripe or tracer on the base color. ●**SEE FIGURE 14–18**.

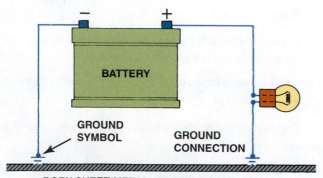

FIGURE 14–16 The return path back to the battery can be any electrical conductor, such as a copper wire or the metal frame or body of the vehicle.

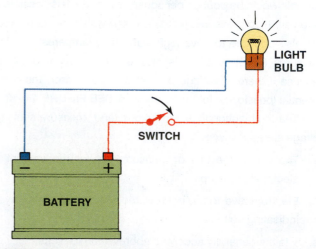

FIGURE 14–17 An electrical switch opens the circuit and no current flows. The switch could also be on the return (ground) path wire.

FIGURE 14–18 The center wire is a solid color wire, meaning that the wire has no other identifying tracer or stripe color. The two end wires could be labeled "BRN/WHT," indicating a brown wire with a white tracer or stripe.

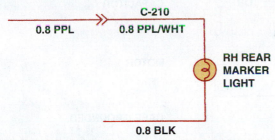

FIGURE 14–19 Typical section of a wiring diagram. Notice that the wire color changes at connection C210. The ".8" represents the metric wire size in square millimeters.

Wires with different color tracers are indicated by both colors with a slash (/) between them. For example, BRN/WHT means a brown wire with a white stripe or tracer.

WIRE SIZE Wire size is shown on all schematics. For example, ● **FIGURE 14–19** illustrates a rear side-marker bulb circuit diagram where ".8" indicates the metric wire gauge size in square millimeters (mm 2) and "PPL" indicates a solid purple wire.

The wire diagram also shows that the color of the wire changes at the number C210. This stands for "connector #210" and is used for reference purposes. The symbol for the connection can vary depending on the manufacturer. The color change from purple (PPL) to purple with a white tracer (PPL/WHT). The ground circuit is the ".8 BLK" wire.

● **SEE FIGURE 14–20**, which shows many of the electrical and electronic symbols that are used in wiring and circuit diagrams.

TYPES OF CIRCUIT FAULTS

Circuits can experience several different types of faults or problems, which often result in improper operation. The types of faults include opens, shorts, and high resistance.

OPEN CIRCUITS An **open circuit** is any circuit that is not complete, or that lacks continuity, such as a broken wire. ● **SEE FIGURE 14–21** on page 263.

Open circuits have the following features.

1. No current will flow through an open circuit.
2. An open circuit may be created by a break in the circuit or by a switch that opens (turns off) the circuit and prevents the flow of current.
3. In any circuit containing a power load and ground, an opening anywhere in the circuit will cause the circuit not to work.
4. A light switch in a home and the headlight switch in a vehicle are examples of devices that open a circuit to control its operation.

NOTE: A blown fuse opens the circuit to prevent damage to the components or wiring in the circuit in the event of an overload caused by a fault in the circuit.

SHORT-TO-VOLTAGE If a wire (conductor) or component is shorted to voltage, it is commonly referred to as being shorted. A **short-to-voltage** occurs when the power side of one circuit is electrically connected to the power side of another circuit. ● **SEE FIGURE 14–22** on page 263.

A short circuit has the following features.

1. It is a complete circuit in which the current usually bypasses some or all of the resistance in the circuit.
2. It involves the power side of the circuit.
3. It involves a copper-to-copper connection (two power side wires touching together).
4. It is also called a short-to-voltage.
5. It usually affects more than one circuit. In this case, if one circuit is electrically connected to another circuit, one of the circuits may operate when it is not supposed to because it is being supplied power from another circuit.
6. It may or may not blow a fuse. ● **SEE FIGURE 14–23** on page 263.

SHORT-TO-GROUND A **short-to-ground** is a type of short circuit that occurs when the current bypasses part of the normal circuit and flows directly to ground. A short-to-ground has the following features.

1. Because the ground return circuit is metal (vehicle frame, engine, or body), it is often identified as having current flowing from copper to steel.
2. A short-to-ground can occur at any place where a power path wire accidentally touches a return path wire or conductor. ● **SEE FIGURE 14–24** on page 263.
3. A defective component or circuit that is shorted to ground is commonly called grounded.
4. A short-to-ground almost always results in a blown fuse, damaged connectors, or melted wires.

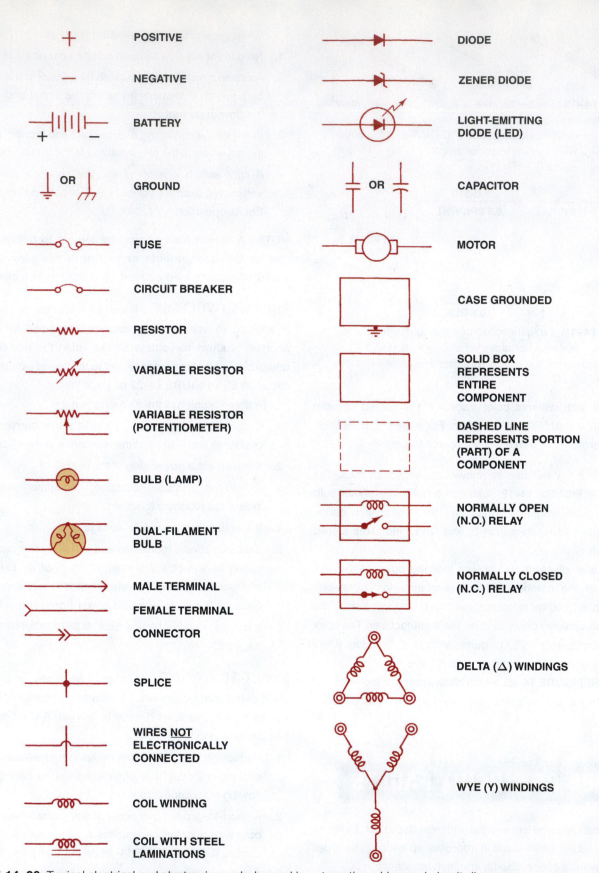

+	POSITIVE			DIODE
—	NEGATIVE			ZENER DIODE
	BATTERY			LIGHT-EMITTING DIODE (LED)
OR	GROUND		OR	CAPACITOR
	FUSE			MOTOR
	CIRCUIT BREAKER			CASE GROUNDED
	RESISTOR			SOLID BOX REPRESENTS ENTIRE COMPONENT
	VARIABLE RESISTOR			DASHED LINE REPRESENTS PORTION (PART) OF A COMPONENT
	VARIABLE RESISTOR (POTENTIOMETER)			NORMALLY OPEN (N.O.) RELAY
	BULB (LAMP)			NORMALLY CLOSED (N.C.) RELAY
	DUAL-FILAMENT BULB			DELTA (△) WINDINGS
	MALE TERMINAL			
	FEMALE TERMINAL			
	CONNECTOR			
	SPLICE			WYE (Y) WINDINGS
	WIRES NOT ELECTRONICALLY CONNECTED			
	COIL WINDING			
	COIL WITH STEEL LAMINATIONS			

FIGURE 14–20 Typical electrical and electronic symbols used in automotive wiring and circuit diagrams.

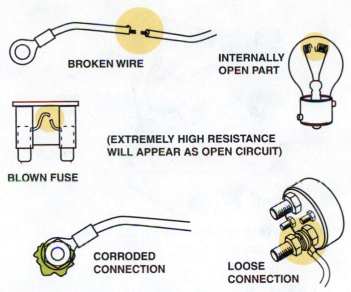

BROKEN WIRE   INTERNALLY OPEN PART

(EXTREMELY HIGH RESISTANCE WILL APPEAR AS OPEN CIRCUIT)

BLOWN FUSE

CORRODED CONNECTION   LOOSE CONNECTION

FIGURE 14–21 Examples of common causes of open circuits. Some of these causes are often difficult to find.

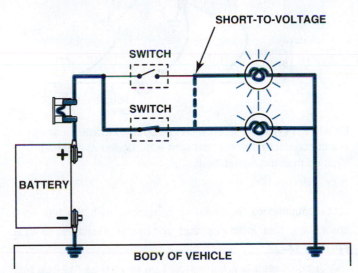

SHORT-TO-VOLTAGE

SWITCH

SWITCH

BATTERY

BODY OF VEHICLE

FIGURE 14–22 A short circuit permits electrical current to bypass some or all of the resistance in the circuit.

HIGH RESISTANCE

High resistance is resistance higher than normal circuit resistance usually caused by any of the following:

- Corroded connections or sockets
- Loose terminals in a connector
- Loose ground connections

If there is high resistance anywhere in a circuit, it may cause the following problems.

1. Slow operation of a motor-driven unit, such as when the transfer case makes a range change.
2. Dim lights
3. "Clicking" of relays or solenoids
4. No operation of a circuit or electrical component

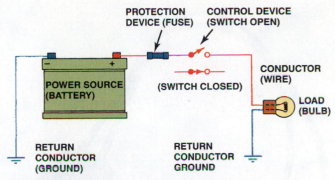

PROTECTION DEVICE (FUSE)   CONTROL DEVICE (SWITCH OPEN)

POWER SOURCE (BATTERY)

(SWITCH CLOSED)

CONDUCTOR (WIRE)

LOAD (BULB)

RETURN CONDUCTOR (GROUND)   RETURN CONDUCTOR GROUND

FIGURE 14–23 A fuse or circuit breaker opens the circuit to prevent possible overheating damage in the event of a short circuit.

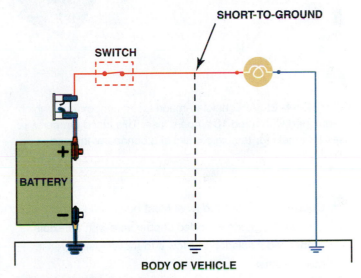

SHORT-TO-GROUND

SWITCH

BATTERY

BODY OF VEHICLE

FIGURE 14–24 A short-to-ground affects the power side of the circuit. Current flows directly to the ground return, bypassing some or all of the electrical loads in the circuit. There is no current in the circuit past the short. A short-to-ground will also cause the fuse to blow.

FUSED JUMPER WIRE

PURPOSE AND FUNCTION

A fused jumper wire is used to check a circuit by bypassing the switch or to provide a power or ground to a component. A fused jumper wire, also called a fused test lead, can be purchased or made by the service technician. ● **SEE FIGURE 14–25.**

It should include the following features:

- *Fuse:* A typical fused jumper wire has a blade-type fuse that can be easily replaced. A 10 ampere fuse (red color) is often the value used.
- *Alligator clip ends:* Alligator clips on the ends allow the fused jumper wire to be clipped to a ground or power source while the other end is attached to the power side or ground side of the unit being tested.

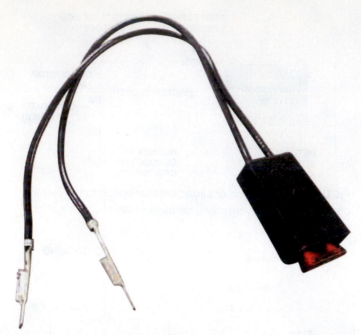

FIGURE 14–25 A technician-made fused jumper lead, which is equipped with a red 10 ampere fuse. This fused jumper wire uses terminals for testing circuits at a connector instead of alligator clips.

- *Good-quality insulated wire:* Most purchased jumper wire is about 14 gauge stranded copper wire with a flexible rubberized insulation to allow it to move easily even in cold weather.

CAUTION: Never use a fused jumper wire to bypass any resistance or load in the circuit. The increased current flow could damage the wiring and could blow the fuse on the jumper lead. Be very cautious when working on or around any computer circuit. Permanent damage to the computer or electronic module could result if power or ground goes to the wrong circuit.

TEST LIGHT

NON-POWERED TEST LIGHT
A 12-volt test light is one of the simplest testers that can be used to detect electricity. A test light is simply a light bulb with a probe and a ground wire attached. ● **SEE FIGURE 14–26.**

A test light is used to detect battery voltage potential at various test points. Battery voltage cannot be seen or felt, and can be detected only with test equipment. The ground clip is connected to a clean ground on either the negative terminal of the battery or a clean metal part of the body and the

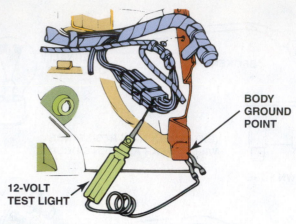

FIGURE 14–26 A 12 volt test light is attached to a good ground while probing for power.

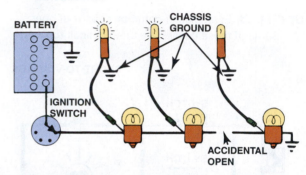

FIGURE 14–27 A test light can be used to locate an open in a circuit. Note that the test light is grounded at a different location than the circuit itself.

probe touched to terminals or components. If the test light comes on, this indicates that voltage is available. ● **SEE FIGURE 14–27.**

A purchased test light should be labeled as "12-volt test light." Do not purchase a test light designed for household current (110 or 220 volts), as it will not light with 12 to 14 volts.

USES OF A 12-VOLT TEST LIGHT
A 12-volt test light can be used to check the following:

- *Electrical power:* If the test light lights, then there is power available. It will not, however, indicate the voltage level or if there is enough current available to operate an electrical load. It only indicates that there is enough voltage and current to light the test light (about 0.25 A).

- *Grounds:* A test light can be used to check for grounds by attaching the clip of the test light to the positive terminal of the battery or any positive 12-volt electrical terminal. The tip of the test light can then be used to touch the ground wire. If there is a ground connection, the test light will light.

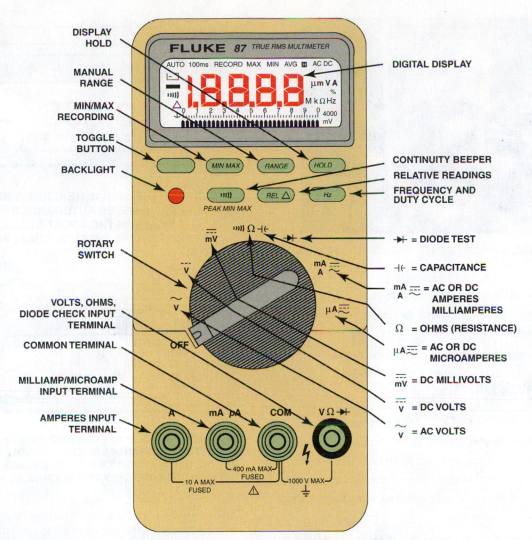

FIGURE 14–28 Typical digital multimeter. The black meter lead always is placed in the COM terminal. The red meter test lead should be in the volt-ohm terminal except when measuring current in amperes.

DIGITAL METERS

TERMINOLOGY Digital multimeter (DMM) and **digital volt-ohm-meter (DVOM)** are terms commonly used to describe digital meters. ● **SEE FIGURE 14–28.**

The common abbreviations for the units that many meters can measure are often confusing. ● **SEE CHART 14–1** for the most commonly used symbols and their meanings.

MEASURING VOLTAGE A **voltmeter** measures the pressure or potential of electricity in units of volts. A voltmeter is connected to a circuit in parallel. Voltage can be measured by selecting either AC or DC volts.

- *DC volts (DCV).* This setting is the most common for automotive use. Use this setting to measure battery voltage and voltage to all lighting and accessory circuits.

SYMBOL	MEANING
AC	Alternating current or voltage
DC	Direct current or voltage
V	Volts
mV	Millivolts (1/1,000 volts)
A	Ampere (amps), current
mA	Milliampere (1/1,000 amps)
%	Percent (for duty cycle readings only)
Ω	Ohms, resistance
kΩ	Kilohm (1,000 ohms), resistance
MΩ	Megohm (1,000,000 ohms), resistance
Hz	Hertz (cycles per second), frequency
kHz	Kilohertz (1,000 cycles/sec.), frequency
Ms	Milliseconds (1/1,000 sec.) for pulse width measurements

CHART 14–1

Common symbols and abbreviations used on digital meters.

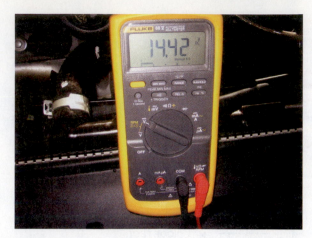

FIGURE 14–29 Typical digital multimeter (DMM) set to read DC volts.

- *AC volts (ACV).* This setting is used to check some computer sensors and to check for unwanted AC voltage from alternators.

- *Range.* The range is automatically set for most meters but can be manually adjusted if needed. ● **SEE FIGURES 14–29 AND 14–30.**

MEASURING RESISTANCE   An **ohmmeter** measures the resistance in ohms of a component or circuit section when no current is flowing through the circuit. An ohmmeter contains a battery (or other power source) and is connected in series with the component or wire being measured. Note the following facts about using an ohmmeter.

- Zero ohms on the scale means that there is no resistance between the test leads, thus indicating continuity or a continuous path for the current to flow in a closed circuit.

- Infinity means no connection, as in an open circuit.

- Ohmmeters have no required polarity even though red and black test leads are used for resistance measurement.

Different meters have different ways of indicating infinity resistance, or a reading higher than the scale allows. Examples of an over-limit display include the following:

- OL, meaning over limit or overload

- Flashing or solid number 1

- Flashing or solid number 3 on the left side of the display

Check the meter instructions for the exact display used to indicate an open circuit or over-range reading. ● **SEE FIGURE 14–31 AND 14–32.**

To summarize, open and zero readings are as follows:

$0.00\ \Omega$ = Zero resistance (component or circuit has continuity)

OL = An open circuit (no current flows) or the reading is higher than the scale selected.

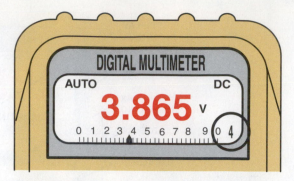

BECAUSE THE SIGNAL READING IS BELOW 4 VOLTS, THE METER AUTORANGES TO THE 4-VOLT SCALE. IN THE 4-VOLT SCALE, THIS METER PROVIDES THREE DECIMAL PLACES.

(a)

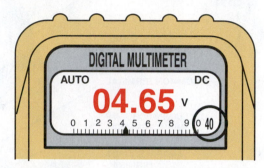

WHEN THE VOLTAGE EXCEEDED 4 VOLTS, THE METER AUTORANGES INTO THE 40-VOLT SCALE. THE DECIMAL POINT MOVES ONE PLACE TO THE RIGHT LEAVING ONLY TWO DECIMAL PLACES.

(b)

FIGURE 14–30 A typical autoranging digital multimeter automatically selects the proper scale to read the voltage being tested. The scale selected is usually displayed on the meter face. (a) Note that the display indicates "4," meaning that this range can read up to 4 volts. (b) The range is now set to the 40 volt scale, meaning that the meter can read up to 40 volts on the scale. Any reading above this level will cause the meter to reset to a higher scale. If not set on autoranging, the meter display would indicate OL if a reading exceeds the limit of the scale selected.

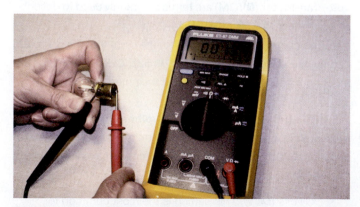

FIGURE 14–31 Using a digital multimeter set to read ohms (Ω) to test this light bulb. The meter reads the resistance of the filament.

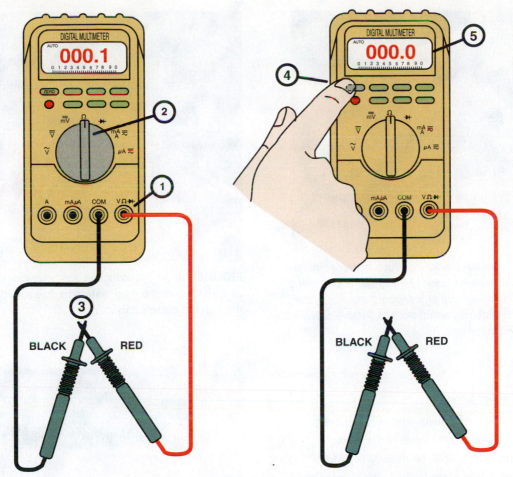

FIGURE 14–32 Many digital multimeters can have the display indicate zero to compensate for test lead resistance. (1) Connect leads in the V Ω and COM meter terminals. (2) Select the Ω scale. (3) Touch the two meter leads together. (4) Push the "zero" or "relative" button on the meter. (5) The meter display will now indicate zero ohms of resistance.

MEASURING AMPERES An **ammeter** measures the flow of current through a complete circuit in units of amperes or milliamperes (1/1,000 of an ampere). The ammeter has to be installed in the circuit (in series) so that it can measure all the current flow in that circuit, just as a water flow meter would measure the amount of water flow (cubic feet per minute, for example). ● **SEE FIGURE 14–33**.

CAUTION: An ammeter must be installed in series with the circuit to measure the current flow in the circuit. If a meter set to read amperes is connected in parallel, such as across a battery, the meter or the leads may be destroyed, or the fuse will blow, by the current available across the battery. Some DMMs beep if the unit selection does not match the test lead connection on the meter. However, in a noisy shop, this beep sound may be inaudible.

Digital meters require that the meter leads be moved to the ammeter terminals. Most digital meters have an ampere scale that can accommodate a maximum of 10 amperes. See the Tech Tip "Fuse Your Meter Leads!"

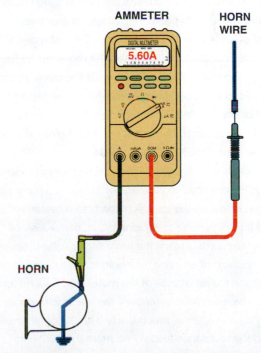

FIGURE 14–33 Measuring the current flow required by a horn requires that the ammeter be connected to the circuit in series and the horn button be depressed by an assistant.

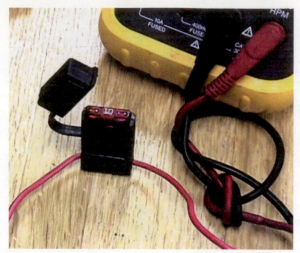

FIGURE 14–34 Note the blade-type fuse holder soldered in series with one of the meter leads. A 10 ampere fuse helps protect the internal meter fuse (if equipped) and the meter itself from damage that may result from excessive current flow if accidentally used incorrectly.

FIGURE 14–35 An inductive ammeter clamp is used with all starting and charging testers to measure the current flow through the battery cables.

 TECH TIP

Fuse Your Meter Leads!

Most digital meters include an ammeter capability. When reading amperes, the leads of the meter must be changed from volts or ohms (V or Ω) to amperes (A) or milliamperes (mA). A common problem may then occur the next time voltage is measured.

Although the technician may switch the selector to read volts, often the leads are not switched back to the volt or ohm position. Because the ammeter lead position results in zero ohms of resistance to current flow through the meter, the meter or the fuse inside the meter will be destroyed if the meter is connected to a battery. Many meter fuses are expensive and difficult to find. To avoid this problem, simply solder an inline 10 ampere blade-fuse holder into one meter lead. ● **SEE FIGURE 14–34**.

Do not think that this technique is for beginners only. Experienced technicians often get in a hurry and forget to switch the lead. A blade fuse is faster, easier, and less expensive to replace than a meter fuse or the meter itself. Also, if the soldering is done properly, the addition of an inline fuse holder and fuse does not increase the resistance of the meter leads. All meter leads have some resistance. If the meter is measuring very low resistance, touch the two leads together and read the resistance (usually no more than 0.2 ohm). Simply subtract the resistance of the leads from the resistance of the component being measured.

FIGURE 14–36 A typical mini clamp-on-type digital multimeter. This meter is capable of measuring alternating current (AC) and direct current (DC) without requiring that the circuit be disconnected to install the meter in series. The jaws are simply placed over the wire and current flow through the circuit is displayed.

INDUCTIVE AMMETERS

OPERATION Inductive ammeters do not make physical contact with the circuit. Inductive ammeters have the advantage of being able to read much higher amperages than 10 amperes. A sensor is used to detect the strength of the magnetic field surrounding the wire carrying the current. The ammeter then uses the strength of the magnetic field to measure the electrical current. ● **SEE FIGURE 14–35**.

AC/DC CLAMP-ON DIGITAL MULTIMETERS An AC/DC clamp-on digital multimeter is a useful meter for automotive diagnostic work. ● **SEE FIGURE 14–36**.

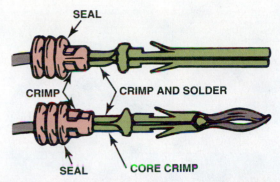

FIGURE 14–37 Some terminals have seals attached to help seal the electrical connections.

The major advantage of the clamp-on-type meter is that there is no need to break the circuit to measure current (amperes). Simply clamp the jaws of the meter around the power lead(s) or ground lead(s) of the component being measured and read the display. Most clamp-on meters can also measure alternating current, which is helpful in the diagnosis of an alternator problem. Volts, ohms, frequency, and temperature can also be measured with the typical clamp-on DMM, but conventional meter leads should be used. The inductive clamp is used to measure only amperes.

THINK OF MONEY Digital meter displays can often be confusing. The display for a battery measured as 12 1/2 volts would be 12.50 V, just as $12.50 is 12 dollars and 50 cents. A 1/2 volt reading on a digital meter will be displayed as 0.50 V, just as $0.50 is half of a dollar. It is more confusing when low values are displayed. For example, if a voltage reading is 0.063 volt, an auto-ranging meter will display 63 millivolts (63 mV), or 63/1,000 of a volt, or $63 of $1,000. (It takes 1,000 mV to equal 1 volt.) Think of millivolts as one-tenth of a cent, with 1 volt being $1.00. Therefore, 630 millivolts are equal to $0.63 of $1.00 (630 tenths of a cent, or 63 cents). To avoid confusion, try to manually range the meter to read base units (whole volts).

If the meter is ranged to base unit volts, 63 millivolts would be displayed as 0.063 or maybe just 0.06, depending on the display capabilities of the meter.

TERMINALS AND CONNECTORS

TERMINOLOGY A **terminal** is a metal fastener attached to the end of a wire, which makes the electrical connection. The term **connector** usually refers to the plastic portion that snaps or connects together, thereby making the mechanical connection. Wire terminal ends usually snap into and are held

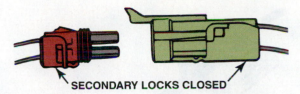

FIGURE 14–38 Separate a connector by opening the lock and pulling the two apart.

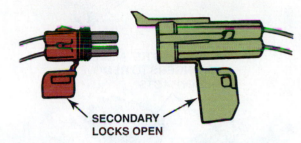

FIGURE 14–39 The secondary locks help retain the terminals in the connector.

by a connector. Male and female connectors can then be snapped together, thereby completing an electrical connection. Connectors exposed to the environment are also equipped with a weather-tight seal. ● **SEE FIGURE 14–37.**

SERVICING TERMINALS Terminals are retained in connectors by the use of a lock tang. Removing a terminal from a connector includes the following steps.

STEP 1 Release the connector position assurance (CPA), if equipped, that keeps the latch of the connector from releasing accidentally.

STEP 2 Separate the male and female connector by opening the lock. ● **SEE FIGURE 14–38.**

STEP 3 Release the secondary lock, if equipped. ● **SEE FIGURE 14–39.**

STEP 4 Using a pick, look for the slot in the plastic connector where the lock tang is located, depress the lock tang, and gently remove the terminal from the connector. ● **SEE FIGURE 14–40.**

WIRE REPAIR

SOLDERING Many manufacturers recommend that all wiring repairs be soldered. Solder is an alloy of tin and lead used to make a good electrical contact between two wires or connections in an electrical circuit. However, a flux must be used to help clean the area and to help make the solder flow. Therefore, solder is made with a resin (rosin) contained in the center, called *rosin-core solder*.

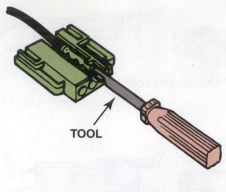

TOOL

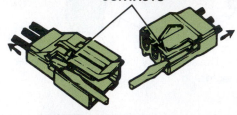

RAISING RETAINING
FINGERS TO REMOVE
CONTACTS

LOCKING WEDGE CONNECTOR

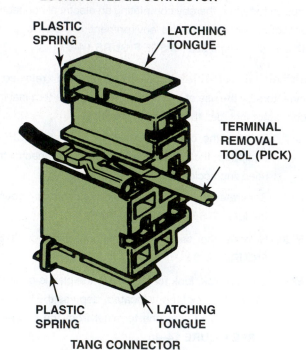

PLASTIC
SPRING

LATCHING
TONGUE

TERMINAL
REMOVAL
TOOL (PICK)

PLASTIC
SPRING

LATCHING
TONGUE

TANG CONNECTOR

FIGURE 14–40 Use a small removal tool, sometimes called a pick, to release terminals from the connector.

CAUTION: Never use acid-core solder to repair electrical wiring as the acid will cause corrosion. ● SEE FIGURE 14–41.

Solder is available with various percentages of tin and lead in the alloy. Ratios are used to identify these various types of solder, with the first number denoting the percentage of tin in the alloy and the second number giving the percentage of lead.

FIGURE 14–41 Always use rosin-core solder for electrical or electronic soldering. Also, use small-diameter solder for small soldering irons. Use large-diameter solder only for large-diameter (large-gauge) wire and higher-wattage soldering irons (guns).

The most commonly used solder is 50/50, which means that 50% of the solder is tin and the other 50 % is lead. The percentages of each alloy primarily determine the melting point of the solder.

- 60/40 solder (60% tin/40% lead) melts at 361°F (183°C).
- 50/50 solder (50% tin/50% lead) melts at 421°F (216°C).
- 40/60 solder (40% tin/60% lead) melts at 460°F (238°C).

SOLDERING PROCEDURE Soldering a wiring splice includes the following steps.

STEP 1 While touching the soldering gun to the splice, apply solder to the junction of the gun and the wire.

STEP 2 The solder will start to flow. Do not move the soldering gun.

STEP 3 Just keep feeding more solder into the splice as it flows into and around the strands of the wire.

STEP 4 After the solder has flowed throughout the splice, remove the soldering gun and the solder from the splice and allow the solder to cool slowly.

The solder should have a shiny appearance. Dull-looking solder may be caused by not reaching a high enough temperature, which results in a cold solder joint. Reheating the splice and allowing it to cool often restores the shiny appearance.

CRIMPING TERMINALS Terminals can be crimped to create a good electrical connection if the proper type of crimping tool is used. Most vehicle manufacturers recommend

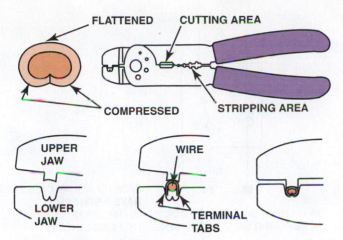

FIGURE 14–42 Notice that to create a good crimp, the open part of the terminal is placed in the jaws of the crimping tool toward the anvil or the W-shape part.

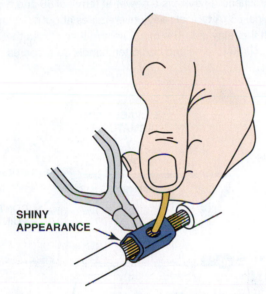

FIGURE 14–43 All hand-crimped splices or terminals should be soldered to be assured of a good electrical connection.

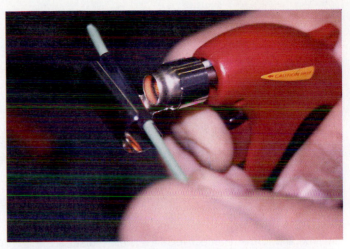

FIGURE 14–44 A butane torch especially designed for use on heat shrink applies heat without an open flame, which could cause damage.

FIGURE 14–45 A typical crimp-and-seal connector. This type of connector is first lightly crimped to retain the ends of the wires and then it is heated. The tubing shrinks around the wire splice, and thermoplastic glue melts on the inside to provide an effective weather-resistant seal.

that a W-shaped crimp be used to force the strands of the wire into a tight space. ● SEE FIGURE 14–42.

Most vehicle manufacturers also specify that all hand-crimped terminals or splices be soldered. ● SEE FIGURE 14–43.

HEAT SHRINK TUBING Heat shrink tubing is usually made from polyvinyl chloride (PVC) or polyolefin and shrinks to about half of its original diameter when heated; this is usually called a 2:1 shrink ratio. Heat shrink by itself does not provide protection against corrosion, because the ends of the tubing are not sealed against moisture. Chrysler Corporation recommends that all wire repairs that may be exposed to the elements be repaired and sealed using adhesive-lined heat shrink tubing. The tubing is usually made from flame-retardant flexible polyolefin with an internal layer of special thermoplastic adhesive. When heated, this tubing shrinks to one-third of its original diameter (3:1 shrink ratio) and the adhesive melts and seals the ends of the tubing. ● SEE FIGURE 14–44.

CRIMP-AND-SEAL CONNECTORS Several vehicle manufacturers recommend the use of crimp-and-seal connectors as the method for wire repair. **Crimp-and-seal connectors** contain a sealant and shrink tubing in one piece and are not simply butt connectors. ● SEE FIGURE 14–45.

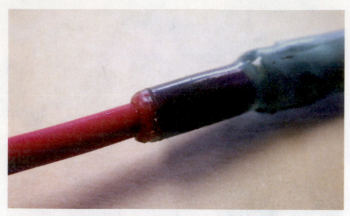

FIGURE 14–46 Heating the crimp-and-seal connector melts the glue and forms an effective seal against moisture.

The usual procedure specified for making a wire repair using a crimp-and-seal connector is as follows:

STEP 1 Strip the insulation from the ends of the wire (about 5/16 inch or 8 mm).

STEP 2 Select the proper size of crimp-and-seal connector for the gauge of wire being repaired. Insert the wires into the splice sleeve and crimp.

NOTE: Use only the specified crimping tool to help prevent the pliers from creating a hole in the cover.

STEP 3 Apply heat to the connector until the sleeve shrinks down around the wire and a small amount of sealant is observed around the ends of the sleeve, as shown in ● **FIGURE 14–46**.

RELAYS

DEFINITION A **relay** is a magnetic switch that uses a movable armature to control a high-amperage circuit by using a low-amperage electrical switch.

TERMINAL IDENTIFICATION Most automotive relays adhere to common terminal identification. The primary source for this common identification comes from the standards established by the International Standards Organization (ISO). Knowing this terminal information will help in the correct diagnosis and troubleshooting of any circuit containing a relay. ● **SEE FIGURES 14–47 AND 14–48.**

Relays are found in many circuits because they are capable of being controlled by computers, yet are able to handle enough current to power motors and accessories. Relays include the following components and terminals.

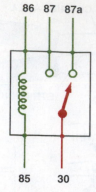

86 - POWER SIDE OF THE COIL
85 - GROUND SIDE OF THE COIL

(MOSTLY RELAY COILS HAVE BETWEEN 50–150 OHMS OF RESISTANCE)

30 - COMMON POWER FOR RELAY CONTACTS
87 - NORMALLY OPEN OUTPUT (N.O.)
87a - NORMALLY CLOSED OUTPUT (N.C.)

FIGURE 14–47 A relay uses a movable arm to complete a circuit whenever there is a power at terminal 86 and a ground at terminal 85. A typical relay only requires about 1/10 ampere through the relay coil. The movable arm then closes the contacts (#30 to #87) and can often handle 30 amperes or more.

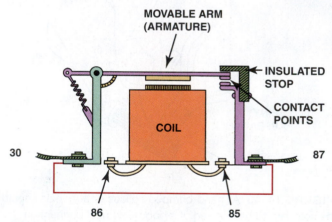

FIGURE 14–48 A cross-sectional view of a typical four-terminal relay. Current flowing through the coil (terminals 86 and 85) causes the movable arm (called the armature) to be drawn toward the coil magnet. The contact points complete the electrical circuit connected to terminals 30 and 87.

1. Coil (terminals 85 and 86)
   ▪ A coil provides the magnetic pull to a movable armature (arm).
   ▪ The resistance of most relay coils is usually between 60 ohms and 100 ohms.
   ▪ The ISO identification of the coil terminals are 86 and 85. The terminal number 86 represents the power to the relay coil and the terminal labeled 85 represents the ground side of the relay coil.

FIGURE 14–49 A typical relay showing the schematic of the wiring in the relay.

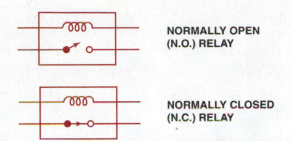

FIGURE 14–50 All schematics are shown in their normal, non-energized position.

- The relay coil can be controlled by supplying either power or ground to the relay coil winding.
- The coil winding represents the control circuit, which uses low current to control the higher current through the other terminals of the relay.
  ● SEE FIGURE 14–49.

2. Other terminals used to control the load current

- The higher amperage current flow through a relay flows through terminals 30 and 87, and often 87a.
- There is power at terminal 85 and a ground at terminal 86 of the relay, a magnetic field is created in the coil winding, which draws the armature of the relay toward the coil. The armature, when energized electrically, connects terminals 30 and 87.

The maximum current through the relay is determined by the resistance of the circuit, and relays are designed to safely handle the designed current flow. ● SEE FIGURES 14–50 AND 14–51.

OHMMETER CHECKS A control switch can be checked by removing it from the circuit and checking it with an ohmmeter.

TECH TIP

Divide the Circuit in Half

When diagnosing any circuit that has a relay, start testing at the relay and divide the circuit in half.

- **High current portion**: Remove the relay and check that there are 12 volts at the terminal 30 socket. If there is, then the power side is okay. Use an ohmmeter and check between terminal 87 socket and ground. If the load circuit has continuity, there should be some resistance. If OL, the circuit is electrically open.

- **Control circuit (low current)**: With the relay removed from the socket, check that there is 12 volts to terminal 86 with the ignition on and the control switch on. If not, check service information to see if power should be applied to terminal 86, then continue troubleshooting the switch power and related circuit.

- **Check the relay itself**: Use an ohmmeter and measure for continuity and resistance.

- Between terminals 85 and 86 (coil), there should be 60 to 100 ohms. If not, replace the relay.

- Between terminals 30 and 87 (high-amperage switch controls), there should be continuity (low ohms) when there is power applied to terminal 85 and a ground applied to terminal 86 that operates the relay. If "OL" is displayed on the meter set to read ohms, the circuit is open which requires that the reply be replaced.

- Between terminals 30 and 87a (if equipped), with the relay turned off, there should be low resistance (less than 5 ohms).

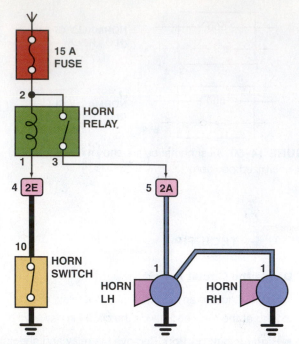

FIGURE 14–51 A typical horn circuit. Note that the relay contacts supply the heavy current to operate the horn when the horn switch simply completes a low-current circuit to ground, causing the relay contacts to close.

- The meter leads are connected to the two terminals of the switch. If there is only one terminal, one meter lead is connected to it, and the other lead is connected to the switch body. Some switches are normally open, and the reading should be high or infinite (OL). Some switches are normally closed, and the reading should be zero ohms.

- When the switch is operated, the reading should change to the opposite value.

- A pressure switch can usually be operated using a specialized tester or by applying air pressure with a rubber-tipped air gun.

The *transmission range (TR)* switch, also called the *manual lever position (MLP)* switch, or neutral start switch, has several circuits and terminals. This switch is checked using service information to determine which terminals should have continuity as the switch is moved through its travel. ● **SEE FIGURE 14–52.**

VOLTMETER CHECKS
A mechanically operated switch can also be checked on the vehicle using a voltmeter.

To test a switch, perform the following steps:

STEP 1 Connect the negative meter lead to a good ground or the switch body and the positive lead to the B+ wire entering the switch. Voltage should be available to the switch.

STEP 2 Move the positive meter lead to the second switch terminal, and operate the switch. As the switch is

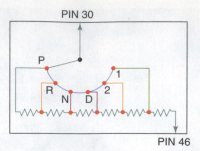

FIGURE 14–52 A typical transmission range switch is also similar to the circuit used for electronic transfer case switches. In this example, power, usually 12 volts, is applied at pin 30 and pin 46 is an input to the PCM. The change in voltage at pin 46 indicates how much resistance the circuit has, which is used to detect the gear selected.

operated, the output voltage should change from zero to the same as the input voltage or vice versa. If the voltage readings are not close to the same, there is a voltage drop, and high resistance in the switch is indicated.

SPEED SENSORS

OPERATION Speed sensors can be either magnetic or Hall-effect-type sensors. A magnetic sensor consists of a notched wheel and a coil consisting of an iron core wrapped with fine wire. The notched wheel causes the magnetic strength changes enough to create a usable varying AC voltage signal. ● **SEE FIGURE 14–53.**

The voltage-generating speed sensor normally uses a two-wire connector and is checked using both an ohmmeter and a voltmeter.

SPEED SENSOR TESTS To test a speed sensor, perform the following steps:

STEP 1 Disconnect the sensor, and connect the two ohmmeter leads to the two sensor terminals.

STEP 2 There should be a complete circuit through the unit, and the resistance reading should fall within the specified range. Excessive or infinite resistance indicates a high resistance or open circuit; too low of a reading indicates a short circuit.

STEP 3 Attach the two leads of a voltmeter to the two sensor connectors, set the meter to AC volts.

STEP 4 Rotate the transmission shaft. As the shaft rotates, the voltmeter should show a fluctuating AC voltage reading, first + and then – of the same value.

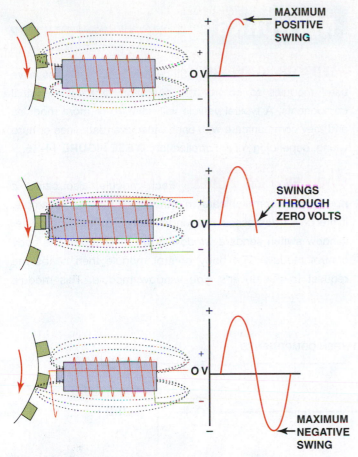

MAXIMUM POSITIVE SWING

SWINGS THROUGH ZERO VOLTS

MAXIMUM NEGATIVE SWING

FIGURE 14–53 A magnetic sensor uses a permanent magnet surrounded by a coil of wire. The notches on the rotating shaft create a variable magnetic field strength around the coil. When a metallic section is close to the sensor, the magnetic field is stronger because metal is a better conductor of magnetic lines of force than air.

Unlike the magnetic pulse generator, the Hall-Effect switch requires a small input voltage to generate an output or signal voltage. **Hall Effect** has the ability to generate a voltage signal in semiconductor material (gallium arsenate crystal) by passing current through it in one direction and applying a magnetic field to it at a right angle to its surface. If the input current is held steady and the magnetic field fluctuates, an output voltage is produced that changes in proportion to field strength. ● **SEE FIGURE 14–54.**

THROTTLE POSITION (TP) SENSOR

PURPOSE AND FUNCTION
The powertrain control module (PCM) uses TP sensor input to determine the amount of throttle opening and the rate of change to determine shift points of an automatic transmission and for engine management.

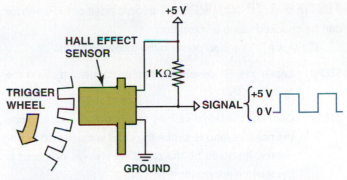

FIGURE 14–54 A Hall-Effect sensor produces an on-off voltage signal whether it is used with a blade or a notched wheel.

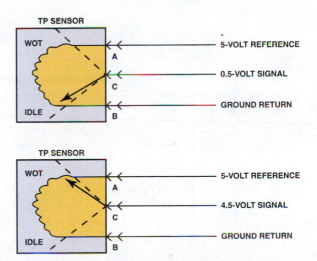

FIGURE 14–55 The signal voltage from a throttle position increases as the throttle is opened because the wiper arm is closer to the 5-volt reference. At idle, the resistance of the sensor winding effectively reduces the signal voltage output to the powertrain control module (PCM).

PARTS AND OPERATION
The TP sensor consists of a **potentiometer,** a type of variable resistor. A potentiometer is a variable-resistance sensor with three terminals. One end of the resistor receives reference voltage, while the other end is grounded. The third terminal is attached to a movable contact that slides across the resistor to vary its resistance. Depending on whether the contact is near the supply end or the ground end of the resistor, return voltage is high or low.

A typical sensor has three wires:

- A 5-volt reference feed wire from the computer
- Signal return
- A ground wire back to the computer

● **SEE FIGURE 14–55.**

TESTING A TP SENSOR A throttle position (TP) sensor can be checked using a voltmeter.

To test a TP sensor, perform the following steps:

STEP 1 Leave the TP sensor connector connected. Turn the ignition "ON."

STEP 2 Connect the negative lead to a good ground, and use the positive lead to probe the input voltage at the connector. It should be the specified voltage indicated in the service information.

STEP 3 Move the positive voltmeter lead to the TP output voltage lead, and measure the voltage as the throttle opens and closes. The output voltage should increase and decrease smoothly as the throttle is opened and closed.

NETWORKS

NEED FOR NETWORK Since the 1990s, vehicles have used modules to control the operation of most electrical components. A typical vehicle will have 10 or more modules and they communicate with each other over data lines or hard wiring, depending on the application. ●**SEE FIGURE 14–56.**

MODULES AND NODES Each module, also called a **node**, must communicate to other modules. For example, if the driver depresses the window-down switch, the power window switch sends a window-down message to the body control module. The body control module then sends the request to the driver's side window module. This module

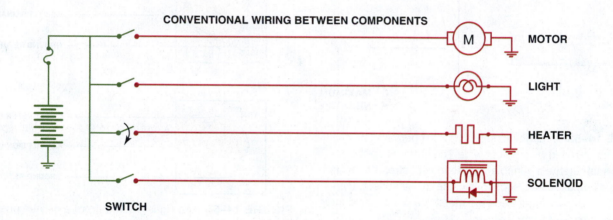

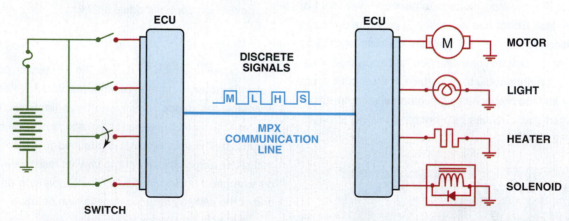

FIGURE 14–56 Module communications makes controlling multiple electrical devices and accessories easier by using simple low-current switches to signal another electronic control module (ECM), which does the actual switching of the current to the device.

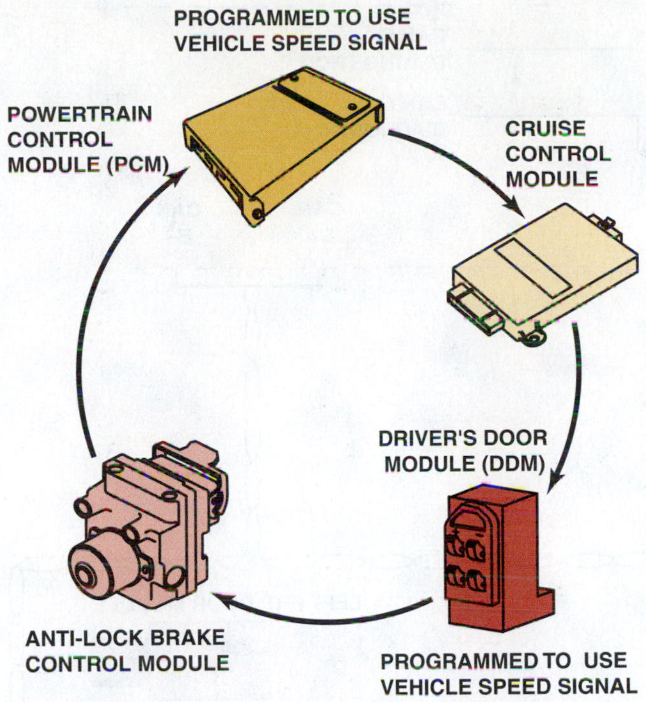

PROGRAMMED TO USE VEHICLE SPEED SIGNAL

POWERTRAIN CONTROL MODULE (PCM)

CRUISE CONTROL MODULE

DRIVER'S DOOR MODULE (DDM)

ANTI-LOCK BRAKE CONTROL MODULE

PROGRAMMED TO USE VEHICLE SPEED SIGNAL

FIGURE 14–57 A network allows all modules to communicate with other modules.

is responsible for actually performing the task by supplying power and ground to the window lift motor in the current polarity to cause the window to go down. The module also contains a circuit that monitors the current flow through the motor and will stop and/or reverse the window motor if an obstruction causes the window motor to draw more than the normal amount of current.

TYPES OF COMMUNICATION The types of communications include the following:

- *Differential.* In the differential form of BUS communication, a difference in voltage is applied to two wires, which are twisted to help reduce electromagnetic interference (EMI). These transfer wires are called a twisted pair.

- *Parallel.* In the parallel type of BUS communication, the send and receive signals are on different wires.

- *Serial data.* The serial data is data transmitted by a series of rapidly changing voltage signals pulsed from low to high or from high to low.

- *Multiplexing.* The process of multiplexing involves the sending of multiple signals of information at the same time over a signal wire and then separating the signals at the receiving end.

This system of intercommunication of computers or processors is referred to as a network. ● **SEE FIGURE 14–57**.

By connecting the computers together on a communications network, they can easily share information back and forth. This multiplexing has the following advantages.

- Elimination of redundant sensors and dedicated wiring for these multiple sensors
- Reduction of the number of wires, connectors, and circuits
- Addition of more features and option content to new vehicles
- Weight reduction due to fewer components, wires, and connectors, thereby increasing fuel economy
- Changeable features with software upgrades versus component replacement

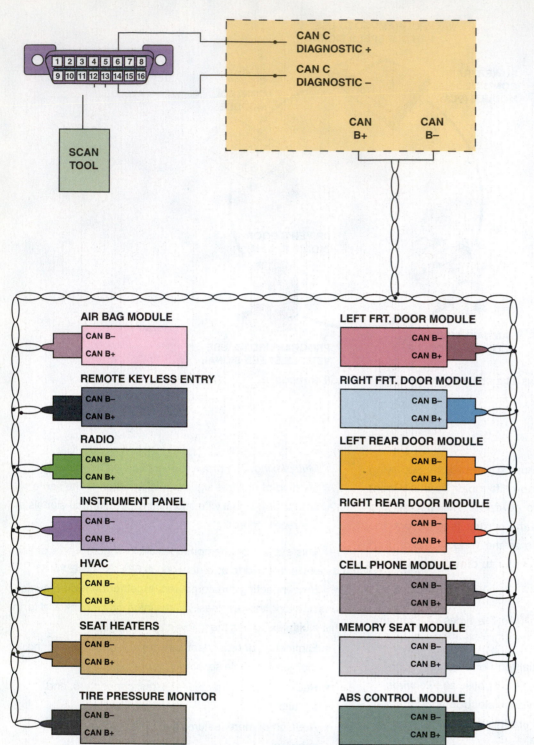

FIGURE 14–58 A typical BUS system showing module CAN communications and twisted pairs of wire.

NETWORK CLASSIFICATIONS

The Society of Automotive Engineers (SAE) standards include the following three categories of in-vehicle network communications.

Class A Low-speed networks, meaning less than 10,000 bits per second (bps, or 10 Kbs), are generally used for trip computers, entertainment, and other convenience features.

Class B Medium-speed networks, meaning 10,000 bps to 125,000 bps (10 Kbs to 125 Kbs), are generally used for information transfer among modules, such as instrument clusters, temperature sensor data, and other general uses.

Class C High-speed networks, meaning 125,000 bps to 1,000,000 bps, are generally used for real-time powertrain and vehicle dynamic control. High-speed BUS communication systems now use a controller area network (CAN). ● **SEE FIGURE 14–58**.

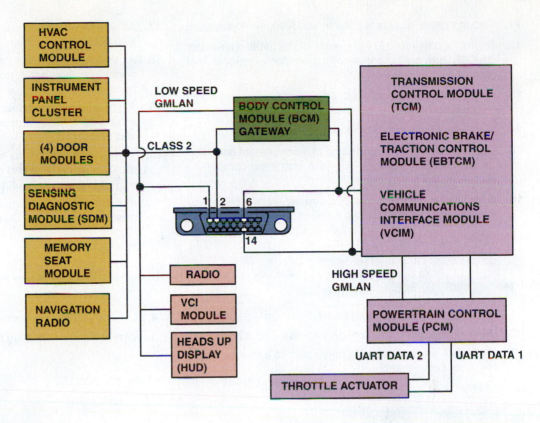

FIGURE 14–59 A schematic of a Chevrolet Equinox shows that the vehicle uses a GMLAN BUS (DLC pins 6 and 14), plus a Class 2 (pin 2). A scan tool can therefore communicate to the transmission control module (TCM) through the high-speed network. Pin 1 connects to the low-speed GMLAN network.

CONTROLLER AREA NETWORK

STANDARD Robert Bosch Corporation developed the CAN protocol, which was called CAN 1.2, in 1993. The CAN protocol was approved by the Environmental Protection Agency (EPA) for 2003 and newer vehicle diagnostics, and a legal requirement for all vehicles by 2008. The CAN diagnostic systems use pins 6 and 14 in the standard 16 pin OBD-II (J-1962) connector. Before CAN, the scan tool protocol had been manufacturer specific. ● **SEE FIGURE 14–59**.

? FREQUENTLY ASKED QUESTION

What Are U Codes?

The "U" diagnostic trouble codes were at first "undefined" but are now network-related codes. Use the network codes to help pinpoint the circuit or module that is not working correctly. Some powertrain-related faults are due to network communications errors and therefore can be detected by looking for "U" diagnostic trouble codes (DTCs).

SUMMARY

1. Electricity is the movement of electrons from one atom to another.

2. In order for current to flow in a circuit or wire, there must be an excess of electrons at one end and a deficiency of electrons at the other end.

3. Automotive electricity uses the conventional theory that electricity flows from positive to negative.

4. The ampere is the measure of the amount of current flow.

5. Voltage is the unit of electrical pressure.

6. The ohm is the unit of electrical resistance.

7. All complete electrical circuits have a power source (such as a battery), a circuit protection device (such as a fuse), a power-side wire or path, an electrical load, a ground return path, and a switch or a control device.

8. A short-to-voltage involves a copper-to-copper connection and usually affects more than one circuit.

9. A short-to-ground usually involves a power path conductor coming in contact with a return (ground) path conductor and usually causes the fuse to blow.

10. An open is a break in the circuit resulting in absolutely no current flow through the circuit.

11. Circuit testers include test lights and fused jumper leads.

12. Digital multimeter (DMM) and digital volt-ohm-meter (DVOM) are terms commonly used for electronic test meters.

13. Ammeters measure current and must be connected in series in the circuit.

14. Voltmeters measure voltage and are connected in parallel.

15. Ohmmeters measure resistance of a component and must be connected in parallel with the circuit or component disconnected from power.

16. A terminal is the metal end of a wire, whereas a connector is the plastic housing for the terminal.

17. All wire repair should use either soldering or a crimp-and-seal connector.

18. All switches and relays on a schematic are shown in their normal position either normally closed (N.C.) or normally open (N.O.).

19. A typical relay uses a small current through a coil (terminals 85 and 86) to operate the higher current part (terminals 30 and 87).

20. The use of a network for module communications reduces the number of wires and connections needed.

21. The SAE communication classifications for vehicle communications systems include Class A (low speed), Class B (medium speed), and Class C (high speed).

REVIEW QUESTIONS

1. What are ampere, volt, and ohm?

2. What is included in a complete electrical circuit?

3. Why must an ohmmeter be connected to a disconnected circuit or component?

4. List and identify the terminals of a typical ISO type relay.

5. Why is a communication network used?

CHAPTER QUIZ

1. An electrical conductor is an element with _____ electrons in its outer orbit.
   a. Less than 2
   b. Less than 4
   c. Exactly 4
   d. More than 4

2. Like charges _____.
   a. Attract each other
   b. Repel each other
   c. Neutralize each other
   d. Add

3. If an insulated wire gets rubbed through a part of the insulation and the wire conductor touches the steel body of a vehicle, the type of failure would be called a(n) _____.
   a. Short-to-voltage
   b. Short-to-ground
   c. Open
   d. Chassis ground

4. High resistance in an electrical circuit can cause _____.
   a. Dim lights
   b. Slow motor operation
   c. Clicking of relays or solenoids
   d. All of the above

5. If two power-side insulated wires were to melt together at the point where the copper conductors touched each other, the type of failure would be called a(n) _____.
   a. Short-to-voltage
   b. Short-to-ground
   c. Open
   d. Floating ground

6. When testing a relay using an ohmmeter, which two terminals should be touched to measure the coil resistance?
   a. 87 and 30
   b. 86 and 85
   c. 87a and 87
   d. 86 and 87

7. Technician A says that a good relay should measure between 60 ohms and 100 ohms across the coil terminals. Technician B says that OL should be displayed on an ohmmeter when touching terminals 30 and 87. Which technician is correct?
   a. Technician A only
   b. Technician B only
   c. Both Technicians A and B
   d. Neither Technician A nor B

8. If a wire repair, such as that made under the hood or under the vehicle, is exposed to the elements, which type of repair should be used?
   a. Wire nuts and electrical tape
   b. Solder and adhesive-lined heat shrink or crimp-and-seal connectors
   c. Butt connectors
   d. Rosin-core solder and electrical tape

9. A module is also known as a _____.
   a. BUS
   b. Node
   c. Terminator
   d. Resistor pack

10. A high-speed CAN BUS communicates with a scan tool through which terminal(s)?
    a. 6 and 14
    b. 2
    c. 7 and 15
    d. 4 and 16

chapter 15

FOUR-WHEEL AND ALL-WHEEL DRIVE

After studying this chapter, the reader should be able to:

1. Prepare for the ASE Manual Drive Train and Axles (A3) certification test content area "F" (Four-Wheel-Drive/All-Wheel-Drive Component Diagnosis and Service).

2. Explain the characteristics of four-wheel-drive (4WD) vehicles.

3. Differentiate between part-time and full-time four-wheel-drive vehicles.

4. Explain the purpose and function of the central differential and transfer case in a four-wheel-drive vehicle.

5. Explain the purpose and function of electronic transfer cases and the power transfer unit of a four-wheel-drive vehicle.

6. Explain the purpose and function of couplers and torque bias devices.

7. Discuss the operation of front drive axles and drive axle/wheel disconnect systems.

All-wheel drive (AWD) 285
Center differential 286
Electronic Shift on-the-Fly (ESOF) 291
Four-wheel drive (4WD) 282
Full-time 4WD 285
Integrated wheel end disconnect 297
Locking hub 284
Manual Shift On-the-Fly (MSOF) 291
Mode shift 283

Open design 296
Part-time four-wheel drive 284
Power transfer unit (PTU) 293
Range shift 284
Rocker pin 291
Torque biasing device (TBD) 294
Transfer case 282
Transfer case control module (TCCM) 291
Viscous coupling 286

FIGURE 15–1 A World War II Jeep on display at the Lemay Museum in Tacoma, Washington.

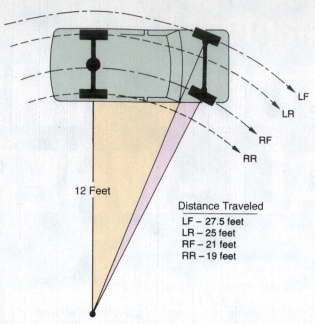

12 Feet

Distance Traveled
LF – 27.5 feet
LR – 25 feet
RF – 21 feet
RR – 19 feet

FIGURE 15–2 If a vehicle makes a right-angle turn with an inside rear-wheel radius of 12 feet, the four tires will travel the distances indicated in the same amount of time; the outside front tire will have to go about 70% faster than the inside rear tire.

FOUR-WHEEL DRIVE

PURPOSE AND FUNCTION Two-wheel-drive vehicles use engine torque to turn either the front or the rear wheels. A differential is required to allow the drive wheels to travel different distances and speeds while cornering or driving over bumps or dips in the road. A four-wheel-drive vehicle, therefore, requires two differentials—one for the front wheels and one for the rear wheels.

NOTE: The term *4 × 4* means a four-wheeled vehicle that has engine torque applied to all four wheels (four-wheel drive). A *4 × 2* means a four-wheeled vehicle that has engine torque applied to only two wheels (two-wheel drive).

The front and the rear wheels of a four-wheel-drive vehicle also travel different distances and speeds whenever cornering or running over dips or rises in the road. Therefore, a four-wheel-drive vehicle also needs a center differential to allow the front wheels to travel different distances than the rear wheels.

BACKGROUND Four-wheel drive (4WD) for cars, pickups, and light trucks has steadily evolved from the somewhat crude but rugged Jeep of World War II to sport cars and sport-utility vehicles. ● **SEE FIGURE 15–1.**

PRINCIPLES A two-wheel-drive vehicle is able to power both drive wheels through the use of a drive axle and a

differential. Powering all four wheels creates some issues such as:

- Not only do the wheels on the outside travel further while turning than the inside wheels, the rear wheels and tires also travel different distances than the front wheels and tires. ● **SEE FIGURE 15–2.**

- There is a need for a unit, usually a **transfer case**, where the engine torque can be split to either one drive axle or both to provide for four-wheel drive.

CONFIGURATIONS 4WD can be based on any drivetrain configuration including:

- **Front engine–RWD**—Most truck-based four-wheel systems use this arrangement.

- **Front engine–FWD**—Many passenger vehicles and sport utility vehicles (SUV) use this arrangement.

- **Mid-engine–RWD**—Some sport cars use this arrangement such as some Porsches.

- **Rear engine–RWD**—Some sport cars use this arrangement such as some Porsches.

● **SEE FIGURE 15–3.**

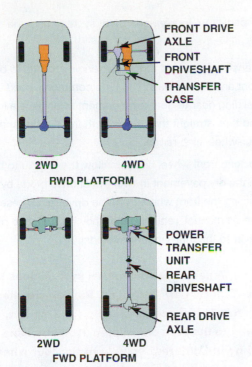

2WD   4WD
RWD PLATFORM

FRONT DRIVE AXLE
FRONT DRIVESHAFT
TRANSFER CASE

2WD   4WD
FWD PLATFORM

POWER TRANSFER UNIT
REAR DRIVESHAFT
REAR DRIVE AXLE

FIGURE 15–3 Four-wheel-drive vehicles can be achieved by using an existing rear-wheel-drive arrangement and adding a transfer case, or a front-wheel-drive arrangement with the addition of rear axle output shaft and center differential assembly.

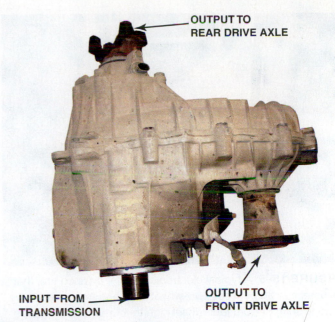

OUTPUT TO REAR DRIVE AXLE

INPUT FROM TRANSMISSION

OUTPUT TO FRONT DRIVE AXLE

FIGURE 15–4 A typical transfer case is attached to the output of the transmission and directs engine torque to the rear or to the front and rear differentials.

TERMINOLOGY

The terms used for four-wheel-drive vehicles can be confusing. The terms and their meaning include the following:

- **Two-Wheel Drive**—In two-wheel drive, engine torque is sent to either the rear (rear-wheel-drive vehicle) or to the front (front-wheel-drive vehicle).

- **Four-Wheel Drive**—In four-wheel drive, engine torque is sent to both the front and rear axles.

- **Part-Time Four-Wheel Drive**—In a vehicle equipped with a part-time four-wheel system, both front and rear axles are mechanically connected and locked together. Driving a part-time four-wheel-drive vehicle on dry pavement can cause the drivetrain to bind unless the front wheels are disconnected usually using locking hubs. With the front hubs locked, the vehicle should only be driven on dirt, mud, or snow to avoid damage caused by driveline windup.

- **Full-Time Four-Wheel Drive**—This type of four-wheel-drive system uses a center (interaxle) differential, which allows for both the front and rear axles to rotate at different speeds. A vehicle equipped with a full-time four-wheel-drive system can be safely driven in four-wheel drive on dry pavement and under all driving conditions.

- **On-Demand Four-Wheel Drive**—With an on-demand type four-wheel-drive system, one axle is driven all the time and engine torque is only sent to the other axle when traction has been lost on the primary axle. This type of system is commonly used in front-wheel-drive-based vehicles where the front axle is driven all the time with engine torque only applied to the rear when the front wheels are starting to slip.

TRANSFER CASES

PURPOSE AND FUNCTION The purpose and function of the transfer case is to control the power flow to both the front and rear axles. Many transfer cases also provide gear reduction to increase the torque applied to the drive wheels. ● SEE FIGURE 15–4.

TYPES OF SHIFTS Most transfer cases also provide for two types of shifts:

- **Mode shift**—Either two-wheel drive or four-wheel drive may be selected. Many transfer cases also have a neutral position. The mode shift is achieved by the use of a floor-mounted lever to engage and disengage a clutch inside the transfer case. This shift is usually performed when the vehicle is stopped. However, new designs allow the mode shift to be performed under most driving conditions.

FIGURE 15–5 A typical electronic transfer case control that is used to shift between two-wheel drive and four-wheel drive (mode shift) or from four-wheel high to four-wheel low (range shift).

> **NOTE: The mode shift is not available on all-wheel-drive vehicles.**

- **Range shift**—A low range may be selected to deliver high torque at low speeds to the drive wheels. Low range gear ratio varies with application. Commonly used ratios are 2:1, 2.5:1, 2.6:1, and 2.72:1 gear reduction. High range (usually 1:1 ratio) simply transfers engine torque at the same speed as the output shaft of the transmission.

● **SEE FIGURE 15–5.**

PART-TIME FOUR-WHEEL DRIVE

PURPOSE AND FUNCTION A part-time four-wheel-drive system does *not* include a center differential therefore it is designed primarily for slow speed, off-road use. Both front and rear drive axles are driven at the same speed, and the tires must slip to compensate for speed differential on turns. Older pickups and Jeep-type vehicles use part-time 4WD that is designed to be used off-road.

PARTS AND OPERATION **Part-time four-wheel drive** has a positive, mechanical connection between the front and rear driveshafts when shifted into 4WD. 4WD is used only where there is poor traction because the front or rear tires *must* be able to slip on the road surface while cornering. Gear train bind up will occur if turns are made on pavement.

A part-time four-wheel-drive system has the following parts:

- Transfer case used to transfer engine torque to both the front and rear wheels. The type commonly used includes a sliding gear to gear arrangement to achieve a low range and then straight through to both front and rear axles for four-wheel high range.

- Locking front wheel hubs to allow the vehicle to be driven on the dry pavement in two-wheel drive mode by disconnecting the front wheel from the drivetrain. These hubs can be manual, requiring that they be switched by the driver to the four-wheel-drive position.

> **CAUTION: A part-time four-wheel system does NOT use a center differential. Therefore, the vehicle should only be driven in four-wheel drive when it is on dirt, mud, or snow, where the tires can slip, to avoid driveline binding caused by the different speeds of the four wheels. The vehicle will likely shake and shutter as wheel torque is applied to the four wheels on dry pavement. The tires will often slip and hop over the pavement as the driveline binds and then the wheels slip and then bind again.**

LOCKING HUBS The transfer case also applies power to the front differential. Power is then applied to the front wheels through the drive axles to the **locking hubs**. In normal 4H driving on hard surfaces, the front hubs *must* be in the unlocked position. The front hubs are locked whenever driving on loose road surfaces to absorb and allow for tire slippage due to the different tire speeds front to back. This type of four-wheel-drive system is called **part-time four-wheel drive** because it can be driven in four-wheel drive only on slippery surfaces. ● **SEE FIGURE 15–6.**

> **CAUTION: Failure to unlock the front wheel hubs while driving on a hard road surface can cause serious driveline vibrations and damage to driveshafts, U-joints, and bearings, as well as to the transfer case, transmission, and even the engine.**

AUTO LOCKING HUBS Another method of locking the hubs on a part-time four-wheel-drive system is with a clutch arrangement built into the hub assembly. Whenever driving on smooth, hard road surfaces, the hubs "free wheel" and allow the front wheels to rotate at different speeds from the rear wheels. When the speed difference between the wheels and the front drive axle is great, the hubs will automatically lock and allow engine torque to be applied to the front wheels. Automatic-locking hubs are unlocked by disengaging

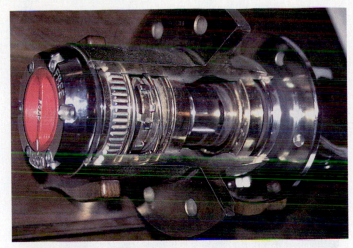

FIGURE 15–6 Cutaway of a manually operated locking hub.

four-wheel drive at the transfer case and driving for several feet.
● **SEE FIGURE 15–7.**

FULL-TIME FOUR-WHEEL DRIVE

PURPOSE AND FUNCTION **Full-time 4WD** is also called **all-wheel drive (AWD)** or *anytime 4WD*. AWD vehicles include a transfer case that has center differential, which allows the front and rear driveshafts to be driven at different speeds to prevent drivetrain binding. AWD transfer cases that deliver power to both driveshafts all of the time are called *mechanically active*. Some AWD vehicles are passenger car based, using AWD to enhance driving on wet or icy roads, such as all Subarus.

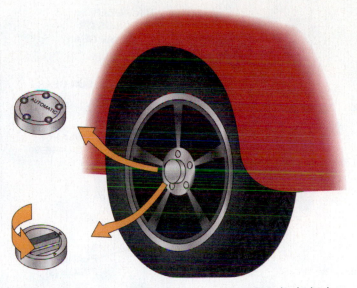

FIGURE 15–7 Manual locking hubs require that the hubs be rotated to the locked position by hand to allow torque to be applied to the front wheels. Automatic locking hubs enable the driver to shift into four-wheel drive from inside the vehicle.

PLANETARY GEAR SET TRANSFER CASE A full-time four-wheel-drive system is designed for on-road use. A center differential allows front to rear speed differential for turns. Both front and rear axles drive the wheels at the same speed.

Many transfer cases use a planetary gear set for gear reduction in low range. A planetary gear set includes the following three elements:

1. **Sun gear.** This gear is in the center, like the position of the sun is in our solar system.

2. **Planet pinions.** The planet pinion gears rotate around the sun gear, like the planets around the sun, and are attached and held in place by a *planet carrier*.

3. **Ring gear.** The outer ring gear has teeth on the inside that mesh with the teeth of the planet pinion gears. The ring gear is also called the *annulus gear* or *internal gear* because the gear teeth are on the inside (rather than the outside) portion of the gear.

The gear teeth of a planetary gear set remain in constant mesh. When gear reduction is needed, the sun gear is often the drive gear and the planet carrier is often the driven gear. The gear ratio reduction depends on the number of teeth on the various gears used in a planetary gear set. To achieve direct 1:1 output from the transfer case, any two of the three elements can be locked together and the entire assembly will rotate as a unit.
● **SEE FIGURE 15–8.**

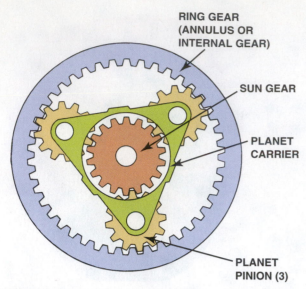

FIGURE 15–8 A typical planetary gear set used in a transfer case.

RING GEAR
(ANNULUS OR
INTERNAL GEAR)

SUN GEAR

PLANET
CARRIER

PLANET
PINION (3)

BEVEL GEAR-TYPE INTERAXLE DIFFERENTIAL

FIGURE 15–9 A bevel gear-type center (interaxle) differential used inside a transfer case. Bevel gear differentials normally split the torque equally between the front and rear drive axles.

CENTER DIFFERENTIAL

PURPOSE AND FUNCTION All-the-time four-wheel-drive, all-wheel-drive, and full-time four-wheel-drive systems use a **center differential**, also called *interaxle differential,* to prevent driveline harshness and vibration, commonly referred to as "driveline windup."

TYPES A center (interaxle) differential can include one of the following:

▪ **Standard bevel gear differential.** The bevel gear differential uses two bevel gears or spider gears attached to the output shaft of the transmission. Two to four differential pinion gears are attached to a carrier, which is

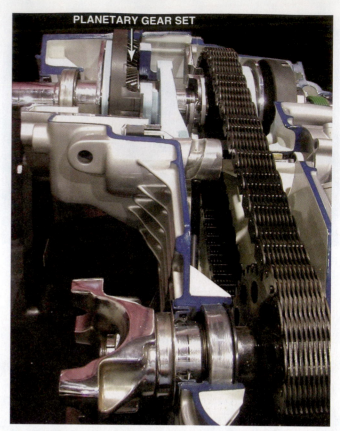

PLANETARY GEAR SET

FIGURE 15–10 Cutaway of a planetary gear set transfer case. Planetary gear differentials are designed split the torque unequally between the front and rear drive axles.

attached to the transfer gears. In other words, it operates in the same fashion as the differential in a rear axle; power is transferred to the tire with the least traction. When there is unequal traction between the front and rear axles, the axle with the most traction is allowed to slip enough to prevent damage to driveline components. Some bevel-type center differentials use an internal clutch mechanism, much like a limited slip unit, to increase torque transfer and still lessen driveline vibration and harshness. ● SEE FIGURE 15–9.

▪ **Planetary gear differential.** A planetary gear set is often incorporated in transfer cases to act as a differential. The torque split can be varied by using a planetary gear set as a center differential by changing the number of teeth on the various elements and how they are interconnected can result in various torque splits front to rear. ● SEE FIGURE 15–10.

▪ **Viscous coupling.** A **viscous coupling** is a series of steel plates housed in a sealed steel drum. The viscous coupling is not active during equal traction conditions. It actively transfers torque during light to moderate cornering, but there is a certain amount of slippage under these conditions to prevent driveline windup. If there is a significant loss of traction, the speed differences between the front and rear axles increase, and this increase in plate speed heats the silicone fluid in the viscous coupling, causing it to thicken to the point that it transfers more torque to the axle that is losing traction. During a severe loss of traction, the viscous fluid thickens enough to lock the plates together, dividing engine torque equally 50/50 between the front and rear axles. ● SEE FIGURE 15–11.

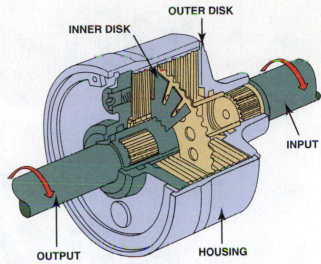

FIGURE 15–11 A viscous coupling is a sealed unit containing many steel discs. One-half of them are splined to the input shaft, with every other disc splined to the output shaft. Surrounding these discs is a thick (viscous) silicone fluid that expands when hot and effectively locks the discs together.

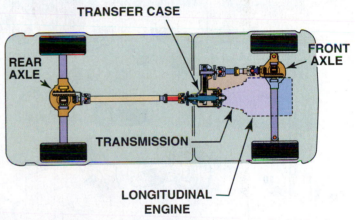

FIGURE 15–12 A typical four-wheel-drive vehicle that uses a longitudinal engine and a transfer case to send engine torque to both the front and rear wheel. Even then a 4WD vehicle can get stuck.

? FREQUENTLY ASKED QUESTION

Can a Four-Wheel-Drive Vehicle Still Get Stuck?

Yes. A four-wheel-drive vehicle can easily get stuck under some conditions depending on the type of system in the vehicle and the type of road surface. ● **SEE FIGURE 15–12.**

   This can occur in the following instances:

- If the front, center, and rear differentials are open type, and if only one wheel is on a slippery surface, then the other wheels will only get the torque required by the wheel on the slippery surface and thus the vehicle may not be able to move.

- In case the rear differential is a limited slip-type and both front and center differentials are open type, then if one of the rear tires was on a slippery surface, then the vehicle could continue to move only if the other rear drive wheel was on dry pavement.

- If one front wheel and one rear wheel were on a slippery surface and the rear axle was limited slip, the vehicle may not be able to move because the center differential is an open type.

- If the vehicle is equipped with a locking center differential and a limited slip differential in the rear, then the vehicle will be equipped to go under almost every road surface condition. However, the locking center differential needs to be unlocked at a higher speed to keep the driveline from binding.

- Current technology allows the electronic brake computer to control traction by applying the wheel brake on the wheel that is spinning to increase the amount of torque that is applied to the side or end of the vehicle with the most traction. This means that many systems use open-type differentials instead of limited slip units and rely on the wheel brakes to maintain traction to all drive wheels.

TRANSFER CASES

PARTS AND OPERATION Engine torque from the transmission is applied directly to the rear differential through the transfer case. ● **SEE FIGURE 15–13.**

   The transfer case permits the driver to select a low-speed, high-power gear ratio inside the transfer case while in four-wheel drive. These positions and their meanings include the following:

- 4H four-wheel drive with no gear reduction in the transfer case.

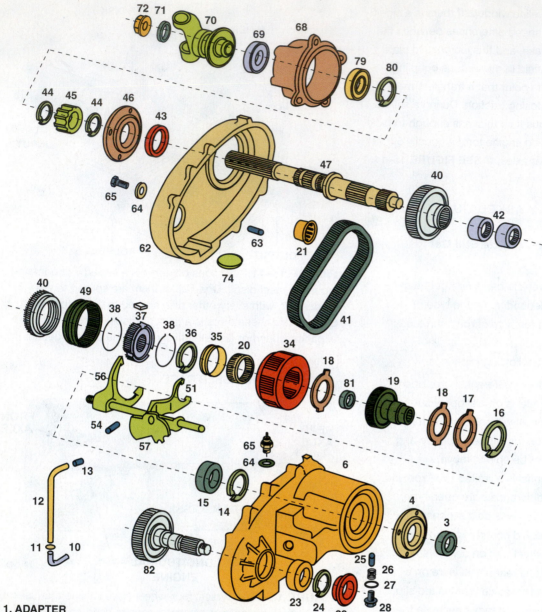

1. ADAPTER
2. LOCKNUT
3. FRONT RETAINER SEAL
4. FRONT BEARING RETAINER
5. RETAINER SCREW
6. FRONT CASE
7. CASE STUD
8. VACUUM SWITCH
9. O-RING
10. VENT
11. CLAMP
12. HOSE
13. HOSE END CAP
14. SNAP RING
15. BEARING
16. SNAP RING
17. RETAINER
18. THRUST WASHER
19. INPUT GEAR
20. PILOT BEARING
21. BEARING
22. OUTPUT SHAFT
23. BEARING

24. SNAP RING
25. DETENT PLUNGER
26. SPRING
27. O-RING
28. PLUG
29. SEAL
30. OIL SLINGER
31. YOKE
32. WASHER
33. NUT
34. LOW RANGE GEAR
35. SHIFT HUB
36. SNAP RING
37. SYNCHRONIZER
38. SPRINGS
39. STOP RING
40. SPROCKET
41. DRIVE CHAIN
42. BEARING
43. SEAL
44. SNAP RING

45. SPEEDOMETER GEAR
46. OIL PUMP
47. MAINSHAFT
48. SHIFT FORK PADS
49. RANGE FORK PADS
50. MODE FORK PADS
51. MODE FORK
52. SPRING
53. SHIFT RAIL
54. PIN
55. BUSHING
56. RANGE FORK
57. SHIFT SECTOR
58. O-RING
59. RETAINER
60. RANGE LEVER
61. NUT
62. REAR CASE
63. ALIGNMENT DOWEL
64. WASHER

65. BOLT
66. CASE BOLT
67. RETAINER SCREW
68. RETAINER
69. SEAL
70. YOKE
71. SEAL
72. YOKE NUT
73. WASHER
74. MAGNET
75. O-RING
76. OIL TUBE
77. TUBE CONNECTOR
78. SCREEN
79. BEARING
80. SNAP RING
81. PLUG
82. FRONT SHAFT
83. SNAP RING
84. GASKET

FIGURE 15–13 An exploded view of a New Venture 241 transfer case.

FIGURE 15–14 Part-time four-wheel-drive transfer cases use a manually controlled lever to perform the mode and range shifts.

- 4L four-wheel drive with gear reduction. Use of this position is usually restricted to low speeds on slippery surfaces.
- 2H two-wheel drive (rear wheels only) in high range, with no gear reduction in the transfer case.

The purpose and function of the transfer case is to direct engine torque to the front and rear axle assemblies. A four-wheel-drive transfer case is basically an auxiliary 2-speed transmission. It uses the transmission output as an input to a secondary gear train or planetary gear set, which provides a low and high range. The transfer of torque to the front axle output shaft can be accomplished either by a gear-to-gear transfer or a gear and chain transfer. A transfer case has one input shaft (connected to the output of the transmission) and two output shafts. The two output shafts are connected to the driveshafts and transfer torque to the front and rear differentials.

The gear ranges can be engaged in a number of ways, such as:

- Manual lever (older vehicles) ● **SEE FIGURE 15–14.**
- Electrical motor (most commonly used) ● **SEE FIGURE 15–15.**

FIGURE 15–15 Most transfer cases today use an electric motor to make the mode and range changes and use a dial or push button for each position.

? FREQUENTLY ASKED QUESTION

What Is a Gear-to-Gear Transfer Case?

Gear-to-gear transfer case is simple in design, and is an older design not currently being used. Three gear shafts are in mesh in the transfer case. One gear shaft is attached to the transmission output shaft. The second shaft acts as an idler, and the third shaft is the output to the front axle. Gear-to-gear transfer cases, in most cases, have two speeds. The first four-wheel drive low is a gear reduction that is usually around two to one (2:1). The second gear in the transfer case is a direct drive. The gears are engaged by sliding collars or synchronizers to lock the gears to the shaft. Neutral is accomplished when neither gear collar is locking a gear in place.

- Vacuum actuators (Usually used to connect and disconnect the front-drive axle when two-wheel drive is selected)

TWO-WHEEL-DRIVE OPERATION When the transfer case controls are in two-wheel drive, the front differential assembly is disconnected from the transfer case. This disconnection is usually accomplished by disconnecting one of the drive axles. The disconnect mechanism in the front axle

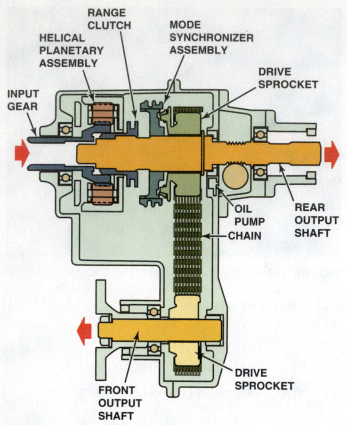

FIGURE 15–16 Two-wheel-drive/high-range torque flow in a NV231 transfer case. The sliding range clutch is shifted to the forward position by the range lever and fork, which connects the input gear to the output shaft and rear axle. The mode synchronizer sleeve is moved out of engagement from the drive sprocket to remove torque from the front axle.

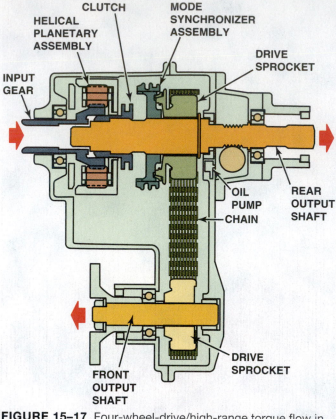

FIGURE 15–17 Four-wheel-drive/high-range torque flow in a NV231 transfer case. The range clutch position remains the same as in two-wheel drive/high-range, but the synchronizer sleeve is moved rearward and engages the drive sprocket clutch teeth. This action connects the drive sprocket to the rear output shaft, thereby applying equal torque to both front and rear output shafts.

and a synchronizer assembly in the transfer case combine to remove torque for the front wheels. ● **SEE FIGURE 15–16.**

FOUR-WHEEL-DRIVE OPERATION
To achieve four-wheel drive, two things must occur.

1. A synchronizer assembly connects the torque from the engine to the front driveshaft in the transfer case.

2. The drive axles must be connected to allow the torque from the front differential.

Full-time 4WD or all-wheel drive (AWD) transfer cases maintain constant power to both the front and rear axles and include a center (interaxle) differential, between the front and rear output shafts.

A chain drive transfer case uses the following parts:

1. An input shaft, which is connected to the output shaft of the transmission.

2. In a planetary gear set transfer case, the input shaft is connected to the sun gear.

3. The output shaft to the rear wheels are connected directly to the output shaft through the range clutch if it is in four-wheel drive high range. In Low range, the torque flows though the planetary gear set and exits through the ring gear.

4. In two-wheel drive, engine torque is sent directly to the output shaft and on to the rear drive axle assembly.

5. In four-wheel drive mode, engine torque is sent through a drive sprocket and a wide chain to the driven sprocket and front output shaft. ● **SEE FIGURE 15–17.**

OIL PUMP
Most transfer cases also use an oil pump that is driven from the output shaft and supplies the lubricating oil throughout the assembly. The lubricating oil is usually

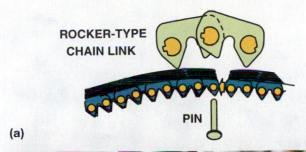

ROCKER-TYPE CHAIN LINK

PIN

(a)

BLACK LINK

(b)

FIGURE 15–18 (a) A pin and rocker-type chain, which is also called a *rocker joint-type* chain, is used in transfer cases because of low noise and high efficiency, which improves fuel economy. (b) A rocker pin-type chain used in a transfer case. The black link faces upward and is used as an indicator to the service technician to help insure that the chain is replaced in the same side up when it is reassembled.

 FREQUENTLY ASKED QUESTION

What Is a Rocker Pin Chain?

The type of chain used in transfer cases is usually assembled from pin links and chain links and is called "**rocker pin**" type chain. The chain links are what contact the teeth of the sprocket and not the pins as with a roller-type chain. ● **SEE FIGURE 15–18**.

---

automatic transmission fluid but can be a special fluid designed for the assembly. Always check service information for the type of fluid used. ● **SEE FIGURE 15–19**.

MANUAL SHIFT ON-THE-FLY SYSTEMS Manual Shift on-the-Fly (MSOF) transfer cases have a selector lever on floor transmission hump and may also have:

OIL PUMP PICKUP SCREEN

OIL PUMP

FIGURE 15–19 The oil pump is driven by the rear output shaft and is removed with the rear part of the case.

- Two sealed automatic front axle locking hubs or
- Two manual front axle hub selectors of "LOCK" and "UNLOCK" or "FREE."

To engage the four-wheel-drive system into four-wheel-drive high range, the vehicle must be moving at a low speed, usually under 50 MPH (80 km/h). To engage the four-wheel-drive low setting, the vehicle must be stopped and the transmission must be shifted to neutral, and then the four-wheel-drive low can be selected.

ELECTRONIC TRANSFER CASES

PURPOSE AND FUNCTION The transfer case motor/encoder assembly is an electric motor which is used to shift the transfer case from two-wheel high to four-wheel high and can also make a range change between four-wheel high and four-wheel low. These are used on vehicles that feature **electronic shift-on-the-fly (ESOF)** transfer cases. In an electronic transfer case the operation of the range clutch and mode synchronizer assembly is controlled by the motor/encoder assembly. ● **SEE FIGURE 15–20**.

MOTOR/ENCODER ASSEMBLY Part of the motor assembly is an *encoder*, which is a position sensor that sends the actual position of the transfer case shift shaft to the **transfer case control module (TCCM)**. The TCCM uses the data from the input and output speed sensor to determine

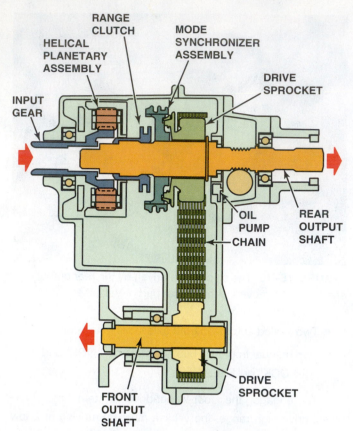

FIGURE 15–20 Four-wheel-drive/low-range torque flow in a NV231 transfer case. The mode synchronizer assembly remains engaged and the range clutch is moved to the rearward position. The annulus (ring) gear is fixed to the case and the input (sun) gear drives the pinion gears, which walk around the stationary annulus gear and drive the planetary carrier and output shaft at a speed lower than the input gear.

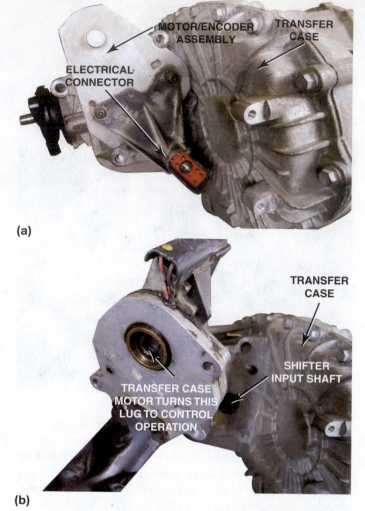

FIGURE 15–21 (a) Electronically controlled transfer cases use an electric motor to make the mode and range shifts. (b) The motor being removed from the transfer case. The assembly includes the DC motor as well as the feedback sensor so the TCCM "knows" the location of the motor.

when to shift the transfer case to four-wheel drive. If the rear wheels start to slip, the TCCM commands the motor/encoder assemble to make the mode shift. The TCCM also sends a signal to the front axle motor or actuator to engage the front axle when the transfer case is engaging four-wheel high mode. ● SEE FIGURE 15–21.

The DC electric motor usually has an attached encoder ring or sensor that indicates the position of the transfer case motor to the TCCM. Some AWD vehicles use *smart transfer cases* that automatically lock up or drive both or either output shaft as needed for the driving conditions. The speed sensors are used to detect unequal wheel speeds and tire slippage and apply the front axle actuator so that engine power is applied to the front and rear drive axles. ● SEE FIGURE 15–22.

TORQUE SPLIT Planetary differentials are designed to split torque unevenly so that 35% goes to the front axle and the remaining 65% goes to the rear axle. The exact ratio or

torque split depends on the gear ratios in the planetary gear set. This makes the vehicle drive like a rear-wheel-drive vehicle. Some transfer cases use a hydraulically applied internal clutch much like the Quadra-Trac II (Hydra-Lok) limited slip differential to connect the front and rear drive axles. The amount of slip of this clutch determines the torque split.

Some AWD vehicles produced by Audi, Land Rover, Lexus, Toyota, and VW use a Torsen® differential for the center differential. Torsen center differentials are designed with a torque bias ratio of 2.5:1 to 3.5:1. The two driveshafts can operate at different speeds without spin-out problems at the front or rear and smooth turning action.

Most non-planetary center differentials, however, split torque equally. It is possible, though, to lift one wheel and not get enough torque to the other three wheels to move the vehicle. ● SEE FIGURE 15–23.

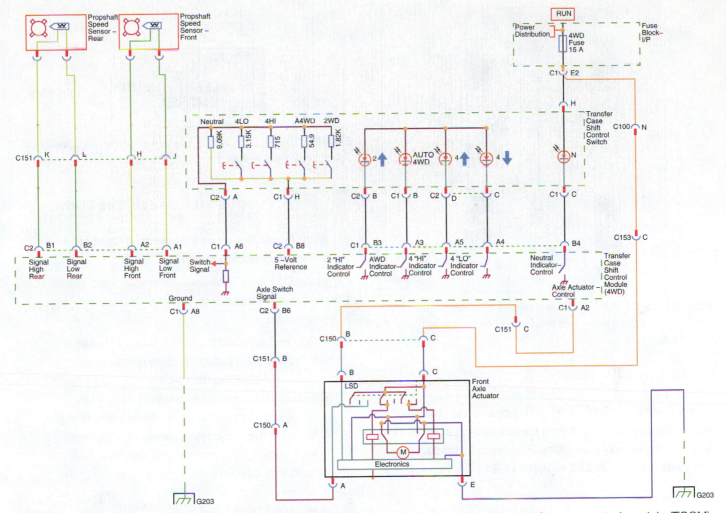

FIGURE 15–22 The driveshaft (prop shaft) speed sensor signals (upper left) are sent to the transfer case control module (TCCM), which then controls the operation of the front axle actuator.

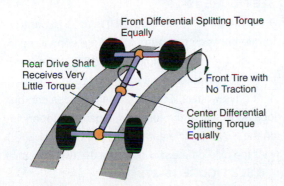

FIGURE 15–23 If the center and front differential split torque equally, an AWD vehicle can become stuck when one wheel loses traction.

NOTE: Some vehicles are equipped with a center differential lockout. With the lockout, at least both drive-shafts and one wheel at each end will be driven.

TECH TIP

Equal Tire Sizes

Full-time four-wheel drive (4WD) and AWD vehicles must have four equal-diameter tires. Unequal diameters produce different axle speeds, and this will cause excessive wear at the drive axle or center differential. A viscous coupling at the center differential will not last if it has to operate constantly.

POWER TRANSFER UNIT

PURPOSE AND FUNCTION   4WD/AWD vehicles that are based on FWD vehicles integrate a **power transfer unit (PTU)** into the transaxle. In its simplest form, a PTU is just a right angle gear set.

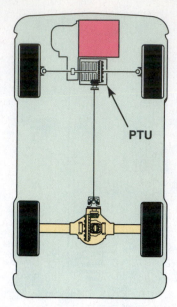

FIGURE 15–24 A PTU has an interaxle differential that drives the front axle differential and the transfer of torque to the rear driveshaft.

PARTS AND OPERATION   This gear set is driven by the front differential, and it can drive the rear driveshaft at the same speed as the front wheels. Some PTUs include a sliding gear or multiplate coupling. ● **SEE FIGURE 15–24**.

COUPLERS AND TORQUE BIAS DEVICES

PURPOSE AND FUNCTION   Couplers are connected in series with other drivetrain members and are used to transfer torque, much like a clutch. They can be active, meaning that they are applied only when needed, or passive and work only after a certain amount of slip has occurred. Torque bias devices use similar components but are connected to the drivetrain in parallel instead of in series.

ELECTROMAGNETIC CLUTCH COUPLER   Active couplers used in on-demand systems are dynamic and are applied as needed. These are usually multiplate clutches that are applied by the speed differential between the input and

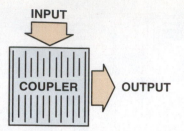

FIGURE 15–25 Coupler is used to transmit engine torque to the drive wheels in series.

? FREQUENTLY ASKED QUESTION

What Is the Difference Between a Coupler and a Torque Biasing Device?

Both of these devices are used in many four-wheel-drive and all-wheel-drive vehicles. The major differences include:

- Couplers are used to control torque between and input and output shafts and are connected in series. ● **SEE FIGURE 15–25**.
- A coupler, such as a viscous coupler, is commonly used in the rear driveshaft to transmit engine torque to the rear drive wheels on a front-wheel-drive vehicle equipped for all-wheel-drive (AWD) operation. Couplers can be located at any of the following locations depending on the exact vehicle and application.
  - Transfer case
  - Power transfer unit
  - Half shafts
  ● **SEE FIGURE 15–26**.
- A **torque biasing device (TBD)** is used to control torque between two outputs and are connected in parallel. The most commonly used TBDs are used to control the torque in a drive axle to the left and right drive wheels. Torque biasing devices can be located at any of the following locations depending on the exact vehicle and application.
  - At the axle differential between the two axle shafts. ● **SEE FIGURE 15–27**.
  - At the center differential between the front and rear driveshafts.
- Both devices may use the same or similar components but how they are connected and used in the system is what separates them from each other.

FIGURE 15–26 A viscous coupling. Note that the unit is attached to the output shaft between the transfer case (or transaxle) and the rear differential. A typical viscous coupling in a sealed unit is serviced as a complete assembly.

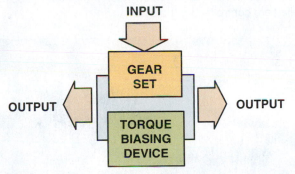

FIGURE 15–27 A TBD is used to control torque to the drive wheel in parallel.

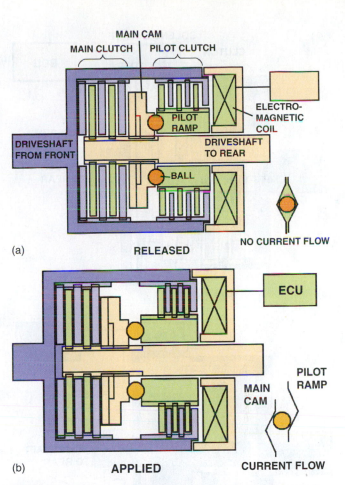

(a)   **RELEASED**

(b)   **APPLIED**

FIGURE 15–28 An electromagnetic coupler in a released (a) and applied (b) condition. When the ECU energizes the electromagnet, the pilot clutch applies to cause a speed differential between the pilot ramp and main cam, and this applies the multiplate clutch.

output shafts. In one design, an electromagnetic clutch applies a pilot clutch that in turn applies the main clutch that transfers power. ● SEE FIGURE 15–28.

Another design uses a solenoid to control hydraulic pressure from a gerotor hydraulic pump and the fluid pressure applies the clutch when needed. ● SEE FIGURE 15–29.

These systems are called:

- *Torque Management*
- *Interactive Torque Management System*
- *Intelligent AWD System*
- *Active Torque Dynamics*

An electromagnetic coil is used to engage a multiplate clutch to transfer torque to the rear drive axle. Electrical current to the clutch is controlled by a 4WD electronic control module (ECM) that uses the wheel speeds sensors. If the front-wheel speed is excessively greater than the rear-wheel speed, the ECM applies the clutch to drive the rear wheels. The rear wheels are driven only when necessary to improve traction.

ELECTRO-HYDRAULIC COUPLER The Haldex all-wheel-drive system is currently being used on several domestic and European vehicles. The system uses a coupling that can be installed onto the rear drive axle to connect it to the FWD system. The coupling uses a multidisc clutch that is applied hydraulically when there is an excessive speed difference between the input and output shafts.

Hydraulic pressure to apply the clutch is generated in the clutch when the input and output shafts turn at different speeds. When there is no speed difference, there will be no pressure. The clutch application rate is controlled electronically by software designed for the particular vehicle. ● SEE FIGURE 15–30.

FRONT DRIVE AXLES

PURPOSE AND FUNCTION The purpose and function of the front drive axle is to transfer engine torque to the front wheels. Unlike the rear drive axle, the front drive axle has to be designed to steer the front wheels as well as transmit engine torque.

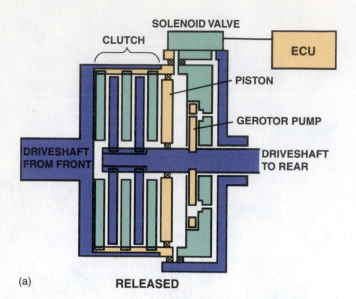

(a) **RELEASED**

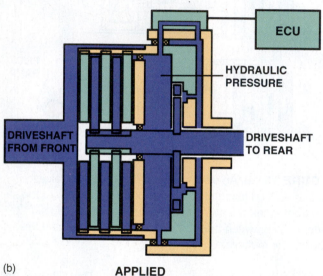

(b) **APPLIED**

FIGURE 15–29 A hydraulic coupler in a released (a) and applied (b) condition. An input shaft–output shaft speed differential will cause the pump to develop hydraulic press, and when the ECU energizes the solenoid valve, the pressure will apply the multiplate clutch.

PARTS AND OPERATION
Except for the outer ends of the axle housing, which allow steering, most early 4WD utility vehicles have a solid front drive axle housing, which is essentially the same as the one used in the rear.

Some of the 4WD vehicles, based on a rear-wheel-drive platform, use a RWD drive axle that is simply rotated so the drive pinion points toward the rear. Axles using reverse-cut gears can be identified by a high-mounted pinion shaft.

FRONT AXLES
Most front drive axles use an **open design** with ball joints for the steering pivots and a Cardan U-joint.
● **SEE FIGURE 15–31.**

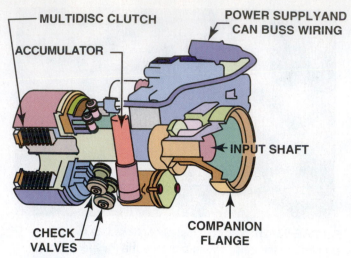

FIGURE 15–30 The Haldex system uses hydraulic pressure to apply the clutch, which can be created as soon as there is a speed differential between the input and output shafts. Hydraulic pressure and speed at which the clutch will be applied are controlled by the ECU.

(a)

(b)

FIGURE 15–31 (a) A double Cardan U-joint used on the output driveshaft from the transfer case to the front differential assembly. (b) A Cardan-type U-joint at the front drive wheels on a Jeep Wrangler.

FIGURE 15–32 Constant velocity (CV) joints are used on the front axles of many four-wheel-drive vehicles like this Chevrolet Blazer.

Some 4WDs mount the differential carrier to the vehicle frame or body and use a fully independent suspension. These designs usually use constant velocity-type joints. ● **SEE FIGURE 15–32**.

DRIVE AXLE/WHEEL DISCONNECT SYSTEMS

PURPOSE AND FUNCTION Some front drive axle assemblies include a feature that allows disconnecting one of the axle shafts. As the vehicle is driven, the wheels will drive the axles, differential, and driveshaft. A collar is shifted to connect or disconnect the two parts of the shaft. Either a vacuum or electric shift motor is used for this with the controls being activated by shifting the transfer case into or out of 4WD. ● **SEE FIGURE 15–33**.

When the transfer case is placed in two-wheel drive, the vacuum is applied to the other side of the diaphragm and the shift collar moves, unlocking the front axles.

The transfer case can disconnect the power from the driveshaft to only one of the drive axles at a time.

- The front axle of RWD-based vehicles
- The rear axle of vehicles based on FWD designs

The wheels of the disconnected axle will still drive the axle shaft and gears as well as the driveshaft, causing unnecessary wear and a decrease in fuel economy (about 0.5 mpg). ● **SEE FIGURE 15–34**.

PARTS AND OPERATION Some 4WD vehicles are equipped with special hubs that can be manually operated to lock or unlock the power flow. An **integrated wheel end disconnect** system is used to connect or disconnect the outboard CV joint with the wheel hub. This is controlled by a 4WD electronic control so that the wheel ends connect when 4WD is engaged and disconnect when shifted back to 2WD. A coupler, which resembles a synchronizer sleeve, is used to connect the CV joint with the wheel hub. The coupler is released by vacuum and engaged by a wave spring. Vacuum remains at the release piston during 2WD operation. A vacuum loss will cause the wheel ends to engage and if the system should fail, 4WD engages. The engine intake manifold provides the vacuum, which is controlled by the vacuum control valve. The control valve is controlled by the mode switch.

CONTINUOUS VACUUM LOCKING HUBS A continuous vacuum locking hub system is similar to a conventional manual locking hub except that a vacuum diaphragm applies the force to the clutch ring into engagement. When the transfer case is shifted into two-wheel drive, the vacuum is released from the hub assembly. This then causes the clutch ring to slide out of engagement. This system requires that all of the vacuum seals be leak free so that the hubs receive a continuous vacuum for proper operation.

PULSE VACUUM LOCKING HUBS Similar to the continuous vacuum system, the pulse vacuum system uses vacuum to engage or disengage the hubs. A continuous supply of vacuum is not required to operate this type of hub disconnect system. Two different levels of vacuum are used to engage and disengage the hubs. The vacuum is applied unto the hub engages or disengages, and then the vacuum is released.

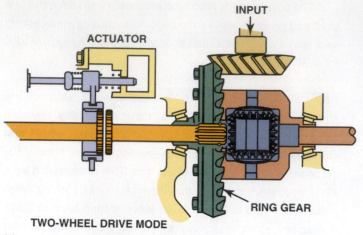

ACTUATOR

INPUT

RING GEAR

TWO-WHEEL DRIVE MODE

(a)

FIGURE 15–33 (a) When one axle shaft is disconnected, both front wheels can rotate independently, reducing excessive tire wear. (b) In four-wheel-drive mode, vacuum is applied to the front part and the opposite side is vented to atmospheric pressure retracting the shift motor stem. The shift fork and collar move into engagement with both axle shaft gears. Engine torque from the front differential can now be applied to both front axles.

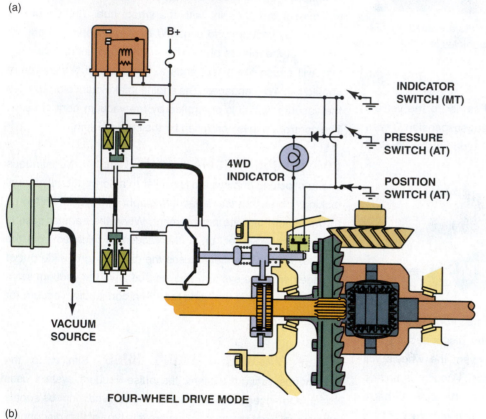

B+

INDICATOR
SWITCH (MT)

PRESSURE
SWITCH (AT)

4WD
INDICATOR

POSITION
SWITCH (AT)

VACUUM
SOURCE

FOUR-WHEEL DRIVE MODE

(b)

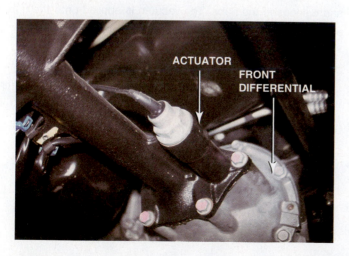

ACTUATOR
FRONT
DIFFERENTIAL

FIGURE 15–34 A General Motors sport utility vehicle front axle showing the electric axle disconnect actuator.

1 The vacuum hubs on this Ford four-wheel-drive truck are leaking and need to be resealed.

2 View of the hub assembly with the wheel removed.

3 The disc brake caliper is removed and supported to prevent causing damage to the brake hose.

4 The outside hub and hub clip are removed.

5 The inner clip is removed.

6 The disc brake rotor is removed.

CONTINUED ▶

7 The caliper support bracket is being removed.

8 The vacuum hose to the wheel hub assembly is disconnected.

9 The wheel hub assembly is removed and set aside.

10 The backside view of the hub assembly.

11 The vacuum part of the hub is being driven out from the backside.

12 The drive axle shaft is removed through the steering knuckle.

13 The old seal is removed.

14 The sealing surfaced is cleaned.

15 The new seal and the driver needed to install the seal.

16 After lubricating the inner seal, the seal is installed on the axle hub.

17 The outer part of the seal is lubricated with engine oil, and then the shaft is reinstalled.

18 The hub assembly is installed.

CONTINUED ▶

19 The caliper mounting bracket is installed and the fasteners torqued to factory specifications.

20 The disc brake caliper is installed and the fasteners are also torqued to factory specifications. After installing the wheel/tire assembly and checking for proper operation, this repair has been completed.

SUMMARY

1. Early 4WD vehicles were based on front engine, RWD vehicles. Many of today's 4WD/AWD vehicles are based on front engine FWD vehicles.
2. A transfer case or power transfer unit drives the second axle.
3. AWD transfer cases/PTUs can include a differential, viscous coupler, or electromechanical clutch to control torque to the front and rear drive axles.
4. Transfer cases can use a gear set or silent chain.
5. Some transfer cases include a planetary gear set.
6. A front drive axle has outboard U-joints or CV joints to allow steering.
7. Front wheel hubs can be disconnected using a mechanical, automatic, or vacuum operation.

REVIEW QUESTIONS

1. Why must there be a center differential in a four-wheel-drive vehicle that is used on hard pavement?
2. What is the difference between a mode shift and a range shift?
3. How can a four-wheel-drive vehicle get stuck if one or more wheels are on a slippery surface?
4. How is front/rear torque split using a planetary gear–type center differential?

CHAPTER QUIZ

1. In 4 × 4, the first 4 refers to _____.
   a. Four-wheel drive
   b. Four wheels on the vehicle
   c. Four speed transfer case
   d. Four speed transmission

2. When a vehicle turns a corner, what is true about the four wheel travel?
   a. Each wheel travels a different distance
   b. The two right side wheels turn the same distance
   c. The two left side wheels turn the same distance
   d. Both b and c are correct

3. What type of four-wheel-drive system does not include a center (interaxle) differential?
   a. All-wheel Drive (AWD)
   b. Full-time four-wheel drive
   c. Part-time four-wheel drive
   d. None of the above

4. Low range in a transfer case is about what ratio?
   a. 2:1 to about 3:1
   b. 8:1
   c. 10:1
   d. 12:1 or higher

5. What can occur if a part-time four-wheel-drive vehicle is driven on hard pavement in four-wheel drive?
   a. The vehicle will shake and shutter as engine torque is applied to the drive wheels
   b. The vehicle will slip and hop over the pavement
   c. The vehicle will experience driveline vibrations and damage to driveshafts, U-joints, and bearings
   d. All of the above can occur

6. What type of chain is commonly used in transfer case?
   a. Roller chain
   b. Double roller chain
   c. Rocker pin
   d. Any of the above depending on application

7. To engage the four-wheel-drive system into four-wheel-drive high range on manual shift on-the-fly (MSOF) transfer case, the vehicle must be moving at about what speed?
   a. Completely stopped
   b. Low speed usually under 50 MPH (80 km/h)
   c. Less than 10 MPH (16 km/h)
   d. At any speed

8. A transfer case used with a transaxle is called a _____.
   a. A coupler device
   b. A torque biasing device
   c. A power transfer unit (PTU)
   d. A torque split unit

9. What type of unit is used as a center differential inside a transfer case?
   a. Planetary gear set
   b. Bevel gear differential
   c. Viscous coupling
   d. Any of the above

10. Most transfer cases are lubricated using _____.
    a. An internal oil pump
    b. Splash lubrication
    c. An external pump
    d. Any of the above depending on the application

SERVICE

LEARNING OBJECTIVES

After studying this chapter, the reader should be able to:

1. Prepare for the ASE certification test for content area "F" (Four-Wheel Drive Component Diagnosis and Repair).

2. Diagnose four-wheel-drive-related problems.

3. Explain the procedure for diagnosing four-wheel drive and transfer case faults.

4. Discuss how to test a four-wheel-drive vehicle using a scan tool.

5. Explain the procedure for front hub removal and replacement.

6. Explain the procedure for transfer case removal and overhaul.

KEY TERMS

Double-lip seal 314

Technical Service Bulletins (TSBs) 310

FOUR-WHEEL-DRIVE PROBLEM DIAGNOSIS

PROCEDURE   The process of diagnosing faults or concerns in four-wheel drives and transfer cases involves the following eight steps.

STEP 1   Verify the customer concern.

STEP 2   Perform a visual inspection.

STEP 3   Check for any stored diagnostic trouble codes (DTCs) and technical service bulletins (TSBs).

STEP 4   Check scan tool data for sensor values and bidirectional control operation (if available).

STEP 5   Check electrical switches and actuators using a digital multi-meter.

STEP 6   Follow service information pinpoint tests to determine the root cause.

STEP 7   Perform the needed repair.

STEP 8   Verify the repair.

VERIFY CUSTOMER CONCERN

VERIFY CUSTOMER CONCERN   The first step is to verify the customer concern. The customer should be asked the following questions in an effort to determine as much about the problem as possible.

- What exactly seems to be the concern? (Ask the customer to be as detailed as possible.)
- When did the problem first appear?
- Is there a problem between two-wheel drive and four-wheel drive (mode change)?
- Is there a problem going between 4-High to 4-Low (range change)?
- Under what conditions do the symptoms occur? (Do they occur first thing in the morning? After the vehicle has been driven for a while?)
- Describe under what driving conditions the problem is noticed, such as when accelerating or while coasting to a stop or some other condition.
- Has the vehicle been serviced recently, such as a fluid change?

Operate the vehicle and drive it under all conditions and in both modes (two-wheel drive and four-wheel drive) and in both ranges (four-wheel high and four-wheel low).

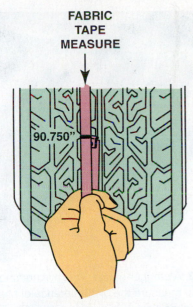

FIGURE 16–1 The measuring tape wrapped around the tire shows the circumference is 90 3/4 inch. The other three tires should measure close to the same, usually within ¼ inch in circumference.

VISUAL INSPECTION

EQUAL SIZE TIRES   All tires of a full-time four-wheel-drive or all-wheel-drive vehicle must be within a 1/16 inch (1.6 mm) tread depth of each other. Always check that all tires are:

- The exact same size
- The same brand (different brands even if the same size can vary in the actual diameter and width of the tire).
- The same tread depth within 2/32 inch (1/16 inch).
- The same inflation pressure within 2 PSI for best results

MEASURING TIRE CIRCUMFERENCE   Tire circumference can be checked by wrapping a cloth tape measure around the tread. ● **SEE FIGURE 16–1.**

A stagger gauge can also be used to measure tire circumference. ● **SEE FIGURE 16–2.**

VISUALLY CHECK DRIVELINE   Hoist vehicle safely and perform a thorough visual inspection of the driveline including the following:

- Driveshaft for damage or mud that could affect the balance of the driveshaft

FIGURE 16–2 A stagger gauge, which is commonly used by racing teams to measure the circumference of tires, is a sliding caliper-type tool calibrated to read in circumference.

FIGURE 16–3 Red rust stain is an indication that metal-to-metal contact is occurring and usually indicates that the part is worn and needs to be replaced such as in this U-joint.

 REAL WORLD FIX

The Case of the Noisy Chevrolet Pickup Truck

A GMC pickup (42,000 mi) had a noise in 4WD and would not shift out of 4WD until coasting in second gear. A test using an electronic noise detecting device such as Chassis Ears®, indicated the whining noise to be coming from the transfer case. A careful check of tire size showed 5/32 inch deeper tread on the rear tires, and a check of tire circumference showed 98 inch at the front and 99 inch at the rear. Replacement of the worn front tires fixed this problem. Apparently, the mix-matched tire sizes caused the drivetrain to bind, which prevented the transfer case to lock up and not be able to be shifted correctly.

- U-joints for damage or looseness (check for "rust dust").
  ● **SEE FIGURE 16–3**.
- Engine and transmission mounts for damage
- Check electrical and mechanical connections to the transfer case
- Check for leaks at the transmission or transfer case

GEAR OIL LEVEL AND CONDITION Most transfer cases and power transfer units have a gear oil-level plug in the side of the case for checking the oil level. ● **SEE FIGURE 16–4**.

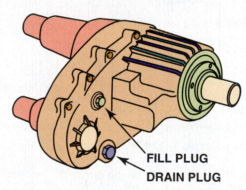

FILL PLUG
DRAIN PLUG

FIGURE 16–4 Always check the fluid level and condition as one of the first items to check when diagnosing a four-wheel-drive customer concern.

As in a manual transmission, the gear oil-level should be at the bottom of the plug opening. Always use the lubricant specified by the manufacturer. The fluid used in transfer cases can include:

- Automatic transmission fluid (ATF)—check service information for the exact type of ATF to use.
- SAE 80W-90 gear oil—check service information for the exact viscosity and API rating required.
- Special specific transfers case fluid. ● **SEE FIGURE 16–5**.

Dirty or discolored fluid gear oil should be replaced by draining the old oil and filling the transfer case with new oil of the correct type to the proper level. Many transfer cases include a drain plug so an oil change is relatively easy.

FIGURE 16–5 Chrysler recommends the use of a specific transfer case lubricant.

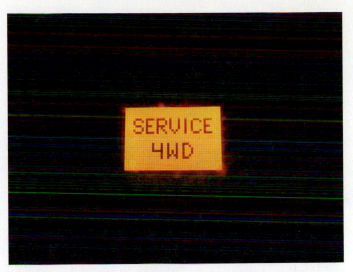

FIGURE 16–6 If the "SERVICE 4WD" warning light is on, check service information for the exact procedures to follow.

CAUTION: Some vehicles use a transfer case made from magnesium with an aluminum oil-level plug. The plug has a small head, and it tends to seize. A wrench will easily slip and round off the small plug head. It is recommended that if the plug does not unscrew using a reasonable amount of force, then heat the case area surrounding the plug. Use a hot-air device and _DO NOT_ use a torch because the magnesium case can ignite and cause a serious fire.

REAL WORLD FIX

The Case of the Skipping Chevrolet Minivan

An AWD Chevrolet SUV (38,000 mi) had an odd skip-miss feeling during acceleration. All the engine management features had been checked, and it appeared the engine was running properly. Tire circumferences were checked, and they were within 1/8" of each other. The transfer case was drained and refilled with the proper fluid, but this did not help.

A second transfer case fluid change was recommended, and this fixed the problem. This transfer case can have a stick/slip problem, similar to a limited slip differential. Apparently, the second fluid change caused the clutch plates to work normally.

TECH TIP

Is the Problem Inside or Outside the Unit?

The purpose of the diagnosis is to determine the cause of the problem.

- Is it due to a fault with the controls (electrical or mechanical)?
- Is it due to the transmission or some other drive-train component instead of the transfer case?

FOUR-WHEEL-DRIVE DIAGNOSTIC PROCEDURES

WARNING LIGHTS   Often in electronic-controlled transfer cases, the controller will light a separate warning lamp to notify that the control system has detected a problem with the system. ● **SEE FIGURE 16–6**.

SCAN TOOLS   Scan tools are the most important tools for any diagnostic work on all vehicles. Scan tools can be divided into the following three basic categories:

1. **Factory scan tools**. These are the scan tools required by all dealers that sell and service a specific brand of vehicle.

    Examples of factory scan tools include the following:
    - General Motors—TECH 2. ● **SEE FIGURE 16–7**.
    - Ford—WDS (Worldwide Diagnostic System) and IDS (Integrated Diagnostic Software)
    - Chrysler—DRB-III, Star Scan, or WiTECH
    - Honda—HDS or Master Tech
    - Toyota—Master Tech and Tech Stream

    All factory scan tools are designed to provide bidirectional capability, which allows the service technician the

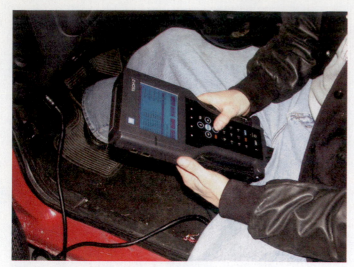

FIGURE 16–7 A TECH 2 scan tool is the factory scan tool used on General Motors vehicles and can be used to diagnose four-wheel-drive concerns.

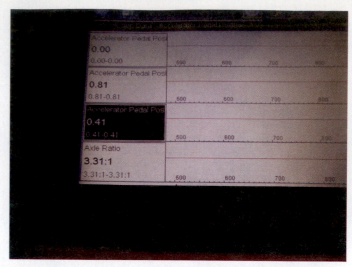

FIGURE 16–8 A Snap-on Solus scan tool is being used to troubleshoot a vehicle. This scan tool can be used on most makes and models of vehicles and is capable of diagnosing other computer systems in the vehicles such as the antilock braking system (ABS) and four-wheel-drive systems.

opportunity to operate components using the scan tool, thereby confirming that the component is able to work when commanded. Also, all factory scan tools are capable of displaying all factory parameters.

2. **Aftermarket scan tools**. These scan tools are designed to function on more than one brand of vehicle. Examples of aftermarket scan tools include the following:

   - Snap-on (various models, including the Ethos, Modis, and Solus). ● **SEE FIGURE 16–8.**
   - OTC (various models, including Pegasus, Genisys, TOUCH, and Task Master).
   - AutoEnginuity and other programs that use a laptop or handheld computer for display.

   While many aftermarket scan tools can display most if not all of the parameters of the factory scan tool, there can be a difference when trying to troubleshoot some faults.

3. **Global scan tools**. Global (generic) scan tools are the lowest-priced scan tools and they are designed to only be able to retrieve emission-related data as per the SAE standard J1979. The vehicle diagnostic trouble codes (DTCs) and data can be acquired by looking at the global (generic) part of the PCM and does not need to have the vehicle information entered into the scan tool. All global scan tools display only emission-related data stream information. The data displayed on this type of scan tool will be emission-related only and will NOT display faults or codes for transmission or transfer cases.

FIGURE 16–9 Connecting a scan tool to the data link connector (DLC) located under the dash on this vehicle.

HOW TO USE A SCAN TOOL   In order to get the most from a scan tool, the technician should read, understand, and follow the operating instructions. To use a scan tool perform the following steps:

STEP 1   Locate the data link connector (DLC). This 16-pin connector is usually located under the dash on the driver's side. It can be located in the center console and may be covered by a panel that can be removed without the use of tools. Check service information for the exact location of the DLC for the vehicle being serviced.

STEP 2   Connect the scan tool to the DLC. ● **SEE FIGURE 16–9.**

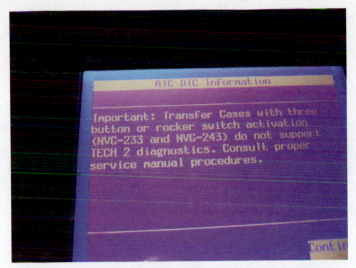

FIGURE 16–10 Not all scan tools are capable of communicating transfer case faults. Check service information for the exact procedures to follow.

DTC	DESCRIPTION
C0300	Rear propeller shaft speed sensor circuit
C0305	Front propeller shaft speed sensor circuit
C0308	Motor A/B circuit, short to ground
C0309	Motor A/B circuit, short to voltage
C0310	Motor A/B circuit, open circuit
C0315	Module ground circuit
C0323	Lock solenoid circuit, open circuit
C0324	Lock solenoid circuit, shorted to voltage
C0327	Encoder feed circuit
C0367	Front axle control circuit, shorted actuator or short to voltage
C0374	Shift control module unable to control slip
C0376	Front and rear propeller shaft speeds greater than 20% difference
C0387	Unable to complete shift as commanded
C0550	Failed shift control module test

CHART 16–1

Typical C-type DTCs associated with faults in the transfer case system.

STEP 3 Turn the ignition key on (engine off). In most cases, the scan tool will come on automatically because the DLC has power and ground connections for the scan tool.

STEP 4 If using a factory or factory-level scan tool, select the vehicle you are scanning and enter the information requested on the screen such as:

- Year (tenth character of the VIN)
- Model (usually the fourth or fifth character of the VIN)
- Engine (usually the eighth character of the VIN)
- Any options that may be on the vehicle

STEP 5 Follow the on-screen instructions. Read and record any stored diagnostic trouble codes (DTCs). ● SEE FIGURE 16–10.

RETRIEVING DIAGNOSTIC TROUBLE CODES Most four-wheel-drive-related trouble codes will be "B" (body) codes, "C" (Chassis) codes, or "U" (network) codes. Global-type scan tools will not be able to access these codes. Codes used for the engine that are emission-related-type codes are "P" (powertrain) codes and do not associate with the transfer case faults except if the speed sensor is faulty.

CODES Most transfer case and four-wheel-drive B and C diagnostic trouble codes are for faults with the transfer case or communication faults between the transfer case the transfer case control module (TCM). For some sample "C" DTCs, ● SEE CHART 16–1.

DTC	DESCRIPTION
C0306 02	Motor A or B circuit shorted to ground
C0306 05	Motor A or B circuit shorted to voltage or open
C0321 01	Transfer case lock circuit shorted to ground
C0321 04	Transfer case lock circuit shorted to voltage or open
C0379 01	Front axle short to voltage
C0379 02	Front axle short to ground
C0379 04	Front axle open circuit

CHART 16–2

Typical DTCs with subcodes associated with faults in the transfer case system.

SUBCODES Sometimes the diagnostic trouble code will also have a two-digit subcode that gives additional information to help the technician find the fault. For example, B0770 DTC indicates that there is a fault in the "AWD Indicator circuit." However, with the addition of a two-digit subcode, the cause that set the code is enhanced such as:

- B0770 01—AWD indicator circuit shorted to voltage
- B0770 06—AWD indicator circuit shorted to ground or open

Note that the last two numbers added at the end of the code gives additional information as to why the code was set. For some sample transfer case-related DTC codes with subcodes, ● SEE CHART 16–2.

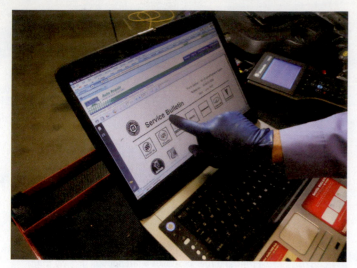

FIGURE 16–11 After checking for stored diagnostic trouble codes (DTCs), the wise technician checks service information for any technical service bulletins that may relate to the vehicle being serviced.

TECH TIP

Ask the Driver

A diagnostic trouble code for a fault with the control switch can be set if the driver switches positions rapidly. This is a common situation when the driver is trying to engage four-wheel-drive and when it does not go into four-wheel-drive immediately, moves the switch back to two-wheel drive and then back into four-wheel-drive. Therefore, if there is a diagnostic trouble code set for a fault in the switch and no fault is found, ask the driver if this might be the case.

	GM ROTARY SWITCH (5 VOLT)	GM PUSH BUTTON (5 VOLT)	GM PUSH BUTTON (8 VOLT)	FORD ROTARY SWITCH (12 VOLT)	FORD PUSH BUTTON (12 VOLT)	DODGE (RAM) (5 VOLT)
2WD	4.1 volts	2.0 volts	3.2 volts	7.5 volts	NA	2.1 volts
AUTO 4WD	3.3 volts	4.6 volts	7.5 volts	NA	1.8 volts	2.7 volts
4WD High	2.5 volts	3.0 volts	4.8 volts	5.5 volts	6.4 volts	3.5 volts
4WD Low	1.6 volts	1.5 volts	2.4 volts	3.7 volts	9.0 volts	4.1 volts
Neutral	0.8 volts	0.9 volts	1.2 volts	NA	NA	NA

CHART 16–3

Typical voltage readings that may be measured at the four-wheel-drive control switch with the key on, engine off (KOEO). Always check service information for the exact specifications and testing procedures for the vehicle being serviced.

EXAMPLE OF A "C" CODE A C0308 diagnostic trouble code will be set when the Transfer Case Control Module (TCCM) determines a short-to-ground in motor control circuit A or B. Once the C0308 code has been activated, all of the 4WD shifter positions will be inoperative and will cause the *SERVICE 4WD* light to turn on.

CHECK TECHNICAL SERVICE BULLETINS After checking for stored diagnostic trouble codes, **technical service bulletins (TSBs)** should be checked to see if there are any faults that are addressed for the codes that have been set. ● **SEE FIGURE 16–11**.

According to studies performed by automobile manufacturers, as many as 30% problem vehicles can be repaired following the information, suggestions, or replacement parts found in a service bulletin. DTCs must be known before searching for service bulletins, because bulletins often include information on solving problems that involve a stored diagnostic trouble code.

CHECK ELECTRICAL COMPONENTS

CHECKING SWITCHES AND CONTROLS When diagnosing a four-wheel-drive fault, use a scan tool or a digital multimeter and check for voltage at the switch for each position of the switch. Typical switches are multiplex switches that use a 5-volt reference and through resistors cause the mode selection signal to change voltage levels. ● **SEE FIGURE 16–12**.

TYPICAL VOLTAGE READINGS Service information should be checked for the exact voltage and resistance readings for the vehicle being serviced. Often the fault with the four-wheel-drive system can be found by checking the switch for proper operation. Then check to see that the proper voltage is being applied to the transfer case control module. For some typical readings, ● **SEE CHART 16–3**.

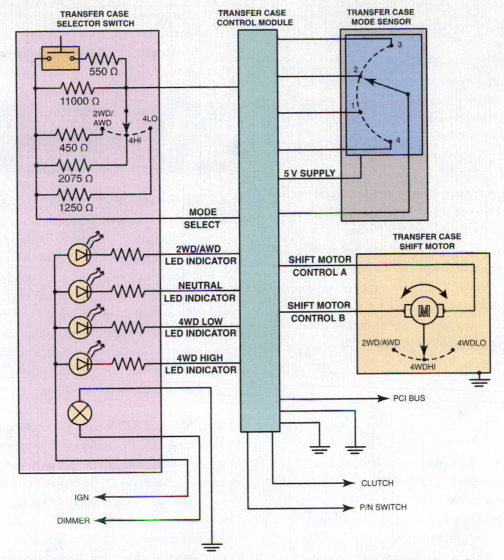

FIGURE 16–12 A typical schematic showing an electronic four-wheel-drive control switch and the wiring connections to the transfer case from the TCCM.

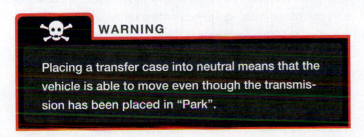

⚠ **WARNING**

Placing a transfer case into neutral means that the vehicle is able to move even though the transmission has been placed in "Park".

CHECKING FOR POWER AND GROUND AT MOTOR The shift control motor operates on 12 volts DC and ground that is routed through the TCCM. To change direction of the motor, the power and ground are reversed inside the TCCM, causing the motor to reverse directions. Most motor assemblies also include a feedback sensor that signals the TCCM the position of the motor. Check service information for the exact test procedures to follow. ● **SEE FIGURE 16–13.**

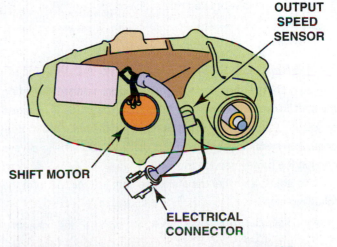

FIGURE 16–13 The voltage to the shift motor and the feedback signal voltage signals can often be tested at the electrical connector using a digital meter or by using a scan tool on some models.

What Is Driveline Windup?

A condition unique to 4WD that may be considered a problem by some vehicle owners is driveline windup. This condition, which should be avoided, occurs when a part-time 4WD vehicle is operated on dry pavement with the transfer case in 4WD and the front hubs engaged.

The different rotating speeds of the front and rear wheels will cause a bindup condition. The result will be a hop, skip, or bounce of the front or rear tires and transfer case locked in gear. This is also called *crow hopping*. Driveline windup can be removed by lifting a wheel off the ground or, more simply, by driving the vehicle in a circle in a direction opposite to what made the windup. With some electric-shifted transfer cases, windup can cause a delay in shifting out of 4WD.

The Case of the Broken Jeep

A Jeep Wrangler (73,500 mi) front axle would not engage. An inspection showed broken and brittle vacuum hoses, some falling off their connectors. The vacuum harness to the vacuum hubs was replaced, which did not fix the problem. However, after looking at a vacuum diagram, it was determined that a clogged vent could be the cause. A visual inspection revealed that the vent was plugged with mud. Cleaning this vent fixed this problem.

TRANSFER CASE SHIFT LINKAGE ADJUSTMENT

Manually shifted transfer cases include a provision for adjusting the shift linkage to ensure that the unit can be properly engaged or disengaged in the various lever positions. The actual adjustment will vary between the makes and models; always consult the proper service manual.

To adjust a typical transfer case shift linkage, perform the following steps:

STEP 1 Remove the shift boot to access the gearshift mechanism.

STEP 2 Place the lever in the correct position. Sometimes a spacer of a certain size is specified to position the lever properly.

STEP 3 Disconnect the linkage rod swivel/trunnion from the shift lever. It should slide freely in and out of the lever. If not, adjust the trunnion position so that it is a free fit in the lever hole.

FRONT HUB REMOVAL AND REPLACEMENT

NORMAL OPERATION Some automatic hubs will not disengage under certain conditions. These hubs are designed to engage automatically when the driving action of the front axles causes the internal cam to lock the hub.

With some vehicles, these hubs need to be released by shifting the transfer case to 2WD and driving in the opposite direction for at least 10 feet (3 m). If this is not done, the front hubs can remain engaged, which will cause front wheel rotation to drive the axle, differential, and opposite axle or both axles, ring and pinion gears, and driveshaft. This can produce a noise problem and unnecessary wear.

SERVICING LOCKING HUBS Locking front hubs should be cleaned periodically, especially if the vehicle has been driven under water or in dusty conditions. Most vehicle manufacturers recommend that the hubs be cleaned and lightly coated with grease at the same time the front wheel bearings are serviced. Check the service information for the exact procedure for the vehicle being serviced. Start the inspection of the front hubs by removing the cover plate. Many problems associated with locking hubs can be corrected by cleaning and lubricating the components. If noise is heard from the hubs, carefully inspect the inner components on both sides of the vehicle. A damaged part can cause noise in the hub on the other side. Service kits are often available for the hubs. These kits contain the gaskets, seals, and retaining rings necessary for installing the hubs correctly after wheel bearing or front brake work has been completed. ● **SEE FIGURE 16–14**.

TYPICAL PROCEDURE FOR REMOVAL Some front hubs are removed by removing the bolts at the wheel hubs and sliding them off the axle and hub. Other wheel hubs have an internal snap ring that secures the splined inner sleeve to the axle. These hubs require partial disassembly in order to remove this snap ring. Some front hubs are built entirely in the wheel hub so the wheel hub encloses the wheel bearings along with the locking mechanism. To remove the hub and rotor in these units, the locking mechanism must be removed to gain access to the wheel bearing locking and adjusting nuts.

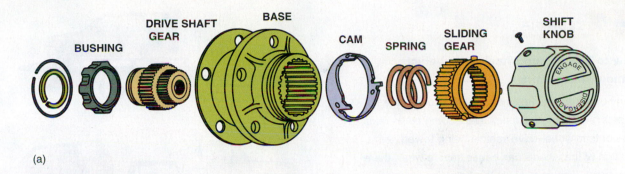

(a)

(b)

FIGURE 16–14 (a) An exploded view of a Dualmatic ® manual locking hub. (b) A Warn ® manual locking hub.

 REAL WORLD FIX

The Case of the Broken Kia

A Kia SUV (63,000 mi) came in with an inoperative 4WD. This vehicle uses vacuum-operated front hubs. Rotted flexible front hub vacuum lines and plugged steel vacuum lines were replaced, but this did not help. New hubs had previously been installed.

The technician found that a seal failure had apparently allowed vacuum to suck all of the grease out of the wheel bearing. This grease probably caused the plugged and rotted vacuum lines, and the grease loss caused wheel and spindle bearing failure. Replacement of the wheel bearings, spindle bearing, spindle, and seal with updated parts fixed this problem.

Always follow the instructions found in service information. Hub replacement is the reverse of the disassembly procedure.

TRANSFER CASE/ UNIT REMOVAL AND REPLACEMENT

TYPICAL REMOVAL PROCEDURE Most transfer cases used on utility vehicles and pickups are bolted to the rear of the transmission and can be removed by following the procedure

 REAL WORLD FIX

The Case of the Broken Chevrolet Suburban

The transfer case of a Chevrolet Suburban would jump into neutral when the vehicle hit a large dip or bump in the road. The vehicle could be shifted back into gear and driven.

After disassembly of the transfer case, it was found that the plastic shift fork inserts had broken off. Replacement of the shift forks fixed this problem.

described here. Service information instructions should be followed and usually includes the following steps.

STEP 1 Raise and support the vehicle securely on a hoist or jack stands.

STEP 2 Remove any skid plates and brace rods that block access to the transfer case.

STEP 3 Disconnect the front and rear driveshafts, being sure to make index marks so that the driveshafts can be reinstalled in the same position.

STEP 4 Disconnect the speed sensors and shift connectors and linkage, including encoder motor harness or other wiring connector. Most will come out with wiring attached, for removal on the bench.

STEP 5 Support the transfer case using a transmission jack, and remove the bolts that secure the transfer case to the transmission.

STEP 6 Slide the transfer case off the rear of the transmission, and remove it from the vehicle.

How to Tow a Four-Wheel-Drive Vehicle without Doing Harm

If any of the drive wheels are on the ground, the wheels are turning the axles. Depending on the exact type of four-wheel-drive vehicle being towed, this rotation of the wheels can cause severe wear; therefore, most experts suggest the following options:

- **Placing the vehicle on a flatbed or trailer.** This keeps all four wheels off the ground and is the safest method for transporting a four-wheel-drive (or all-wheel-drive) vehicle without doing any harm.

- **Hoisting the front wheels off the ground and placing the rear wheels on a dolly.** This procedure also keeps all wheels off the ground and therefore prevents any damage being done to the powertrain as a result of towing. Always check with vehicle specific information for exact towing procedures.

    If the transfer case has a neutral position, this will allow the vehicle to be towed with all four wheels on the ground. Always check the owner's manual or service information for the recommend method to use. ● **SEE FIGURE 16–15.**

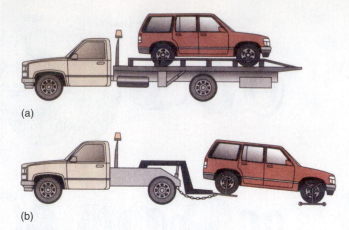

(a)

(b)

FIGURE 16–15 If a four-wheel-drive vehicle must be towed, it should be either on (a) a flatbed truck or (b) a dolly.

The Case of the Noisy Range Rover

A Land Rover, Range Rover (100,000 mi) has a ratcheting type noise that seems to be coming from the back seat. The transfer case was removed and disassembled. The chain appeared to be stretched because the new, replacement chain was about an inch shorter. Replacement of the drive chain fixed this problem.

REPLACEMENT OR REPAIR DECISION After the transfer case fault has been diagnosed and the fault is found to be inside the unit itself, the customer and repair shop have the following options:

1. Repair the unit and replace all needed parts.
2. Replace the unit with a used assembly from a wrecking (salvage) yard.
3. Replace the assembly with a remanufactured unit.
4. Replace with a new assembly.

Which option to use depends on the skills and talents of the shop personnel and the budget of the customer.

TRANSFER CASE INSTALLATION Installation of most transfer cases is the reverse of the removal procedure. Make sure that the gasket and seals between the transfer case and the transmission are in good condition and that the bolts are tightened to the correct torque. Some units use a **double-lip seal**, which is a seal that prevents fluid from moving to and from the transfer case to the transmission.

NOTE: If this double-lip seal where to leak, the fluid from the transfer case could be forced into the automatic transmission or the other way around. Therefore, if the fluid level is found to be low in one unit, always check the level in the other unit.

TRANSFER CASE/UNIT OVERHAUL

SERVICE PROCEDURE Because overhaul procedures and adjustments vary, service information instructions are required when repairing transfer cases. Most of the operations are the same as those used in transmissions, transaxles, and drive axles. The operations include:

- Disassembly
- Gear and bearing inspection
- Shift fork clearance and operation
- Chain wear check, shaft inspection
- Seal replacement
- Reassembly with adjustments for gear end float and bearing clearance or preload

NV-242 TRANSFER CASE SERVICE

1 The identification plate on the housing indicates the transfer case is a New Venture (New Process) model #242 and has a low-range gear ratio of 2.72:1.

2 Rear output shaft housing being removed.

3 Before the case can be separated, the bearing retaining snap ring must be removed using snap-ring pliers.

4 The lubricating oil pump is visible after the cover and bearing assembly have been removed.

5 The two case halves are being separated.

6 The oil pump assembly, pickup screen, and tube are visible on the backside of the case cover.

CONTINUED ▶

FOUR-WHEEL DRIVE DIAGNOSIS AND SERVICE **315**

7 The rear output shaft and sprocket are visible on the right. The front output shaft and sprocket are visible on the left connected by the drive chain.

8 View of the shift levers and the center differential after the chain has been removed.

9 Differential being removed.

10 Center differential assembly after removal from the transfer case.

11 Mode shift fork (upper fork) is used to change two-wheel drive and four-wheel drive. The fork is attached to the range hub, which changes four-wheel-drive high to four-wheel drive low.

12 Main shaft showing the range hub (left), which changes the transfer case between four-wheel high and four-wheel low.

13 The chain used on the NV-242 (right) is larger than the chain used in the smaller version NV-231 (left).

14 Reinstalling the components and the drive chain.

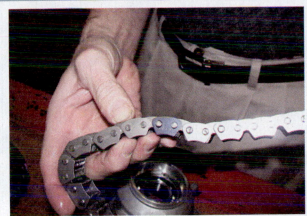

15 The drive chain should be installed with the black (dark) link(s) up.

16 Install all snap rings so that the sharpest tips face up so snap-ring pliers can grab onto the tips for easier removal.

17 Assembling the case halves.

18 The parting surface should be sealed with RTV silicone. Do not use too much or the oil pump screen can become clogged.

CONTINUED ▶

19 After attaching the oil pump and tube, the output shaft housing is installed.

20 The output shaft speed sensor drive gear is correctly installed in this photo. The slip yoke of the drive shaft slips onto the splines and inside the nylon gear.

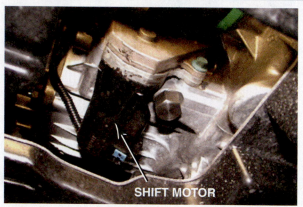

SHIFT MOTOR

21 The electronically-shifted version of the case is identical except that the shifting is achieve an electric motor, shown here installed in a vehicle.

1. Transfer cases/gear sets must have clean gear oil at the proper level and of the proper type.
2. The cause of improper 4WD/AWD operation is determined using several diagnostic steps.
3. Electronic control and shift motor problems can set a diagnostic trouble code (DTC).
4. Transfer case/gear set disassembly and reassembly varies between makes and models.
5. Locking hubs need routine service including cleaning and lubricating to keep them working properly.
6. Parts must be clean before they can be fully inspected.

REVIEW QUESTIONS

1. What are the eight steps of the diagnostic procedure?
2. What type of lubricant does a transfer case require?
3. What type of scan tool should be used to diagnose transfer case problems?
4. Why is the vehicle free to move if the transfer case is placed into neutral but the automatic transmission is in the park position?
5. If a transfer case is found to be defective internally, what are the repair options?

CHAPTER QUIZ

1. The lubricant in a transfer case is being checked. What type of fluid is used in transfer cases?
   a. ATF
   b. Gear oil such as SAE 80W-90
   c. Special transfer case fluid
   d. Any of the above depending on make, model and year of vehicle

2. The tires on a full-time four-wheel-drive or AWD vehicle should be _____.
   a. Inflated to the same inflation pressure
   b. The same size
   c. The same brand of tire
   d. All of the above

3. What type of scan tool should NOT be used to diagnose transfer case faults?
   a. Global (generic)
   b. Factory scan tool
   c. Enhanced aftermarket scan tool
   d. Either b or c

4. "Rust dust" is a sign of what type of fault?
   a. Old contaminated transfer case fluid
   b. Worn steel parts such as U-joints
   c. High resistance in electrical wiring
   d. Worn powertrain mounts

5. What type of diagnostic trouble code is usually not associated with a transfer case problem?
   a. P codes
   b. U codes
   c. B codes
   d. C codes

6. Transfer case binding or driveline windup can occur when _____.
   a. Driving an AWD vehicle on dry pavement
   b. Unequal tire sizes are used on a full-time four-wheel-drive vehicle
   c. Driving a part-time four-wheel-drive vehicle on dirt, mud, or snow
   d. Driving a four-wheel-drive vehicle in two-wheel drive

7. Most electronic transfer case controls (push button or rotary) use what type of switch?
   a. On or off
   b. Serial data
   c. Multiplex
   d. Relay

8. If a transfer case is placed into neutral, what happens if the automatic transmission is in park?
   a. The vehicle can be towed
   b. The vehicle will be able to roll
   c. The transfer case will be lockup if the transmission is in park
   d. Both a and b

9. If the transfer case fluid level is low, why should the technician check the level of the automatic transmission?
   a. Both use the same oil pan
   b. Both use ATF
   c. There may be a leaking double lip seal between the two units
   d. The fluid levels are checked using the same access plug

10. Electronic transfer cases use what type of motor?
    a. AC synchronous
    b. DC motor
    c. Stepper motor
    d. AC induction motor

chapter 17

VIBRATION AND NOISE DIAGNOSIS AND CORRECTION

LEARNING OBJECTIVES

After studying this chapter, the reader will be able to:

1. Prepare for Suspension and Steering (A4) ASE certification test content area "C" (Related Suspension and Steering Service).

2. List the possible vehicle components that can cause a vibration or noise.

3. Explain the vibration speed ranges and the method to determine the frequency of the vibration.

4. Discuss the methods for measuring driveshaft U-joint phasing and balancing the driveshaft.

5. Diagnose and correct noise problems.

KEY TERMS

Companion flange 329
Driveline angles 328
Driveshaft runout 329
EVA 326
Frequency 323
Hertz (Hz) 323
Neutral run-up test 323
NVH 321
Rolling circumference 325
Vibration order 324
Witness mark 321

FIGURE 17–1 Many vehicles, especially those equipped with four-cylinder engines, use a dampener weight attached to the exhaust system or drive axle as shown to dampen out certain frequency vibrations.

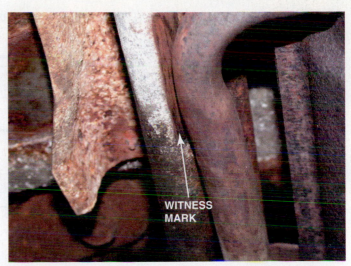

FIGURE 17–2 The exhaust was found to be rubbing on the frame rail during a visual inspection. Rubber exhaust system hangers are used to isolate noise and vibration from the exhaust system from entering the interior. These rubber supports can fail causing the exhaust system to be out of proper location. It was found by looking for evidence of **witness marks**.

Vibration and noise are two of the most frequent complaints from vehicle owners and drivers. If something is vibrating, it can move air; changes in air pressure (air movement) are what we call noise. Though anything that moves vibrates, wheels and tires account for the majority of vehicle vibration problems.

CAUSES OF VIBRATION AND NOISE

Vehicles are designed and built to prevent most vibrations and to dampen out any vibrations that cannot be eliminated. For example, engines are designed and balanced to provide smooth power at all engine speeds. Some engines, such as large four-cylinder or 90 degree V-6's, require special engine mounts to absorb or dampen any remaining oscillations or vibrations. Dampening weights are also fastened to engines or transmissions in an effort to minimize **noise, vibration,** and **harshness** (called **NVH**).

If a new vehicle has a vibration or noise problem, then the most likely cause is an assembly or parts problem. This is difficult to diagnose because the problem could be almost anything, and a careful analysis procedure should be followed as outlined later in this chapter.

If an older vehicle has a vibration or noise problem, the first step is to question the vehicle owner as to when the problem first appeared. Some problems and possible causes include the following:

Problem	Possible Causes
Vibration at idle	Engine mount could be defective or not reinstalled correctly after an engine or transmission repair.
Noise/vibration	Exhaust system replacement or repair. ● SEE FIGURE 17–1.

NOTE: A typical exhaust system can "grow" or lengthen up to 2 inch (1 cm) when warm, as compared with room temperature. Always inspect an exhaust system when warm, if possible, being careful to avoid being burned by the hot exhaust components.

Vibration at higher vehicle speeds	Incorrect driveshaft angles could be the result of a change in the U-joints, springs, transmission mounts, or anything else that can cause a change in driveshaft angles.
Noise over rough roads	Exhaust system or parking brake cables are often causes of noise while driving over rough road surfaces. ● SEE FIGURE 17–2. Defective shock absorbers or shock absorber mountings are also a common cause of noise.

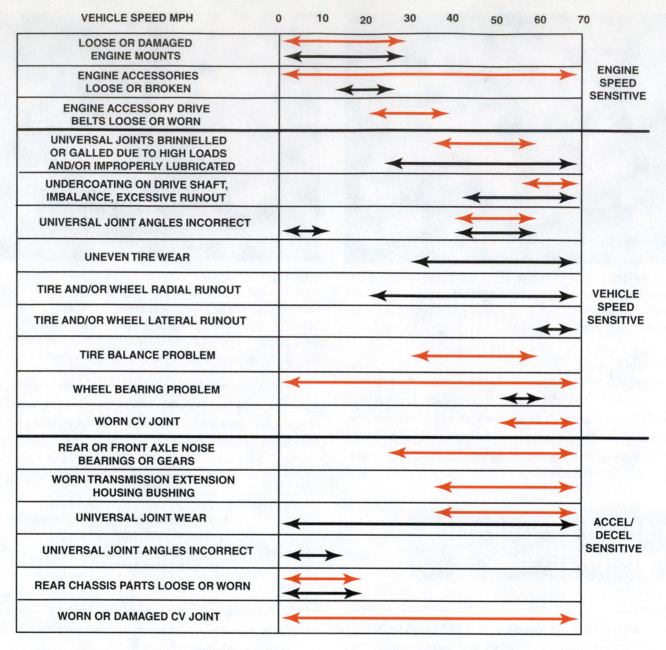

FIGURE 17–3 A chart showing the typical vehicle and engine speeds at which various components will create a noise or vibration and under what conditions.

TEST-DRIVE

The first thing a technician should do when given a vibration or noise problem to solve is to duplicate the condition. This means the technician should drive the vehicle and observe when and where the vibration is felt or heard. See the chart in ● **FIGURE 17–3**.

Though there are many possible sources of a vibration, some simple observations may help to locate the problem quickly:

1. If the vibration is felt or seen in the steering wheel, dash, or hood of the vehicle, the problem is most likely to be caused by defective or out-of-balance *front* wheels or tires. ● **SEE FIGURE 17–4**.

2. If the vibration is felt in the seat of the pants or seems to be all over the vehicle, the problem is most likely to be caused by defective or out-of-balance *rear* wheels or tires. In a rear-wheel-drive vehicle, the driveshaft (propeller shaft) and related components might also be the cause.

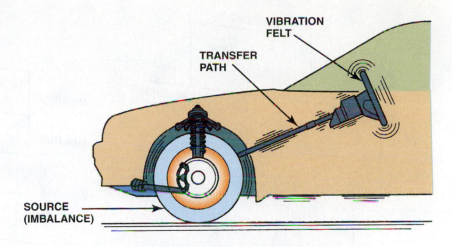

FIGURE 17–4 Vibration created at one point is easily transferred to the passenger compartment. MacPherson strut suspensions are more sensitive to tire imbalance than SLA-type suspensions.

VIBRATION FELT

TRANSFER PATH

SOURCE (IMBALANCE)

While on the test-drive, try to gather as much information about the vibration or noise complaint as possible.

STEP 1 Determine the vehicle speed (mph or km/h) or engine speed (RPM) where the vibration occurs. Drive on a smooth, level road and accelerate up to highway speed, noting the vehicle speed or speeds at which the vibration or noise occurs.

STEP 2 To help pin down the exact cause of the vibration, accelerate to a speed slightly above the point of maximum vibration. Shift the vehicle into neutral and allow it to coast down through the speed of maximum vibration. If the vibration still exists, then the cause of the problem could be wheels, tires, or other rotating components, *except* the engine.

If the vibration is eliminated when shifted out of gear, the problem is related to the engine or transmission.

NOTE: If the engine or transmission has been removed from the vehicle, such as during a clutch replacement, carefully observe the location and condition of the mounts. If an engine or transmission mount is defective or out of location, engine and driveline vibrations are often induced and transmitted throughout the vehicle.

NEUTRAL RUN-UP TEST

The **neutral run-up test** is used to determine if the source of the vibration is engine-related. With the transmission in neutral or park, slowly increase the engine RPM and with a tachometer observe the RPM at which the vibration occurs. **Do Not Exceed The Manufacturer's Recommended Maximum Engine RPM.**

If the fault is found in the engine itself, further engine testing is needed to find the root cause.

VIBRATION DURING BRAKING

A vibration during braking usually indicates out-of-round brake drums, warped disc brake rotors, or other braking system problems. The *front* rotors are the cause of the vibration if the steering wheel is also vibrating (moving) during braking. The *rear* drums or rotors are the cause of the vibration if the vibration is felt throughout the vehicle and brake pedal, but *not* the steering wheel. Another way to check if the vibration is due to rear brakes is to use the parking brake to stop the vehicle. If a vibration occurs while using the parking brake, the rear brakes are the cause.

NOTE: Wheels should *never* be installed using an air impact wrench. Even installation torque is almost impossible to control, and overtightening almost always occurs. The use of impact wrenches causes the wheel, hub, and rotor to distort, resulting in vibrations and brake pedal pulsations. Always tighten wheel lugs in the proper sequence and with proper torque value, using a torque wrench or torque-limiting adapter bars.

VIBRATION SPEED RANGES

FREQUENCY *Vibration* describes an oscillating motion around a reference position. The number of times a complete motion cycle takes place during a period of one second is called **frequency** and is measured in **hertz (Hz)** (named for Heinrich R. Hertz (1857–1894), a nineteenth-century German physicist). ● **SEE FIGURES 17–5 AND 17–6.**

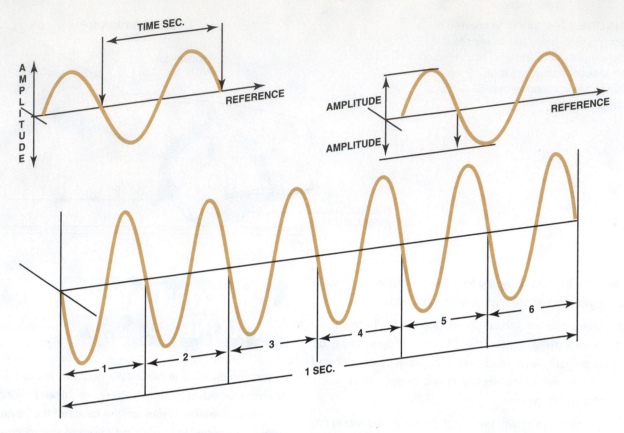

FIGURE 17–5 Hertz means *cycles* per *second*. If six cycles occur in one second, then the frequency is 6 Hz. The amplitude refers to the total movement of the vibrating component.

 TECH TIP

The Duct Tape Trick

A clicking noise heard at low speeds from the wheels is a common noise complaint. This noise is usually most noticeable while driving with the windows lowered. This type of noise is caused by loose disc brake pads or noisy wheel covers. Wire wheel covers are especially noisy. To confirm exactly what is causing the noise, simply remove the wheel covers and drive the vehicle. If the clicking noise is still present, check the brakes and wheels for faults. If the noise is gone with the wheel covers removed, use duct tape over the inner edge of the wheel covers before installing them onto the wheels. The duct tape will cushion and dampen the wheel cover and help reduce the noise. The sharp prongs of the wheel cover used to grip the wheel will pierce through the duct tape and still help retain the wheel covers.

The unit of measure for frequency was originally cycles per second (CPS). This was changed to Hz in the 1960s.

To help understand frequency, think of the buzzing sound made by some fluorescent light fixtures. That 60 Hz hum is the same frequency as the alternating current. A 400 Hz sound is high-pitched. In fact, most people can only hear sounds between 20 and 15,000 Hz. Generally, low-frequency oscillations between 1 and 80 Hz are the most disturbing to vehicle occupants.

VIBRATION ORDER **Vibration order** is the number of vibrations created in one revolution of a component. A single high spot on a tire, for example, will cause one bump per revolution, which is a first-order vibration. If the tire rotates 10 times per second, there are 10 disturbances per second, which is also called a first-order vibration of 10 Hz. If there are two bumps on a tire, a second-order vibration is created that would generate a vibration of 20 Hz if the tire were rotating 10 times per second.

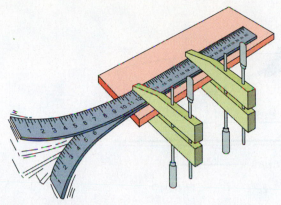

FIGURE 17–6 Every time the end of a clamped yardstick moves up and down, it is one cycle. The number of cycles divided by the time equals the frequency. If the yardstick moves up and down 10 times (10 cycles) in two seconds, the frequency is 5 Hertz (10 ÷ 2 = 5).

 REAL WORLD FIX

S-10 Pickup Truck Frame Noise

The owner of a Chevrolet S-10 pickup truck complained of a loud squeaking noise, especially when turning left. Several technicians attempted to solve the problem and replaced shock absorbers, ball joints, and control arm bushings without solving the problem. The problem was finally discovered to be the starter motor hitting the frame. A measurement of new vehicles indicated that the clearance between the starter motor and the frame was about 1/8 inch (0.125 inch) (0.3 cm)! The sagging of the engine mount and the weight transfer of the engine during cornering caused the starter motor to rub up against the frame. The noise was transmitted through the frame throughout the vehicle and made the source of the noise difficult to find.

TIRE AND WHEEL VIBRATIONS   Typical vehicle components that can cause vibration in specific frequency ranges at 50 mph (80 km/h) include the following:

LOW FREQUENCY (5–20 HZ).   This frequency range of vibration is very disturbing to many drivers because this type of vibration can be seen and felt in the steering wheel, seats, mirrors, and other components. Terms used to describe this type of vibration include *nibble*, *shake*, *oscillation*, *shimmy*, and *shudder*.

Tires and wheels are the most common source of vibration in the low-frequency range. To determine the *exact* frequency for the vehicle being checked, the following formula and procedure can be used.

Tire rolling frequency is calculated as follows:

$$Hz = \frac{mph \times 1.47}{tire\ circumference\ in\ feet}$$

This formula works for all vehicles regardless of tire size. The circumference (distance around the tread) can be measured by using a tape measure around the tire. The **rolling circumference** of the tire is usually shorter due to the contact patch. To determine the rolling circumference, follow these easy steps:

STEP 1   Inflate the tire(s) to the recommended pressure. Park the vehicle with the valve stem pointing straight down and mark the location on the floor directly below the valve stem.

STEP 2   Slowly roll the vehicle forward (or rearward) until the valve stem is again straight down. Mark the floor below the valve stem.

STEP 3   Measure the distance between the marks in feet. ● **SEE FIGURE 17–7.** To change inches to feet, divide by 12 (for example, 77 inch divided by 12 inch = 6.4 feet). To determine the rolling frequency of this tire at 60 mph, use 6.4 feet as the tire circumference in the formula.

$$Frequency = \frac{60\,mph \times 1.47}{6.4\,ft} = 13.8\,Hz$$

NOTE: Tire circumference is critical on four-wheel-drive vehicles. The transfer case can be damaged and severe vibration can occur if the rolling circumference is different by more than 0.6 inch (15 mm) on the same axle, or more than 1.2 inch (30 mm) front to rear.

DRIVELINE VIBRATIONS

MEDIUM FREQUENCY (20–50 HZ).   This frequency range of vibrations may also be described as a shake, oscillation, or shimmy. These higher frequencies may also be called *roughness* or *buzz*. **Components become blurred and impossible to focus on above a vibration of 30 Hz.**

ENGINE-RELATED VIBRATIONS

HIGH FREQUENCY (50–100 HZ).   Vibrations in this range may also be *heard* as a moan or hum. The vibration is high enough that it may be felt as a numbing sensation that can put the driver's hands or feet to sleep. Engine-related vibrations vary with engine speed, regardless of road speed. Frequency of the vibration from an engine is determined from the engine speed in revolutions per minute (RPM).

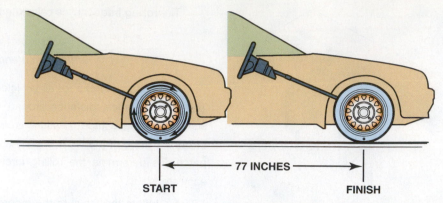

FIGURE 17–7 Determining the rolling circumference of a tire.

$$\text{Frequency in Hz} = \frac{\text{engine RPM}}{60}$$

For example, if a vibration occurs at 3000 engine RPM, then the frequency is 50 Hz.

$$\text{Hz} = \frac{3000\,\text{RPM}}{60} = 50\,\text{Hz}$$

FREQUENCY

MEASURING FREQUENCY Knowing the frequency of the vibration greatly improves the speed of tracking down the source of the vibration. Vibration can be measured using a reed tachometer or an **electronic vibration analyzer (EVA)**. ● **SEE FIGURE 17–8.**

FIGURE 17–8 An electronic vibration analyzer.

A reed tachometer is placed on the dash, console, or other suitable location inside the vehicle. The vehicle is then driven on a smooth, level road at the speed where the vibration is felt the most. The reeds of the reed tachometer vibrate at the frequency of the vibration.

NOTE: Other types of vibration diagnostic equipment may be available from vehicle or aftermarket manufacturers.

CORRECTING LOW-FREQUENCY VIBRATIONS A low-frequency vibration (5–20 Hz) is usually due to tire/wheel problems, including the following:

1. Tire and/or wheel imbalance. ● **SEE FIGURES 17–9 THROUGH 17–11.**

2. Tire and/or wheel radial or lateral runout.

3. Radial force variation within the tire itself.

4. If front-wheel drive, a bent or damaged drive axle joint or shaft.

5. Warped rotors.

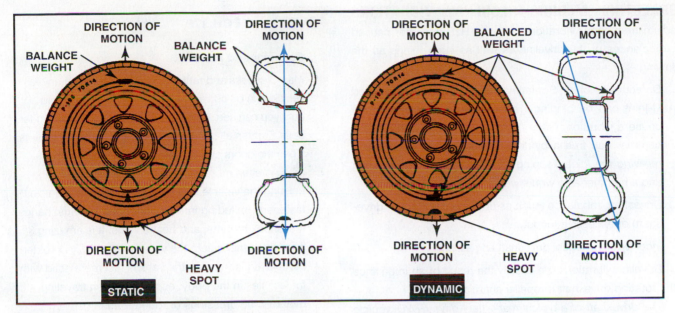

FIGURE 17–9 Properly balancing all wheels and tires solves most low-frequency vibrations.

FIGURE 17–10 An out-of-balance tire showing scallops or bald spots around the tire. Even if correctly balanced, this cupped tire would create a vibration.

FIGURE 17–11 Another cause of a vibration that is often blamed on wheels or tires is a bent bearing hub. Use a dial indicator to check the flange for runout.

Tires that are out of round or defective will be most noticeable at low speeds, will get better as speed increases, and then will vibrate again at highway speeds.

Tires that are out of balance will tend not to be noticeable at low speeds, and will be most noticeable at highway speeds.

NOTE: High-performance tires are manufactured with different carcass and belt package angles as well as a stiffer, harder tread rubber compound than standard tires. While these construction features produce a tire that allows sporty handling, the tire itself causes a stiff ride, often with increased tire noise. High-performance tires also generate and transmit different frequencies than regular tires. Using replacement high-performance tires on a vehicle not designed for this type of tire may create noise and vibration concerns for the driver/owner that the technician cannot correct.

CORRECTING MEDIUM-FREQUENCY VIBRATIONS

Medium-frequency vibrations (20–50 Hz) can be caused by imbalances of the driveline as well as such things as the following:

1. **Defective U-joints.** Sometimes an old or a newly installed U-joint can be binding. This binding of the U-joint can cause a vibration. Often a blow to the joint with a brass hammer can free a binding U-joint. This is often called *relieving the joint.* Tapping the joint using a brass punch and a hammer also works well.

2. Driveshaft imbalance (such as undercoating on the driveshaft) or excessive runout.

3. Incorrect or unequal driveshaft angles.

Driveline vibrations are usually the result of an imbalance in the rotating driveshaft (propeller shaft) assembly.

The driveshaft of a typical rear-wheel-drive (RWD) vehicle rotates at about three times the speed of the drive wheels. The differential gears in the rear end change the direction of the power flow from the engine and driveshaft, as well as provide for a gear reduction. Front-wheel-drive (FWD) vehicles do not have medium-frequency vibration caused by the driveshaft because the differential is inside the transaxle and the drive axle shafts rotate at the same speed as the wheels and tires.

All driveshafts are balanced at the factory, and weights are attached to the driveshaft, if necessary, to achieve proper balance. A driveshaft should be considered one of the items checked if the medium-frequency vibration is felt throughout the vehicle or in the seat of the pants.

NOTE: If a vibration is felt during heavy acceleration at low speeds, a common cause is incorrect universal joint angles. This often happens when the rear of the vehicle is heavily loaded or sagging due to weak springs. If the angles of the U-joints are not correct (excessive or unequal from one end of the driveshaft to the other), a vibration will also be present at higher speeds and is usually torque-sensitive.

CORRECTING HIGH-FREQUENCY VIBRATIONS

High-frequency vibrations (50–100 Hz) are commonly caused by a fault of the clutch, torque converter, or transmission main shaft that rotates at engine speed; in the engine itself, they can be caused by items such as the following:

1. A defective spark plug wire
2. A burned valve
3. Any other mechanical fault that will prevent any one or more cylinders from firing correctly
4. A defective harmonic balancer

TECH TIP

Squeaks and Rattles

Many squeaks and rattles commonly heard on any vehicle can be corrected by tightening all bolts and nuts you can see. Raise the hood and tighten all fender bolts. Tighten all radiator support and bumper brackets. Open the doors and tighten all hinge and body bolts.

An even more thorough job can be done by hoisting the vehicle and tightening all under-vehicle fasteners, including inner fender bolts, exhaust hangers, shock mounts, and heat shields. It is amazing how much this quiets the vehicle, especially on older models. It also makes the vehicle feel more solid with far less flex in the body, especially when traveling over railroad crossings or rough roads.

If the engine is the cause, run in neutral at the same engine speed. If the vibration is present, perform a complete engine condition diagnosis. Some engines misfire only under load and will not vibrate while in neutral without a load being placed on the engine, even though the engine is being operated at the same speed (RPM).

Exhaust system pulses occur at the following conditions:

4-cylinder engine	2 × engine RPM
6-cylinder engine	3 × engine RPM
8-cylinder engine	4 × engine RPM

If the exhaust system is touching the body, it will transfer these pulses as a vibration. Exhaust system vibrations vary with engine speed and usually increase as the load on the engine increases.

CORRECTING DRIVELINE ANGLES

Incorrect **driveline angles** are usually caused by one or more of the following:

1. Worn, damaged, or improperly installed U-joints.
2. Worn, collapsed, or defective engine or transmission mount(s).
3. Incorrect vehicle ride height. (As weight is added to the rear of a rear-wheel-drive vehicle, the front of the differential rises and changes the working angle of the rear U-joint.)
4. Bent or distorted driveshaft.

CHECKING DRIVESHAFT RUNOUT

Check to see that the driveshaft is not bent by performing a **driveshaft runout** test using a dial indicator. Runout should be measured at three places along the length of the driveshaft.

The maximum allowable runout is 0.030 inch (0.76 mm). If runout exceeds 0.030 inch, remove the driveshaft from the rear end and reindex the driveshaft onto the **companion flange** at 180 degrees from its original location. Remeasure the driveshaft runout. If the runout is still greater than 0.030 inch, the driveshaft is bent and needs replacement *or* the companion flange needs replacement.

MEASURING DRIVESHAFT U-JOINT PHASING

Measuring driveshaft U-joint phasing involves checking to see if the front and rear U-joints are directly in line or parallel with each other. With the vehicle on a drive-on lift, or if using a frame-contact hoist, support the weight of the vehicle on stands placed under the rear axle. Place an inclinometer on the front U-joint bearing cup and rotate the driveshaft until horizontal; note the inclinometer reading. Move the inclinometer to the rear U-joint. The angles should match. If the angles are not equal, the driveshaft is out of phase and should be replaced. Incorrect phasing is usually due to a twisted driveshaft or an incorrectly welded end yoke.

COMPANION FLANGE RUNOUT

The companion flange is splined to the rear axle pinion shaft and provides the mounting for the rear U-joint of the driveshaft. Two items should be checked on the companion flange while diagnosing a vibration:

1. The companion flange should have a maximum runout of 0.006 inch (0.15 mm) while being rotated. If the flange was pounded off with a hammer during a previous repair, the deformed flange could cause a vibration.

2. Check the companion flange for a missing balance weight. Many flanges have a balance weight that is spot-welded onto the flange. If the weight is missing, a driveline vibration can result.

BALANCING THE DRIVESHAFT

If the driveshaft (propeller shaft) is within runout specification and a vibration still exists, the balance of the shaft should be checked and corrected as necessary.

Checking for driveshaft balance is usually done with a strobe balancer. The strobe balancer was commonly used to balance tires on the vehicle and was very popular before the universal use of computer tire balancers. A strobe balancer uses a magnetic sensor that is attached to the pinion housing of the differential. The sensor causes a bright light to flash (strobe) whenever a shock force is exerted on the sensor. The procedure for testing driveshaft balance using a strobe balancer includes the following:

NOTE: Driveshaft balance is more important than front drive axle shaft balance because a driveshaft rotates much faster. A typical driveshaft rotates about three times faster than the drive wheels due to the gear reduction in the differential. Drive axle shafts rotate at the same speed as the drive wheels.

STEP 1 Raise the vehicle and mark the driveshaft with four equally spaced marks around its circumference. Label each mark with a 1, 2, 3, and 4. ● **SEE FIGURE 17–12.**

STEP 2 Attach the strobe balancer sensor to the bottom of the differential housing as close to the companion flange as possible. ● **SEE FIGURE 17–13.**

NOTE: The sensor does not rotate with the driveshaft but picks up the vibration of the driveshaft through the differential housing.

STEP 3 With the vehicle securely hoisted and the drive wheels off the ground, start the engine and put the transmission into gear to allow the drive wheels to rotate.

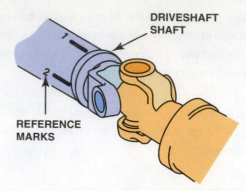

FIGURE 17–12 When checking the balance of a driveshaft, make reference marks around the shaft so that the location of the unbalance may be viewed when using a strobe light.

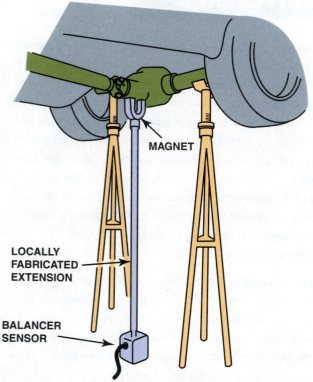

NOTE: LOCALLY FABRICATED EXTENSION FOR BALANCER PICKUP CONSISTS OF 3/8" TUBE AND COMPRESSION FITTINGS

FIGURE 17–13 Using a strobe balancer to check for driveline vibration requires that an extension be used on the magnetic sensor. Tall safety stands are used to support the rear axle to keep the driveshaft angles the same as when the vehicle is on the road.

STEP 4 Hold the strobe light close to the marks on the driveshaft.

    a. If the light does *not* flash, the driveshaft is balanced and no corrective action is necessary.

    b. If the light *does* flash, observe what number mark is shown by the flashing light.

STEP 5 Apply hose clamps so that the screw portion of the clamp(s) is *opposite* the number seen with the strobe light. The screw portion of the hose clamp is the corrective weight. Remember, the strobe light sensor

was mounted to the *bottom* of the differential housing. The strobe light flashes when the heavy part of the driveshaft is facing *downward*. If the heavy part of the driveshaft is down, then corrective weight must be added to the opposite side of the driveshaft. ● SEE **FIGURES 17–14 AND 17–15**.

NOISE DIAGNOSIS

Noise diagnosis is difficult because a noise is easily transmitted from its source to other places in the vehicle. For example, if a rear shock absorber mount is loose, the noise may be heard as coming from the middle or even the front of the vehicle. As the axle moves up and down, the noise is created where metal touches metal between the shock absorber bolt and the axle shock mount. The noise is then transmitted throughout the frame of the vehicle, and therefore causes the sound to appear to come from "everywhere." To help pin down the exact location of the sound, perform a thorough test-drive, including driving beside parked vehicles or walls with the vehicle windows open. (See the following chart for driveline and bearing-type noise diagnosis.)

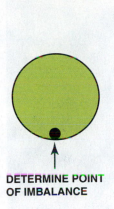

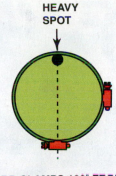

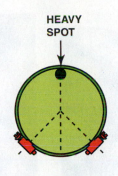

HEAVY SPOT

HEAVY SPOT

FIGURE 17–14 Typical procedure to balance a driveshaft using hose clamps.

DETERMINE POINT OF IMBALANCE

ADD CLAMPS 180° FROM POINT OF IMBALANCE UNTIL THEY BECOME THE HEAVY SPOT

ROTATE TWO CLAMPS EQUALLY AWAY FROM EACH OTHER UNTIL BEST BALANCE IS ACHIEVED

Noise	Diagnostic Procedure
Tire noise	Change tire pressure; if no change, then the problem is not tires but bearings, or other components.
	Drive on various road surfaces—smooth asphalt reduces tire noise.
	Rotate the tires front to rear, if possible.
	Various tread designs can cause added noise (● **SEE FIGURE 17–16**).
Engine/exhaust noise	Operate the engine at various speeds and loads.
	Drive faster than the speed where the noise occurs, place the transmission in neutral, and "coast" down through the speed of maximum noise.
	Determine if the engine speed or vehicle speed is the cause of the noise.
Wheel bearing noise (● **SEE FIGURE 17–17**)	Drive the vehicle slowly on a smooth road.
	Make left and right turns with the vehicle.
	Wheel bearing noise changes as weight is transferred side to side.
	If noise occurs when turning to the right, then the left bearing is the cause.
	If noise occurs when turning to the left, then the right bearing is the cause.
	Hoist the vehicle and rotate the wheel by hand to verify the roughness.
Differential side bearing noise	Drive the vehicle slowly on a smooth road.
	Differential bearing noise is a low-pitch noise that does not change when turning.
	The noise varies with vehicle speed.
Differential pinion bearing noise	A whine noise increases with the vehicle speed.
	Drive on a smooth road and accelerate, coast, and hold a steady speed (float). A defective front pinion bearing may be louder on acceleration. A defective rear pinion bearing may be louder on deceleration.
	Pinion bearing noise usually peaks in a narrow speed range.
U-joint noise	Drive slowly on a smooth road surface.
	Drive in reverse and forward.
	U-joints usually make a "chirp, chirp, chirp" noise in reverse because of lack of lubrication and brinelling from driving forward. Driving in reverse changes the force on the needle bearings in the U-joint, and noise is created.
Clutch noise	**Transmission input bearing:** Start the engine with the transmission in neutral and the parking brake set. The clutch should be engaged (foot off the clutch pedal). If the bearing noise is heard, the transmission input bearing is the source.
	Release (throw-out) bearing: Start the engine with the transmission in neutral and the parking brake set. Lightly depress the clutch pedal just enough to take up freeplay (usually 1 inch or less). If the noise is now heard, the source is the release (throw out) bearing as the clutch fingers make contact with the bearing.
	Pilot bearing: Start the engine with the transmission in neutral and the parking brake set. Push the clutch pedal fully to the floor (disengage the clutch). If the bearing noise is heard with the clutch disengaged, it is caused by the pilot bearing.

FIGURE 17–15 Two clamps were required to balance this front driveshaft of a four-wheel-drive vehicle. Be careful when using hose clamps that the ends of the clamps do not interfere with the body or other parts of the vehicle.

FIGURE 17–16 Tire wear caused by improper alignment or driving habits, such as high-speed cornering, can create tire noise. Notice the feather-edged outer tread blocks.

Some noises may be normal; a similar vehicle should be driven and compared before replacing parts that may not be defective. Noises usually become louder and easier to find as time and mileage increase. An occasional noise usually becomes a constant noise.

NOISE CORRECTION

The proper way to repair a noise is to repair the cause. Other methods that have been used by technicians include the following:

FIGURE 17–17 This bearing was found on a vehicle that had been stored over the winter. This corroded bearing produced a lot of noise and had to be replaced.

? FREQUENTLY ASKED QUESTION

What are "Chassis Ears"?

Chassis Ears is a brand name for a tool that uses microphones that can be attached to parts under the vehicle and transmit noise to a receiver. The receiver can be tuned so that a technician can listen to one microphone at a time while someone else is driving. This tool makes finding the source of a noise easier. ● **SEE FIGURE 17–18**.

🔧 TECH TIP

RAP It

Many technicians who service transmissions and differentials frequently replace *all* bearings in the differential when there is a noise complaint. While this at first may seem to be overkill, these technicians have learned that one defective bearing may put particles in the lubricant, often causing the destruction of all the other bearings. This practice has been called *RAP* (replace all parts), and in the case of differentials, RAP may not be such a bad idea.

1. Insulating the passenger compartment to keep the noise from the passengers.
2. Turning up the radio!

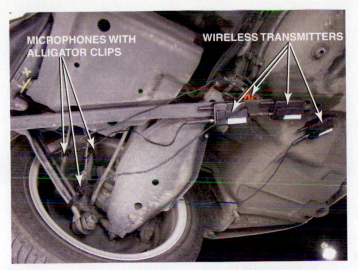

FIGURE 17–18 Chassis Ears microphones attached to various suspension components using the integral clamps. The sound is transmitted wirelessly to the receiver inside the vehicle where an assistant technician can listen for noises while the vehicle is being driven.

While these methods are usually inexpensive, the noise is still being generated, and if a noisy bearing or other vehicle component is not corrected, more expensive damage is likely to occur. Always remember: *Almost all vehicle faults cause noise first—do not ignore the noise because it is the early warning signal of more serious and possibly dangerous problems.*

Some of the things that can be done to correct certain vibrations and noise include the following:

1. Check all power steering high-pressure lines, being certain that they do not touch any part of the body, frame, or engine except where they are mounted.

 REAL WORLD FIX

Engine Noise

An experienced technician was assigned to diagnose a loud engine noise. The noise sounded like a defective connecting rod bearing or other major engine problem. The alternator belt was found to be loose. Knowing that a loose belt can "whip" and cause noise, the belt was inspected and the alternator moved on its adjustment slide to tighten the belt. After tightening the belt, the engine was started and the noise was still heard. After stopping the engine, the technician found that the alternator belt was still loose. The problem was discovered to be a missing bolt that attached the alternator mounting bracket to the engine. The forces on the alternator caused the bracket to hit the engine. This noise was transmitted throughout the engine. Replacing the missing bracket bolt solved the loud engine noise and pleased a very relieved owner.

2. Carefully check, tighten, and lubricate the flexible couplings in the exhaust system. Use a drive-on lift to ensure normal suspension positioning to check the exhaust system clearances. Loosen, then tighten, all exhaust clamps and hangers to relieve any built-up stress.

3. Lubricate all rubber bushings with rubber lube and replace any engine or transmission mounts that are collapsed.

4. Replace and/or tighten all engine drive belts and check that all accessory mounting brackets are tight.

SUMMARY

1. Vibration and noise are two of the most frequently heard complaints from vehicle owners. Noise is actually a vibration (vibrations cause the air to move, creating noise).

2. A vibration felt in the steering wheel, dash, or hood is usually due to out-of-balance or defective front tires. A vibration felt in the seat of the pants or throughout the entire vehicle is usually due to out-of-balance or defective rear tires.

3. Defective engine or transmission mounts, warped rotors, and out-of-round brake drums can all cause a vibration.

4. Vibration is measured by an electronic vibration analyzer (EVA) or a reed tachometer and measured in units called Hertz.

5. Low-frequency vibrations (5–20 Hz) are usually due to tires or wheels.

6. Medium-frequency vibrations (20–50 Hz) are usually caused by driveline problems on rear-wheel-drive vehicles.

7. High-frequency vibrations (50–100 Hz) are usually caused by an engine problem.

8. Driveshafts should be inspected for proper U-joint working angles and balance.

REVIEW QUESTIONS

1. Describe how you can tell if the source of a vibration is at the front or the rear of a vehicle during a test-drive.

2. Explain the terms *cycle* and *Hertz*.

3. List two types of frequency-measuring instruments.

4. Discuss why the balance of a driveshaft on a rear-wheel-drive vehicle is more important than the balance of a front-wheel-drive axle shaft.

5. Explain how to check and balance a driveshaft on a rear-wheel-drive vehicle.

CHAPTER QUIZ

1. A vibration that is felt in the steering wheel at highway speeds is usually due to _____.
   a. Defective or out-of-balance rear tires
   b. Defective or out-of-balance front tires
   c. Out-of-balance or bent driveshaft on a RWD vehicle
   d. Out-of-balance drive axle shaft or defective outer CV joints on a FWD vehicle

2. A vibration during braking is usually caused by _____.
   a. Out-of-balance tires
   b. Warped front brake rotors
   c. A bent wheel
   d. An out-of-balance or bent driveshaft

3. The rolling circumference of both tires on the same axle of a four-wheel-drive vehicle should be within _____.
   a. 0.1 inch (2.5 mm)
   b. 0.3 inch (7.6 mm)
   c. 0.6 inch (15 mm)
   d. 1.2 inch (30 mm)

4. The maximum allowable driveshaft runout is _____.
   a. 0.030 inch (0.8 mm)
   b. 0.10 inch (2.5 mm)
   c. 0.50 inch (13 mm)
   d. 0.015 inch (0.4 mm)

5. A driveshaft can be checked for proper balance by marking the circumference of the shaft in four places and running the vehicle drive wheels to spot the point of imbalance using a _____.
   a. Reed tachometer
   b. Strobe light
   c. Electronic vibration analyzer
   d. Scan tool

6. A defective clutch release (throw out) bearing is usually heard when the clutch is _____.
   a. Engaged in neutral
   b. Disengaged in a gear
   c. Depressed to take up any freeplay
   d. Engaged in first gear or reverse

7. Wheel/tire imbalance is the most common source of vibrations that occur in what frequency range?
   a. 5–20 Hz
   b. 20–50 Hz
   c. 50–100 Hz
   d. 100–150 Hz

8. Driveline vibrations due to a bent or out-of-balance driveshaft on a rear-wheel-drive vehicle usually produce a vibration that is _____.
   a. Felt in the steering wheel
   b. Seen as a vibrating dash or hood
   c. Felt in the seat or all over the vehicle
   d. Felt by the rear passengers only

9. Rubber is used for exhaust system hangers because the exhaust system lengthens as it gets hot and rubber helps isolate noise and vibration from the passenger compartment.
   a. True
   b. False

10. A vibration is felt in the steering wheel during braking only. A common cause of the vibration is _____.
   a. Worn idler arm
   b. Out-of-balance front tires
   c. Loose or defective wheel bearing(s)
   d. Warped or nonparallel front disc brake rotors

appendix 1
SAMPLE ASE-TYPE CERTIFICATION TEST

CLUTCH DIAGNOSIS AND REPAIR (6 QUESTIONS)

1. An owner of a manual transmission vehicle complained that the clutch slipped during hard acceleration. Technician A says that the clutch linkage may need adjustment. Technician B says the clutch may require replacement. Which technician is correct?
   a. Technician A only
   b. Technician B only
   c. Both Technicians A and B
   d. Neither Technician A nor B

2. A clutch engages close to the floor and will often not disengage. What is the most likely cause?
   a. Worn clutch disc
   b. Misadjusted clutch linkage
   c. Weak pressure plate
   d. Worn flywheel

3. An owner of a vehicle equipped with a manual transmission and a cable-operated clutch complained that the transmission is difficult to shift without grinding the gears. Which is the least likely cause?
   a. Incorrect gear lube in the transmission
   b. Bulkhead (firewall) flex
   c. Incorrect clutch adjustment
   d. Misadjusted clutch switch

4. A loud squeak is heard every time the clutch pedal is depressed or released. What is the most likely cause?
   a. A defective release (throw out) bearing
   b. A defective input shaft bearing
   c. A cracked diaphragm spring on the pressure plate
   d. The clutch pedal linkage needs lubrication

5. A clutch is chattering when it is engaged. What is the most likely cause?
   a. Oil or grease on the friction surface(s)
   b. A worn release (throw out) bearing
   c. A worn clutch fork
   d. A defective pilot bearing (bushing)

6. Two technicians are discussing clutch linkage adjustment. Technician A says that most hydraulic clutches are self-adjusting and that no adjustment is needed. Technician B says that many cable-operated clutches are self-adjusting and that no adjustment is needed. Which technician is correct?
   a. Technician A only
   b. Technician B only
   c. Both Technicians A and B
   d. Neither Technician A nor B

TRANSMISSION DIAGNOSIS AND REPAIR (7 QUESTIONS)

7. Which component cannot be removed before removing the transmission/transaxle from the vehicle?
   a. Vehicle speed sensor
   b. Reverse (backup) light connector
   c. Front bearing retainer (quill)
   d. Drive axle shaft(s)

8. A customer complained of hard shifting particularly into first gear and reverse. Technician A says that the blocking ring may be worn. Technician B says that the clutch may be defective or out of adjustment. Which technician is correct?
   a. Technician A only
   b. Technician B only
   c. Both Technicians A and B
   d. Neither Technician A nor B

9. A manual transmission is difficult to shift into all gears but only when the outside temperature is below freezing point (32°F or 0°C). Technician A says that the brass blocking ring could be defective. Technician B says that incorrect gear lubricant could be the cause. Which technician is correct?
   a. Technician A only
   b. Technician B only
   c. Both Technicians A and B
   d. Neither Technician A nor B

10. Various lubricants are used in a manual transmission except _____.
    a. Automatic transmission fluid (ATF)
    b. High temperature chassis grease
    c. SAE 80W-90 gear lube
    d. Engine oil

11. A manual five-speed transmission in a rear-wheel-drive vehicle is noisy in all gears except fourth. Technician A says that the main shaft bearing(s) is likely to be defective. Technician B says that the countershaft bearing(s) is likely to be defective. Which technician is correct?
    a. Technician A only
    b. Technician B only
    c. Both Technicians A and B
    d. Neither Technician A nor B

12. A five-speed manual transmission jumps out of fifth gear while driving. What is the most likely cause?
    a. A worn input shaft bearing
    b. A worn shift lever
    c. Low on lubricating oil
    d. A cracked synchronizer ring

13. A transmission is low on lubricant. Which component is the least likely to fail?
    a. Synchronizer assembly
    b. Speed gear bearing(s)
    c. Input shaft bearing
    d. Shift forks

TRANSAXLE DIAGNOSIS AND REPAIR (7 QUESTIONS)

14. The owner of a vehicle equipped with a manual transaxle complained that gear clash was heard whenever shifting. Which is the *least likely* to be the cause?
    a. Worn blocking ring
    b. Misadjusted clutch linkage
    c. Defective output shaft bearing
    d. Defective pilot bearing

15. Technician A says that the clearance between the synchronizer ring (blocking ring) and the speed gear should be measured with a feeler (thickness) gauge. Technician B says that a worn synchronizer ring (blocking ring) can cause gear clash when shifting. Which technician is correct?
    a. Technician A only
    b. Technician B only
    c. Both Technicians A and B
    d. Neither Technician A nor B

16. The owner of a front-wheel-drive vehicle complains that the shift lever is difficult to move in all positions. Which is the most likely cause?
    a. A seized pilot bearing
    b. A misadjusted clutch
    c. A worn release (throw out) bearing
    d. Dirty/corroded shift linkage

17. A growling sound is heard with the engine running and the transaxle is in neutral with the clutch engaged (foot off of the clutch pedal). What is the most likely cause?
    a. Excessive main shaft endplay
    b. An input shaft bearing
    c. An output bearing
    d. A pilot bearing

18. A transaxle has been overheated. What is the *most likely* cause?
    a. The driver was slipping the clutch
    b. Worn synchronizer sleeve(s)
    c. A lack of or low on lubricating oil
    d. Defective input shaft bearings

19. A five-speed manual transaxle is noisy in all gears. Which is the least likely cause?
    a. A pilot bearing
    b. An input shaft bearing
    c. An output shaft bearing
    d. Final drive side (differential) bearings

20. A paper blocker ring is used in a manual transaxle. What type of lubricant will harm this type of blocker ring?
    a. SAE 80W-90 gear lube
    b. ATF
    c. Engine oil
    d. Manual transmission fluid

DRIVE SHAFT AND U-JOINT/CV JOINT DIAGNOSIS AND REPAIR (5 QUESTIONS)

21. A rear-wheel-drive vehicle shutters or vibrates when first accelerating from a stop. The vibration is less noticeable at higher speeds. What is the most likely cause?
    a. Drive shaft unbalance
    b. Excessive U-joint working angles
    c. Unequal U-joint working angles
    d. Brinelling of the U-joint

22. Two technicians are discussing U-joints. Technician A says that a defective U-joint could cause a loud "clunk" noise when the transmission is shifted between drive and reverse. Technician B says a worn U-joint can cause a clicking or squeaking sound when driving the vehicle in reverse, but not while moving forward. Which technician is correct?
    a. Technician A only
    b. Technician B only
    c. Both Technicians A and B
    d. Neither Technician A nor B

23. Incorrect or unequal U-joint working angles are most likely to be caused by _____.
    a. A bent drive shaft
    b. A collapsed engine or transmission mount
    c. A dry output shaft spline
    d. Defective or damaged U-joints

24. An owner of a front-wheel-drive minivan complained that the front of the vehicle made a clicking sound whenever turning a corner. Technician A says that defective wheel bearings are the most likely cause. Technician B says that defective inner CV joint(s) may be the cause. Which technician is correct?
    a. Technician A only
    b. Technician B only
    c. Both Technicians A and B
    d. Neither Technician A nor B

25. A vehicle owner complained that a severe vibration was felt throughout the entire vehicle at highway speeds. What is the least likely cause?
    a. Excessive driveshaft working angles
    b. A bent driveshaft
    c. Worn CV joints
    d. A defective rear tire(s)

REAR AXLE DIAGNOSIS AND REPAIR (7 QUESTIONS)

26. A service technician removed the inspection/fill plug from the differential of a rear-wheel-drive vehicle and gear lube started to flow out. Technician A says that the technician should quickly replace the plug to prevent any more loss of gear lube. Technician B says the fluid should be allowed to drain. Which technician is correct?
    a. Technician A only
    b. Technician B only
    c. Both Technicians A and B
    d. Neither Technician A nor B

27. A growling sound is heard from the rear of a rear-wheel-drive vehicle while turning left only. Technician A says that defective rear axle bearings may be the cause. Technician B says that defective side bearings may be the cause. Which technician is correct?
    a. Technician A only
    b. Technician B only
    c. Both Technicians A and B
    d. Neither Technician A nor B

28. Technician A says that if the backlash is okay, then the side bearing preload is also okay. Technician B says that a ring gear tooth pattern check will indicate if the drive pinion depth is correct. Which technician is correct?
    a. Technician A only
    b. Technician B only
    c. Both Technicians A and B
    d. Neither Technician A nor B

29. Two technicians are discussing which lubricants are used in a limited slip differential. Technician A says to use SAE 80W-140. Technician B says that most vehicle manufacturers usually specify SAE 80W-90 be used with or without special limited slip additives. Which technician is correct?
    a. Technician A only
    b. Technician B only
    c. Both Technicians A and B
    d. Neither Technician A nor B

30. Two technicians are discussing the pinion depth adjustment in a differential. Technician A says that the pinion depth is adjusted using a shim. Technician B says that the pinion depth is adjusted by adjusting the pinion nut. Which technician is correct?
    a. Technician A only
    b. Technician B only
    c. Both Technicians A and B
    d. Neither Technician A nor B

31. A differential pinion seal is leaking. What should be used to remove the pinion nut?
    a. Air impact wrench
    b. Torque wrench
    c. Socket and wrench while companion flange is being held with a holding tool.
    d. Gear puller

32. A ring gear and pinion are being replaced. Which part(s) usually requires replacement?
    a. Ring gear bolts
    b. Differential side bearings
    c. Axle seals
    d. Pinion bearings

FOUR-WHEEL-DRIVE COMPONENT DIAGNOSIS AND REPAIR (8 QUESTIONS)

33. The owner of a full-size four-wheel-drive pickup truck complains that whenever turning sharply and accelerating rapidly, a severe vibration is felt. Technician A says that the transfer case may be defective. Technician B says that this is normal if conventional Cardan U-joints are used to drive the front wheels. Which technician is correct?
    a. Technician A only
    b. Technician B only
    c. Both Technicians A and B
    d. Neither Technician A nor B

34. A transfer case is extremely noisy in all selections except in two-wheel drive and neutral (N) whenever the vehicle is moving. Technician A says the drive chain may be stretched causing the noise as it hits the inside of the case. Technician B says that one or more of the transfer case bearings could be defective. Which technician is correct?
    a. Technician A only
    b. Technician B only
    c. Both Technicians A and B
    d. Neither Technician A nor B

35. A transfer case is difficult to shift from four-wheel low to four-wheel high (range shift). Technician A says that the shift linkage or shift fork may be worn, damaged, or mis-adjusted. Technician B says that incorrect lubricant could be the cause. Which technician is correct?
    a. Technician A only
    b. Technician B only
    c. Both Technicians A and B
    d. Neither Technician A nor B

36. Transfer cases use what lubricant?
    a. Automatic transmission fluid (ATF)
    b. Special fluid
    c. SAE 80W-90 gear lube
    d. Any of the above depending on application

37. A grinding sound is heard when the driver attempts to shift into four-wheel low range from four-wheel high range while traveling at about 20 MPH (32 km/hr). Technician A says that the drive chain could be slipping on the sprockets thus causing this sound. Technician B says that a center differential inside the transfer case could be the cause. Which technician is correct?
    a. Technician A only
    b. Technician B only
    c. Both Technicians A and B
    d. Neither Technician A nor B

38. The owner of an all-wheel-drive sport utility vehicle (SUV) complained that the vehicle tends to vibrate and hop when turning a corner. A visual inspection showed that the viscous coupling on the rear drive shaft was blue and looked as if it had been overheated. Which is the most likely cause?
    a. Mismatched tire sizes
    b. Worn output shaft bearings
    c. Frozen U-joints on the front or rear drive shaft
    d. Excessive slack in the transfer case chain

39. A four-wheel-drive vehicle is noisy in four-wheel low, but not in four-wheel high or two-wheel drive. Which is the most likely cause?
    a. Excessive axial play in the planetary gears
    b. A loose drive chain
    c. A defective input bearing
    d. A defective rear output bearing

40. A vehicle equipped with all-wheel drive with 20,000 miles on new tires has a blowout on the left front due to road debris. Technician A says to replace the left front tire only. Technician B says to replace both front tires. Which technician is correct?
    a. Technician A only
    b. Technician B only
    c. Both Technicians A and B
    d. Neither Technician A nor B

1. c	11. b	21. c	31. c
2. b	12. d	22. c	32. a
3. d	13. a	23. b	33. b
4. d	14. c	24. d	34. c
5. a	15. c	25. c	35. c
6. c	16. d	26. b	36. d
7. c	17. b	27. a	37. d
8. b	18. c	28. b	38. a
9. b	19. a	29. b	39. a
10. b	20. a	30. a	40. d

MLR— Maintenance & Light Repair
AST— Auto Service Technology (Includes MLR)
MAST— Master Auto Service Technology (Includes MLR and AST)

MANUAL DRIVE TRAIN AND AXLES (A3)

TASK	PRIORITY	MLR	AST	MAST	TEXT PAGE #	TASK PAGE #
A. GENERAL: DRIVE TRAIN DIAGNOSIS						
1. Identify and interpret drive train concerns; determine necessary action.	P-1		✓	✓	86–96; 133–138; 227–233; 305–310; 321–327	11, 26, 27, 33
2. Research applicable vehicle and service information, fluid type, vehicle service history, service precautions, and technical service bulletins.	P-1	✓	✓	✓	2–4; 120–122; 228–230	3, 4, 21, 45, 59
3. Check fluid condition; check for leaks; determine necessary action.	P-1	✓	✓	✓	120–122; 228–230	20, 64
4. Drain and refill manual transmission/transaxle and final drive unit.	P-1	✓	✓	✓	120–122	21
B. CLUTCH DIAGNOSIS AND REPAIR						
1. Diagnose clutch noise, binding, slippage, pulsation, and chatter; determine necessary action.	P-1		✓	✓	86–89	11
2. Inspect clutch pedal linkage, cables, automatic adjuster mechanisms, brackets, bushings, pivots, and springs; perform necessary action.	P-1		✓	✓	79–80; 86	12
3. Inspect and replace clutch pressure plate assembly, clutch disc, release (throw-out) bearing and linkage, and pilot bearing/bushing (as applicable).	P-1		✓	✓	89–102	14
4. Bleed clutch hydraulic system.	P-1		✓	✓	95–96	15
5. Check and adjust clutch master cylinder fluid level; check for leaks.	P-1	✓	✓	✓	87–88	13
6. Inspect flywheel and ring gear for wear and cracks; determine necessary action.	P-1		✓	✓	90–91	16
7. Measure flywheel runout and crankshaft end play; determine necessary action.	P-2		✓	✓	91–92	17
C. TRANSMISSION/TRANSAXLE DIAGNOSIS AND REPAIR						
1. Inspect, adjust, and reinstall shift linkages, brackets, bushings, cables, pivots, and levers.	P-2		✓	✓	115–117; 134	25

TASK	PRIORITY	MLR	AST	MAST	TEXT PAGE #	TASK PAGE #
2. Describe the operational characteristics of an electronically controlled manual transmission/transaxle.	P-3	✓	✓	✓	60	9
3. Diagnose noise concerns through the application of transmission/transaxle powerflow principles.	P-2			✓	136–138	24
4. Diagnose hard shifting and jumping out of gear concerns; determine necessary action.	P-2			✓	135–137	24
5. Diagnose transaxle final drive assembly noise and vibration concerns; determine necessary action.	P-3			✓	143–145; 148	26
6. Disassemble, inspect clean, and reassemble internal transmission/transaxle components.	P-3			✓	141–151; 155–160	23

D. DRIVE SHAFT AND HALF SHAFT, UNIVERSAL AND CONSTANT-VELOCITY (CV) JOINT DIAGNOSIS AND REPAIR

TASK	PRIORITY	MLR	AST	MAST	TEXT PAGE #	TASK PAGE #
1. Diagnose constant-velocity (CV) joint noise and vibration concerns; determine necessary action.	P-1		✓	✓	175	27
2. Diagnose universal joint noise and vibration concerns; perform necessary action.	P-2		✓	✓	175–177	27
3. Inspect, remove, and replace front-wheel drive (FWD) bearings, hubs, and seals.	P-1	✓ (P-2)	✓	✓	181–182	28
4. Inspect, service, and replace shafts, yokes, boots, and universal/CV joints.	P-1	✓ (P-2)	✓	✓	181–185	28
5. Check shaft balance and phasing; measure shaft runout; measure and adjust driveline angles.	P-2		✓	✓	179–180; 329–332	28

E. DRIVE AXLE DIAGNOSIS AND REPAIR

E.1 RING AND PINION GEARS AND DIFFERENTIAL CASE ASSEMBLY

TASK	PRIORITY	MLR	AST	MAST	TEXT PAGE #	TASK PAGE #
1. Clean and inspect differential housing; check for leaks; inspect housing vent.	P-2	✓	✓	✓	229; 312	33, 34
2. Check and adjust differential housing fluid level.	P-1	✓	✓	✓	229	34
3. Drain and refill differential housing.	P-1	✓	✓	✓	229; 251	34
4. Diagnose noise and vibration concerns; determine necessary action.	P-2			✓	321–333	60
5. Inspect and replace companion flange and pinion seal; measure companion flange runout.	P-2		✓	✓	236–238	35
6. Inspect ring gear and measure runout; determine necessary action.	P-3			✓	239–240	36
7. Remove, inspect, and reinstall drive pinion and ring gear, spacers, sleeves, and bearings.	P-3			✓	240–250	37
8. Measure and adjust drive pinion depth.	P-3			✓	241–244	38
9. Measure and adjust drive pinion bearing preload.	P-3			✓	243–244	39
10. Measure and adjust side bearing preload and ring and pinion gear total backlash and backlash variation on a differential carrier assembly (threaded cup or shim types).	P-3			✓	245–250	40
11. Check ring and pinion tooth contact patterns; perform necessary action.	P-3			✓	245–246	41
12. Disassemble, inspect, measure, and adjust or replace differential pinion gears (spiders), shaft, side gears, side bearings, thrust washers, and case.	P-3			✓	241–242	42
13. Reassemble and reinstall differential case assembly; measure runout; determine necessary action.	P-3			✓	245–247	43

TASK	PRIORITY	MLR	AST	MAST	TEXT PAGE #	TASK PAGE #
E.2 LIMITED SLIP DIFFERENTIAL						
1. Diagnose noise, slippage, and chatter concerns; determine necessary action.	P-3			✓	220; 223; 250	44
2. Measure rotating torque; determine necessary action.	P-3			✓	232–233	46
E.3 DRIVE AXLES						
1. Inspect and replace drive axle wheel studs.	P-1	✓ (P-2)	✓	✓	233–234	30
2. Remove and replace drive axle shafts.	P-1		✓	✓	233–236	29
3. Inspect and replace drive axle shaft seals, bearings, and retainers.	P-2		✓	✓	233–236	29
4. Measure drive axle flange runout and shaft end play; determine necessary action.	P-2		✓	✓	231–232	29
5. Diagnose drive axle shafts, bearings, and seals for noise, vibration, and fluid leakage concerns; determine necessary action.	P-2			✓	229–231	29
F. FOUR-WHEEL DRIVE/ALL-WHEEL DRIVE COMPONENT DIAGNOSIS AND REPAIR						
1. Inspect, adjust, and repair shifting controls (mechanical, electrical, and vacuum), bushings, mounts, levers, and brackets.	P-3		✓	✓	283–284; 289; 299–302; 299–313	59, 60
2. Inspect front-wheel bearings and locking hubs; perform necessary action(s).	P-3	✓	✓	✓	284–285; 312–313	63
3. Check for leaks at drive assembly seals; check vents; check lube level.	P-3	✓ (P-2)	✓	✓	312	64
4. Identify concerns related to variations in tire circumference and/or final drive ratios.	P-3		✓	✓	305–306	66
5. Diagnose noise, vibration, and unusual steering concerns; determine necessary action.	P-3			✓	306–307; 321–333	66
6. Diagnose, test, adjust, and replace electrical/electronic components of four-wheel drive systems.	P-3			✓	307–311	65
7. Disassemble, service, and reassemble transfer case and components.	P-3			✓	314–318	62

GLOSSARY

Aboveground storage tank (AGST)   A storage tank that stores used oil and is located above ground.

Active radius   The longer the distance between the centerline of the friction material and the centerline of the clutch disc, the higher the torque capacity of the clutch disc.

All-wheel drive (AWD)   A drive system that can drive both the front and rear wheels through all phases of operation. (Also called full-time 4WD.)

Ammeter   A meter used to measure electrical current.

Amperes (A, amp)   The unit of measurement for electric flow.

Anaerobic sealant   A chemical that cures in tight, smooth areas to form a gasket to prevent fluid leaks.

Antifriction bearings   Bearings that use steel balls or rollers to reduce friction.

Asbestosis   A health condition where asbestos causes scar tissue to form in the lungs, causing shortness of breath.

Automatic transmission   A transmission that automatically changes forward gear speeds.

Axial load   A force in line (same axis) as the centerline of the bearing or shaft.

Backlash   The clearance between gears; also called *lash*.

Backlash variation   The variation in backlash caused by ring gear runout.

Ball bearing   A nonfriction bearing that uses steel balls as the rolling element.

Battery Council International (BCI)   A trade organization of battery manufacturers.

Bearing retained axle   An axle that is retained at the outer end of the axle.

Bearing spacer   Shim used to position bearings and maintain bearing preload.

Bench grinder   A type of electric motor driven grinder that mounts to a bench.

Belleville spring   A conical steel spring that gives a spring action because of its resistance to flattening.

Bevel gear   Gears that are cut at an angle and used to transfer power between nonparallel shafts.

Blocker ring clearance   A check to determine the amount of blocker ring wear.

Blocker rings   *See* Synchronizer ring.

Bolt   The major type of threaded fastener used with a nut to secure parts together.

Breaker bar   A long-handled socket drive tool.

Brinelling   A wear pattern that presses or wears a series of grooves or dents in a bearing surface.

Bump cap   A hard plastic hat to protect the head from bumps.

Cage   The support for rollers or ball bearings.

Calibration codes   Codes used on many powertrain control modules.

Campaign   A recall where vehicle owners are contacted to return a vehicle to a dealer for corrective action.

Cardan joint   The common U-joint used in most RWD driveshafts.

Carrier   The casting section of a drive axle that contains the differential and ring and pinion gears.

Carrier bearing preload   The load placed on carrier bearings during assembly.

Carrier bearings   The bearings that support the differential carrier.

Casting number   An identification code cast into an engine block or other large cast part of a vehicle.

Clean Air Act (CAA)   Federal legislation passed in 1970 and updated in 1990 that established national air quality standards.

C-lock   A "C" shaped locking device used to retain an axle shaft. Often called a C-clip.

C-lock-retained axle   An axle that is retained by a C-lock on the inner end of the axle.

Center differential   A differential used with AWD to allow a speed difference between the front and rear axles.

Center support bearing   A bearing used between the two parts of a two-piece drive shaft. Also called a steady bearing or hanger bearing.

Cheater bar   A bar used on a wrench to increase the amount of torque that can be applied to a fastener. Not recommended.

Chisels   A type of hand tool used with a hammer to cut or mark metal and other materials.

Clutch   A device that controls the power transfer between two points by either allowing or not allowing a transfer.

Clutch disc   The clutch member that transmits torque to the transmission input shaft.

Clutch pedal free travel   The amount that the clutch pedal moves before the release bearing contacts the release levers.

Clutch plate   *See* Clutch disc.

Clutch shaft   A part of the main drive gear; the transmission input shaft.

Clutch slippage   A clutch problem in which the clutch does not transmit the torque load and the engine overrevs.

Clutch spin down   A diagnostic test to determine clutch drag.

Coast   A load condition in which the vehicle is driving the engine, as during deceleration.

Coast side   The concave side of a gear tooth.

Code of Federal Regulations (CFR)   A compilation of the general and permanent rules published in the federal register by the executive departments and agencies of the federal government.

Coefficient of friction   A reference to the amount of friction between two surfaces.

Coil spring style   A type of clutch pressure plate that uses coil springs

Collapsible spacer   *See* Crush sleeve.

Companion flange   The input flange at the differential pinion gear.

Complete circuit   A complete path from battery B+ to ground required for electrical current to flow.

Composite rings   Synchronizer rings that are lined with carbon, metal, or paper-based composite material.

Conductors   A material that conducts electricity and heat. A metal that contains fewer than four electrons in its atom's outer shell.

Cone (inner ring)   The inside race of a bearing.

Cone clutch   A type of clutch that uses conical driving and driven members.

Connector   The plastic part of an electrical connection.

Constant mesh gear   A transmission in which each gear (with the possible exception of the reverse idler gear) is constantly meshed with its mating gear.

Constant-velocity joint (CV joint)   A V-joint that can transmit power without changing the velocity.

Contact pattern   See Gear contact pattern.

Contamination   Scratches, pitting, or scoring in a scattered pattern.

Continuity   A circuit or component that has a complete path for current to flow.

Continuously variable transmission (CVT)   A transmission that varies the gear ratio in a continuous, rather than stepwise, manner.

Control module   Electronic device that controls electrical circuits.

Conventional theory   The theory that electricity flows from positive (+) to negative (–).

Countershaft   The shaft that supports some cluster gears.

Countertrack   A plunge-type CV joint that uses eight drive balls.

Coupler   A clutchlike device that can connect or disconnect the power flow between two components.

Cover   The outer part of a pressure plate assembly that contains the other parts.

Crack   A surface break that appears as a line.

Crimp-and-seal connectors   A type of electrical connector that has glue inside which provides a weather-proof seal after it is heated.

Cross and yoke joint   Most common type of U-joint, also known as a Cardan joint.

Cross groove joint   A plunge joint similar to a Rzeppa joint.

Crosstrack   A fixed-type CV joint that uses eight drive balls.

Crush sleeve   A collapsible spacer used to maintain pinion bearing preload.

Cup (outer ring)   The outer race of a bearing

Cushioned disc   A clutch disc with a damper assembly.

Cushion spring   In the space between the friction surfaces of a clutch disc which is a wavy spring steel material.

CV joint boot   The rubber or plastic bellow-shaped covering for the CV joints used to keep lubricating grease in the joint and protected from the moisture and dirt.

Damper   A device that reduces the torsional vibrations between the engine and transmission.

Dead axle   An axle that supports a wheel but does not transmit power.

Decelerate   To reduce speed.

Deflection   The bending or movement caused by a load.

Department of Transportation (DOT)   A governmental agency that is concerned with transportation.

Detent   A spring-loaded device used to position a shift fork correctly.

Diagnostic trouble code (DTC)   Codes generated by a control module that are used to help with troubleshooting.

Dial indicator   A measuring instrument that is used to measure travel/clearance.

Diaphragm   A type of pressure plate assembly that uses a diaphragm spring.

Diaphragm spring   A round, conical-shaped spring; a Belleville spring.

Diaphragm spring style   This style is the most commonly used pressure plate design. It uses one large, round, steel spring, called a Belleville spring to apply even force on the clutch disc.

Differential   A gear arrangement that allows the drive wheels to be driven at different speeds.

Differential case clearance   A check to determine the amount of differential wear.

Digital multimeter (DMM)   A meter that has multiple functions for measuring electrical activity and uses a digital read out.

Digital volt-ohm-meter (DVOM)   A meter that has multiple functions for measuring electrical activity and uses a digital read out. Also called a DMM.

Diode   An electrical one-way check valve.

Direct current (DC)   An electrical current that flows only in one direction.

Direct drive   A 1:1 gear ratio.

Disc alignment   The procedure of aligning a new disc to the flywheel before replacing the pressure plate.

Disc runout   The checking procedure to make sure that a clutch disc runs true.

Dog clutch   A type of clutch that uses gearlike, one male and one female, driving and driven members. It is engaged when one is slid over the other.

Dog clutch teeth   The set of teeth on a speed gear that engage the synchronizer sleeve.

Dogs   See Keys.

Double-Cardan joint   Two Cardan joints separated by a ball and spring to maintain equal operating angles.

Double cone   A synchronizer design that uses two or more cones.

Double-lip seal   Used to seal two lubricant containing units so the lubricant will not pass between them.

Double-offset joint   A plunging CV joint typically used as the inboard CV joint on FWD shafts.

Dowel   A round metal pin attached to a casting, which ensures proper alignment as a hole in another casting is placed onto it.

Drag   The resistance or friction created by one object passing by another.

Drive   A load condition in which the engine is applying power to the drive wheels.

Drive axle   An axle that supports the vehicle and provides a method of driving the wheels.

Drive Axle shaft   A short drive shaft used in front –wheel-drive vehicles. Also called a half shaft.

Driveline angles   The angle of the front and rear U-joints.

Drive sizes   The size in fractions of an inch of the square drive for sockets.

Driveline   Another name for a driveshaft.

Drive pinion gear   The smaller drive gear in a ring and pinion gear set.

Drive side   The convex side of a gear tooth.

Driveshaft   A device that transmits power from one unit to another.

Driveshaft runout The amount of radial movement of a driveshaft as it is rotated.

Dual-mass flywheel A two-part flywheel that drives the secondary flywheel through a set of long damper springs.

Dynamic friction The relative amount of friction between two surfaces that have different speeds.

Dynamic seals Seals used between two surfaces where there is movement.

Dynamic shift test A shift test that is made with the engine running.

Dynamometer A machine used to measure engine torque.

Eccentric Two circles that do not have the same center.

Electric arcing A series of small burn marks around a bearing or shaft caused by electrical sparks.

Electricity The movement of free electrons from one atom to another.

Electron theory The theory that electricity flows from negative (-) to positive (+).

Electronic control module (ECM) An electronic device that uses various inputs to determine the needed output reaction to efficiently operate the system.

Electronic Shift on-the-Fly (ESOF) A type of four-wheel-drive system that allows shifting into and out of four-wheel-drive while the vehicle is moving.

Electronic traction control (ETC) A system that prevents wheels from spinning to increase overall vehicle traction.

Electronic vibration analyzer (EVA) A tester that measures vibration and displays the results in hertz and amplitude.

Electrostatic discharge (ESD) A momentary flow of electricity that occurs when an excess of electric charge finds a path to ground.

End float *See* End play.

End play Free movement of a part in a sideways direction.

Energy The ability to do work.

Engagement modulation The ability to engage the clutch in order to produce a smooth, slip-free engagement.

Engine support A device that supports the engine so the transaxle can be removed.

Environmental Protection Agency (EPA) A governmental agency that is charged with protecting human health and with safeguarding the natural environment: air, water, and land.

Excessive wear Wear that causes a part to become unusable.

Extensions A socket wrench tool used between a ratchet or breaker bar and a socket.

Extension rod *See* Stabilizer bar.

Extreme-pressure (EP) A lubricant designed to stay in place and keep parts from touching when under extremely high pressure.

Eye wash station A water fountain designed to rinse the eyes with a large volume of water.

Face The area of a gear tooth above the pitch line.

Face runout The checking procedure to make sure that the face of the clutch housing is true to the flywheel.

Facing The friction material on a clutch disc.

Feeler gauge Thin metal strips of precise thickness, used to measure the clearance between two parts.

Fiber composites A mixture of fiber threads (glass, graphite, or other materials) and a resin.

Files A type of hand tool used to smooth metal and other materials.

Final drive The last set of reduction gears before the power flows to the differential gears and drive axles.

Final drive ring gear The larger driven gear in a ring and pinion gear set.

Fire blanket A fire-proof wool blanket used to cover a person who is on fire to smother the fire.

Fire extinguisher classes The classification of fire extinguishers by the type of fires they are designed to handle.

Fixed joint A CV joint that does not change length.

Flank The area of a gear tooth below the pitch line.

Float A load condition in which two parts are turning at the same speed with no driving force between them; also when a shaft is supported by a gear, the gear in turn is supported by a bearing.

Fluid clutch A type of clutch that drives through fluid; similar to a torque converter.

Flywheel The rotating metal mass attached to the crankshaft that helps even out power surges and provides a mounting point and friction surface for the clutch.

Force A push or pull measured in units of weightlike pounds or kilograms.

Formed-in-place gasket (FIPG) A gasket material that comes from a tube, which is applied to metal surfaces before assembly.

Four-wheel drive (4WD) A drive system that can drive both the front and rear wheels.

Frequency The number of times a waveform repeats in one second, measured in Hertz (Hz), frequency band.

Fretting Small particles that decay and break off bearing races.

Friction The resistance in motion between two bodies in contact with each other.

Friction disc A flat disc that is faced with friction materials; it is driven when it is clamped between two flat metal surfaces.

Friction modifier An additive that increases the slipperiness of a lubricant.

Front bearing retainer The transmission front bearing retainer has a long, hollow tube extending toward the engine. The release bearing sleeve slides on the outer surface of this tube, which is also commonly called (slang) a Quill, Quill shaft or Candlestick.

Front drive axle The driving axle at the front of a 4WD vehicle.

Front-wheel drive (FWD) A drive system that drives the front wheels.

Fulcrum The pivot or supporting point for a lever.

Full-floating axle An axle supported by two bearings at the wheel end that transfers vehicle weight from the axle housing to the wheel.

Full-time 4WD *See* All-wheel drive (AWD).

Fuse A circuit protection device that will break (open) a circuit if the current flow exceeds the rating of the fuse.

Fusible link A circuit protection device that is made of wires that are four gauge size smaller than the circuit wire. The wire will melt (open) if the current flow exceeds the ability of the wire to pass the current.

Galling Wear that transfers metal and is caused by metal-to-metal contact without proper lubrication.

Garter spring A spring used around the lip of a seal.

Gasket A compressible material used as a seal between two mating surfaces.

Gauge (wire) The cross-section size of a wire. AWG gauges use low numbers for large wires and higher numbers for smaller wires.

GAWR Abbreviation for gross axle weight rating.

GC-LB A grease rating for GC is the highest rating for wheel bearing grease and LB is the highest rating for chassis grease. A GC-LB grease, therefore, can be used.

Gear A metal wheel with teeth that transmit power or motion to another gear.

Gear clash The noise created when gears rotating at different speeds are tried to move into mesh.

Gear marking compound A paint compound that is placed on the gear teeth to make the gear contact pattern more visible.

Gear ratio The ratio of the number of teeth on the driving and driven gears; it is calculated by dividing the number of teeth on the driven gear by the number of teeth on the driving gear.

Gear rattle A noise created when one of the gears in mesh tries to change speed.

Grade The strength rating of a bolt.

Gravity bleeding A method of removing air from the hydraulic system using gravity.

Grease A thick lubricant typically made of oil and lithium soap.

Grease seal A rubber seal with a steel backing used to keep grease in a bearing assembly from leaking.

GVWR Abbreviation for gross vehicle weight rating.

Hacksaws A type of hand tool that is used to cut metal and other materials.

Half shaft The driveshaft used to connect the differential to the drive wheels on drive axles with independent suspension.

Hall Effect A type of sensor that creates a square wave output signal.

Hammers A type of hand tool used to force objects into position using a swinging motion.

Hazardous waste materials Chemicals or components that are no longer needed and pose a danger to the environment or people.

Heel The outer end of a bevel or hypoid ring gear tooth.

Helical gear A gear with teeth cut at an angle.

Hertz A unit of measurement of frequency. One Hertz is one cycle per second, abbreviated Hz. Named for Heinrich R. Hertz, a 19th-century German physicist.

HEPA vacuum High efficiency particulate air filter vacuum used to clean brake dust.

HEV Hybrid electric vehicle.

High efficiency particulate air (HEPA) A type of air filter that can theoretically remove at least 99.97% of airborne particles.

High resistance A type of electrical circuit fault where excessive resistance reduces proper current flow.

Horsepower A measure of engine power derived from the torque and engine speed on revolutions per minute measurements.

Hub The center part of a wheel; the surface where a wheel mounts.

Hunting *See* Hunting gear set.

Hunting gear set A gear set in which the driving gear will mesh with every tooth on the driven gear as they rotate.

Hypoid gear A special form of bevel gear that positions the gear axis on nonintersecting planes and is commonly used in drive axles.

Hypoid gear set A matched set of hypoid gears.

Idler gear A gear positioned between two other gears such that it causes a change in the direction of rotation.

Inclinometer A device used to measure mounting positions relative to true level.

Independent rear suspension (IRS) A type of rear suspension in which the two rear wheels can move vertically without changing the other's position.

Inertia The physical property maintaining that a body at rest tends to remain at rest and a body in motion tends to remain in motion and travel in a straight line.

Input shaft The shaft that carries the driving torque into a gear box.

Insulators A material that does not readily conduct electricity and heat. A nonmetal material that contains more than four electrons in its atom's outer shell.

Integral carrier A rear axle carrier that is integrated with the axle housing so it cannot be removed for service.

Integrated wheel end disconnect A system that is used to connect and disconnect the outboard CV joint with the wheel hub.

Interlock A transmission mechanism that prevents two shift rails or forks from moving at the same time.

Intermediate shaft The output shaft of the transmission portion of a transaxle that drives the differential.

Keys A synchronizer part that pushes the synchronizer rings into contact with the gear cone.

LED Light emitting diode.

Limited slip differential (LSD) A differential that uses internal clutches to limit the speed difference between the axles.

Live axle An axle that transmits power.

Locked differential A differential that will not allow differential action to occur.

Locking hub A 4WD front hub that will unlock the hubs for highway use and lock for off-road use.

Longitudinal engine The term used to describe when the engine is installed length wise in the vehicle.

Lubricant checks A check to determine the fluid level.

Main drive gear The transmission's input gear.

Main shaft The transmission's output shaft.

Manual Shift on-the-Fly (MSOF) A type of four-wheel-drive system that allows shifting into and out of four-wheel-drive while the vehicle is moving.

Manual transmission A transmission device in which the gear ratios are changed by manually.

Manual transmission fluid (MTF) The lubricant required for a transmission that uses composite synchronizer rings.

Marcel spring A large series of wave springs between the two lining sections of a clutch disc.

Material safety data sheets (MSDSs) Forms containing data regarding the properties of a particular substance.

Mercury A heavy metal that is liquid at room temperature.

Metric bolts Bolts manufactured and sized in the metric system of measurement.

Misalignment A wear pattern that leaves a diagonal polish on bearing races.

Mode shift When either two-wheel drive or four-wheel drive may be selected in a four-wheel-drive vehicle.

National Lubricating Grease Institute (NLGI) Organization that establishes grease specifications.

Needle rollers A type of bearing that uses small rollers called needle rollers to reduce friction.

Neutral run-up test The neutral run-up test is used to determine if the source of the vibration is engine-related. With the transmission in Neutral or Park, slowly increase the engine RPM and with a tachometer observe the RPM at which the vibration occurs.

Node Another name for an electronic module.

Non-hunting A gear ratio that allows contact of the same drive and driven gear teeth each revolution of the gear set.

Nut A threaded fastener that is used with a bolt.

NVH Noise, vibration and harshness

Occupational Safety and Health Administration (OSHA) A governmental agency that regulates workplace safety.

Ohmmeter A meter used to measure the resistance of a circuit or component.

Ohms (Ω) Unit of measurement for resistance.

Open circuit A break or interruption in a circuit that will not allow current to flow.

Open design A design used for most 4WD that has ball joints and Cardan joints.

Open differential A differential that will split torque equally between axles and does not limit the speed difference between the axles.

Output shaft The shaft that carries the torque out of a gear box.

Overdrive A gear arrangement that causes the output shaft to turn faster than the input shaft.

Overhung pinion A pinion that hangs over from the support bearing.

Partial non-hunting A gear ratio that allows contact of the same drive and driven gear teeth in a regular pattern.

Part-time 4WD A 4WD vehicle that allows the front drive axle to be disconnected for highway use and applied for off-road use. Commonly called *4WD*.

Peeling A slight scraping away of material from a bearing race.

Pilot bearing A bearing in the end of the crankshaft used to support the front end of the transmission input shaft.

Pin bushings The pins used to hold a chain together.

Pinch bolt A bolt used to retain a ball joint in some designs of suspensions.

Pinch weld seam A strong section under a vehicle where two body panels are welded together.

Pinion bearing preload The load placed on the pinion bearings during assembly.

Pinion gear A small gear that meshes with a larger gear.

Pitch The distance between threads of a bolt and nut; the relative number of teeth or spacing of the teeth on a gear.

Pitch diameter The effective diameter of a gear; midpoint of gear tooth. (Also called *pitch line*.)

Pitch line The line of contact between driving and driven gears.

Planet carrier The part of a planetary gear set that contains the planetary pinion gears.

Planetary gear set A gear system composed of a sun gear, a planet carrier with planet pinions, and a ring gear that can produce one or more gear ratios.

Plunge joint A CV joint that allows a driveshaft to change length.

Pliers A type of hand tool that has two moveable parts and are used to hold or rotate an object or fastener.

Positraction The brand name of limited slip differentials used in Chevrolets.

Potentiometer A 3-terminal variable resistor that varies the voltage drop in a circuit.

Power transfer unit (PTU) A gear box added to a FWD transaxle to control the power flow to a rear drive axle.

PPE Personal protective equipment.

Preload An adjustment that removes all clearance and places a load on the parts.

Pressure plate The metal disc that applies pressure onto the friction disc to transmit torque.

Prevailing torque nut A nut that designed to not become lose from vibration. Usually a a design that uses a deformed thread area to help keep the nut from loosening.

Propeller shaft *See* Driveshaft.

Punches A type of hand tool used with a hammer to drive pins or other similar uses.

Radial load The load applied to a bearing 90 degrees from the axis. The weight of the vehicle applies a radial load to the wheel bearing.

Range shift The switch from four-wheel-drive low or from four-wheel-drive to high or the other way around.

Ratchet A hand tool used to drive a socket wrench that is capable of being changed to tighten or loosen a fastener.

Rear-wheel drive (RWD) A drive system that drives the rear wheels.

Recall A notification to the owner of a vehicle that a safety issue needs to be corrected.

Relay A device that uses a small current to control a large current.

Release bearing The bearing that is forced against the pressure plate assembly to release a clutch. (Also called *throwout bearing*.)

Removable carrier A rear axle carrier that can be removed from the housing for service.

Resource Conservation and Recovery Act (RCRA) This law states that hazardous material users are responsible for hazardous materials from the time they become a waste until the proper waste disposal is completed.

Retainer plate-type axle A type of rear axle that uses a retainer plate instead of a C-clips to keep the axle retained to the axle housing.

Reverse idler shaft The shaft that supports the reverse idler gear.

Right-to-know laws Laws that state that employees have a right to know when the materials they use at work are hazardous.

Ring gear *See* Annulus gear.

Ring gear runout The side-to-side wobble of the ring gear as it is rotated.

Rocker pin The type of chain used in transfer cases is usually assembled from pin links and chain links and is called a "rocker pin" type chain.

Roller bearings Antifriction bearings that use hardened steel rollers between the inner and outer races.

Rolling circumference The distance traveled by a rotating tire in one revolution.

Room-temperature vulcanizing (RTV) A formed-in-place gasket material; a rubberlike material that vulcanizes at room temperature.

Rust dust The orange-colored dust that surrounds a steel part that has rusted.

Rzeppa joint The most commonly used outboard CV joint.

Schematic a wiring diagram showing components and connecting wires

Screwdrivers A type of hand tool designed to remove screws.

Seizing Parts that are partially or completely welded together by friction-generated heat.

Semiconductor An element with exactly four elections in its outer orbit.

Semi-floating axle A rear drive axle that is supported at one end by a bearing and the differential side gear at the other end.

Service spacer Shims used to space the carrier bearings and maintain carrier bearing preload.

Shift fork The part that transfers motion from the shift shaft to the synchronizer sleeve.

Shim A thin metal spacer used to adjust clearance or preload.

Short-to-ground A short circuit in which the current bypasses some or all the resistance of the circuit and flows to ground. Because ground is usually steel in automotive electricity, a short-to-ground (grounded) is a "copper-to-steel" connection.

Short-to-voltage A circuit in which current flows, but bypasses some or all the resistance in the circuit. A connection that results in a "copper-to-copper" connection.

Side bearings See Carrier bearings.

Side gears See Axle gears.

Slave cylinder The hydraulic cylinder attached to the throw-out bearing as part of a hydraulic clutch activating system.

Sliding sleeve A part of a synchronizer assembly. Also called a synchronizer sleeve

Snips A type of hand tool used to cut sheet metal and other thin materials.

Socket A type of tool that fits over the top and used to remove a threaded fastener.

Socket adapter An adapter that allows the use of one size of driver (ratchet or breaker bar) to rotate another drive size of socket.

Solvent Usually colorless liquids that are used to remove grease and oil.

Spalling A condition where surface metal breaks away from a bearing race.

Special service tools (SSTs) Tools that are developed by OEM so service or repair procedures can be done.

Speed gears The gears that are meshed with the cluster gear that transfer motion to the synchronizer assembly.

Spider A part of a simple universal joint where the two Y-shaped yokes are connected.

Spiral bevel gear A type of bevel gear that uses curved teeth that are spirally cut to provide quieter operation.

Spline bind A condition where the splines on the yoke of a driveshaft bind and then release as a vehicle is first accelerated after a stop.

Spontaneous combustion Self-ignition of oily rags without the use of an ignition source.

Spur gear A gear with teeth cut parallel to the axis of the gear.

Static seal A seal used between two surfaces that are not moving.

Static shift test A shift test that is made with the engine off.

Stop ring Another name for a blocker ring which is a part of a synchronizer assembly used in a manual transmission/transaxle.

Straddle mounting Mounting a gear between two bearings.

Struts See Keys.

Stud A short rod with threads on both ends.

Sun gear The gear in the center of a planetary gear set.

Synchronizer keys Small, spring-loaded detent keys, a part of a synchronizer assembly. Also called a synchronizer strut.

Synchronizer ring Part of a synchronizer assembly that blocks a shift until the speeds are synchronized.

Synthetic retainers A type of retention method for holding together parts of a universal joint.

Tapered roller bearing A nonfriction bearing that uses tapered steel rollers as the rolling element.

Technical service bulletin (TSB) A form that describes a particular vehicle concern and the recommended correction procedure.

Tensile strength The maximum stress used under tension (lengthwise force) without causing failure.

Terminal The metal end of a wire that fits into a plastic connector and is the electrical connection part of a junction.

Throwout bearing See Release bearing.

Toe The inner end of a bevel or hypoid ring gear tooth.

Torque A turning or twisting effort that is normally measured in foot-pounds or Newton-meters.

Torque biasing device (TBD) A torque biasing device is used to control torque between two outputs and are connected in parallel. The most commonly used TBDs are used to control the torque in a drive axle to the left and right drive wheels.

Torque bias ratio (TBR) The relative amount of torque that each drive wheel will receive.

Torque converter A type of fluid coupling that is used with automatic transmissions that will multiply engine torque. It self-releases to allow the vehicle to stop with the engine running and the transmission in gear.

Torque steer Torque steer occurs in front-wheel-drive vehicles when engine torque causes a front wheel to change its angle (toe) from straight ahead. The resulting pulling effect of the vehicle is most noticeable during rapid acceleration, especially whenever upshifting of the transmission creates a sudden change in torque.

Torsen® Torque-sensing worm gear differential.

Torsional dampers Springs used in clutch discs to absorb engine torque.

Transaxle A transmission that is combined with the final drive and differential and is normally used in FWD and mid-engine vehicles.

Transfer case An auxiliary transmission used in most 4WD vehicles to divide and control the power flow to the front and rear drive axles.

Transfer case control module (TCCM) The electronic control module that is controls the operation of an electronic transfer case.

Transmission A device in the powertrain that provides different forward gear ratios, a neutral, and a reverse.

Transverse engine An engine that is mounted sideways in a vehicle.

Trouble light A light used to help a service technician see while performing service work on a vehicle.

Trunnion   The projecting arms of a U-joint cross that form the bearing journals.

U-joint   An abbreviation of universal joint which is a joint in a steering or drive shaft that allows torque to be transmitted at an angle.

UNC   Unified national coarse.

Underground storage tank (UST)   Underground storage tank used to store used oil.

UNF   Unified national fine.

Universal joint (U-joint)   A mechanical device used to transfer power and motion at changeable angles.

Used oil   Any petroleum-based or synthetic oil that has been used.

Vehicle emission control information (VECI)   An underhood label with emission control information.

Vibration order   A term used to define how often a vibration occurs.

VIN   Vehicle identification number.

Viscosity   A fluid's resistance to flow.

Viscous coupling   A sealed clutch filled with a viscous fluid that will transfer power as the fluid is heated.

Visual inspection   A careful inspection of a part or vehicle using sight and feel.

Voltmeter   A meter that can measure voltage.

Volts (V)   Unit of measurement for electrical pressure.

Washer   A thin metal disk with a hole used to support the load of a threaded fastener.

WHMIS   Workplace Hazardous Materials Information Systems.

Wiring schematic   A drawing showing the wires and the components in a circuit using symbols to represent the components.

Witness mark   A mark showing where two objects have made contact.

Workplace Hazardous Materials Information Systems (WHMIS)   A Canadian form that contains data regarding the properties of a particular substance.

Worm gear   A type of gear with teeth that resemble screw threads.

Wrench   Any of various hand or power tools, often having fixed or adjustable jaws, used for gripping, turning, or twisting objects such as nuts, bolts, or pipes.

INDEX

W